Researching the Family

Researching the Family:

A Guide to Survey and Statistical Data on U.S. Families

Edited by
Nicholas Zill and Margaret Daly

Contributing Authors:
Connie Blumenthal
Brett Brown
Mary Jo Coiro
Margaret Daly
Kristin A. Moore
Donna Ruane Morrison
Christine Winquist Nord
Nancy O. Snyder
Barbara Sugland
Nicholas Zill

Child Trends, Inc.

Prepared for the
Office of the Assistant Secretary for Planning and Evaluation
Office of the Secretary
U.S. Department of Health and Human Services

Washington, DC

Child Trends
2100 M Street, Suite 610
Washington, DC 20037
(202) 223-6288

Table of Contents

Acknowledgements

The preparation of this guide was supported by Contract No. HHS-100-88-0041, Delivery Order No. 17, U.S. Department of Health and Human Services.

The authors gratefully acknowledge the review and comments of the following people:

Patricia Adams, Paula Baker, Patrick Benton, Sanford Braver, Ronette Breifel, Vaughn Call, Carmen Campbell, Dennis Carroll, Aurora D'Amico, Kathryn Dawson, Carol Emig, Joan Gaffney, Joe Gfroerer, Steve Gorman, Lawrence Greenfeld, Ruth Harris, Martha Hill, Gerry Hendershot, Sandra Hofferth, Gerald Joireman, Joleen Kirschenman, Robert Kominski, Enrique Lamas, Felicia LeClere, Gordon Lester, Kathryn London, Eleanor Maccoby, Steve McClaskie, Jack McNeil, Marie Moreno, Frank Mott, Martin O'Connell, Patrick O'Malley, Jeffrey Owings, Mark Peterson, Paul Placek, Peggy Quinn, Pat Rhoton, Charlotte Schoenborn, Christopher Sempos, Virgil Sheets, Tom Smith, Tracy Snell, Murray Straus, Arland Thornton, Doreen Trammell, Stephanie Ventura, Jim Warden, Greg Weyland, Chris Williams, Barbara Foley Wilson, and Linda Young-DeMarco.

The authors also wish to acknowledge James L. Peterson and Carolyn C. Rogers for their work on earlier editions of this guide, and James McGrath Morris for his patience and good advice in producing this guide

The opinions expressed herein do not necessarily reflect the positions of the U.S. Department of Health and Human Services or the agencies that sponsor the data collection programs described.

Introduction

The family is a basic building block of American society, fulfilling a variety of important functions for the young, the elderly, and those in the middle years of life. Over the last three decades, living arrangements and behavior patterns have changed rapidly. These changes have increased public concern over family issues and have stimulated a growth in family-oriented research in a wide variety of disciplines.

During this same period there has been a great increase in the number and quality of survey and administrative data sets with which one can perform family research of all sorts. Much of this valuable data is not used due both to a lack of access and to a lack of familiarity with the contents of the databases. The problem of access is now being addressed in a number of innovative ways. For example, many data sets are now available on CD-ROM, a development that promises to greatly increase access to all sorts of data. In 1992, the first archive of family studies on compact disk was produced by Sociometrics Corporation with support from the National Institute of Child Health and Human Development. This "archive on a disk" contains 14 data sets for family research, nearly all of which are reviewed in this guide.

This guide to family data is intended as a tool to increase the familiarity of the research community with the rich resources of existing databases. The databases described here have not been analyzed to produce anything like the wealth of facts, insights, and hypothesis tests that they could potentially yield. More often than not, research begins with a question rather than a data set. Using this guide, researchers can determine which if any existing databases contain the information needed to pursue their particular research questions.

The guide can also be of use to those who have no intention of carrying out analytic studies themselves, but want the best available answers to pressing questions about family trends. The guide catalogs the data resources that are potentially available to answer such questions, lists articles that have made use of major data sets, and gives names, addresses, and phone numbers of knowledgeable persons who can provide additional information on each database.

The production of the guide was sponsored by the Office of the Assistant Secretary for Planning and Evaluation of the U.S. Department of Health and Human Services. In underwriting the guide, that agency hoped to encourage more analysts to make use of available data for studies of individuals and families for both basic research and policy-relevant research.

Defining "The Family"

Most of the data sets described here adopt a definition of "the family" that is similar to the standard Census Bureau definition. That is, "a family is a group of two persons or more...related by birth, marriage, or adoption and residing together." Some researchers may wish to use a different definition of family, such as one that includes men and women who are not formally wed but live together as unmarried partners. Others may want to consider adults who live elsewhere but provide regular assistance or financial support as family members, or include gay or lesbian couples in their definition of family. Some data sets contain information that would allow for analyses based on alternative definitions of family, but others do not. Information is included in the database descriptions to assist researchers in determining whether or not such analyses are possible.

A Family-Based Approach To Social Policy

Understanding what families look like and how they function in contemporary society may provide insights into a variety of social problems, including educational underachievement, poverty, welfare dependence, domestic violence, delinquency and crime, mental illness, and substance abuse. Family factors seem important in the development and enactment of positive behaviors such as community participation, parents' involvement in their children's schools, and adult children's provision of care for their elderly parents. There are several reasons why a family-based approach to the analysis of social behaviors may be a useful supplement to conventional individual-based approaches. First of all, most people live in families, and virtually all have relatives with whom they interact, either within or outside their places of residence. Family members may make demands, require assistance, or provide support. Understanding family influences and interaction patterns can help us understand the context of people's lives. Of course, the quality of family relationships may be as important or more important than the fact that family members do or do not live together.

Dynamics within families have an influence on the well-being and functioning of individual members. Quality-of-life surveys have repeatedly shown that a person's sense of how well his or her family life is going is closely linked to overall life satisfaction. There are significant variations across families in the frequency of problems such as poverty, medical care use, and crime victimization. The reasons for these variations are not fully understood. Some families experience multiple problems, whereas other families are relatively problem free. One type of disease, such as alcoholism or drug addiction, may lead to the development of other family problems, such as frequent unemployment, family violence, or child neglect. Multiple-problem families may require different kinds of interventions or more intensive services than single-problem families.

Despite their problems, families usually carry out functions like rearing children and caring for frail or disabled adults more effectively and inexpensively than bureaucracies do. When families fail to perform certain functions or perform them badly, it makes sense for social agencies to seek ways to help families do a better job. In this way, a family-based approach may make social programs more cost-effective.

For all of these reasons, many policy makers and service providers have been advocating a shift away from the categorical and individual-oriented programs that have dominated health, education, and welfare policies in the United States. What they propose instead are more integrated and family-centered schemes for delivering services. In order to develop such schemes, new kinds of data and analyses are needed.

Data Implications of A Family-Based Approach

The first requirement of a family-based approach is to know how many families are affected by a particular social problem. For example, how many families have been victims of a crime in the last year? How many have one or more members who suffer from a chronic mental illness? How do these proportions vary by economic, social, and geographic characteristics?

It is important to know these things because when a person experiences illness, unemployment, crime victimization, or other negative happenings, his or her family members are also affected, sometimes in dramatic ways. Thus, a family-based analysis may provide a more accurate measure of the total impact of a given disease or social problem on American society. Conventional tabulations based on individuals provide only a partial indication of the number of families that are touched by a disease or dislocation, and give only a partial picture of the social and economic characteristics of the affected families.

A family-based approach also requires tabulation of data on the receipt of specific services with the family as the unit of analysis (for example, in how many families do one or more members receive a particular benefit or service?). Beyond this, information is needed on the problem "clusters" that families experience (for example, families caring for dependent elderly members as well as young children). Needed too is information on the combinations of private and public benefits and services that families receive or are eligible for (for example, how many low-income families receive publicly subsidized child care *and* Medicaid or employer-provided health insurance for their children?). Such information can lead to better appraisals of the adequacy of existing programs and delivery systems. Data are also needed on the direct provision of care by family members, how much they pay for care provided by others, and the ways in which family members act as agents or intermediaries between the affected individual and health care or social service agencies.

Although some of these data elements are not available currently, most of them are. They are contained in existing survey archives, but appropriate family-level analyses have rarely been carried out. This guide may assist researchers in pursuing family-oriented analyses of a variety of social problems.

Analyzing Links Between The Family And The Individual

In addition to family-based tabulations of problem occurrence and service receipt, the databases described in this guide can be used to analyze links between family situations and the functioning and well-being of individuals. These analyses can look at the effects of family circumstances on individual well-being, or look at the impact of individual behavior on the functioning of the family. Taking one tack, the researcher can examine whether being in particular family situations enhances or detracts from the performance or well-being of individual family members. For example, do married men who live with their wives and children tend to be more steadily employed and to work more hours per week than separated, divorced, or never married men of the same age and educational background? What are the family dynamics present when a young person drops out of high school?

Taking the opposite tack, the researcher can examine whether the behavior or health of individual members has favorable or unfavorable consequences for the functioning of their families. For example, are mothers and fathers who suffer from depression less likely to read to their young children regularly or play with them in intellectually stimulating ways? Are couples who have a child with retardation more likely to become divorced than comparable couples who do not have such a child?

On either tack, when significant associations between individual behavior and family functioning are found, researchers have to heed the old injunction not to confuse correlation with causality. For example, marital status and work effort may be related because men with a strong work ethic are more attractive as mates and hence more likely to get and stay married than men with less diligence. Since random experiments on family behavior are usually not possible, researchers have to seek ways of controlling statistically for confounding and selection bias. New econometric methods have recently become available to assist the researcher in this task.

Types of Surveys and Statistical Data Covered in the Guide

The body of the guide consists of descriptions of over 60 major survey and statistical databases that contain useful information about the characteristics, experiences, and behaviors of American families. These can be used by researchers who wish to carry out a study of a particular issue to locate a suitable database. The surveys described deal with an assortment of substantive issues, including health, education, employment and unemployment, poverty, crime, family formation and dissolution, child development, and substance abuse. The surveys are similar in that most are federally funded and nearly all are based on large national data collections using true probability samples of the population. A probability sample means that all persons in the sampled universe have a known chance of being included in the study. If such a sample is properly implemented and reasonable cooperation obtained, the survey findings should be generalizable, within a margin of sampling error, to the population as a whole. Furthermore, the various subgroups in the sample should accurately reflect the diversity of the U.S. population.

Characteristics of families in specific geographic areas. Although the surveys described here have samples that number in the thousands, most are not large enough to allow estimates at the local level, as for a particular city or county. Also, most have not been designed to yield estimates for specific states of the U.S. On the other hand, nearly all of the surveys yield valid estimates for different regions of the U.S., (e.g., the Northeast, Midwest, South, and West), and for urban, suburban, and rural areas within those regions.

Databases that permit one to assess the characteristics of families in specific states, cities, or counties, are the Decennial Census of the population and the Vital Statistics system. The latter includes:

- the birth registration system (from which natality statistics are derived);
- the death registration system (from which mortality statistics are extracted); and
- less comprehensive systems for registering marriages and divorces (which provide indicators of family formation and dissolution).

Trends in family living. In addition to the Decennial Census and the Vital Statistics system, a data collection program that all family researchers should be familiar with is the Current Population Survey (CPS). The CPS is an ongoing national survey that the Census Bureau conducts each month for the Bureau of Labor

Statistics. It is the federal government's primary mechanism for measuring trends in employment and unemployment. The CPS is also a major source of trend information about the nation's families, including trends in the marital situations of adults, the living arrangements of children, and family poverty. Recurring supplements to the CPS focus on topics such as family income and benefit receipt, child support and alimony, fertility, and school enrollment.

Family transitions and activity patterns. Four longitudinal studies and one cross-sectional survey described in the guide provide fertile ground for studies of the causes and consequences of family transitions. They are the Panel Study of Income Dynamics (PSID); the National Longitudinal Surveys of Labor Market Experience, including the National Longitudinal Survey of Youth (NLSY), sponsored by the Bureau of Labor Statistics; the National Survey of Families and Households; and the Survey of Income and Program Participation (SIPP). The last is a recurring panel survey, with each panel lasting a relatively short time (two and a half years). Topical modules of the SIPP cover issues such as retrospective information about the families of origin of adults in the survey, non-parental care arrangements for children, child support, functional limitations and disabilities of family members, support for non-household members, and the financing of post-secondary education.

The National Survey of Families and Households (NSFH) is a two-wave survey, which covers a wide range of family-related topics, including communication patterns, childrearing practices, family activities, division of household chores and responsibilities, family decision-making, marital satisfaction, community involvement, and contact with relatives outside the household. The National Survey of Family Growth (NSFG), a cross-sectional, recurring federal survey, focuses explicitly on issues related to family planning, childbearing, and infertility.

Child and youth development. Several of the studies profiled in the guide deal with families with children and contain data that make it possible to relate family structure and functioning to aspects of children's development and well-being. These surveys include the National Survey of Children (NSC), the National Commission on Children's Survey of Children and Parents, the National Health Interview Survey Child Health Supplements

(NHIS-CH), and the Child-Mother Data Supplements to the NLSY.

Post-divorce family functioning. Two important subnational studies provide information on divorce, child custody, and post-divorce family functioning. They are the Stanford Child Custody and Adolescent Custody Studies and the Noncustodial Parents Survey. National surveys that contain extensive information on marital separation and its consequences include the NSFH, the NSC, the NHIS-CS, the SIPP, and the Child Support and Fertility supplements to the CPS.

Public opinion on family matters. A number of the data sets described here contain information on public attitudes about family values, family behavior, and family policy and show how these attitudes have changed over time. Relevant surveys include the General Social Survey (GSS) and the Study of American Families, as well as polls done for the National Commission on Children, the NSFH, and the NSC. The Public Opinion Location Library can guide the researcher to privately-sponsored opinion polls that contain questions on specific family-related topics of interest. Trends in youthful attitudes about family matters are tracked in an annual survey of high school seniors, Monitoring the Future.

Health, education, crime and other specific topics. The principal source of national data on family expenditure patterns is the Consumer Expenditure Survey. In the years between censuses, data on the housing of American families is provided by the American Housing Survey. Major health surveys described in the guide include the National Health Interview Survey (NHIS), which is conducted annually; the National Health and Nutrition Examination Survey (NHANES), which includes direct measures of physiological and biochemical variables, as well as interview-based information; and the National Medical Expenditure Survey (NMES).

Data on an important set of health-related behaviors, namely smoking, alcohol consumption, and use of illicit drugs are obtained in the National Household Survey on Drug Abuse. Self-reports of smoking and substance abuse by high school students are obtained in the annual school-based survey, Monitoring the Future.

In the area of education, the major surveys covered include three National Education Longitudinal Surveys (NELS), the National Assessment of Educational Progress (NAEP), and the National Household Education Survey (NHES), a recently begun series of cross-sectional surveys. Both the NAEP and the NELS involve direct testing of the academic achievement of representative samples of American youth.

Information on crime from the victim's perspective is gathered in the National Crime Victimization Survey (NCVS). Information about the family circumstances and backgrounds of offenders is obtained in a series of periodic surveys of inmates of various correctional institutions, such as the Survey of Juveniles in Custody. Data on family violence are obtained in the National Surveys of Family Violence and the Study of the National Incidence and Prevalence of Child Abuse and Neglect.

Families with elderly members. There is a growing body of survey data on families containing elderly members. Examples are the 1984 Supplement on Aging to the National Health Interview Survey, and its followup, the Longitudinal Study of Aging; the NHANES I Epidemiological Followup Study; the National Long Term Care Surveys; and the Current Beneficiary Survey of Medicare Recipients. Due to time and space limitations, these surveys are not covered in this guide. For further information on these and other relevant databases, the reader is directed to a publication of the National Center for Health Statistics entitled *Health Statistics on Older Persons*. Additional guidance may be obtained from the National Institute on Aging, the Agency for Health Care Policy and Research, and the Health Care Financing Administration.

Format of Database Descriptions

For each survey or statistical program described in this guide, material is presented on the purpose of the effort, the sponsoring agency, and the design of the survey or other data gathering procedure. Design information includes who was covered in the survey universe, how large the sample was, how often the survey has been conducted, and what completion rate was achieved. The content of the survey instrument or data collection form is summarized by listing topics covered, especially those involving potential causes or consequences of family behavior.

In the "Limitations" section of each survey write-up, we have tried to alert the analyst to gaps and biases in the data, particularly those that may cause difficulties or lead to erroneous conclusions for family-based studies. The "Availability" section tells where and how to get the data files, and gives the name, address, and phone number of one or more contact persons. The "Publications" section gives a short bibliography of selected articles and reports that have made use of the data set in question.

The last three pages of each database write-up consist of checklists that show what the survey questionnaire or data collection form provides in the way of descriptive material about the families covered in the sample. These checklists show the varieties of families that can be identified in the database and the sorts of family-related variables against which other variables (such as measures of the prevalence of various social problems) can be tabulated. This is critical information for the analyst who is deciding whether or not the database can be used to investigate a particular issue.

The first checklist is composed of items pertaining to family-level characteristics; i.e., those that apply to the family as a whole. The second consists of items describing the characteristics of adult family members, and the third, of items on the characteristics of children in the family. The following sections give illustrations of the specific items included in the checklists.

Family-level characteristics. These include attributes that relate to the composition, social status, geographic location, life cycle stage, and functioning of the family. Specific items include the following:

Family composition (What do we know about who is in the family? About how they are related to one another? Is there information about part-time household members? About family members who no longer live in the household? About relatives who live nearby, but not in the household?);

Socioeconomic variables (Can we determine the family income level, or whether the family is below the official poverty line? Do we know whether the family receives welfare payments or food stamps or other non-cash benefits? Can we tell whether a language other than English is spoken in the home?);

Geographic/community variables (Does the database indicate in which region, state, county or city, zip code or telephone area code the family resides? Is there coded data pertaining to neighborhood quality or the state of the local labor market at the time of the survey?);

Stage in the family life cycle (Do we know the age of the adult respondent or his or her spouse/partner? Can we differentiate adults who were never married from those who were formerly married? Or those who have not yet had children from those who no longer have children living at home? Or those who are retired from those who are unemployed or not in the labor force for other reasons?); and

Family functioning (Does the database provide any information about family activities or time use patterns? About the family's level of community involvement? Do we know how much family members communicate with one another or how family decisions are made? Are there indicators of marital conflict or marital happiness or satisfaction? Do we know whether the family has a history of marital separations, family violence, or receipt of marital counseling?)

Two important distinctions relating to family composition are captured in the family-level checklists. The first involves whether or not a complete roster of household members is taken as part of the data collection procedure. A full roster means that one person in the household is defined as the reference person, and all household members are listed by age, sex, and relationship to the reference person.

The full roster is most useful from a family analysis perspective. It enables the analyst to derive information about family size, number of siblings, presence of extended relatives, and presence of non-related adults or children. However, some studies take only a partial roster of household members, or just collect summary information about the number of adults or the number of children in the household. When the roster is less complete, the analytic possibilities are obviously more constrained. Indeed, if no relationship information is collected, it may not even be possible to tell whether the household contains a family at all.

A second important distinction captured in the checklist is whether relationships between family members have been captured in exact terms or approximate terms. Exact relationships mean, for example, that when a person is described as a child's mother, the interviewer probes to find out whether the mother is the child's birth mother, adoptive mother, stepmother, foster mother, or other female guardian. Likewise for the child's father. Sibling relationships are similarly specified as to whether, for example, two brothers are full brothers, half brothers, adoptive brothers, or stepbrothers.

It is only when family relationships have been determined exactly that it becomes possible to identify stepfamilies, or "blended" families, or adoptive families, and carry out separate or comparative analyses of these family forms. In addition, specification of exact relationships opens up possibilities for twin or sibling studies that try to separate family environmental influences from genetic influences on children's development, learning, and behavior.

Characteristics of adult family members. In the checklist on adult characteristics, separate note is taken of the information provided about the focal adult or adult reference person, his or her current spouse who resides in the household, and a current or former spouse who does not live in the household at the time of the survey. Typically, the most family-related information is obtained about the reference adult, considerably less about the resident spouse, and much less, if any, about a former or non-resident spouse.

Specific types of items contained in the adult checklist include the following:

basic demographic data (age, gender, race and Hispanic origin);

more detailed background information (ethnic origins other than Hispanic, country of birth, immigrant status, fluency in English, residential mobility, religious affiliation and level of religious participation);

marriage, fertility, and parenting patterns (cohabitation status and history, marital status and history, parental status, age at first birth, number of children ever born or sired, existence of children who live elsewhere, payment of child support);

educational data (aptitude or achievement test score, years of education, degrees attained);

employment and earnings information (employment status, annual employment pattern, main occupation, earnings, wage rate, work-related attitudes); and

physical and mental well-being (health and disability status, measures of self-concept and subjective well-being).

Characteristics of child family members. In the checklist on child characteristics, information provided about a focal or reference child and information provided about other children in the family are separately coded. Even in surveys that focus on children or youth, it is often the case that much more information is obtained about a reference child than about other children in the family. This restricts analyses that seek to describe a family's children as a group, or that try to examine similarities or differences among different children in the same family. In some surveys, however, questions are asked about all children in a given age range. Alternatively, questions may be obtained about a random subset of children, such as two but no more. In these cases, relationships among family members can be analyzed.

Specific types of information contained in the child checklist include the following:

basic demographic data (month and year of birth, current age, gender, race and Hispanic origin, exact relationship to adult family members, exact relationship to other children in household);

more detailed background information (ethnic origins other than Hispanic, country of birth and immigrant status, fluency in English, religious affiliation and participation);

educational data (aptitude or achievement test score, enrollment in daycare, preschool, or regular school, grade attainment and grade repetition);

physical health and psychological well-being (health status, handicapping conditions, measures of subjective well-being, delinquent behavior); and

employment, marriage, fertility, and parenting patterns of older youth (if relevant: marital status and history, pregnancy and birth history, parental status and history, employment status and history).

We conclude this introduction by alerting the reader to the advantages and drawbacks of using the data sets described in this guide to study family circumstances and behavior. We also note some needed improvements in the collection of survey data on families, improvements that would make these data far more useful to researchers and policy analysts.

Advantages of Working With Large-Scale Databases

There are a number of advantages to be gained by carrying out a study of family behavior by means of secondary analysis of a data set described in this guide as opposed to the collection and analysis of new data. The benefits include the following:

The analysis of existing data usually takes far less time and costs less money than gathering and analyzing new data.

The sample of families on which conclusions are based is likely to be larger and more representative of the general population.

Sampling methods are explicitly defined and implemented, and the completion rate achieved in the study is clearly specified. This is often not the case in non-federal studies using small samples, volunteer samples, or samples of convenience.

Information about demographic and socioeconomic characteristics of family members is gathered in well-established ways.

Existing data sets can be used to study historical trends in family behavior and group differences in behavior at earlier points in time.

Conclusions based on existing data sets may be less biased by demand characteristics that are often introduced when an investigator sets out to do a new survey on a specific topic, such as the effects of divorce on children.

Drawbacks of Using Existing Databases

Although studying family behavior through analysis of existing data has distinct advantages, the researcher should also be aware of the limitations of the method. Among the drawbacks are the following:

Many of the data sets described in this volume do not contain measures of family process, information greatly desired by many researchers.

A good deal of manipulation may be required to produce family-level information from survey files, which are typically organized with the individual respondent as the unit of data collection and analysis.

Because of their individual orientation, many surveys lack appropriate weights for producing national estimates of the number of families (as opposed to the number of individuals) for whom a given characteristic applies.

Rarely do the measures included in a national study emerge from a coherent theoretical framework.

Most of the measures used in large-scale studies consist of single items or short scales, and some of the scales have low reliability or are not well-validated.

Most of the behavioral measures contained in large-scale data sets are based on self-reports of survey respondents, which have inherent limitations and biases.

Many data sets lack information that would permit the analyst to identify certain types of families, e.g., stepfamilies or families with adopted children.

Even large databases usually contain relatively few cases of rare family types, and caution should be exercised in generalizing from these small subsamples.

Balancing the Strengths and Weaknesses of Survey Data

Some researchers who have not worked with survey data take extreme positions on the value of such data. They either accept survey data in an uncritical fashion, or reject them out of hand as hopelessly biased and invalid. The truth is rather more complicated. Although survey measures are often blurred by both random noise and systematic bias, they generally contain real "signal" as well. Experienced survey researchers can tease valid conclusions out of imperfect measures by looking at patterns of relationships rather than single numbers. Also, the imperfections of questionnaire-based measures have to be balanced against the virtues of large probability samples. These samples represent the full range of variation in attitudes, behaviors, and living arrangements, and include segments of the population that are often missing from small-scale studies based on samples of convenience. We hope this guide will inspire many researchers with an interest in families who have not tried secondary analysis studies to conduct family-oriented tabulations and multivariate studies employing the data described in this volume.

Needed Improvements in Survey Data on Families

The process of reviewing and appraising the data sets described in this guide caused the authors to develop definite ideas about the kinds of changes needed to make survey data on families more useful to both academic researchers and policy analysts. We conclude by summarizing these recommendations.

First, the field of family research would benefit greatly if a standard set of family descriptors were used throughout the federal statistical system. This would make it possible, for example, to draw a more rounded picture of the health and well-being of specific types of families, of the problems they experience and the services they receive. By having uniform descriptors, information that is obtained in different surveys can be integrated at the subgroup level. The family-level checklist used in this guide illustrates the kinds of variables that ought to be contained in the standard set of descriptors.

Second, secondary research on families would be more fruitful if large-scale surveys made use of concepts and measures that matched the realities of modern family life. One of those realities is the challenge of balancing work and family responsibilities in two-earner and single-parent families. While many families balance family and work on full-time work schedules, other adults follow part-time, part-year, or staggered work schedules. One or both parents work only part-time, or for part of the year only, or on shifts that reduce the need for child care or enable one parent to be home when the children are home. Getting information about year-round work schedules and coordination of shifts between parents, rather than just asking about each adult's employment in the last week or two, would yield a better understanding of the changing patterns of work life.

Another reality of modern life is that many families have members who live elsewhere but maintain contact with the family or provide financial support or assistance with child care. This member may be a separated, divorced, or never-married parent, or a grandmother or other family member who lives in the neighborhood but not in the household. Surveys should collect more information about non-resident family members and family interactions that cross household boundaries.

Family research would be aided if surveys obtained data on more than one family member at a time. This would make it possible, for example, to examine the influence of the health-related behavior of one family member on the parallel behavior of other family members. When, as is often the case, only one random adult per family is selected for study, such within-family effects cannot be analyzed.

Methodological research is needed to develop more accurate methods of assessing basic conditions of family living. Chief among these are indicators of the basic economic well-being of families. Current measures of family income suffer from substantial missing data and deliberate under-reporting of some forms of income because of fears that the respondent may be penalized by the government if she or he reports truthfully. Assessments of levels of living based on consumption or expenditure patterns (the goods and services available to the family) may prove more useful than assessments based on income. Better measures of neighborhood and community characteristics and family supports should also be developed.

Finally, family researchers could certainly make use of data sets that provide more information about how families are functioning as a unit. This means questions or observations about communication patterns and the division of chores and responsibilities within the family, on how family decisions are made, and how the family adjusts to changing economic circumstances and to developments in the education, work, and health situations of individual members. Obtaining valid data on these topics at reasonable cost may prove challenging. But federal agencies and private survey sponsors have to take on this challenge if we are to learn how family life is changing and find better ways of assisting families in carrying out their critical functions.

American Housing Survey

PURPOSE The American Housing Survey (AHS) is a source of current information on the quality and quantity of America's housing stock. The survey provides a current and continuous series of data on selected housing and demographic characteristics to researchers, planners, and policymakers on the national, local, and corporate levels. Topics covered in the survey include: housing costs, the physical condition and age of the unit, equipment available (such as a heating system), residential mobility, neighborhood services available to residents, and needed improvements for all types of public and private housing in various locations. Basic demographic and income data are collected for the members of each household in the survey. Data are also collected in occasional survey supplements on topics such as energy conservation, commuting, and disabilities.

SPONSORSHIP The survey is designed and funded by the Division of Housing and Demographic Analysis, Office of Policy Development and Research, Department of Housing and Urban Development. The Bureau of the Census is responsible for the collection, tabulation, and publication of the survey data.

DESIGN The American Housing Survey is divided into two separate components: a national longitudinal sample of housing units from urban and rural areas surveyed in odd-numbered years, and a longitudinal metropolitan sample. In 1985, the national sample was redesigned, with the selection of housing units based on data from the 1980 decennial census and information on new construction. The national sample comprises 46,000 to 52,000 housing units drawn from listings stratified according to housing as well as household characteristics. The sample for the 1973-1983 surveys was stratified only by household characteristics; thus, the redesigned sample, though smaller, is a better representation of the housing stock. In most national AHS surveys, there is an extra sample of approximately 6,000 rural units for more accurate rural estimates. For years in which a neighbor sample is drawn, however, no rural sample is selected. In each survey, new dwelling units are added to replace lost units and to represent new construction. As in 1985 and 1989, a special neighbors sample will be drawn in 1993. For each of 660 members of the national sample, a sample of ten neighbors are selected and interviewed. With this sample, one may look at such issues as the degree of homogeneity among both housing unit and the inhabitant characteristics within neighborhoods.

The metropolitan survey is conducted in 44 metropolitan areas interviewed on a rotating basis (11 each year). Each metropolitan area is surveyed once every four years. Metropolitan areas covered were originally selected to represent the largest and fastest growing of such areas in the country. The sample consists of units included in previous enumerations supplemented by new construction and by units from any new geographic areas added to the metropolitan area definition between 1970 and 1980.

The American Housing Survey is a survey of housing units, not of individuals or families. For occupied housing units, the respondent must be a knowledgeable household member 16 years of age or over who provides information on the housing unit, household composition, and income. Typically, the person selected as the household respondent is the householder or spouse of the householder. For vacant housing units, the landlord, owner, real estate agent, or a knowledgeable neighbor provides data on the housing unit. Occupants of group quarters are not interviewed.

An initial sample of housing units was drawn in 1973 and followed through 1983. All housing units in the 50 states and the District of Columbia, including vacant units, are represented. Interviewers return to the same housing unit in the sample to interview current residents of the unit. The sample size of the first national survey conducted in 1973 was 60,000 units. In 1974, the sample size was increased by 16,000 rural units. These units were dropped from the 1981 survey due to budget constraints, but were subsequently reinstated for the 1983 survey. The 1985 national survey, redesigned based on the 1980 census, was conducted in the fall of 1985, with a sample size of approximately 53,000 units.

The metropolitan survey was initially called the SMSA survey; the name was changed in 1984 to reflect changes in the definition and composition of such areas. The original SMSA survey consisted of 60 SMSAs divided into three groups of 20 SMSAs each. These groups were interviewed on a rotating basis beginning in 1974; each group had a total sample size of 140,000. Beginning in 1978, this was changed to four groups of 15 SMSAs due to budget constraints. Further budgetary considerations in 1982 required a reduction in the number of SMSAs to be interviewed annually and also a reduction in the sample size by about 50%. The 1986 and subsequent metropolitan survey samples includes 11 metropolitan areas each year. In 1991, the sample size per metropolitan area was 3,800.

PERIODICITY Interviewing for the first national survey was conducted in 1973. The survey was conducted annually from 1973 to 1981; thereafter, it was conducted biennially. The national sample was redesigned in 1985 based on data from the 1980 decennial census. The metropolitan survey was first conducted in 1974 and has been continued each year during the period mid-March through December. The metropolitan survey is conducted on a four-year cycle, with a quarter of the cities being studied each year.

CONTENT A large volume of information is collected on the characteristics and condition of the housing unit, the type of utilities used, the age and condition of kitchen appliances, the condition of the plumbing, heating, and cooling systems, the neighborhood, housing costs and values, and the mobility of the residents. Information is also collected about the geographical characteristics of the place where the housing unit is located, such as the size of the community and whether it is in a central city, an urbanized suburb, a suburb, and so on. More limited information is collected on household composition, relationship of household members to the reference person, and the characteristics and income of household members. Occasional supplements have collected information on commuting patterns, second homes, mobile homes, disabilities and handicaps of members of the household, and assets such as ownership of cars and major appliances.

Although exact relationships among household members cannot be identified (e.g., stepchildren of the reference person are not distinguished from biological children), it is possible to identify

3

married-couple households with and without children, and households maintained by a never-married adult or by a divorced or separated adult. Because the ages of all household residents are obtained, it is also possible to identify households maintained by the elderly or in which young children are living. The AHS could thus be used to describe the living conditions and neighborhoods of selected types of families. For example, it is possible to determine which types of families are more apt to live in a house or apartment that is uncomfortably cold during the winter, has breakdowns of the heating system, peeling plaster or a leaky roof, or other such conditions. To the extent that sample size permits, a comparison of the living conditions and neighborhoods of families living in different types of communities could also be made, such as between single-parent families living in central cities and in suburbs.

Because the AHS has been collected since 1973 and many of the same items have been asked repeatedly, it is possible to use the AHS to examine how the living conditions of various types of families have changed over time.

LIMITATIONS Information on household residents is not as detailed as in most other federal surveys of its size. There are no direct measures of family functioning. Finally, because households and not residents are the units of analysis, persons are lost to the survey whenever they move. Strengths of the survey include the detailed information on the housing unit and the neighborhood, though the neighborhood measures are subjective evaluations of the reference person.

AVAILABILITY Public use data tapes are available from:

> HUD User
> Box 6091
> Rockville, MD 20850
> 800/245-2691
> 301/251-5154

For information concerning the content of the survey contact:

> Paul Burke
> Office of the Assistant Secretary for
> Policy Development and Research
> Department of Housing and Urban Development
> Washington, DC 20410
> 202/708-1060

PUBLICATIONS

The Bureau of the Census publishes data for both the national and metropolitan sample surveys as joint HUD-Census reports, approximately 15-18 months after the end of data collection. A regular series of reports is produced: the national reports are contained in *Current Housing Reports*, Series H-150; reports on occasionally covered topics such as commuting, disabilities, and second homes are covered in *Current Housing Reports*, Series H-151; and the metropolitan reports are published separately for each metropolitan area as *Current Housing Reports*, Series H-170. A number of reports unique to each metropolitan area are also published.

A complete listing of reports are available from:

> HUD User
> Box 6091
> Rockville, MD 20850
> 800/245-2691
> 301/251-5154

In addition, Abt Associates, Inc., sells several useful publications about the American Housing Survey, including a codebook that covers both the national and metropolitan surveys for the years 1973 to 1993 entitled, *Codebook for the American Housing Survey Data Base: 1973 to 1993*. This directory provides unweighted frequency distributions for each variable, a cross-reference to tape locations and questionnaire items for all surveys information on allocation variables and copies of the questionnaires used in the surveys. These publications can be obtained by contacting:

AHS Data Project
Abt Associates, Inc.
55 Wheeler Street
Cambridge, MA 02138
617/497-7182

American Housing Survey
Year of Questionnaire: 1991
Sample size: approximately 46,400 occupied housing units
FAMILY-LEVEL CHARACTERISTICS

Family Composition
● Full roster of household members (first name, age, sex, and relationship to reference person of each member)
○ Partial roster of household members
● Number of adults in household
● Number of children in household
● Approximate relationship of family members to householder, child, or one another
○ Exact relationship of family members to householder, child, or one another
○ Information about part-time household member
○ Information about family members no longer living in household
○ Information about relatives who live nearby but not in household

Socioeconomic
● Total family income
○ Number of persons who depend on family income
● Sources of income
● Income amounts identified separately by source
● Poverty status[1]
● Welfare status
● Food Stamps receipt
● Child support receipt
○ Medicaid coverage
○ Private health insurance
● Home ownership/renters
○ Assets (other than home ownership)
● Public housing status
○ Telephone in household
○ Language other than English spoken in home

Geographic/Community Variables
● Region of country
● State of residence
● County/city/MSA of residence
● Size/type of community
○ Zip code
○ Telephone area code
● Metropolitan residence
● Neighborhood quality
○ Local labor market

Stage in Family Life Cycle
● Age of adult respondent or spouse/partner
● Marital status of adult respondent or spouse/partner
○ Employment status of adult respondent or spouse/partner
● Presence of own children in household
● Age of youngest own child in household
● Age of oldest own child in household
○ Existence of own children who have left home
○ Intention to have (more) children in future

7

Family Functioning
- Family activities or time use
- Community involvement (civic, religious, recreational)
- Family communication patterns
- Family decision-making
- Marital conflict
- Marital happiness/satisfaction
- Parent-child conflict
- History of marital separations
- History of family violence
- History of marital counselling

CHARACTERISTICS OF ADULT FAMILY MEMBERS

Adult Respondent or Reference Person	Current Spouse in HH	Current or Former Spouse Not in HH	
●	●	○	Age
●	●	○	Gender
●	●	○	Race
●	●	○	Hispanic origin
●	●	○	Other origin/ethnicity[2]
○	○	○	Religious affiliation
○	○	○	Religious participation
○	○	○	Country of birth
○	○	○	Immigrant status
○	○	○	English fluency
●	●	○	Current marital status
○	○	○	Marital history
○	○	○	Cohabitation status
○	○	○	Cohabitation history
○	○	○	Parental status
○	○	○	Number children ever born/sired
○	○	○	Age at first birth
○	○	○	Age of youngest child
○	○	○	Children living elsewhere
●	●	○	Duration at current address
●	●	○	Residential mobility
●	●	○	Educational attainment
○	○	○	Degrees attained
○	○	○	GED or regular HS diploma
○	○	○	Current enrollment
○	○	○	Current employment status
○	○	○	Hours usually worked (ft/pt)
○	○	○	Weeks worked
○	○	○	Annual employment pattern
○	○	○	Main occupation
●	●	○	Earnings
○	○	○	Wage rate
○	○	○	Payment of child support
○	○	○	Aptitude or achievement score
○	○	○	Health/disability status
○	○	○	Self-esteem
○	○	○	Locus of control or efficacy
○	○	○	Depression or subjective well-being
○	○	○	Work-related attitudes

CHARACTERISTICS OF CHILD FAMILY MEMBERS

Reference Child or Youth Respondent	Children (in HH)	
O	●	Age
O	O	Month and year of birth
O	●	Gender
O	●	Race
O	●	Hispanic origin
O	O	Other origin/ethnicity
O	O	Religious affiliation
O	O	Religious participation
O	O	Country of birth
O	O	Immigrant status
O	O	English fluency
O	O	Exact relationship to adult family members
O	O	Exact relationship to other children in HH
O	●	Marital status/history[3]
O	O	Parental status/history
O	O	Current enrollment in regular school
O	O	Current enrollment in preschool/daycare
O	●	Highest grade completed[3]
O	O	Grade now enrolled
O	O	Employment status/history
O	O	Health status
O	O	Handicapping conditions
O	O	Grade repetition
O	O	Aptitude or achievement score
O	O	Pregnancy/birth history
O	O	Psychological well-being
O	O	Delinquency

NOTES
1. Reports total *household* income as percent of poverty level.
2. Possible to identify American Indian, Aleutian, Eskimo, or Alaskan Native and Asian or Pacific Islander.
3. Asked for persons 14 years of age and older.

Consumer Expenditure Surveys

PURPOSE The Consumer Expenditure Surveys are designed to provide a current and continuous series of data on consumer expenditures and other related characteristics. The data are used to determine the need to revise the Consumer Price Index (CPI) and also to study family expenditures and related issues. The surveys provide timely and detailed information on the consumption patterns of different types of families. Rapidly changing economic conditions and use of the CPI to adjust many prices and benefits have made frequent data collection necessary; consequently, the Consumer Expenditure Surveys have been conducted on a continuing basis.

SPONSORSHIP The data collection effort is designed by the Bureau of Labor Statistics, with the Bureau of the Census responsible for conducting the survey.

DESIGN The surveys are based upon a nationally representative probability sample of the total noninstitutional U.S. population; a rotating sample of households in 106 Primary Sampling Units (PSUs) is selected. All 50 states and the District of Columbia are included. There are two components: the Quarterly Interview Survey and the Diary Survey. In November 1985, a sample design based on the 1980 census was introduced for the Quarterly Interview Survey. New PSUs were introduced in the Diary Survey in December 1985. With the new samples, the Quarterly Interview Survey has approximately 7,000 designated addresses quarterly and the Diary Survey has approximately 7,000 designated addresses annually.

In the Quarterly Interview Survey, each address is visited five times, once per quarter for five consecutive quarters, spanning 15 months. The Quarterly Interview Survey obtains data on large or regular expenditures.

In the Diary Survey, respondents are asked to keep two one-week diaries for recording purchases. The Diary Survey provides data on items not covered in detail in the Quarterly Interview Survey.

Data are collected by means of an in-person interview, except for the Diary Survey, which is left for the respondent to complete. The household respondent, who must be a knowledgeable household member 16 years old or older, provides information for the entire household. A "respondent" is a consumer unit defined in terms of financial independence. Five people living together constitute five units if they are financially independent from one another. On the other hand, a family of five is one consumer unit. A sample of 5,000 consumer units are interviewed in the Diary Survey, and another sample of 5,000 consumer units are interviewed in the Quarterly Interview Survey (panel study).

PERIODICITY The Consumer Expenditure Surveys are continuing surveys, with interviews conducted throughout the month. Twenty percent of the respondents are replaced each quarter. The surveys began in 1980.

CONTENT The Quarterly Interview Survey collects detailed information on large expenditures and some other purchases which occur on a fairly regular basis, that is, those expenditures which respondents can be expected to recall fairly accurately over a three-month period or for which records are readily available. The Diary Survey obtains data on all purchases made during a week, providing detailed information on small, frequently purchased items (food, meals, personal care products and services, housekeeping supplies) as well as small expenditure items that are occasionally purchased. Although the focus of the surveys is on consumption patterns, data are also collected on a number of characteristics of consumers, including income, family structure, and the age and sex of children.

LIMITATIONS The surveys focus on expenditure patterns of consumer units, and the family is treated as one unit. Demographic characteristics are collected for each member of the consumer unit.

AVAILABILITY Data are integrated from the Diary and Interview Surveys and are published in an annual report and a biannual bulletin. The integrated data provide a complete accounting of consumer unit expenditures and income, which neither survey component alone is designed to do. Survey data shown at the same level of detail published in the bulletin are available on diskettes shortly after publication of the annual report. Interview Survey data are published in quarterly reports. Public use tapes with data from the Interview Survey and Diary Survey are made available a few months after publication of the annual report. For further information or to order a data tape, contact:

> Stephanie Shipp or Eva Jacobs
> Consumer Expenditure Survey
> Bureau of Labor Statistics
> Washington, DC 20212
> 202/606-6900

PUBLICATIONS

Hanson, S.L. & Ooms, T. (1991). The economic costs and rewards of two-earner, two-parent families. *Journal of Marriage and the Family, 53*(3), 622-634.

U.S. Department of Labor. (August 1991). *Consumer Expenditures Survey, 1988-89.* Bureau of Labor Statistics Bulletin 2383. Washington, DC: GPO.

U.S. Department of Labor. (December 1992). *Consumer expenditures in 1991.* Bureau of Labor Statistics Report No. 835. Washington, DC: GPO.

Consumer Expenditure Surveys
Interview and Diary Public Use Tapes
Year of Questionnaire: 1991
Sample size: 5,000 consumer units for each survey
FAMILY-LEVEL CHARACTERISTICS

Family Composition
- ● Full roster of household members (first name, age, sex, and relationship to reference person of each member)
- ○ Partial roster of household members
- ○ Number of adults in household
- ○ Number of children in household
- ○ Approximate relationship of family members to householder, child, or one another
- ○ Exact relationship of family members to householder, child, or one another
- ○ Information about part-time household member
- ○ Information about family members no longer living in household
- ○ Information about relatives who live nearby but not in household

Socioeconomic
- ● Total family income
- ○ Number of persons who depend on family income
- ● Sources of income
- ● Income amounts identified separately by source
- ● Poverty status[1]
- ○ Welfare status
- ● Food Stamps receipt
- ● Child support receipt
- ● Medicaid coverage
- ● Private health insurance
- ● Home ownership/renters
- ● Assets (other than home ownership)
- ● Public housing status
- ● Telephone in household[2]
- ○ Language other than English spoken in home

Geographic/Community Variables
- ● Region of country
- ○ State of residence
- ○ County/city/MSA of residence
- ○ Size/type of community
- ○ Zip code
- ○ Telephone area code
- ○ Metropolitan residence
- ○ Neighborhood quality
- ○ Local labor market

Stage in Family Life Cycle
- ● Age of adult respondent or spouse/partner
- ● Marital status of adult respondent or spouse/partner
- ● Employment status of adult respondent or spouse/partner
- ● Presence of own children in household
- ● Age of youngest own child in household
- ● Age of oldest own child in household
- ○ Existence of own children who have left home
- ○ Intention to have (more) children in future

Family Functioning

○ Family activities or time use
○ Community involvement (civic, religious, recreational)
○ Family communication patterns
○ Family decision-making
○ Marital conflict
○ Marital happiness/satisfaction
○ Parent-child conflict
○ History of marital separations
○ History of family violence
○ History of marital counselling

CHARACTERISTICS OF ADULT FAMILY MEMBERS

Adult Respondent or Reference Person	Current Spouse in HH	Current or Former Spouse Not in HH	
●	●	○	Age
●	●	○	Gender
●	●	○	Race
●	●	○	Hispanic origin
○	○	○	Other origin/ethnicity
○	○	○	Religious affiliation
○	○	○	Religious participation
○	○	○	Country of birth
○	○	○	Immigrant status
○	○	○	English fluency
●	●	○	Current marital status
○	○	○	Marital history
○	○	○	Cohabitation status
○	○	○	Cohabitation history
●	●	○	Parental status
○	○	○	Number children ever born/sired
○	○	○	Age at first birth
○	○	○	Age of youngest child
○	○	○	Children living elsewhere
○	○	○	Duration at current address
○	○	○	Residential mobility
●	●	○	Educational attainment
○	○	○	Degrees attained
●	●	○	GED or regular HS diploma
●	●	○	Current enrollment
●	●	○	Current employment status
●	●	○	Hours usually worked (ft/pt)
●	●	○	Weeks worked
○	○	○	Annual employment pattern
●	●	○	Main occupation
●	●	○	Earnings
○	○	○	Wage rate
●	●	○	Payment of child support
○	○	○	Aptitude or achievement score
○	○	○	Health/disability status
○	○	○	Self-esteem
○	○	○	Locus of control or efficacy
○	○	○	Depression or subjective well-being
○	○	○	Work-related attitudes

CHARACTERISTICS OF CHILD FAMILY MEMBERS

Reference Child or Youth Respondent	Other Children (in HH)	
○	●	Age
○	○	Month and year of birth
○	●	Gender
○	●	Race
○	●	Hispanic origin
○	○	Other origin/ethnicity
○	○	Religious affiliation
○	○	Religious participation
○	○	Country of birth
○	○	Immigrant status
○	○	English fluency
○	●	Exact relationship to adult family members
○	●	Exact relationship to other children in HH
○	○	Marital status/history
○	○	Parental status/history
○	○	Current enrollment in regular school
○	○	Current enrollment in preschool/daycare
○	○	Highest grade completed
○	○	Grade now enrolled
○	●	Employment status/history[3]
○	○	Health status
○	○	Handicapping conditions
○	○	Grade repetition
○	○	Aptitude or achievement score
○	○	Pregnancy/birth history
○	○	Psychological well-being
○	○	Delinquency

NOTES
1. Collected on Interview Survey only.
2. If they have bought a telephone and/or paid any telephone bills.
3. Over age 14.

15

Current Population Survey —Core Survey

PURPOSE The Current Population Survey (CPS) is designed to provide estimates of employment, unemployment, and other characteristics of the general labor force, the population as a whole, and various subgroups of the population. Monthly labor force data for the nation, the 11 largest states, New York City, and Los Angeles are used by the Bureau of Labor Statistics to determine the distribution of funds under the Job Training Partnership Act.

In addition to the collection of labor force data, the CPS's basic funding provides annual data on work experience, income, and migration (the annual March income and demographic supplement), and school enrollment of the population (the October supplement). Other supplements are conducted as part of the CPS but are separately funded; these include the child support and alimony supplement (April), the fertility and birth expectations supplement (June), and the supplement on the immunization status of the population (most recently collected in September 1985).

SPONSORSHIP The Core Survey is funded by the Bureau of the Census and the Bureau of Labor Statistics. The Census Bureau has the responsibility for sample design, data collection, and tabulation. Since July 1959, the Bureau of Labor Statistics has been responsible for the analysis and publication of CPS data on unemployment and characteristics of the labor force. The supplements are funded by a variety of sponsors.

DESIGN The Current Population Survey is designed to be representative of the civilian, noninstitutional population of the United States, and of Armed Forces personnel living off base or on base with their families. The total sample size is approximately 71,000 households per month, located in 729 primary sampling units (PSUs), comprising 1,973 counties and independent cities with coverage in every state and in the District of Columbia. About 57,000 households are interviewed in the monthly survey. The remainder of the assigned housing units are found to be vacant, converted to non-residential use, to contain persons with residence elsewhere, or are not interviewed because the residents are not found at home after repeated calls, are temporarily absent, or are unavailable for other reasons. The household respondent must be a knowledgeable household member 15 years old or older; the respondent provides information for each household member.

Since its inception in 1940, various revisions and expansions of the CPS sample have taken place. This description refers to the most recent change to a state-based design, which was phased in from April 1984 to July 1985 and is currently in place. Data from the 1980 Decennial Census were used to select independent samples for the 50 states and the District of Columbia. The combined samples allow the CPS to produce reliable monthly estimates for the nation and the 11 largest states, as well as reliable estimates for all states and selected metropolitan areas on an annual average basis. The sample will be revised again based on the results of the 1990 Census. Changes will be phased in between April 1994 and July 1995.

The CPS is a probability sample based on a multistage stratified sampling scheme. Each month's sample is divided into eight approximately equal rotation groups. A rotation group is interviewed for four consecutive months, then temporarily leaves the sample for eight months, and returns for four more consecutive months before retiring permanently from the CPS (a total of eight interviews). Only 25% of the households differ between consecutive months. The end result of this rotation pattern (in use since July 1953) is an improvement in the reliability of the estimates of month to month change as well as estimates of year to year change.

PERIODICITY The CPS has been conducted monthly by the Bureau of the Census since 1942 in response to a need that emerged in the late 1930s for reliable and up-to-date estimates of unemployment. It is a continuing survey, with interviews conducted during the week containing the 19th of each month.

CONTENT. The CPS Core collects employment data on all household members aged 15 and older. For those who are employed, information is gathered on usual number of hours worked, number of hours worked in the last week, time off from work in the last week for any reason including illness or a holiday, whether the person worked overtime or at more than one job in the last week, whether the person received wages or salary for time off, and the person's occupation and industry. For those who are not employed, information is gathered about whether they looked for work in the previous four weeks, the reasons they began looking for work, how long they have looked, whether they have been looking for full or part time work, when they last worked full time at a job or business for two weeks or longer, when they last worked at a full or part time job, and the reasons that they left that position.

In addition to the core questionnaire, the CPS uses a control card which also contains useful background demographic and socioeconomic data for household members, including their marital status and highest grade completed. The control card also obtains the family's total income in the past 12 months. Several revisions to the control card were made in October 1978 to improve the collection of data on household relationship, race, and ethnicity. In January 1979, the CPS began collecting children's demographic data on a monthly basis. These items include relationship to the reference person, parent's line number, age, sex, race, and origin. In 1988, the coding of relationship to the reference person was expanded so that it became possible to distinguish natural/adopted, step, foster, and grandchildren.

The information from the control card and the Core can be used to provide basic demographic information about families such as family structure, family income, and the educational attainment of the head of household. It can also be used to examine the combined work patterns of husbands and wives to determine, for example, whether the family consists of two full time workers, of one full time and one part time worker, or of a breadwinner-homemaker family. Issues of joblessness and idleness, by which is meant youth who are not in school and not in the labor force, can also be studied.

More detailed information on selected topics can be obtained from the supplements. Some supplements are conducted on a regular basis (annual or biennial), whereas others are done one time only. The supplements are sponsored by various government agencies as well as by the Bureau of the Census. Data on the following topics have been collected:

January	1990—displaced workers
	1991—job training
February	1990—unemployment compensation
March	1991—annual demographic and income supplement
April	1990—child support and alimony
	1991—work place drug abuse programs
May	1988—employee benefits
	1989—volunteer workers
	—shift work/flexitime
	1991—multiple jobs, flexitime, shift work, and work at home
June	1990—marital history, fertility, and birth expectations
	1991—immigration, emigration
August	1988—health insurance coverage of retirees
	1990—job training
September	1985—immunization status
	1991—veterans
October	1991—annual school enrollment
November	1990—voting and registration
December	1989—receipt of pension benefits

LIMITATIONS Because the main objective of the CPS is to provide information about the labor force, the types of information collected about families is rather limited. For example, the CPS contains no information on internal dynamics within the family. Thus, the implications for family life of differential patterns of labor force participation and other such issues cannot be examined.

Moreover, although state data are available from the CPS, the small sample size restricts its usefulness. Cross-tabulations of state data can be produced in detail only by averaging several months of data. It is also possible to combine several years of data.

AVAILABILITY Public use microdata files are available from the Bureau of the Census for months in which there is a supplement; these files are usually made available within six months to one year after data collection. The first year for which microdata files are available is 1968.

For information about the availability of data for a particular month, contact:

> Data User Services Division
> U.S. Bureau of the Census
> Washington, DC 20233
> 301/763-4100

For further information on the content of CPS files, contact:

> Ronald Tucker
> Current Population Surveys Branch
> Demographic Surveys Division
> U.S. Bureau of the Census
> Washington, DC 20233
> 301/763-2773

> Gloria Green
> Division of Data Users
> Bureau of Labor Statistics
> 441 G Street NW
> Washington, DC 20212
> 202/606-6376

PUBLICATIONS The Bureau of Labor Statistics first releases monthly employment data approximately two weeks after the end of data collection in the form of a press release. The final report, *Employment and Earnings*, is published by the Bureau approximately six weeks after data collection. On a quarterly basis, earnings data for persons in the labor force are published in the form of a press release, and data on the characteristics of persons not in the labor force are published in *Employment and Earnings*. The Bureau of Labor Statistics also publishes the *Monthly Labor Review*.

The Census Bureau usually releases advance reports on supplement data approximately three to six months after data collection, and final reports for supplements are typically released within 12 to 18 months. Published tabulations are available in the *Current Population Reports*, Series P-20 (population characteristics), Series P-23 (special studies), Series P-25 (population estimates and projections), and Series P-60 (consumer income).

A joint publication of the Bureau of Labor Statistics and the Census Bureau covers the changes made in the CPS between 1942 and 1975. This useful publication is entitled, "Concepts and Methods Used in Labor Force Statistics derived from the Current Population Survey".

Current Population Survey—Core Survey
Year of Questionnaire: 1990, obtained monthly
FAMILY-LEVEL CHARACTERISTICS
Sample size: 57,000 households

Family Composition
- ● Full roster of household members (first name, age, sex, and relationship to reference person of each member)[1]
- ○ Partial roster of household members
- ● Number of adults in household[2]
- ● Number of children in household[2]
- ● Approximate relationship of family members to householder, child, or one another
- ○ Exact relationship of family members to householder, child, or one another
- ○ Information about part-time household member
- ○ Information about family members no longer living in household
- ○ Information about relatives who live nearby but not in household

Socioeconomic
- ● Total family income
- ● Number of persons who depend on family income[3]
- ○ Sources of income
- ○ Income amounts identified separately by source
- ○ Poverty status
- ○ Welfare status
- ○ Food Stamps receipt
- ○ Child support receipt
- ○ Medicaid coverage
- ○ Private health insurance
- ● Home ownership/renters
- ○ Assets (other than home ownership)
- ○ Public housing status
- ● Telephone in household[4]
- ○ Language other than English spoken in home

Geographic/Community Variables
- ● Region of country
- ● State of residence
- ● County/city/MSA of residence
- ● Size/type of community[5]
- ○ Zip code
- ○ Telephone area code
- ● Metropolitan residence[5]
- ○ Neighborhood quality
- ○ Local labor market

Stage in Family Life Cycle
- ● Age of adult respondent or spouse/partner
- ● Marital status of adult respondent or spouse/partner
- ● Employment status of adult respondent or spouse/partner
- ● Presence of own children in household
- ● Age of youngest own child in household[2]
- ● Age of oldest own child in household[2]
- ○ Existence of own children who have left home
- ○ Intention to have (more) children in future

22

Family Functioning
- O Family activities or time use
- O Community involvement (civic, religious, recreational)
- O Family communication patterns
- O Family decision-making
- O Marital conflict
- O Marital happiness/satisfaction
- O Parent-child conflict
- O History of marital separations
- O History of family violence
- O History of marital counselling

CHARACTERISTICS OF ADULT FAMILY MEMBERS
Sample size: 107,000 persons 18 and older

Adult Respondent or Reference Person	Current Spouse in HH	Current or Former Spouse Not in HH	
●	●	O	Age
●	●	O	Gender
●	●	O	Race
●	●	O	Hispanic origin
●	●	O	Other origin/ethnicity
O	O	O	Religious affiliation
O	O	O	Religious participation
O	O	O	Country of birth
O	O	O	Immigrant status
O	O	O	English fluency
●	●	O	Current marital status
O	O	O	Marital history
O	O	O	Cohabitation status
O	O	O	Cohabitation history
O	O	O	Parental status
O	O	O	Number children ever born/sired
O	O	O	Age at first birth
O	O	O	Age of youngest child
O	O	O	Children living elsewhere
O	O	O	Duration at current address
O	O	O	Residential mobility
●	●	O	Educational attainment
O	O	O	Degrees attained
O	O	O	GED or regular HS diploma
●	●	O	Current enrollment
●	●	O	Current employment status
●	●	O	Hours usually worked (ft/pt)
O	O	O	Weeks worked
O	O	O	Annual employment pattern
●	●	O	Main occupation
●	●	O	Earnings
O	O	O	Wage rate
O	O	O	Payment of child support
O	O	O	Aptitude or achievement score
O	O	O	Health/disability status
O	O	O	Self-esteem
O	O	O	Locus of control or efficacy
O	O	O	Depression or subjective well-being
O	O	O	Work-related attitudes

CHARACTERISTICS OF CHILD FAMILY MEMBERS
Sample size: 44,000 children under 18

Reference Child or Youth Respondent	Other Children (in HH)	
O	●	Age
O	O	Month and year of birth
O	●	Gender
O	●	Race
O	●	Hispanic origin
O	●	Other origin/ethnicity
O	O	Religious affiliation
O	O	Religious participation
O	O	Country of birth
O	O	Immigrant status
O	O	English fluency
O	O	Exact relationship to adult family members
O	O	Exact relationship to other children in HH
O	●	Marital status/history[7]
O	O	Parental status/history
O	O	Current enrollment in regular school
O	O	Current enrollment in preschool/daycare
O	●	Highest grade completed[7]
O	O	Grade now enrolled
O	●	Employment status/history[7]
O	O	Health status
O	O	Handicapping conditions
O	O	Grade repetition
O	O	Aptitude or achievement score
O	O	Pregnancy/birth history
O	O	Psychological well-being
O	O	Delinquency

NOTES
1. First name not coded on data tapes, but is contained on control card.
2. Obtained by cycling through individual records.
3. Number of persons in primary family.
4. Telephone availability is asked in March, July, and November.
5. Within confidentiality restrictions.
6. Obtained only for persons aged 16 to 24.
7. Obtained for persons 15 and older.

CPS—Child Support and Alimony Supplement

PURPOSE The Child Support and Alimony Supplement is designed to provide national estimates of the award and receipt of child support payments following separation and divorce. The supplement also presents information on support payments for children of never-married parents who are not living together. In addition, data on alimony payments are obtained for currently separated and ever-divorced men and women.

SPONSORSHIP The supplement was first conducted in April 1979 and was jointly sponsored by the Bureau of the Census and the Department of Health and Human Services (then Department of Health, Education, and Welfare). Since then the April supplements have been conducted by the Bureau of the Census and sponsored, in part, by the Office of Child Support Enforcement, Department of Health and Human Services.

DESIGN A description of the basic design of the Current Population Survey is provided in the write-up of the core survey. Although the content of the supplement and the universe have been redefined several times since its inception, the basic design of the supplement has been as follows: the child support and alimony questions were asked of all women 18 years and over in sample households who met eligibility requirements based upon marital status, divorce history, and the presence of children under 21 in the household. Questions were asked only of the woman herself; no proxy responses were accepted. Beginning in April 1992, however, custodial fathers were included in the universe.

Until 1992, child support questions were asked about children fathered or adopted by the respondent's most recently divorced spouse. In 1992, they were asked regarding the respondent's youngest child. By changing the universe in this way, information about child support from parents who never married each other is also obtained.

The information obtained in the April supplement is also combined with data on annual work experience, income and poverty

25

status collected in the annual March income and demographic supplement. A data file is created by matching persons in the March CPS file with the April file, with about three-fourths of the sample interviewed in both months.

PERIODICITY The child support and alimony supplement has been conducted in April of 1979, 1982, 1984, 1986, 1988, and 1990. The supplement was conducted in April 1992 using a revised instrument.

CONTENT The April supplement collects data on the award of child support and the amount received. Currently separated and ever-divorced respondents are asked about the award and receipt of alimony as well as the amount. Previous versions of the supplement gathered information from ever-divorced women on the receipt and type of property settlement following divorce.

Beginning in 1988, useful information on joint-custody and visitation privileges as well as whether or not the non-custodial parent resides in the same state as the custodial parent was collected.

Among the other questions currently asked are whether the child(ren) is covered by a child support order; the year in which the agreement was made; any changes in the amount of the award that have been made by the court or other agency; the arrangements for receiving payment of child support; if applicable, reasons for why payment was not supposed to be received in 1991; whether health insurance is included as part of the agreement; whether a child support office, department of social services or any other state or local government agency has been contacted to assist in obtaining child support; and if so the type of assistance provided.

Basic demographic and other background characteristics can be obtained from the matched March/April CPS supplements which allows researchers to analyze socioeconomic differences among persons receiving child support and alimony. Additional questions available on some supplements pertain to the respondent's working status at the time of divorce/separation and 5 years prior to that time and AFDC recipiency status in the previous year.

LIMITATIONS The Child Support and Alimony Supplement is an important source of national-level data that can be used to inform researchers and policy makers about the post-divorce economic and custodial arrangements of families involving children. The addition of custodial fathers to the sample is an improvement over the previous focus on custodial mothers only. Unfortunately, no sociodemographic data are collected on non-custodial parents, which means that valuable information such as the parent's age, sex, race, and income cannot be ascertained from the supplement. Two data items on absent fathers were included in the 1979 supplement but were subsequently dropped due to low response rates. These questions covered the father's responsibility for the support of other children and the current income of ex-husbands.

Prior to 1992, information on child support payments was collected only for children from the most recent divorce or separation. Thus, data on support from previous marital disruptions were not considered. As of 1992, child support information is collected only about the youngest child; thus, data on support for older children are not available.

Another possible limitation of these CPS data is potential under-reporting of child support payment among women receiving AFDC. The Child Support Enforcement amendments to the 1973 Social Security Act provided for AFDC child support payments contributed by the father to be paid directly to the welfare agency and not to the parent with whom the child lives. Thus, some AFDC recipients may be unaware that the child's biological father is contributing child support. Moreover, as in most household surveys, estimates of money income derived from the March CPS are somewhat less than the comparable estimates derived from independent sources such as the Bureau of Economic Analysis.

Plans for 1994 include the use of computer-based equipment which will allow a greater number of questions to be asked.

AVAILABILITY Refer to the description in the core survey. Machine-readable micro-data files are available. To obtain the data and to ask substantive questions contact:

> Gordon Lester
> Income Statistics Branch
> Housing & Household
> Economic Statistics Division
> U.S. Bureau of the Census
> Washington, D.C. 20233
> 301/763-8576

PUBLICATIONS Annual reports based on the child support and alimony supplement appear in:

U.S. Bureau of the Census. (1991). Child Support and Alimony: 1989, *Current Population Reports, Series P-60*, No. 173. Washington, D.C.: U.S. Government Printing Office.

CPS - Child Support and Alimony Supplement
Year of Questionnaire: March and April, 1990
Sample size: 39,474 Housing Units[1]
FAMILY-LEVEL CHARACTERISTICS

Family Composition
- ○ Full roster of household members (first name, age, sex, and relationship to reference person of each member)
- ● Partial roster of household members
- ● Number of adults in household
- ● Number of children in household
- ● Approximate relationship of family members to householder, child, or one another
- ○ Exact relationship of family members to householder, child, or one another
- ○ Information about part-time household member
- ○ Information about family members no longer living in household
- ○ Information about relatives who live nearby but not in household

Socioeconomic
- ● Total family income
- ○ Number of persons who depend on family income
- ○ Sources of income
- ○ Income amounts identified separately by source
- ○ Poverty status
- ○ Welfare status
- ○ Food Stamps receipt
- ● Child support receipt
- ○ Medicaid coverage
- ● Private health insurance
- ● Home ownership/renters
- ○ Assets (other than home ownership)
- ○ Public housing status
- ● Telephone in household
- ○ Language other than English spoken in home

Geographic/Community Variables
- ● Region of country
- ● State of residence
- ● County/city/MSA of residence
- ● Size/type of community
- ○ Zip code
- ○ Telephone area code
- ● Metropolitan residence
- ○ Neighborhood quality
- ○ Local labor market

Stage in Family Life Cycle
- ● Age of adult respondent or spouse/partner
- ● Marital status of adult respondent or spouse/partner
- ● Employment status of adult respondent or spouse/partner
- ● Presence of own children in household
- ● Age of youngest own child in household
- ● Age of oldest own child in household
- ○ Existence of own children who have left home
- ○ Intention to have (more) children in future

Family Functioning

- ○ Family activities or time use
- ○ Community involvement (civic, religious, recreational)
- ○ Family communication patterns
- ○ Family decision-making
- ○ Marital conflict
- ○ Marital happiness/satisfaction
- ○ Parent-child conflict
- ○ History of marital separations
- ○ History of family violence
- ○ History of marital counselling

CHARACTERISTICS OF ADULT FAMILY MEMBERS

Sample Size: 43,018 women ages 18 or older (or 15-17 if they had children)

Adult Respondent or Reference Person	Current Spouse in HH	Current or Former Spouse Not in HH	
●	●	○	Age
●	●	○	Gender
●	●	○	Race
●	●	○	Hispanic origin
●	●	○	Other origin/ethnicity
○	○	○	Religious affiliation
○	○	○	Religious participation
○	○	○	Country of birth
○	○	○	Immigrant status
○	○	○	English fluency
●	●	○	Current marital status
●	○	○	Marital history[2]
○	○	○	Cohabitation status
○	○	○	Cohabitation history
●	○	○	Parental status
●	○	●	Number children ever born/sired[3]
○	○	○	Age at first birth
○	○	○	Age of youngest child
●	○	○	Children living elsewhere
○	○	○	Duration at current address
○	○	○	Residential mobility
●	●	○	Educational attainment
○	○	○	Degrees attained
○	○	○	GED or regular HS diploma
●	●	○	Current enrollment
●	●	○	Current employment status
●	●	○	Hours usually worked (ft/pt)
○	○	○	Weeks worked
○	○	○	Annual employment pattern
●	●	○	Main occupation
●	●	○	Earnings
●	●	○	Wage rate
○	○	●	Payment of child support
○	○	○	Aptitude or achievement score
○	○	○	Health/disability status
○	○	○	Self-esteem
○	○	○	Locus of control or efficacy
○	○	○	Depression or subjective well-being
○	○	○	Work-related attitudes

CHARACTERISTICS OF CHILD FAMILY MEMBERS

Reference Child or Youth Respondent	Children (in HH)	
O	●	Age
O	O	Month and Year of Birth
O	●	Gender
O	●	Race
O	●	Hispanic Origin
O	●	Other origin/ethnicity
O	O	Religious affiliation
O	O	Religious participation
O	O	Country of birth
O	O	Immigrant status
O	O	English fluency
O	●	Exact relationship to adult family members
O	O	Exact relationship to other children in HH
O	O	Marital status/history
O	O	Parental status/history
O	O	Current enrollment in regular school
O	O	Current enrollment in preschool/daycare
O	O	Highest grade completed
O	O	Grade now enrolled
O	O	Employment status/history
O	O	Health status
O	O	Handicapping conditions
O	O	Grade repetition
O	O	Aptitude or achievement score
O	O	Pregnancy/birth history
O	O	Psychological well-being
O	O	Delinquency

NOTES
1. 3,544 women interviewed in March were given imputed child support and alimony information for April.
2. Partial; we know if respondent is divorced.
3. We know if any children living with respondent were fathered by ex-spouse.

CPS-Fertility Supplement

PURPOSE The Fertility Supplement to the CPS is designed to provide national estimates of women's childbearing experience and future birth expectations. Additionally, information on child spacing was provided in the June 1971, 1975, 1980, 1985, and 1990 supplements. Data on the fertility of foreign-born women were obtained in the April 1983 and June 1986 and 1988 supplements.

SPONSORSHIP The supplemental questions on children ever born and birth expectations are sponsored and conducted entirely by the Bureau of the Census. The detailed marital and fertility history supplements of June 1971, 1975, 1980, 1985, and 1990 were funded by the National Institute of Child Health and Human Development (NICHD), as was the April 1983 supplement on the fertility of foreign-born women. The Immigration and Naturalization Service sponsored the June 1986 and 1988 supplements.

DESIGN A description of the basic design of the Current Population Survey is provided in the write-up of the core survey. The supplemental questions are asked of women in sampled households who meet certain eligibility requirements.

The age range of women included in the supplement has varied from year to year; however, certain core ages have been included annually. Questions on children ever born have usually been asked of ever-married women 15 to 44 years old and of never-married women 18 to 44 years old. On occasion, the upper age limit has been extended. The questions on birth expectations have been consistently asked of women 18 to 34 years old regardless of marital status. In selected years, the upper age limit has been extended to 39 or 44 years of age. Never-married women were first introduced into the sample in June of 1976. Beginning in June 1990, fertility items were asked of women 15 to 17 years old, regardless of marital status.

In previous marital and fertility history supplements, men were asked detailed marriage history questions. In 1985 and 1990, however, men were only asked the number of times they had been married. Thus, no data are available on their dates of marriage, separation, or divorce.

PERIODICITY The supplement has been conducted annually in June since 1971. Questions on fertility were asked of women in June 1958 and February 1965, but these were asked of a restricted universe and are not comparable to the data obtained in the surveys from 1971 on.

Questions on birth expectations were asked every year since 1971, with the exception of 1984. The June 1990 supplement contained the basic questions on childbearing and birth expectations. Current plans are to continue asking these basic questions whenever fertility supplements are proposed.

By order of OMB, as of 1988 the June fertility supplement was restricted to a biennial supplement. OMB stated fertility rates did not change rapidly enough to justify an annual supplement. Hence, the June CPS fertility supplement was not collected in either 1989 or 1991.

CONTENT The basic supplement collects data on children ever born and birth expectations. Data are also obtained on the socioeconomic characteristics of women and allow for analysis of fertility differentials. Data on children ever born can also be used to estimate the fertility rate for the 12 months ending in June (the number of births per 1000 women 18-44 years old).

The June 1992 supplement collected data on the date of first marriage for ever-married women, and the number of children ever born for all women 15 to 44 years old. The dates of birth for the woman's first and last born child were also obtained. Additionally, women 18 to 34 were asked questions on their birth expectations.

A detailed marital and fertility history supplement was conducted in June of 1971, 1975, 1980, 1985, and 1990. These supplements provide additional data on marriages and child spacing. In June 1990, women 15 to 65 years of age were asked questions about the number of times they had been married, how their first, second, and most recent marriages ended, and the dates when the marriages ended. Women whose marriages ended in divorce were also asked when they had stopped living with their spouse. Thus, both the dates of separation and divorce can be obtained.

Detailed marriage history questions were not asked of men in the June 1990 supplement. Similar questions had been asked of men in previous surveys but these were dropped in 1985 and also in 1990 due to the high rate of proxy responses and the resulting uncertainty as to the quality of the data for men. Thus, ever-married men were asked only the number of times they had been married and whether their first marriage had ended in widowhood or divorce. The detailed fertility portion of the June 1990 supplement obtained information on the date of birth for the woman's first through fourth child and her last child, as well as the sex of the child and where the child currently lived.

The June 1988 immigration and fertility supplements collected data on country of birth for persons of all ages and their parents. For persons born in foreign countries, citizenship and period of immigration are also available. Marital and fertility information was obtained for women aged 18 to 44; these data include date of first marriage, number of births, and dates of birth for the woman's first and last born child. Birth expectations data were also collected for all women 18 to 39 years old.

The fertility supplement can also be used to obtain estimates of the number of women whose first child had been born or conceived out of wedlock. (See O'Connell and Rogers (1989), referenced in the final section of this write-up, for greater detail.)

LIMITATIONS The basic supplement is quite brief, and thus more detailed information on fertility-related topics is available only on an occasional basis. The variability in the age range of women eligible for the supplement in different survey years has limited comparisons over time to women 18 to 44 years old for data on children ever born and to women 18 to 34 for birth expectations data. Furthermore, birth expectations of single women were not asked until 1976 and thus previous data are restricted to ever-married women.

Moreover, because of the sensitive nature of asking never-married women under 18 about their childbearing experience, these women had previously been excluded from the supplement. Thus, period measures of out-of-wedlock births to younger teenagers were not available in prior surveys. However, estimates of out-of-wedlock childbearing can be obtained by cohort analysis (see O'Connell and Rogers, 1984, referenced in the final section of this write-up) for years prior to 1990.

Basic socio-demographic characteristics of women can be obtained from the supplement; however, no data are collected on the woman's earnings. The June supplement lacks the detailed income data collected on the annual March income and demographic supplement to CPS. Thus, family income is the only measure that can be used to approximate the woman's economic standing.

Only limited data on men's marital histories can be obtained from the marital and fertility history supplements conducted in June 1975, 1985, and 1990.

AVAILABILITY Refer to the description of the core survey. Machine-readable micro-data files are available for June since 1971. To learn about the latest data tape currently available from the supplement, contact:

Martin O'Connell
Fertility Statistics Branch
Population Division
U.S. Bureau of the Census
Washington, DC 20233
301/763-5303

For information on the marital history supplements, contact:

Donald J. Hernandez
Marriage & Family Statistics Branch
Population Division
U.S. Bureau of the Census
Washington, DC 20233
301/763-7987

PUBLICATIONS

U.S. Bureau of the Census. (1991). Fertility of American women: June 1990. *Current Population Reports*, Series P-20, No. 454. Washington, DC:GPO.

U.S. Bureau of the Census. (1991). Studies on American fertility. *Current Population Reports*, Series P-23, No. 162. Washington, DC:GPO.

Norton, A.J., & Moorman, J.E. (1987). Current trends in marriage and divorce among American women. *Journal of Marriage and the Family, 49*(1), 3-14.

O'Connell, M. & Rogers, C.C. (1984). Out-of-wedlock births, premarital pregnancies and their effect on family formation and dissolution. *Family Planning Perspectives, 16*(4), 157-162.

CPS—Fertility Supplement
Years of Questionnaire: 1988, 1990
FAMILY-LEVEL CHARACTERISTICS
Sample Size: 57,000 households

Family Composition
- Full roster of household members (first name, age, sex, and relationship to reference person of each member)[1]
- ○ Partial roster of household members
- Number of adults in household[2]
- Number of children in household[2]
- Approximate relationship of family members to householder, child, or one another
- ○ Exact relationship of family members to householder, child, or one another
- ○ Information about part-time household member
- ○ Information about family members no longer living in household
- ○ Information about relatives who live nearby but not in household

Socioeconomic
- Total family income
- Number of persons who depend on family income[3]
- ○ Sources of income
- ○ Income amounts identified separately by source
- ○ Poverty status
- ○ Welfare status
- ○ Food Stamps receipt
- ○ Child support receipt
- ○ Medicaid coverage
- ○ Private health insurance
- Home ownership/renters
- ○ Assets (other than home ownership)
- ○ Public housing status
- ○ Telephone in household
- ○ Language other than English spoken in home

Geographic/Community Variables
- Region of country
- State of residence
- County/city/MSA of residence
- Size/type of community[4]
- ○ Zip code
- ○ Telephone area code
- Metropolitan residence[4]
- ○ Neighborhood quality
- ○ Local labor market

Stage in Family Life Cycle
- Age of adult respondent or spouse/partner
- Marital status of adult respondent or spouse/partner
- Employment status of adult respondent or spouse/partner
- Presence of own children in household
- Age of youngest own child in household[2]
- Age of oldest own child in household[2]
- Existence of own children who have left home[5]
- Intention to have (more) children in future[6]

37

Family Functioning

- Family activities or time use
- Community involvement (civic, religious, recreational)
- Family communication patterns
- Family decision-making
- Marital conflict
- Marital happiness/satisfaction
- Parent-child conflict
- History of marital separations
- History of family violence
- History of marital counselling

CHARACTERISTICS OF ADULT FAMILY MEMBERS
Sample size: 107,000 persons 18 and older

Adult Respondent or Reference Mother	Current Father in HH	Current or Former Spouse Not in HH	
●	●	○	Age
●	●	○	Gender
●	●	○	Race
●	●	○	Hispanic origin
●	●	○	Other origin/ethnicity
○	○	○	Religious affiliation
○	○	○	Religious participation
●	●	○	Country of birth[7]
●	●	○	Immigrant status[7]
○	○	○	English fluency
●	●	○	Current marital status
●	●	○	Marital history[8]
○	○	○	Cohabitation status
○	○	○	Cohabitation history
●	●	○	Parental status[5]
●	●	○	Number children ever born/sired [5]
●	●	○	Age at first birth[5]
●	●	○	Age of youngest child[9]
●	●	○	Children living elsewhere
○	○	○	Duration at current address
○	○	○	Residential mobility
●	●	○	Educational attainment
●	●	○	Degrees attained
○	○	○	GED or regular HS diploma
●	●	○	Current enrollment[10]
●	●	○	Current employment status
●	●	○	Hours usually worked (ft/pt)
●	●	○	Weeks worked
●	●	○	Annual employment pattern
○	○	○	Main occupation
○	○	○	Earnings
○	○	○	Wage rate
○	○	○	Payment of child support
○	○	○	Aptitude or achievement score
○	○	○	Health/disability status
○	○	○	Self-esteem
○	○	○	Locus of control or efficacy
○	○	○	Depression or subjective well-being
○	○	○	Work-related attitudes

CHARACTERISTICS OF CHILD FAMILY MEMBERS
Sample size: 44,000 children under 18

Reference Child or Youth Respondent	Other Children (in HH)	
○	●	Age
○	○	Month and year of birth
○	●	Gender
○	●	Race
○	●	Hispanic origin
○	○	Other origin/ethnicity
○	○	Religious affiliation
○	○	Religious participation
○	●	Country of birth[7]
○	●	Immigrant status[7]
○	○	English fluency
○	○	Exact relationship to adult family members
○	○	Exact relationship to other children in HH
○	●	Marital status/history[8]
○	●	Parental status/history[5]
○	○	Current enrollment in regular school
○	○	Current enrollment in preschool/daycare
○	●	Highest grade completed[11]
○	○	Grade now enrolled
○	●	Employment status/history[11]
○	○	Health status
○	○	Handicapping conditions
○	○	Grade repetition
○	○	Aptitude or achievement score
○	○	Pregnancy/birth history
○	○	Psychological well-being
○	○	Delinquency

NOTES
1. First name not coded on data tapes, but is contained on control card.
2. Obtained by cycling through individual records
3. Number of persons in primary family
4. Within confidentiality restrictions
5. In 1988 fertility questions were asked of women 18-44. In 1990 fertility questions were asked of women 15-65. In 1990, if any of a respondent's oldest three or last born children were not living in her household, she was asked where those children lived.
6. Birth expectations questions asked only of women 18 to 39
7. Available *only* in 1988 from Immigration Supplement that was also asked in June.
8. In 1988, the date of first marriage was asked of a restricted universe. In 1990, ever-married men and women ages 15 to 65 were asked about their marital history.
9. It is possible to calculate age of youngest child because the file contains information on month and year of birth of last born child.
10. In 1988 and 1990 asked of persons ages 16 - 24.
11. Obtained for persons 15 and older

CPS—Income and Demographic Supplement

PURPOSE The March Income and Demographic Supplement to the Current Population Survey collects data on employment and income for the previous calendar year. The reference period differs from the monthly core survey which collects data on unemployment, employment, and labor force characteristics pertaining to the preceding week. Thus, the income supplement provides additional data to study the work experience of the population in a given year (including job changes, lay-offs, and part-year employment), data which cannot be obtained from the monthly core survey.

In addition to earnings and work experience data, the income and demographic supplement collects more detailed income data, including sources of income and receipt of child support, alimony, and AFDC payments. Other topics include health insurance coverage and migration. Furthermore, the March Supplement provides extensive detail on marital status, family and household composition, and living arrangements. All questions within the core survey are also asked in the March survey.

SPONSORSHIP The supplement has been jointly sponsored by the Bureau of Labor Statistics and the Bureau of the Census, with the data collection being conducted by the Census Bureau.

DESIGN A description of the basic design of the Current Population Survey is provided in the write-up of the core survey. Income and demographic supplement questions are asked of all persons age 15 and over in sampled households. Certain questions pertain to the household or family as a whole, such as housing tenure, subsidized housing, receipt of energy assistance, food stamps, and household composition. Other questions refer to persons, including marital status, earnings and employment patterns, migration, and educational attainment.

Data pertaining to the family are constructed from the data collected for persons and households. The relationship code is used to construct measures such as the presence of children in the family.

The March 1988 supplement contained changes in the relationship coding which improved the study of household and family composition. The parent line number and spouse line number were edited, making it possible to link children to their parents. This procedural change makes it possible to identify all children with parents in the household.

Additionally, the coding of relationship to the reference person was expanded to include new categories. It is now possible to determine natural/adopted children, step children, foster children, and grandchildren, data previously not available. Thus, more complex parent-child combinations and other relationships within families and households are able to be identified.

PERIODICITY The supplement has been conducted in March each year since 1947. Plans are to continue the basic income and demographic supplement into the foreseeable future.

CONTENT The income and demographic supplement collects data pertaining to households and individuals. Examples of household data include the number of housing units in the structure, the type of household, housing tenure, receipt of a rent subsidy, receipt of food stamps, and the receipt of free or reduced price lunches at school.

The public use microdata file contains three types of records: household, family, and person. There is one household record per household; there is one family record for each family within the household; there is one person record for each person within the household, including children.

Family types include primary, related subfamily, and unrelated subfamily. The primary family includes as members all persons related to the householder. Related subfamilies are those family units headed by an individual who is related to the householder. Unrelated subfamilies are composed of families headed by persons not related to the householder. There is extensive income and family composition data for each family unit within the household.

Individual data are available for each person age 15 and over in the sampled household. Questions cover employment history in the previous year, including the number of weeks worked, hours worked, reasons for not working, reasons for part-time work, number of different jobs held, earnings from employment, and unemployment or worker's compensation. Questions are also asked about income from a variety of sources, including Social Security, Supplemental Security, survivors benefits, disability benefits, pensions, interest, dividends, rents and royalties, public assistance, veterans benefits, child support and alimony, and other sources. Additional questions are asked about migration in the last 12 months as well as coverage by health and retirement benefits.

The income and demographic supplement collects marital status and living arrangements data as well as household and family composition data in extensive detail. Trends in the age at first marriage, the postponement of marriage, the divorce ratio, and the number of unmarried couples can be determined from the supplement. Data are also presented on the living arrangements of children under 18 and the number of children in one-parent families. Basic demographic and socioeconomic characteristics of households and families are also collected and tabulated.

Since March 1983, the annual report *Marital Status and Living Arrangements*, has included data on the living arrangements of children under 18 by marital status and selected characteristics of the parent (Table 9 in the report). Parental characteristics include age, education, and employment status. Other characteristics of the child's household include the number of siblings in the household, the presence of other adults, family income, housing tenure, and area of residence. Additionally, the tabulation is shown separately for three age groups of children (under 6 years old, 6 to 11 years old, and 12 to 17 years old). This enables the data user to ascertain the type of household environment and family resources available to children at different stages of development.

LIMITATIONS Many of the published tabulations from the income and demographic supplement use the household or family as the unit of analysis. However, the type of data collected about families is primarily demographic or economic in nature. And almost no information is collected about family members living outside the household. Thus, it is not possible to use the CPS to study family dynamics or the influence on the family of members residing elsewhere. Moreover, tables based on the individual are generally restricted to persons 15 years or older, as these are the persons who are asked the detailed work experience and income questions in the supplement. Child-based tabulations were not produced until March 1983.

Income data may be under-reported in the March supplement. As in most household surveys, estimates of money income derived from the March CPS are somewhat less than the comparable estimates derived from independent sources such as the Bureau of Economic Analysis. Although wage and salary income may be only slightly under-reported, income from sources such as public assistance and welfare, unemployment compensation, and property income tends to be under-reported to a greater extent.

AVAILABILITY Refer to the description of the Core Survey. Public-use microdata files are available for March since 1968.

For information on marriage and family statistics, contact:

> Donald J. Hernandez
> Marriage and Family Statistics Branch
> Population Division
> U.S. Bureau of the Census
> Washington, D.C. 20233
> 301/763-7987

For information on income statistics, contact:

> Edward Welniak
> Income Statistics Branch
> Population Division
> U.S. Bureau of the Census
> Washington, D.C. 20233
> 301/763-8576

PUBLICATIONS Reports from the income and demographic supplement appear in *Current Population Reports*, Series P-20 (marital status and living arrangements, household and family composition), Series P-23 (special studies), Series P-25 (projections of the number of households and families), and Series P-60 (consumer income).

Beginning with the March 1988 supplement, an expanded report is published on marriage and family statistics. This report consists of an analysis of several topics, such as stepchildren, using not only CPS data but also data from other surveys (such as the Survey of Income and Program Participation) and decennial censuses. A variety of topics will be covered in these analytical reports which will vary from year to year.

The following articles use the family as the unit of analysis and are based upon CPS and decennial census data:

Hernandez, D.J. (1986). Childhood in socio-demographic perspective, *Annual Review of Sociology, 12*, 159-80.

Moorman, J., & Hernandez, D.J. (1989). Families with biological, step and adopted children, *Demography, 26*(2), 267-277.

CPS—March Income and Demographic Supplement
Year of Questionnaire: 1990; asked annually in March
FAMILY-LEVEL CHARACTERISTICS
Sample size: 57,000 households

Family Composition
- Full roster of household members (first name, age, sex, and relationship to reference person of each member)
○ Partial roster of household members
- Number of adults in household
- Number of children in household
- Approximate relationship of family members to householder, child, or one another
○ Exact relationship of family members to householder, child, or one another
○ Information about part-time household member
○ Information about family members no longer living in household
○ Information about relatives who live nearby but not in household

Socioeconomic
- Total family income
○ Number of persons who depend on family income
- Sources of income
- Income amounts identified separately by source
- Poverty status
- Welfare status
- Food Stamps receipt
- Child support receipt
- Medicaid coverage
- Private health insurance
- Home ownership/renters
○ Assets (other than home ownership)
- Public housing status
- Telephone in household
○ Language other than English spoken in home

Geographic/Community Variables
- Region of country
- State of residence
- County/city/MSA of residence
- Size/type of community
○ Zip code
○ Telephone area code
- Metropolitan residence
○ Neighborhood quality
○ Local labor market

Stage in Family Life Cycle
- Age of adult respondent or spouse/partner
- Marital status of adult respondent or spouse/partner
- Employment status of adult respondent or spouse/partner
- Presence of own children in household
- Age of youngest own child in household
- Age of oldest own child in household
○ Existence of own children who have left home
○ Intention to have (more) children in future

Family Functioning
○ Family activities or time use
○ Community involvement (civic, religious, recreational)
○ Family communication patterns
○ Family decision-making
○ Marital conflict
○ Marital happiness/satisfaction
○ Parent-child conflict
○ History of marital separations
○ History of family violence
○ History of marital counselling

CHARACTERISTICS OF ADULT FAMILY MEMBERS
Sample size: 107,000 persons 18 and older

Adult Respondent or Reference Person	Current Spouse in HH	Current or Former Spouse Not in HH	
●	●	○	Age
●	●	○	Gender
●	●	○	Race
●	●	○	Hispanic origin
●	●	○	Other origin/ethnicity
○	○	○	Religious affiliation
○	○	○	Religious participation
○	○	○	Country of birth
○	○	○	Immigrant status
○	○	○	English fluency
●	●	○	Current marital status
○	○	○	Marital history
○	○	○	Cohabitation status
○	○	○	Cohabitation history
○	○	○	Parental status
○	○	○	Number children ever born/sired
○	○	○	Age at first birth
○	○	○	Age of youngest child
○	○	○	Children living elsewhere
○	○	○	Duration at current address
○	○	○	Residential mobility
●	●	○	Educational attainment
○	○	○	Degrees attained
○	○	○	GED or regular HS diploma
●	●	○	Current enrollment[1]
●	●	○	Current employment status
●	●	○	Hours usually worked (ft/pt)
●	●	○	Weeks worked
●	●	○	Annual employment pattern
●	●	○	Main occupation
●	●	○	Earnings
●	●	○	Wage rate
○	○	○	Payment of child support
○	○	○	Aptitude or achievement score
○	○	○	Health/disability status
○	○	○	Self-esteem
○	○	○	Locus of control or efficacy
○	○	○	Depression or subjective well-being
○	○	○	Work-related attitudes

CHARACTERISTICS OF CHILD FAMILY MEMBERS
Sample size: 44,000 children under 18

Reference Child or Youth Respondent	Other Children (in HH)	
O	●	Age
O	O	Month and year of birth
O	●	Gender
O	●	Race
O	●	Hispanic origin
O	●	Other origin/ethnicity
O	O	Religious affiliation
O	O	Religious participation
O	O	Country of birth
O	O	Immigrant status
O	O	English fluency
O	●	Exact relationship to adult family members[2]
O	O	Exact relationship to other children in HH
O	●	Marital status/history[3]
O	O	Parental status/history
O	●	Current enrollment in regular school[1]
O	O	Current enrollment in preschool/daycare
O	●	Highest grade completed[3]
O	●	Grade now enrolled[3]
O	●	Employment status/history[3]
O	O	Health status
O	●	Handicapping conditions[3]
O	O	Grade repetition
O	O	Aptitude or achievement score
O	O	Pregnancy/birth history
O	O	Psychological well-being
O	O	Delinquency

NOTES
1. Available for persons 16-24 years of age.
2. Beginning in 1988, stepchildren are identified as distinct from natural or adopted children. Foster children are also separately identified.
3. Available for persons 15 and older.

CPS—Multiple Jobholding and Work Schedules Supplement

PURPOSE The Multiple Jobholding and Work Schedules Supplement to the CPS is designed to obtain more information about these topics for the nation and to update similar data collected from 1969 through 1980 and in 1985. These data are also used to reconcile differences in estimates of employment statistics obtained from the CPS and other sources of employment data used by the Bureau of Labor Statistics.

SPONSORSHIP The Supplement is jointly sponsored by the Bureau of the Census and the Bureau of Labor Statistics.

DESIGN A description of the basic design of the Current Population Survey is provided in the write-up of the Core Survey. The supplementary questions on multiple jobholdings and work schedules are asked of persons aged 15 and older who were employed in the week prior to the survey.

PERIODICITY The Multiple Jobholding and Work Schedules Supplement was asked in May 1989 and 1991. As noted above, similar data were collected annually between 1969 and 1980 and in 1985.

CONTENT The 1989 and 1991 versions of the supplement are not identical. The 1991 version modified some of the questions asked in 1989 and expanded the information collected. In 1989, respondents were asked about the hours per week they usually worked and whether they were on flexitime or some other schedule that allowed them to vary the time they began and ended their workday. Those who said they had a flexible schedule were asked for the main reason that they worked such a schedule. In 1991, respondents were asked about the usual number of hours they worked per week and per day, the usual number of days per week that they worked, and the specific days of the week that they usually worked. They were also asked about the time of day they began and ended work on most days in the previous week and whether their schedule might best be described as a regular daytime schedule, a regular evening shift, a regular night shift, a rotating shift (one that changes periodically from days to evenings or nights), a split shift, an irregular schedule, or some other shift. They were then asked the main reasons they worked the type of shift that they did. After answering these questions, respondents were asked if they were on flexitime or some other schedule that allowed them to vary the time they began and ended their work day. They were also asked if, as part of their job, they did any work at home and, if yes, approximately how many hours of work they did at home for the job in the previous week and whether they got paid for the additional work done at home.

To learn about multiple job holding, in both 1989 and 1991 respondents were asked if they did any other work for pay in the previous week for other employers and, if so, for how many employers they worked. They were also asked whether they operated their own businesses, professions, or farms in the previous week or whether they had another job or business at which they did not work last week. If they did have a second job, they were asked questions about that job such as the type of business or industry it was, the type of work they did, whether the job was in the private sector, the federal government, state government, local government, or, if self-employed, whether the business was incorporated or unincorporated. In both years respondents were asked about the hours they usually worked at the second job, the amount of money they earned, whether any of the work was performed at home, and, if so, how much was performed at home, and the main reason that they worked at more than one job. In addition to these questions, respondents in 1991 were also asked the number of days per week they usually worked at the additional job, the specific days of the week that they worked at that job, and the time of day that they began and ended work at the job on most days in the previous week.

The information collected in this supplement can provide important information on the work schedules and time constraints of families of different types and whether child care demands influence work schedules. It can also be used to examine the joint work schedules of husbands and wives and how schedules vary by the presence of children of different ages. The information on multiple job holdings provides additional information about how adult family members spend their time.

LIMITATIONS The supplement would be more useful to researchers interested in families if it could be combined with the more detailed family composition and income information collected in the March Income and Demographic Supplement. In particular, the data on work schedules and multiple jobholdings would help to provide insights into issues surrounding poverty such as how families who work can still be in poverty and the lengths to which some families must go to avoid poverty.

AVAILABILITY Refer to the description of the CORE Survey. Machine-readable micro-data files are available. For substantive questions about the supplement, contact:

> Diane Herz
> Division of Labor Force Statistics
> Bureau of Labor Statistics
> Department of Labor
> Washington, DC 20212

For questions about specific variables or issues related to the survey design, contact:

> Jim Warden
> Demographic Surveys Division
> Bureau of the Census
> Washington, DC 20233
> 301/763-2773

PUBLICATIONS

Stinson, John F. Jr. (1990). Multiple jobholding up sharply in the 1980s. *Monthly Labor Review, 113(7),* 3-10.

CPS-Multiple Jobholding and Work Schedules
Year of Questionnaire: May 1989, 1991
Sample Size: 57,000 households
FAMILY-LEVEL CHARACTERISTICS

Family Composition
- Full roster of household members (first name, age, sex, and relationship to reference person of each member)[1]
- ○ Partial roster of household members
- Number of adults in household[2]
- Number of children in household[2]
- Approximate relationship of family members to householder, child, or one another
- ○ Exact relationship of family members to householder, child, or one another
- ○ Information about part-time household member
- ○ Information about family members no longer living in household
- ○ Information about relatives who live nearby but not in household

Socioeconomic
- Total family income
- Number of persons who depend on family income[3]
- ○ Sources of income
- ○ Income amounts identified separately by source
- ○ Poverty status
- ○ Welfare status
- ○ Food Stamps receipt
- ○ Child support receipt
- ○ Medicaid coverage
- ○ Private health insurance
- Home ownership/renters
- ○ Assets (other than home ownership)
- ○ Public housing status
- ○ Telephone in household
- ○ Language other than English spoken in home

Geographic/Community Variables
- Region of country
- State of residence
- County/city/MSA of residence
- Size/type of community[4]
- ○ Zip code
- ○ Telephone area code
- Metropolitan residence[4]
- ○ Neighborhood quality
- ○ Local labor market

Stage in Family Life Cycle
- Age of adult respondent or spouse/partner
- Marital status of adult respondent or spouse/partner
- Employment status of adult respondent or spouse/partner
- Presence of own children in household
- Age of youngest own child in household[2]
- Age of oldest own child in household[2]
- ○ Existence of own children who have left home
- ○ Intention to have (more) children in future

Family Functioning
○ Family activities or time use
○ Community involvement (civic, religious, recreational)
○ Family communication patterns
○ Family decision-making
○ Marital conflict
○ Marital happiness/satisfaction
○ Parent-child conflict
○ History of marital separations
○ History of family violence
○ History of marital counselling

CHARACTERISTICS OF ADULT FAMILY MEMBERS

Adult Respondent or Reference Person	Current Spouse in HH	Current or Former Spouse Not in HH	
●	●	○	Age
●	●	○	Gender
●	●	○	Race
●	●	○	Hispanic origin
●	●	○	Other origin/ethnicity
○	○	○	Religious affiliation
○	○	○	Religious participation
○	○	○	Country of birth
○	○	○	Immigrant status
○	○	○	English fluency
●	●	○	Current marital status
○	○	○	Marital history
○	○	○	Cohabitation status
○	○	○	Cohabitation history
○	○	○	Parental status
○	○	○	Number children ever born/sired
○	○	○	Age at first birth
○	○	○	Age of youngest child
○	○	○	Children living elsewhere
○	○	○	Duration at current address
○	○	○	Residential mobility
●	●	○	Educational attainment
○	○	○	Degrees attained
○	○	○	GED or regular HS diploma
●	●	○	Current enrollment[5]
●	●	○	Current employment status
●	●	○	Hours usually worked (ft/pt)
○	○	○	Weeks worked
○	○	○	Annual employment pattern
●	●	○	Main occupation
●	●	○	Earnings
○	○	○	Wage rate
○	○	○	Payment of child support
○	○	○	Aptitude or achievement score
○	○	○	Health/Disability status
○	○	○	Self-esteem
○	○	○	Locus of control or efficacy
○	○	○	Depression or subjective well-being
○	○	○	Work-related attitudes

CHARACTERISTICS OF CHILD FAMILY MEMBERS

Reference Child or Youth Respondent	Other Children (in HH)	
O	●	Age
O	O	Month and year of birth
O	●	Gender
O	●	Race
O	●	Hispanic origin
O	●	Other origin/ethnicity
O	O	Religious affiliation
O	O	Religious participation
O	O	Country of birth
O	O	Immigrant status
O	O	English fluency
O	O	Exact relationship to adult family members
O	O	Exact relationship to other children in HH
O	●	Marital status/history[6]
O	O	Parental status/history
O	O	Current enrollment in regular school
O	O	Current enrollment in preschool/daycare
O	●	Highest grade completed[6]
O	O	Grade now enrolled
O	●	Employment status/history[6]
O	O	Health status
O	O	Handicapping conditions
O	O	Grade repetition
O	O	Aptitude or achievement score
O	O	Pregnancy/birth history
O	O	Psychological well-being
O	O	Delinquency

NOTES
1. First name not coded on data tapes but is contained on control card.
2. Obtained by cycling through individual records.
3. Number of persons in primary family.
4. Within confidentiality restrictions.
5. Obtained only for persons aged 16 to 24.
6. Obtained for persons 15 and older.

CPS—School Enrollment Supplement

PURPOSE The School Enrollment Supplement is designed to provide national estimates of school enrollment by demographic and socioeconomic characteristics of the population, from nursery school through college. College students are included as residents of their parents' households, even if temporarily away at school, to provide socioeconomic characteristics of most young college students.

SPONSORSHIP The Supplement has been jointly sponsored by the Bureau of Labor Statistics and the Bureau of the Census, with the data collection being conducted by the Census Bureau. Occasionally, the Department of Education sponsors additional questions. The National Institute of Child Health and Human Development sponsored the December 1984 supplement on the after-school care of school-age children.

DESIGN A description of the basic design of the Current Population Survey is provided in the write-up of the Core Survey. The questions in the School Enrollment Supplement are asked of all persons aged 3 and over in sampled households.

PERIODICITY The Supplement has been conducted each October since 1946. Plans are to continue the basic school enrollment supplement in 1992 and beyond.

CONTENT The Basic School Enrollment Supplement collects data on highest grade completed, enrollment status, grade or level, type of school (public or private), college attendance (full-time or part-time), type of college (two-year or four-year), and high school graduation status and date. Data are also collected on school enrollment in the last year, which yields a measure of the number of dropouts for a given year.

Occasional topics include homework for elementary and secondary school students (October 1983); use of computers at school and at home (October 1989); and private school tuition, technical or vocational education, degrees sought by college students, and whether high school was completed by means of a high school equivalency test such as the GED (October 1991).

By combining information in the supplement with information in the core, it is possible to examine the decisions that families make about the education of their children and whether family structure influences these decisions.

LIMITATIONS The Supplement is quite brief. A number of useful topics are not covered, such as educational outcomes, degrees earned other than high school graduation, participation in SAT or other testing programs, and skipped or repeated grades. Those topics included on an occasional basis (for example, field of study and degrees sought) would be more useful if continued on a regular basis.

Additionally, information on class rankings and on students' finances are not part of the data set, but such data would add to the usefulness of the supplement. Inclusion of additional questions is dependent upon the needs and funding of other agencies. Also, some data which could be reasonably derived from administrative records or personal interviews may not be appropriately asked of a household respondent.

AVAILABILITY Machine-readable micro-data files are available for October since 1968. For information about the availability of data, contact:

> Data User Services Division
> U.S. Bureau of the Census
> Washington, DC 20233
> 301/763-4100

For substantive questions about the School Enrollment Supplement, contact:

> Paul Siegel
> Education & Social Stratification Branch
> Population Division
> U.S. Bureau of the Census
> Washington, DC 20233
> 301/763-1154

PUBLICATIONS Reports from the supplement appear in the *Current Population Reports*, Series P-20 (annual reports), and Series P-23 (special reports).

Kominski, R., & Roodman, S. (1991). School enrollment - Social and economic characteristics of students: October 1989. *Current Population Reports* (Series P-20, No. 452). Washington, DC: GPO.

CPS—School Enrollment Supplement
FAMILY-LEVEL CHARACTERISTICS
Year of Questionnaire: October 1991
Sample size: 57,000 households

Family Composition
- ● Full roster of household members (first name, age, sex, and relationship to reference person of each member)[1]
- ○ Partial roster of household members
- ● Number of adults in household[2]
- ● Number of children in household[2]
- ○ Approximate relationship of family members to householder, child, or one another
- ○ Exact relationship of family members to householder, child, or one another
- ○ Information about part-time household member
- ○ Information about family members no longer living in household
- ○ Information about relatives who live nearby but not in household

Socioeconomic
- ● Total family income
- ● Number of persons who depend on family income[3]
- ○ Sources of income
- ○ Income amounts identified separately by source
- ○ Poverty status
- ○ Welfare status
- ○ Food Stamps receipt
- ○ Child support receipt
- ○ Medicaid coverage
- ○ Private health insurance
- ● Home ownership/renters
- ○ Assets (other than home ownership)
- ○ Public housing status
- ○ Telephone in household
- ○ Language other than English spoken in home

Geographic/Community Variables
- ● Region of country
- ● State of residence
- ● County/city/MSA of residence
- ● Size/type of community[4]
- ○ Zip code
- ○ Telephone area code
- ● Metropolitan residence[4]
- ○ Neighborhood quality
- ○ Local labor market

Stage in Family Life Cycle
- ● Age of adult respondent or spouse/partner
- ● Marital status of adult respondent or spouse/partner
- ● Employment status of adult respondent or spouse/partner
- ● Presence of own children in household
- ● Age of youngest own child in household[2]
- ● Age of oldest own child in household[2]
- ○ Existence of own children who have left home
- ○ Intention to have (more) children in future

Family Functioning
○ Family activities or time use
○ Community involvement (civic, religious, recreational)
○ Family communication patterns
○ Family decision-making
○ Marital conflict
○ Marital happiness/satisfaction
○ Parent-child conflict
○ History of marital separations
○ History of family violence
○ History of marital counselling

CHARACTERISTICS OF ADULT FAMILY MEMBERS
Sample size: 107,000 persons 18 and older

Adult Respondent or Reference Person	Current Spouse in HH	Current or Former Spouse Not in HH	
●	●	○	Age
●	●	○	Gender
●	●	○	Race
●	●	○	Hispanic origin
●	●	○	Other origin/ethnicity
○	○	○	Religious affiliation
○	○	○	Religious participation
○	○	○	Country of birth
○	○	○	Immigrant status
○	○	○	English fluency
●	●	○	Current marital status
○	○	○	Marital history
○	○	○	Cohabitation status
○	○	○	Cohabitation history
○	○	○	Parental status
○	○	○	Number children ever born/sired
○	○	○	Age at first birth
○	○	○	Age of youngest child
○	○	○	Children living elsewhere
○	○	○	Duration at current address
○	○	○	Residential mobility
●	●	○	Educational attainment
○	○	○	Degrees attained
●	●	○	GED or regular HS diploma[5]
●	●	○	Current enrollment[6]
●	●	○	Current employment status
●	●	○	Hours usually worked (ft/pt)
○	○	○	Weeks worked
○	○	○	Annual employment pattern
●	●	○	Main occupation
●	●	○	Earnings
○	○	○	Wage rate
○	○	○	Payment of child support
○	○	○	Aptitude or achievement score
○	○	○	Health/disability status
○	○	○	Self-esteem
○	○	○	Locus of control or efficacy
○	○	○	Depression or subjective well-being
○	○	○	Work-related attitudes

CHARACTERISTICS OF CHILD FAMILY MEMBERS
Sample size: 44,000 children under 18

Reference Child or Youth Respondent	Children (in HH)	
O	●	Age
O	O	Month and year of birth
O	●	Gender
O	●	Race
O	●	Hispanic origin
O	●	Other origin/ethnicity
O	O	Religious affiliation
O	O	Religious participation
O	O	Country of birth
O	O	Immigrant status
O	O	English fluency
O	O	Exact relationship to adult family members
O	O	Exact relationship to other children in HH
O	●	Marital status/history
O	O	Parental status/history
O	●	Current enrollment in regular school[6]
O	●	Current enrollment in preschool/daycare[7]
O	●	Highest grade completed[6]
O	●	Grade now enrolled
O	●	Employment status/history[6]
O	O	Health status
O	O	Handicapping conditions
O	O	Grade repetition
O	O	Aptitude or achievement score
O	O	Pregnancy/birth history
O	O	Psychological well-being
O	O	Delinquency

NOTES
1. First name not coded on data tapes, but contained on control card.
2. Obtained by cyling through individual records.
3. Number of persons in primary family.
4. Within confidentiality restrictions.
5. Asked of persons 15-24.
6. Asked of persons 15 and older.
7. Asked about children ages 3 to 14.

59

Decennial Census of Population and Housing

PURPOSE The Decennial Census is designed to be a complete enumeration of the population and housing stock of the United States. The data are used to apportion seats in the U.S. House of Representatives and also in state and local legislative districts. The data are also used in the allocation of revenue-sharing and other federal and state funds among approximately 39,000 governmental units. Additional information on the demographic, social, and economic characteristics of the population are also obtained from the Decennial Census. These data are used in marketing studies, academic research, federal, state, and local planning, affirmative action programs, and many other purposes.

SPONSORSHIP The Decennial Census is designed, conducted, and funded by the U.S. Bureau of the Census, Department of Commerce.

DESIGN The Decennial Census employs two types of questionnaire forms: a short form, with a small set of basic population and housing questions asked of all households, and a long form, with all the questions asked in the short form plus additional detailed questions on population and housing. In 1990, nineteen additional questions about the housing unit and twenty-six additional questions about each household member were asked on the long form. The questionnaire is designed to be understood and completed without enumerator assistance and then returned by mail.

The proportion of households receiving the long form is dependent upon the size of the locality, with smaller locality households sampled at a higher rate to assure sufficient precision. For 1990, about 17% of the housing units nationwide were given the long form.

PERIODICITY As mandated by the U.S. Constitution, a census of the population has been conducted every decade since 1790.

No two censuses have been conducted in exactly the same manner. Decade-to-decade changes in content and processing have been made reflecting the attendant changes in our society, economy, and technology. On the whole, however, there is a great deal of continuity across adjacent censuses. Substantive differences between the 1980 and 1990 censuses are detailed below.

CONTENT In the 1980 census, the short form obtained the following information on each household member: relationship to the person filling out the census form (the person in whose name the home is owned or rented), sex, race, age, year and month of birth, marital status, Hispanic origin. The short form housing questions asked about the number of living quarters at the address, access to the housing unit, completeness of plumbing facilities, number of rooms, tenure, condominium status, acreage and commercial establishment status, and value of the property (owned) or monthly rent (rental units). The short form questions for 1990 differ in several small respects from those asked in 1980: they no longer ask for month of birth, questions concerning access to the housing unit and the number of living quarters at a single address. A new housing question asks whether meals are included in the rent. Minor wording changes have been made to several of the questions.

The 1980 long form included all short form items plus twenty additional housing questions and twenty-three additional population questions. These questions covered educational attainment, place of birth, citizenship and year of immigration, current language and ability to speak English, ancestry, residence five years ago, activity five years ago, veteran status and period of service, disability, children ever born, marital history, employment status, place of work and journey to work, year last worked, industry, occupation and class of worker, work experience, and amount and source of income.

The short and long form population questions in the 1990 Decennial Census are basically the same as those in the 1980 census. In 1990, however, no question was asked about activity five years ago; also, no data was collected on marital history. Another change in 1990 concerns the question on educational attainment. The question has been rephrased to ask for the degree received instead of the number of years of school completed. Additionally, the categories of household relationship on the 1990 census form have been changed, enabling data users to distinguish between natural/adopted children and step children, and also to identify foster children in the household.

The long form housing questions in 1980 pertained to number and type of units in the structure, number of stories in the structure and presence of an elevator, farm status, source of water, sewage disposal, year the structure was built, year the householder moved into the unit, heating equipment, fuels used for home heating, water heating, and cooking, cost of utilities and fuels, completeness of kitchen facilities, number of bedrooms, number of bathrooms, telephone, air conditioning, number of automobiles, vans and light trucks, and selected shelter costs for homeowners (including real estate property taxes, annual premiums for fire and hazard insurance, and mortgage on the property).

The long form housing questions for 1990 differed in the following ways: questions concerning the number of stories in the building, the presence of an elevator, and the fuels used for home heating have been eliminated; questions concerning home equity loans, the amount of second mortgages, condominium fees, and mobile home fees are new.

There are many minor changes in the wording of questions between the 1980 and 1990 censuses which were not covered above. For full details, the Census Customer Services Branch will provide a publication which details all of the changes. It is a reprint of an article which appeared in the magazine *American Demographics.*

LIMITATIONS A unique advantage of the one-in-six long form sample of the population is that it provides reliable social, economic, and demographic data for relatively small geographic areas and subgroups of the population. Several aspects of the census limit its usefulness as a research and planning tool.

The major limitation of the census is the fact that it is taken only once every ten years. By the second half of each decade, the data are too old to be useful for many purposes.

A significant limitation of the 1990 census for those interested in marriage is the elimination of the marital history questions which were present in 1980. Finally, there are no direct family functioning measures in the census. This limits its utility for analyses of family function and dysfunction.

For those interested in doing micro analyses on family issues, the configuration of the data in the census public use micro-data files is not optimal. For each household, there is a household record which contains housing information and selected household level characteristics (e.g. total household income), followed by a record containing data for each individual within the household. Unlike the Current Population Survey, there is no family level data as such. This is a problem if there is more than one family sharing a household. Family data can be generated from the individual person records because each person has a subfamily identifier in their record, but it is a great deal of trouble for the individual researcher.

Several limitations which existed in the 1980 census in identifying exact relationships between household members have been eliminated for 1990. In the 1980 census, nuclear family relationships within the household were defined as relationships by birth, marriage, or adoption. One could not distinguish between biological, step, and adoptive parent-child relationships nor measure the size and characteristics of these important subgroups of children. The revised categories of the household relationship item in the 1990 census addresses this problem in part by allowing for the separate identification of step-children. In addition, the 1990 census now allows for the separate identification of foster children.

AVAILABILITY Decennial Census data products are prepared by the Bureau of the Census and are available through the Data User Services Division. The census products for 1990 are listed and described, complete with projected release dates, in the Census publication *1990 Census of Population and Housing: Tabulation and Publication Program*, which can be ordered through the Customer Services Branch listed at the end of this entry. The following types of data products are available from the census:

Summary data on computer tape files (STFs): The statistical information provided on computer tape is similar to data found in printed reports, but is often more detailed and covers gerographic areas not covered in the printed materials. The short form items on the social, economic and housing characteristics of the U.S., states, and specified areas are contained on STF 1 and 2; sample data are contained on STF 3 and 4. The content of STF 1-4 in 1990 will be similar to 1980. Data are offered as a series of frequencies and cross-tabulations on two or more characteristics, at various levels of geography.

In these files, data are available at some or all of the following levels of geography: state, metropolitan area, zip code area, congressional district, county, minor civil division or census county division (MCD/CCD), place, census tract or block numbering area (tract/BNA), block group (BG), and block. Different versions of the STF files offer data on different subsets of these geographic levels. For a complete listing of the various versions of STF files available and the geographic levels covered by each version, order the Census publication *Census '90 Basics*, from the Customer Services Branch. Many of these files are available on CD-ROM as well as computer tape.

Microfiche: Microfiche records are used to disseminate selected reports not available in a printed format. Data from some computer summary tapes are also available on microfiche.

Microdata on tape: Public-use microdata samples provide the responses from a sample of long form questionnaires (with names, addresses, and detailed geography deleted to protect confidentiality) which can be tabulated by data users to meet various statistical needs. These are of particular use to researchers. For 1980 and 1990, tapes can be purchased which contain data for 1% and 5% of the population. The check list at the end of this entry corresponds to what is available for these microdata files. The 1990 files are scheduled for release in 1993. For 1990, the Census may, in addition, produce a special microdata tape for the elderly population.

Maps: Maps are available for all geographic areas for which data are tabulated. In addition to maps which primarily show census functional boundaries, the Census Bureau produces maps which display data by geographic area (for example, income data).

The TIGER/line file is a coordinate-based digital map information system for the entire United States, Puerto Rico, and the Virgin Islands. This computerized system of maps can be purchased on computer tape or CD-ROM for individual states or for the country as a whole.

Special tabulations: Statistical information is also specially prepared by the Census Bureau at the request and expense of the data user. These data are furnished on computer tape, printouts, or microfiche. Contact:

> Customer Services Branch
> Data User Services Division
> U.S. Bureau of the Census
> Washington, DC 20233
> 301/763-4100

PUBLICATIONS Many reports are published, including summary social, economic, and housing characteristics for the U.S., states, and sub-state areas (e.g. cities and counties). Titles of selected published reports from short form data include:

Summary Population and Housing Characteristics, Number of Inhabitants for the U.S. and States, Summary Characteristics for the United States, General Population Characteristics for the U.S. and States, and *General Housing Characteristics for the U.S. and States.* Reports based on sample population data include the *Summary Social, Economic, and Housing Characteristics* and a series of subject reports covering selected topics in greater detail.

In addition, a number of monographs on various subjects have been commissioned to be written using data from the 1990 and earlier censuses. Completed monographs include:

Bianchi, S. & Spain, D. (1986). *American Women in Transition.* New York: Russell Sage Foundation.

Farley, R. & Allen, W.R. (1987). *The Color Line and the Quality of Life in America.* New York: Russell Sage Foundation.

Levy, F. (1987). *Dollars and Dreams: The Changing American Income Distribution.* New York: Russell Sage Foundation.

Other monographs cover the following topics: families and households, housing, neighborhoods, regional and metropolitan growth, Hispanic population, geographic mobility, Native Americans, aging, immigration, rural and small town America, work in the American economy, children since the Depression, Asian and Pacific Island population, and ethnic and racial groups. The monograph on children covers the changing economic, social and demographic circumstances of children from 1940 to 1980.

Plans for 1990 are to produce a series of about thirty-five to forty population and housing reports.

Decennial Census Public Use Microdata File
Year of Questionnaire: 1990
Approximately 3,060,000 persons for 1% sample
and 15,300,000 persons for 5% sample
FAMILY-LEVEL CHARACTERISTICS

Family Composition
● Full roster of household members (first name, age, sex, and relationship to reference person of each member)
○ Partial roster of household members
● Number of adults in household
● Number of children in household
● Approximate relationship of family members to householder, child, or one another
○ Exact relationship of family members to householder, child, or one another
○ Information about part-time household member
○ Information about family members no longer living in household
○ Information about relatives who live nearby but not in household

Socioeconomic
● Total family income
○ Number of persons who depend on family income
● Sources of income[1]
● Income amounts identified separately by source[1]
● Poverty status
● Welfare status[1]
○ Food Stamps receipt
○ Child support receipt
○ Medicaid coverage
○ Private health insurance
● Home ownership/renters
○ Assets (other than home ownership)
○ Public housing status
● Telephone in household
● Language other than English spoken in home

Geographic/Community Variables
● Region of country
● State of residence
● County/city/MSA of residence
● Size/type of community
○ Zip code
○ Telephone area code
● Metropolitan residence
● Neighborhood quality[2]
○ Local labor market

Stage in Family Life Cycle
● Age of adult respondent or spouse/partner
● Marital status of adult respondent or spouse/partner
● Employment status of adult respondent or spouse/partner
● Presence of own children in household
● Age of youngest own child in household[1]
● Age of oldest own child in household[1]
○ Existence of own children who have left home
○ Intention to have (more) children in future

67

Family Functioning
O Family activities or time use
O Community involvement (civic, religious, recreational)
O Family communication patterns
O Family decision-making
O Marital conflict
O Marital happiness/satisfaction
O Parent-child conflict
O History of marital separations
O History of family violence
O History of marital counselling

CHARACTERISTICS OF ADULT FAMILY MEMBERS

Adult Respondent or Reference Person	Current Spouse in HH	Current or Former Spouse Not in HH	
●	●	O	Age
●	●	O	Gender
●	●	O	Race
●	●	O	Hispanic origin
●	●	O	Other origin/ethnicity
O	O	O	Religious affiliation
O	O	O	Religious participation
●	●	O	Country of birth
●	●	O	Immigrant status
●	●	O	English fluency
●	●	O	Current marital status
O	O	O	Marital history
●	●	O	Cohabitation status
O	O	O	Cohabitation history
O	O	O	Parental status
●	●	O	Number of children born/sired[3]
O	O	O	Age at first birth
●	●	O	Age of youngest child
O	O	O	Children living elsewhere
O	O	O	Duration at current address
●	●	O	Residential mobility
●	●	O	Educational attainment
●	●	O	Degrees attained
●	●	O	GED or regular HS diploma
●	●	O	Current enrollment
●	●	O	Current employment status
●	●	O	Hours usually worked (ft/pt)
●	●	O	Weeks worked
O	O	O	Annual employment pattern
●	●	O	Main occupation
●	●	O	Earnings
O	O	O	Wage rate
O	O	O	Payment of child support
O	O	O	Aptitude or achievement score
●	●	O	Health/disability status
O	O	O	Self-esteem
O	O	O	Locus of control or efficacy
O	O	O	Depression or subjective well-being
O	O	O	Work-related attitudes

CHARACTERISTICS OF CHILD FAMILY MEMBERS

Reference Child or Youth Respondent	Children (in HH)	
○	●	Age
○	○	Month and year of Birth
○	●	Gender
○	●	Race
○	●	Hispanic origin
○	●	Other origin/ethnicity
○	○	Religious affiliation
○	○	Religious participation
○	●	Country of birth
○	●	Immigrant status
○	●	English fluency
○	○	Exact relationship to adult family members
○	○	Exact relationship to other children in HH
○	●	Marital status/history
○	○	Parental status/history
○	●	Current enrollment in regular school
○	○	Current enrollment in preschool/daycare
○	●	Highest grade completed
○	○	Grade now enrolled
○	●	Employment status/history
○	○	Health status
○	●	Handicapping conditions
○	○	Grade repetition
○	○	Aptitude or achievement score
○	○	Pregnancy/birth history
○	○	Psychological well-being
○	○	Delinquency

NOTES
1. Can be calculated from person records.
2. For 1970 neighborhood sample only.
3. Females only.

General Social Survey

PURPOSE The General Social Survey (GSS) collects data on social attitudes and behaviors of interest to a broad range of sociologists and political scientists. Its primary purpose is to provide data to facilitate the study of social trends. A second objective is to provide current high quality data to scholars and analysts across the country.

SPONSORSHIP The GSS has been conducted by the National Opinion Research Center (NORC), with primary support from the National Science Foundation. James A. Davis of Harvard and Tom W. Smith of NORC are the principal investigators.

DESIGN The survey is representative of the total non-institutionalized English-speaking population of the United States ages 18 and older. The GSS is a face-to-face interview lasting about an hour and a half. It is conducted among a probability sample of households from which an adult is randomly selected as the respondent, with only one interview conducted per household. (Therefore, individuals in households containing many adults are less likely to be chosen. There is a weight factor to adjust for this, if desired.) African American families were oversampled in 1982 and 1987.

The 1991 GSS interview was conducted among 1,517 respondents in all geographic regions and in both urban and rural areas. Respondents included parents with minor children, parents with adult children, and childless adults. In 1993, the GSS interview of 1,500 cases will be conducted using a ninety-minute interview. Beginning in 1994 there will be two separate surveys of 1,500 cases each.

PERIODICITY The General Social Surveys have been conducted annually during February through April of 1972-1978, 1980, 1982-1991, and 1993. Beginning in 1994 and continuing in even-numbered years, there will be biennial, split-sample surveys of 3,000 respondents.

CONTENT The GSS is a good source of trend data on family related attitudes. It also has included questions on marital happiness, satisfaction with family, and, in some years, extramarital sexual activity. The survey contains such measures of adult functioning as score on a brief word knowledge test, hours worked, perceived job stability, spells of unemployment, children produced, and overall life satisfaction. Three types of items are included in the GSS: permanent questions that are identical in each survey; rotating questions that are posed to two-thirds of the respondents every year; and occasional questions or modules that are included in only one year. One such module is a set of questions in the 1990 survey on parental concerns and family issues and policies sponsored by the National Commission on Children. Survey content generally covers a variety of topics, ranging from income, social activities, and political attitudes, to race relations, religion, and health. Beginning in 1994, the traditional core of replicating questions will be cut in half to allow for a larger number of new and changing topics.

An International Social Survey Program (ISSP) uses the GSS to field the United States portion of its questions which are also posed to respondents in Australia, Austria, Bulgaria, Canada, Czechoslovakia, Germany, Hungary, Ireland, Israel, Italy, Japan, the Netherlands, New Zealand, Norway, the Philippines, Russia, and the United Kingdom. Family and sex roles were surveyed in most of these nations in 1988 and 1989. Religion is the subject of the 1991 ISSP module. The 1994 survey will include a module on women, work, and the family.

LIMITATIONS For the study of adult attitudes and behaviors in different family situations, the GSS sample is relatively small. This is especially so as the sample contains a substantial proportion of respondents who do not live in family households. Also, the use of "split-ballot" questionnaires to broaden the range of issues addressed means that not every respondent is asked each item. Only self-report methods are used to assess family related attitudes and behaviors. Inasmuch as children and adolescents are not eligible to be respondents, no data are available on their attitudes and behaviors. However, the survey can provide data on the social and psychological characteristics of the family environments of children and youth.

AVAILABILITY Cumulative tapes (including surveys from 1972 to 1991), SPSS Control Cards, and a 989-page codebook with univariate tabulations for 1972-1982, the 1982 black oversample, 1983-1987, the 1987 black oversample, and 1988-1991 individually are available from:

>
> The Roper Center for Public
> Opinion Research
> P.O. Box 440
> Storrs, CT 06268
> 203/486-4440
>
> Inter-University Consortium for Political
> and Social Research (ICPSR)
> P.O. Box 1248
> Ann Arbor, MI 48106-1248
> 313/763-5010

Reprints of published articles are available from:

>
> GSS
> National Opinion Research Center (NORC)
> 1155 East 60th Street
> Chicago, IL 60637
> 312/753-7500

A free newsletter, titled *GSS NEWS*, is also available from the above address. An annotated bibliography of papers using GSS is available from ICPSR at the University of Michigan. For substantive questions on the GSS, contact:

>
> Tom W. Smith
> NORC
> 312/753-7877.

PUBLICATIONS Some recent articles based on the GSS include:

Alwin, D.F. (1989). *Family size and cohort differences in vocabulary knowledge in the United States adult population.* Chicago: NORC.

Alwin, D.F. (1989). The times they are a-changin': Qualities valued in children, 1964 to 1984. *Social Science Research, 18,* 195-236.

Ellison, C.G. & Sherkat, D.E. (1993). Conservative Protestantism and support for corporal punishment. *American Sociological Review,* 58, 131-144.

Funk, W. (1991, January). *Family and changing sex-roles: Some preliminary findings about sex-role attitudes in Germany and the United States.* Chicago: NORC.

Greeley, A.M., Michael, R.T., & Smith, T.W. (1990). A most monogamous people: Americans and their sexual partners. *Society,* 27 (July/August), 36-42.

Thornton, A. (1988). *Changing attitudes towards family issues in the United States.* Ann Arbor, MI: Institute for Social Research.

General Social Survey
Year of Questionnaire: 1991
Sample size: 1,517 households
FAMILY-LEVEL CHARACTERISTICS

Family Composition
○ Full roster of household members (first name, age, sex, and relationship to reference person of each member)
○ Partial roster of household members
● Number of adults in household
● Number of children in household
● Approximate relationship of family members to householder, child, or one another
○ Exact relationship of family members to householder, child, or one another
○ Information about part-time household member
○ Information about family members no longer living in household
○ Information about relatives who live nearby but not in household

Socioeconomic
● Total family income
○ Number of persons who depend on family income
○ Sources of income
○ Income amounts identified separately by source
● Poverty status
○ Welfare status
○ Food Stamps receipt
○ Child support receipt
○ Medicaid coverage
○ Private health insurance
● Home ownership/renters
○ Assets (other than home ownership)
○ Public housing status
● Telephone in household
○ Language other than English spoken in home

Geographic/Community Variables
● Region of country
○ State of residence
○ County/city/MSA of residence
● Size/type of community
○ Zip code
○ Telephone area code
● Metropolitan residence
● Neighborhood quality
○ Local labor market

Stage in Family Life Cycle
● Age of adult respondent or spouse/partner
● Marital status of adult respondent or spouse/partner
● Employment status of adult respondent or spouse/partner
○ Presence of own children in household
● Age of youngest own child in household
● Age of oldest own child in household
○ Existence of own children who have left home
● Intention to have (more) children in future

74

Family Functioning
○ Family activities or time use
● Community involvement (civic, religious, recreational)
○ Family communication patterns
○ Family decision-making
○ Marital conflict
● Marital happiness/satisfaction
○ Parent-child conflict
○ History of marital separations
○ History of family violence
○ History of marital counselling

CHARACTERISTICS OF ADULT FAMILY MEMBERS

Adult Respondent or Reference Person	Current Spouse in HH	Current or Former Spouse Not in HH	
●	○	○	Age
●	●	○	Gender
●	○	○	Race
●	●	○	Hispanic origin
●	●	○	Other origin/ethnicity
●	●	○	Religious affiliation
●	●	○	Religious participation
○	○	○	Country of birth
●	○	○	Immigrant status
○	○	○	English fluency
●	○	○	Current marital status
●	○	○	Marital history
○	○	○	Cohabitation status
○	○	○	Cohabitation history
●	○	○	Parental status
●	○	○	Number children ever born/sired
○	○	○	Age at first birth
○	○	○	Age of youngest child
○	○	○	Children living elsewhere
○	○	○	Duration at current address
○	○	○	Residential mobility
●	●	○	Educational attainment
●	○	○	Degrees attained
○	○	○	GED or regular HS diploma
○	○	○	Current enrollment
●	●	○	Current employment status
●	●	○	Hours usually worked (ft/pt)
○	○	○	Weeks worked
○	○	○	Annual employment pattern
●	●	○	Main occupation
●	○	○	Earnings
○	○	○	Wage rate
○	○	○	Payment of child support
●	○	○	Aptitude or achievement score
●	○	○	Health/disability status
○	○	○	Self-esteem
○	○	○	Locus of control or efficacy
○	○	○	Depression or subjective well-being
●	○	○	Work-related attitudes[1]

CHARACTERISTICS OF CHILD FAMILY MEMBERS

Reference Child or Youth Respondent	Other Children (in HH)	
O	O	Age
O	O	Month and Year of Birth
O	O	Gender
O	O	Race
O	O	Hispanic origin
O	O	Other origin/ethnicity
O	O	Religious affiliation
O	O	Religious participation
O	O	Country of birth
O	O	Immigrant status
O	O	English fluency
O	O	Exact relationship to adult family members
O	O	Exact relationship to other children in HH
O	O	Marital status/history
O	O	Parental status/history
O	O	Current enrollment in regular school
O	O	Current enrollment in preschool/daycare
O	O	Highest grade completed
O	O	Grade now enrolled
O	O	Employment status/history
O	O	Health status
O	O	Handicapping conditions
O	O	Grade repetition
O	O	Aptitude or achievement score
O	O	Pregnancy/birth history
O	O	Psychological well-being
O	O	Delinquency

NOTES

1. The 1991 survey includes an extensive set of questions on this topic.

Monitoring the Future: A Continuing Study of the Lifestyles and Values of Youth

PURPOSE One of the study's main purposes is to gather information on the prevalence and incidence of the illicit drug use of high school seniors. In addition, it contains questions designed to describe and explain changes in many important values, behaviors, and lifestyle orientations of American youth.

SPONSORSHIP The study has been designed and carried out by The Survey Research Center, Institute for Social Research, University of Michigan. Funding for the study has been provided by a research grant from the National Institute on Drug Abuse.

DESIGN This is a national survey of high school seniors in approximately 125 public and private schools in the coterminous United States. A multi-stage probability sample method is used, selecting geographically defined primary sampling units, high schools within units, and seniors within high schools. The final sample size varies year to year but is generally around 16,000 to 17,000 seniors. The response rate has ranged from 77% to 84%. The data are collected through self-administered questionnaires completed in a supervised classroom setting. A subsample of 2,400 students from each class has been randomly selected and followed longitudinally for more than ten years.

From 1975 to 1988, five different questionnaire forms were used and distributed to five virtually identical subsamples; thus, questions appearing on only one form were administered to a random one-fifth of the total sample. Beginning in 1989, a sixth form was added, and thereafter, questions appearing on only one form are administered to a random one-sixth of the total sample. About one-third of each form contains core questions which are common to all forms.

PERIODICITY The study was first conducted in the spring of 1975 and has been conducted annually since then.

CONTENT The main focus of the study is on drug use and attitudes related to it. Questions are also asked about other delinquent behaviors in the last year, such as participation in gang fights, fighting at school, assault, larceny, shoplifting, car theft, trespassing, arson, vandalism, and getting into trouble with the police. Questions on victimization experiences also refer to the previous twelve months, and cover incidents of theft, property damage, and assault. Some other topics include attitudes about government, social institutions, race relations, changing roles for women, educational aspirations, occupational aims, and marital and family plans. Questions on background and demographics were also included.

LIMITATIONS Those who have dropped out of school by the spring of senior year (about 15-20%) are not included in this study. There may also be a bias introduced by not including absentee students. However, the researchers included a question in the study asking students how many days of school they had missed in the previous four weeks. Assuming that the absence on the day of the administration of the survey is a random event, the researchers were able to use students with high absentee rates to represent all students with such an absentee rate, including those who were actually absent that day. Using this method, they found that absentees as a group have much higher than average use of all licit and illicit drugs. However, they found that this group is such a small proportion of the total target sample that they do not affect cross-time trend estimates. Users of the data can find the necessary components needed to do corrective weighting for absenteeism if they choose.

Although this survey is very rich in data on drug use and attitudinal questions, there is a limited information on characteristics of the respondents' families. Furthermore, though the sample is large, only the core set of questions are asked of all respondents. For the preponderance of questions, data are available on only one-fifth of the sample through 1988 (one-sixth thereafter).

The survey from the class of 1975 was subject to missing data problems. Followup surveys of the class of 1976 were subject to low response rate problems. Changes in procedures in 1978 have put the response rates over 80% on followups of the class of 1977 and subsequent classes.

AVAILABILITY The Survey Research Center produces a publication annually which presents descriptive results on each variable by sex, race, region, college plans, and drug use. Trend data on drug use and related attitudes are available from the National Institute on Drug Abuse. A listing of other available articles, chapters and occasional papers is available from the principal investigators. Micro-data tapes are available through the Inter-University Consortium for Political and Social Research, Institute for Survey Research, University of Michigan, Ann Arbor, MI 48106-1248, 313/763-5010. Data on the longitudinal follow-ups are not publicly available, but results are published in relevant papers and monographs.
Contacts:

> Patrick O'Malley
> Institute for Social Research
> University of Michigan
> Ann Arbor, MI 48106-1248
> 313/763-5043

PUBLICATIONS

Herzog, A.R., Bachman, J.G., & Johnson, L.D. (1983). Paid work, child care, and housework: A national survey of high school seniors' preferences for sharing responsibilities between husband and wife. *Sex Roles, 9*(1), 109-135.

Johnson, L.D., Bachman, J.G., & O'Malley, P.M. (1991). *Monitoring the future: Questionnaire responses from the nation's high school seniors*. Michigan: Institute for Social Research.

Monitoring the Future
Year of Questionnaire: 1988
Sample size: 16,795 high school seniors
FAMILY-LEVEL CHARACTERISTICS

Family Composition
○ Full roster of household members (first name, age, sex, and relationship to reference person of each member)
○ Partial roster of household members
● Number of adults in household
● Number of children in household
○ Approximate relationship of family members to householder, child, or one another
○ Exact relationship of family members to householder, child, or one another
○ Information about part-time household member
○ Information about family members no longer living in household
○ Information about relatives who live nearby but not in household

Socioeconomic
○ Total family income
○ Number of persons who depend on family income
○ Sources of income
○ Income amounts identified separately by source
○ Poverty status
○ Welfare status
○ Food Stamps receipt
○ Child support receipt
○ Medicaid coverage
○ Private health insurance
○ Home ownership/renters
○ Assets (other than home ownership)
○ Public housing status
○ Telephone in household
○ Language other than English spoken in home

Geographic/Community Variables
● Region of country
○ State of residence
○ County/city/MSA of residence
● Size/type of community[1]
○ Zip code
○ Telephone area code
● Metropolitan residence
○ Neighborhood quality
○ Local labor market

Stage in Family Life Cycle
○ Age of adult respondent or spouse/partner
○ Marital status of adult respondent or spouse/partner
○ Employment status of adult respondent or spouse/partner
● Presence of own children in household
○ Age of youngest own child in household
○ Age of oldest own child in household
○ Existence of own children who have left home
○ Intention to have (more) children in future

Family Functioning

- ○ Family activities or time use
- ○ Community involvement (civic, religious, recreational)
- ○ Family communication patterns
- ● Family decision-making[2]
- ○ Marital conflict
- ○ Marital happiness/satisfaction
- ● Parent-child conflict[2]
- ○ History of marital separations
- ○ History of family violence
- ○ History of marital counselling

CHARACTERISTICS OF ADULT FAMILY MEMBERS

Adult Respondent or Reference Person	Current Spouse in HH	Current or Former Spouse Not in HH	
○	○	○	Age
○	○	○	Gender
○	○	○	Race
○	○	○	Hispanic origin
○	○	○	Other origin/ethnicity
○	○	○	Religious affiliation
○	○	○	Religious participation
○	○	○	Country of birth
○	○	○	Immigrant status
○	○	○	English fluency
○	○	○	Current marital status
○	○	○	Marital history
○	○	○	Cohabitation status
○	○	○	Cohabitation history
○	○	○	Parental status
○	○	○	Number children ever born/sired
○	○	○	Age at first birth
○	○	○	Age of youngest child
○	○	○	Children living elsewhere
○	○	○	Duration at current address
○	○	○	Residential mobility
●	○	○	Educational attainment[3]
○	○	○	Degrees attained
○	○	○	GED or regular HS diploma
○	○	○	Current enrollment
○	○	○	Current employment status
○	○	○	Hours usually worked (ft/pt)
○	○	○	Weeks worked
○	○	○	Annual employment pattern
○	○	○	Main occupation
○	○	○	Earnings
○	○	○	Wage rate
○	○	○	Payment of child support
○	○	○	Aptitude or achievement score
○	○	○	Health/disability status
○	○	○	Self-esteem
○	○	○	Locus of control or efficacy
○	○	○	Depression or subjective well-being
○	○	○	Work-related attitudes

CHARACTERISTICS OF CHILD FAMILY MEMBERS

Reference Child or Youth Respondent	Other Children (in HH)	
●	○	Age
●	○	Month and year of birth
●	○	Gender
●	○	Race
○	○	Hispanic origin
○	○	Other origin/ethnicity
●	○	Religious affiliation
●	○	Religious participation
○	○	Country of birth
○	○	Immigrant status
○	○	English fluency
●	○	Exact relationship to adult family members[4]
○	○	Exact relationship to other children in HH
●	○	Marital status/history
○	○	Parental status/history
●	○	Current enrollment in regular school
○	○	Current enrollment in preschool/daycare
●	○	Highest grade completed
●	○	Grade now enrolled
●	○	Employment status/history
●	○	Health status[2]
○	○	Handicapping conditions
○	○	Grade repetition
○	○	Aptitude or achievement score
○	○	Pregnancy/birth history
●	○	Psychological well-being
●	○	Delinquency

NOTES
1. Size/type of community where R grew up.
2. Asked only of subsample; not on all 5 forms.
3. Asks educational attainment regarding parents who raised R.
4. Only partial relationship can be ascertained.

National Assessment of Educational Progress

PURPOSE The National Assessment of Educational Progress is a survey of the educational achievement of American students and changes over time in that achievement. NAEP was developed in 1969 as an educational indicator and for the past 23 years has assessed the knowledge, understanding, skills and attitudes of young Americans in a number of different subject areas. The areas assessed include reading, writing, mathematics, and science, U.S. history, world geography, and, on occasion, special topics such as health. Past assessments also covered the subjects of citizenship, social studies, history, computer competence, literature, art, music, and career and occupational development.

SPONSORSHIP NAEP is a congressionally mandated project of the National Center for Education Statistics (NCES), U.S. Department of Education. Since 1986, the National Assessment has been funded by the Office of Educational Research and Improvement (OERI) of the U.S. Department of Education (NAEP is a line item in the OERI budget). Prior to that time, the Assessment was supported by the National Institute of Education (1979-1986), the National Center for Education Statistics (1974-79) and, before that, by the U.S. Office of Education (1968-74). The forerunner of NAEP was the Committee on Assessing the Progress of Education. It was initiated in 1963 by Francis Keppel, then U.S. Commissioner of Education, who asked the Carnegie Corporation to present a means for determining the educational levels attained through American education. The earliest assessments (in 1969) were carried out with both private and federal funding.

From its inception through 1983, NAEP was administered by the Education Commission of the States in Denver, with field work conducted by the Research Triangle Institute in North Carolina. The Educational Testing Service (ETS) in Princeton has now assumed responsibility for the administration of NAEP, after carrying out a major redesign study and winning a grant competition in 1982. The sample design and field work are conducted by

Westat, Inc. in Rockville, Maryland, and scoring is performed by Computer Systems in Iowa City, Iowa.

In the 1988 Hawkins-Stafford Amendments (P.L. 100-297), Congress created the National Assessment Governing Board to formulate the policy guidelines for NAEP. The governing board's 23 members include teachers, curriculum specialists, state legislators, measurement experts, chief state school officers, state and local school board members, school superintendents, principals, and representatives from business and the general public.

DESIGN The National Assessment is designed to measure change in the educational attainment of young Americans through the periodic replication of cross-sectional surveys that assess the knowledge of the student population at three age levels (9-, 13-, and 17-year-olds in the 4th, 8th, and 12th grades). The populations covered by the NAEP surveys are students enrolled in public or private schools in the 50 states and the District of Columbia. Students and young adults are excluded if they are non-English speaking, institutionalized, or physically, emotionally, or mentally handicapped in such a way that they cannot respond to the exercises as administered.

The sampling plans for both the school-based and household-based surveys follow multi-stage probability designs. The primary sampling units (PSUs) are counties or groups of counties stratified by region of the country and by the size and type of communities contained within the counties. Within each selected PSU, schools are sampled from a list of all schools that is stratified by size and socioeconomic level. Within each selected school, students are randomly selected from lists of all students of the target ages and randomly assigned to one of the assessment packages scheduled for that school. Beginning with the ETS-administered surveys, samples have been drawn of students in the modal grade for each assessment age (e.g., grade 4 for 9-year-olds; grade 8 for 13-year-olds; and grade 12 for 17-year-olds.)

Between 75,000 and 100,000 students are included in each assessment. Response rates have varied across age groups and assessments, but typical figures for recent school-based assessments are about 90% cooperation from the selected schools and over 90% participation by the selected students within cooperating schools, for an overall response rate of more than 80 percent.

In 1988, Congress added a new dimension to NAEP by authorizing voluntary participation in state-level assessments on a trial basis in 1990 and 1992. Designed to provide results comparable to the nation and other participating states, trial state assessments include eighth-grade mathematics as well as fourth-grade mathematics and reading in 1992.

PERIODICITY The original plan for NAEP called for nationwide surveys to be conducted every year, with 10 different subject areas being assessed on a rotating schedule, so that each subject would be assessed at least once every 3 to 6 years. The plan has since been altered over time by budgetary constraints and shifting educational priorities, design modifications instituted by the Educational Testing Service, and more recently by Congress. In 1988 Congress established a schedule for the administration of NAEP assessments: reading and math are to be assessed every 2 years, science and writing every 4 years, while U.S. history and world geography will be assessed every 6 years. There is the possibility that this schedule may be revised as well. Congress will be considering a proposal for testing to take place annually beginning in 1995.

Subjects	Completed Assessments
Reading	70-71,74-75,79-80,83-84,85-86,87-88,89-90
Writing	69-70,73-74,78-79,83-84,87-88
Mathematics	72-73,76-77,77-78,81-82,85-86,89-90
Science	69-70,72-73,76-77,81-82,85-86,89-90
Citizenship	69-70,75-76,81-82 (partial)
Social Studies	71-72,75-76,81-82 (partial)
Literature	70-71,79-80,86 (19-year-olds)
Music	71-72,78-79

Subjects	Completed Assessments
Art	74-75,78-79
Career and Occupational Development	73-74
Computer Competence	85-86
Young Adult Literacy	85-86 (ages 21-25)
U.S. History	85-86 (17-year-olds),87-88
Geography	87-88 (17-year-olds)

The rationale for assessing reading and mathematics biennially is that it will heighten the pace with which important barometers of educational progress can be brought before the public and the educational community. The use of 2- and 4-year cycles also serves to align the assessment intervals to the number of years intervening between the age levels sampled. Thus, the same student cohort assessed at age 9 (although not the same individual students) will be assessed again at ages 13 and 17. This introduces a quasi-longitudinal element into the assessment design, helps to control for cohort differences in a given subject area, and should assist in the interpretation of achievement trends.

CONTENT NAEP gathers a great deal of specific information about what students know and can do at the different ages. In the reading assessments, for example, students are tested on their ability to understand words and word relationships; comprehend graphic materials; follow written directions; use reference materials; glean significant facts from written passages; recognize the main ideas and organization of a passage; draw inferences from what they read; and read critically. Exercises are also grouped into higher order clusters and results are reported in terms of the average percent correct on such clusters. In the reports issued prior to the 1984 assessment, exercise clusters were formed solely on the basis of expert judgment. One of the main thrusts of the ETS redesign is to put these composite scores on a sounder and more sophisticated psychometric basis. Wherever possible, results are now reported on proficiency scales, and at intervals on the scale there are descriptors of what students know and can do. Beginning with the 1992 assessments, there are descriptors of what students *should* know and do.

While the NAEP at one time included affective exercises and attitude survey questions in each assessment to tap students' attitudes towards learning, Congress eliminated these items from the assessment as part of a series of changes made to the NAEP in 1988. Within each age group, assessment results are typically reported for the nation as a whole and for each of the four broad geographic regions, as well as by sex; race/ethnicity (black, white, Hispanic); parental education level (where known by the student) and by the size and type of community which the school serves. Three "extreme" types of community (advantaged urban, disadvantaged urban, and rural) are defined by an occupational profile of the area served by the school. Other communities are classified by population size.

More recently, results have also been reported by the grade in which the student is enrolled, by the percent of minority enrollment in the school, and by the student's "achievement class." The last variable divides students into quartiles based on their performance on the whole booklet of exercises they take. Particular attention is paid to students in the top and bottom quartiles.

LIMITATIONS The initial design of the NAEP intentionally avoided any appearance that a national curriculum and testing program were being imposed on state education agencies and local school systems. NAEP was deliberately designed to make it difficult if not impossible to use the assessment findings to evaluate the performance of any particular school or school system or even to link assessment results to specific educational practices. This was done in order to secure the cooperation of state and local agencies and to help insure the political survival of NAEP. However, the design features that may have made the program more palatable to school administrators have severely limited the usefulness of the NAEP database for educational research and for influencing educational policy and practice.

Since 1984, the Educational Testing Service has made NAEP achievement data more useful for educational research and policy-making by developing better composite measures of achievement from the assessment exercises and by collecting additional information about the backgrounds of the students assessed and about their experiences in schools and educational programs. The kinds of student background data ETS collects include enhanced demographic descriptors; non-NAEP measures of achievement; information about participation in special programs; measures of interests and aspirations; measures of time spent studying, reading, watching TV, in other activities, and, for older students, in employment; and measures of a variety of family status and process characteristics. The kinds of school and program data ETS collects include measures of the racial, ethnic, and socioeconomic composition of the student body; descriptors of the size and type of school; information about the availability of special programs; types of curricula, tracking arrangements, and extracurricular activities; measures of resource utilization; and indicators of school climate and image.

Of course, obtaining valid and reliable measures of some of these student and school characteristics is not a simple matter. Previous research has shown that it is desirable to go to the parents to get valid information about some aspects of family background, such as family income level or parental employment history. Likewise, valid measurement of how the school functions could be enhanced by some direct observation of the school in operation. To date, ETS has not been given congressional authorization to collect such data.

ETS intends to collect more detailed information about which students are being left out of the NAEP samples because of the policy of excluding handicapped and non-English-speaking students from the assessments. Adjustments are also made for the bias that is introduced by absenteeism on the days that the assessment exercises are administered in a given school. NCES hopes to reinstate the practice of testing 17-year-olds who are not in school because they have dropped out or graduated early, perhaps using the sample frame for the Current Population Survey or another Census survey to locate suitable respondents. Again, however, there is a question as to whether sufficient funds will be available to pay for these improvements.

AVAILABILITY To order public use data tapes (or CD version) from the 1990 assessment, contact:

> Roger Herriott
> NCES
> 555 New Jersey Avenue NW, Room 408
> Washington, DC 20208-5654
> 202/219-1837

To obtain tapes for all previous years, contact:

> NAEP/ETS
> P.O. Box 6710
> Princeton, NJ 08541-6710
> 800/223-0267

The National Center for Education Statistics also makes available almanacs of computer-generated tables of information on a nationally representative samples for some assessments. Almanacs are available on 3.5 or 5.25 inch IBM-compatible diskettes. For more information on the almanacs, send a formatted diskette of either size and a note to:

> U.S. Department of Education
> OERI/NCES/EAD
> Capitol Place, Room 308
> 555 New Jersey Avenue NW
> Washington, DC 20208-5653
> 202/219-1937

For substantive questions on the NAEP survey, contact:

> Steve Gorman, Ph.D.
> National Center for Education Statistics
> Educational Assessment Division
> 555 New Jersey Ave, NW
> Washington, DC 20208-5653
> 202/219-1937

PUBLICATIONS More than 300 reports have been published describing NAEP objectives and procedures, the results of specific assessments, and changes over time in student performance. Most of the reports present assessment results in nontechnical, summary terms along with straightforward tables that show group results on individual exercises and exercise clusters. There is also a technical report or appendix for each assessment that presents the results in more detail. A catalog of 1984-1988 NAEP publications as well as the publications themselves may be obtained from Steve Gorman at the above address.

A detailed description of the content and methods of the 1990 and 1992 assessment can be found in *The NAEP Guide*, revised edition, prepared November 1991 by Educational Testing Service under a contract from The National Center for Education Statistics.

National Assessment of Educational Progress
Year of Questionnaire: 1990
Sample size: 3,000 to 100,000 students (depending on subject being assessed)
FAMILY-LEVEL CHARACTERISTICS

Family Composition
○ Full roster of household members (first name, age, sex, and relationship to reference person of each member)
○ Partial roster of household members
● Number of adults in household
○ Number of children in household
○ Approximate relationship of family members to householder, child, or one another
○ Exact relationship of family members to householder, child, or one another
○ Information about part-time household member
○ Information about family members no longer living in household
○ Information about relatives who live nearby but not in household

Socioeconomic[1]
○ Total family income
○ Number of persons who depend on family income
○ Sources of income
○ Income amounts identified separately by source
○ Poverty status
○ Welfare status
○ Food Stamps receipt
○ Child support receipt
○ Medicaid coverage
○ Private health insurance
○ Home ownership/renters
○ Assets (other than home ownership)
○ Public housing status
○ Telephone in household
● Language other than English spoken in home

Geographic/Community Variables
● Region of country
● State of residence
● County/city/MSA of residence
● Size/type of community
● Zip code
○ Telephone area code
○ Metropolitan residence
○ Neighborhood quality
○ Local labor market

Stage in Family Life Cycle
○ Age of adult respondent or spouse/partner
○ Marital status of adult respondent or spouse/partner
○ Employment status of adult respondent or spouse/partner
○ Presence of own children in household
○ Age of youngest own child in household
○ Age of oldest own child in household
○ Existence of own children who have left home
○ Intention to have (more) children in future

Family Functioning

- ● Family activities or time use[2]
- ○ Community involvement (civic, religious, recreational)
- ○ Family communication patterns
- ○ Family decision-making
- ○ Marital conflict
- ○ Marital happiness/satisfaction
- ○ Parent-child conflict
- ○ History of marital separations
- ○ History of family violence
- ○ History of marital counselling

CHARACTERISTICS OF ADULT FAMILY MEMBERS

Adult Respondent or Reference Person	Current Spouse in HH	Current or Former Spouse Not in HH	
○	○	○	Age
○	○	○	Gender
○	○	○	Race
○	○	○	Hispanic origin
○	○	○	Other origin/ethnicity
○	○	○	Religious affiliation
○	○	○	Religious participation
○	○	○	Country of birth
○	○	○	Immigrant status
○	○	○	English fluency
○	○	○	Current marital status
○	○	○	arital history
○	○	○	Cohabitation status
○	○	○	Cohabitation history
○	○	○	Parental status
○	○	○	Number children ever born/sired
○	○	○	Age at first birth
○	○	○	Age of youngest child
○	○	○	Children living elsewhere
○	○	○	Duration at current address
●	○	○	Residential mobility
○	○	○	Educational attainment
○	○	○	Degrees attained
●	○	○	GED or regular HS diploma
○	○	○	Current enrollment
○	○	○	Current employment status
○	○	○	Hours usually worked (ft/pt)
○	○	○	Weeks worked
○	○	○	Annual employment pattern
○	○	○	Main occupation
○	○	○	Earnings
○	○	○	Wage rate
○	○	○	Payment of child support
○	○	○	Aptitude or achievement score
○	○	○	Health/disability status
○	○	○	Self-esteem
○	○	○	Locus of control or efficacy
○	○	○	Depression or subjective well-being
○	○	○	Work-related attitudes

CHARACTERISTICS OF CHILD FAMILY MEMBERS

Reference Child or Youth Respondent	Other Children (in HH)	
●	○	Age
●	○	Month and year of birth
●	○	Gender
●	○	Race
●	○	Hispanic origin
●	○	Other origin/ethnicity
○	○	Religious affiliation
○	○	Religious participation
○	○	Country of birth
○	○	Immigrant status
○	○	English fluency
○	○	Exact relationship to adult family members
○	○	Exact relationship to other children in HH
○	○	Marital status/history
○	○	Parental status/history
●	○	Current enrollment in regular school
○	○	Current enrollment in preschool/daycare
○	○	Highest grade completed
●	○	Grade now enrolled
○	○	Employment status/history
○	○	Health status
●	○	Handicapping conditions[3]
○	○	Grade repetition
○	○	Aptitude or achievement score
○	○	Pregnancy/birth history
○	○	Psychological well-being
○	○	Delinquency

NOTES

1. Along with language spoken in home, presence of reading materials in the home and parents' educational attainment are the only socioeconomic indicators obtained.
2. Student reports time spent on homework and how often someone helps with homework.
3. Functionally disabled and educable mentally retarded children are excluded from NAEP samples.

National Child Care Survey, 1990

PURPOSE The National Child Care Survey (NCCS), 1990, was designed to provide current information on where American children under age 13 spend their day. It provides information on what child care and preschool programs families are using, how child care affects work patterns, and how parents make their choices concerning child care for their children.

SPONSORSHIP The study was jointly sponsored by the Administration for Children, Youth, and Families of the U.S. Department of Health and Human Services and by the National Association for the Education of Young Children. Additional funding was provided by the Assistant Secretary for Planning and Evaluation (DHHS) and the Department of the Navy.

DESIGN This is a nationally representative, cross-sectional survey of 4,392 parents with children under age 13. The survey was designed by The Urban Institute. The design of the NCCS was coordinated with the design of the Profile of Child Care Settings conducted by Mathematica Policy Research, Inc., for the U.S. Department of Education. Both surveys collected data in the same 100 primary sampling units.

The NCCS was a national random-digit-dial telephone survey. Respondents were interviewed by telephone about the early education and care arrangements made for their children. The 40-minute survey asked about children's care arrangements, the alternatives available, and how child care choices were made. In addition, parents were asked whether they provided care in their own homes for other children. Parents contacted in the consumer survey were asked to provide their caregivers' phone numbers so that the providers could also be interviewed. These providers were asked questions about schedules, enrollment and daily activities. Two additional sub-studies were also conducted: 1) a telephone survey of low-income households with children under 13, and 2) a telephone interview of military households with children under 13 that included a followup telephone interview with the child care provider of the youngest child in the household.

PERIODICITY The NCCS was fielded between October 1989 and May 1990 by Abt Associates.

CONTENT The central focus of the survey was on the types of child care arrangements received by children less than 13 years old residing in the household. Questions were geared to the age of the child, types of arrangements used, and whether they were currently enrolled in school. Characteristics of child care arrangements attended on a regular basis for at least one week for the past two weeks were ascertained for each child. Information was gathered about the type of care (e.g., day care center; nursery school; kindergarten, regular school; relative care; lessons, clubs, sports, or similar activities), location, and sponsorship. Detailed information on cost (including information about non-paid arrangements) and payment schedule was obtained for the youngest child, with summary information on total expenditures for all children. Additional detail focused on arrangements made for the youngest child. Respondents were asked to describe the factors they considered in choosing an arrangement and what, if any, alternatives were perceived to be available and considered. Respondents were also asked how they learned about their current arrangement(s) and their satisfaction with it. The survey included questions related to the type of arrangement they would prefer for each child and the aspects of quality that they consider to be most important.

Attention was given to the unique aspects of various types of care. For example, non-users of self-care were asked which factors would be most important in deciding when to allow their child to care for him/herself, and users of sibling care were asked whether a reliable neighbor is available in an emergency. The education and training of child care providers, group size and number of staff, the goals and objectives of formal programs, and distance and availability of different types of arrangements were among the items ascertained. In addition, the survey gathered information about the employment schedule and history of the respondent and spouse; receipt of employment sponsored children benefits; their background characteristics, including family income; and a roster of other household members.

LIMITATIONS The data provide rich detail about the child care experiences of the nation's children and have the particular benefit of providing insight into the decision-making process and parents' perceptions of alternatives. The survey is cross-sectional and covers a single time period; however, the possibility of linking it with the child care provider survey make the data well-suited for policy evaluation purposes.

AVAILABILITY A public data tape is available from:

> Sociometrics Corporation
> 170 State Street, Suite 260
> Los Altos, CA 94022
> 800/846-3475

For substantive information on the NCCS, contact:

> Dr. Sandra Hofferth
> The Urban Institute
> 2100 M Street, NW
> Washington, DC 20037
> 202/857-8617

PUBLICATIONS The first report on the NCCS is currently available from:

> University Press of America
> 4720-A Boston Way
> Lanham, MD 20706
> 301/459-3366

Other publications include:

Brayfield, A., Deich, S., & Hofferth, S. (1991). *Caring for children in low-income families: A substudy of the National Child Care Survey 1990*. Washington, DC: The Urban Institute.

Deich, S., Brayfield, A., & Hofferth, S. (1991). *National Child Care Survey, 1990: Military Substudy.* Washington, DC: The Urban Institute.

Hofferth, S. (1992). The demand for and supply of child care in the 1990s. In Booth, A. (Ed.), *Child care in the 1990s: Trends and consequences.* Hillsdale, NJ: Lawrence Erlbaum Associates.

Hofferth, S., Brayfield, A., Deich, S., & Holcomb, P. (1991). *The National Child Care Survey 1990.* Washington, DC: The Urban Institute.

Hofferth, S., & Kisker, E. (1991). *Family day care in the U.S. 1990.* Washington, DC: The Urban Institute.

Hofferth, S., & Kisker, E. (1992). The changing demographics of family day care in the United States. In D. Peters & A. Pence (Eds.), *Family day care: Current research for informed public policy.* New York: Teachers College Press.

Willer, B., Hofferth, S., Kisker, E., Hawkins, P., Farquhar, E., & Glantz, F. (1991). *The demand and supply of child care in 1990: Joint findings from the National Child Care Survey 1990 and the Profile of Child Care Settings.* Washington, DC: National Association for the Education of Young Children.

National Child Care Survey, 1990
Sample size: 4,392 parents with children under age 13 in household
FAMILY-LEVEL CHARACTERISTICS

Family Composition
- Full roster of household members (first name, age, sex, and relationship to reference person of each member)
- ○ Partial roster of household members
- Number of adults in household
- Number of children in household
- ○ Approximate relationship of family members to householder, child, or one another
- Exact relationship of family members to householder, child, or one another[1]
- ○ Information about part-time household member
- ○ Information about family members no longer living in household
- Information about relatives who live nearby but not in household[2]

Socioeconomic
- Total family income
- ○ Number of persons who depend on family income
- Sources of income
- ○ Income amounts identified separately by source
- ○ Poverty status
- Welfare status
- ○ Food Stamps receipt
- Child support receipt
- ○ Medicaid coverage
- Private health insurance[3]
- Home ownership/renters
- ○ Assets (other than home ownership)
- ○ Public housing status
- Telephone in household
- ○ Language other than English spoken in home

Geographic/Community Variables
- Region of country
- State of residence
- County/city/MSA of residence
- ○ Size/type of community
- Zip code
- ○ Telephone area code
- Metropolitan residence
- ○ Neighborhood quality
- ○ Local labor market

Stage in Family Life Cycle
- Age of adult respondent or spouse/partner
- Marital status of adult respondent or spouse/partner
- Employment status of adult respondent or spouse/partner
- Presence of own children in household
- Age of youngest own child in household
- Age of oldest own child in household
- ○ Existence of own children who have left home
- ○ Intention to have (more) children in future

Family Functioning
O Family activities or time use
O Community involvement (civic, religious, recreational)
O Family communication patterns
O Family decision-making
O Marital conflict
O Marital happiness/satisfaction
O Parent-child conflict
O History of marital separations
O History of family violence
O History of marital counselling

CHARACTERISTICS OF ADULT FAMILY MEMBERS

Mother	Current Father in HH	Current or Former Spouse Not in HH	
●	●	O	Age
●	●	O	Gender
●	O	O	Race
●	O	O	Hispanic origin
●	O	O	Other origin/ethnicity
●	O	O	Religious affiliation
●	O	O	Religious participation
●	O	O	Country of birth
O	O	O	Immigrant status
O	O	O	English fluency
●	●	O	Current marital status
O	O	O	Marital history
●	●	O	Cohabitation status
O	O	O	Cohabitation history
●	O	O	Parental status[4]
O	O	O	Number children ever born/sired
O	O	O	Age at first birth
●	O	O	Age of youngest child
O	O	O	Children living elsewhere
●	O	O	Duration at current address
O	O	O	Residential mobility
●	●	O	Educational attainment
O	O	O	Degrees attained
O	O	O	GED or regular HS diploma
●	●	O	Current enrollment
●	●	O	Current employment status
●	●	O	Hours usually worked (ft/pt)
●	●	O	Weeks worked
●	●	O	Annual employment pattern
●	●	O	Main occupation
●	●	O	Earnings
●	●	O	Wage rate
O	O	O	Payment of child support
O	O	O	Aptitude or achievement score
O	O	O	Health/disability status
O	O	O	Self-esteem
O	O	O	Locus of control or efficacy
O	O	O	Depression or subjective well-being
●	O	O	Work-related attitudes

CHARACTERISTICS OF CHILD FAMILY MEMBERS
Sample size: 7,575

Reference Child or Youth Respondent	Other Children (in HH)	
●	●	Age
●	●	Month and year of birth
●	●	Gender
○	○	Race
○	○	Hispanic origin
○	○	Other origin/ethnicity
○	○	Religious affiliation
○	○	Religious participation
○	○	Country of birth
○	○	Immigrant status
○	○	English fluency
●	○	Exact relationship to adult family members
●	●	Exact relationship to other children in HH [5]
○	○	Marital status/history
○	○	Parental status/history
●	●	Current enrollment in regular school
●	●	Current enrollment in preschool/daycare
○	○	Highest grade completed
●	●	Grade now enrolled
○	○	Employment status/history
●	●	Health status
○	○	Handicapping conditions
○	○	Grade repetition
○	○	Aptitude or achievement score
○	○	Pregnancy/birth history
○	○	Psychological well-being
○	○	Delinquency

NOTES
1. Relationship to youngest child in household.
2. Some limited information obtained if relative provides child care to a child in household.
3. Possible to determine if respondent or spouse have health insurance through employer.
4. Only if child lives in household.
5. Exact relationship to youngest child in household.

National Crime Victimization Survey

PURPOSE The purpose of the survey is to assess the character and extent of criminal offenses reported by victims of crime. The survey ascertains the characteristics of the victims, the circumstances surrounding the incidents, the characteristics of the offenders, and the consequences of the crimes for the victims. The offenses covered for individuals are rape, robbery, assault, and personal larceny. Burglary, household larceny, motor vehicle theft, and vandalism are covered for households.

SPONSORSHIP Formerly known as the National Crime Survey, the survey was originally planned and designed by the Law Enforcement Assistance Administration. When that agency was dissolved, the survey was transferred to the Bureau of Justice Statistics. The survey is funded by the Department of Justice. The data are collected by the U.S. Bureau of the Census.

DESIGN The survey is designed to collect data regarding persons aged 12 and over living in households in the 50 states and the District of Columbia. A three-stage stratified probability sample is used. First, 376 geographically defined primary sampling units are selected; then enumeration districts within sampling units are chosen; finally, segments of about four housing units each are chosen to be contacted within enumeration districts. Each person in the household aged 12 or over is interviewed regarding his or her experience as a victim of crime. Information about crimes against victims aged 11 or younger is not obtained.

The sample of households is divided into six rotation groups, each interviewed every six months for three years (a total of seven interviews). The first interview is done in person; subsequent interviews may be done by telephone. Information is gathered on approximately 100,000 individuals in 49,000 households. Early surveys also included a sample of business establishments to gather data on crimes committed against businesses. This aspect of the survey was dropped in 1977 because it measured only robbery and burglary and did not provide comprehensive commercial data.

While the first of the seven interviews does collect data about victimization incidents in the recent past, its primary purpose is to establish a boundary for the next interview. The interview time periods then serve as a reference period for reports of victimization.

Longitudinal data are available for the household. To the extent that the same family or individual occupied the household during the three year period, longitudinal data are available for the family or individual as well. The NCVS was redesigned in 1990. The new instrument obtains more comprehensive information about victim characteristics and includes screening questions for vandalism.

PERIODICITY The survey was begun in 1973, and data have been collected regularly since then. Households are interviewed twice a year for three years. New households come into the survey at each interview period, while one-sixth of the others are completing their three-year stints.

CONTENT Information is collected both about the household as a whole and about individual members of the household aged 12 or over. On a household basis, data are gathered on the type of structure, tenure, household size and composition, family income, and incidents of victimization against the household (such as larceny, illegal entry, vandalism.)

On an individual basis, information is gathered on basic personal demographic characteristics and on each incident of victimization against persons (aged 12 or over) in the household. The victimization data include information on the nature of the incident, the circumstances surrounding it, when it took place, the use of threats, force, or violence, damage or injury inflicted, the number and characteristics of offenders, the relationship of victim to offender, victim response, and whether the incident was reported to the police. Since 1986, additional questions have been asked about the experience of the victim with the criminal justice system. Questions are also asked about the nature of the police response.

LIMITATIONS The survey currently does not collect any victimization data on persons under 12 (age, sex, race, and origin are the only data available on children under 12). Since July 1986, respondents aged 12 and 13 have been interviewed directly rather than by proxy as was previously done. If the adults in the household refuse to allow the interview, however, an adult is interviewed as a proxy for the 12 or 13 year old.

The data can be used to assess the age and other characteristics of offenders. In this way, information about juveniles as offenders may be obtained. But these data are subject to the errors in the judgment of victims about the ages of their assailants.

AVAILABILITY Basic tabulations of results are published by the Bureau of Justice Statistics for each survey year in a report titled *Criminal Victimization in the United States*. Similar reports are available for each of the 21 most populous states. Preliminary data are released in April of each year for the previous calendar year and final data are released in the BJS *Bulletin* each October. Approximately seven to nine special and technical reports are released each year on topics such as specific crimes (e.g., rape, burglary, robbery), demographic groups (e.g., teenagers, the elderly), and other topics of interest. These reports aggregate data over a number of years and provide more detail than is presented in the annual reports. Public use tapes are available through the Inter-University Consortium for Political and Social Research of the University of Michigan (see below). Files are available for victims and non-victims and for victims only. Longitudinal files for households covering a period of three years are also available. Data are also available on microfilm from the Bureau of Justice Statistics.

For information about reports, contact:

NCJ Reference Service
P.O. Box 6000
Rockville, MD 20850
800/732-3277

To order public use tapes, contact:

> Inter-University Consortium
> for Political and Social Research
> P.O. Box 1248
> Ann Arbor, MI 48106-1248
> 313/763-5010

PUBLICATIONS

U.S. Department of Justice. (1991, June). *Criminal victimization in the United States, 1989*. (National Crime Survey Report, NCJ-129391). Washington, DC: Author.

U.S. Department of Justice. (1986, August). *Preventing domestic violence against women*. (Bureau of Justice Statistics Special Report, NCJ-102037). Washington, DC: Author.

U.S. Department of Justice. (1984, April). *Family violence*. (Bureau of Justice Statistics Special Report, NCJ-93449). Washington, DC: Author.

National Crime Victimization Survey
Year of Questionnaire: 1990
FAMILY-LEVEL CHARACTERISTICS
Sample size: 47,600 households

Family Composition
○ Full roster of household members (first name, age, sex, and relationship to reference person of each member)
○ Partial roster of household members
● Number of adults in household
● Number of children in household
● Approximate relationship of family members to householder, child, or one another
○ Exact relationship of family members to householder, child, or one another
○ Information about part-time household member
○ Information about family members no longer living in household
○ Information about relatives who live nearby but not in household

Socioeconomic
● Total family income
○ Number of persons who depend on family income
○ Sources of income
○ Income amounts identified separately by source
○ Poverty status
○ Welfare status
○ Food Stamps receipt
○ Child support receipt
● Medicaid coverage[1]
● Private health insurance[1]
● Home ownership/renters
○ Assets (other than home ownership)
○ Public housing status
● Telephone in household
○ Language other than English spoken in home

Geographic/Community Variables
● Region of country
○ State of residence
○ County/city/MSA of residence
● Size/type of community
○ Zip code
○ Telephone area code
● Metropolitan residence
○ Neighborhood quality
○ Local labor market

Stage in Family Life Cycle
○ Age of adult respondent or spouse/partner
○ Marital status of adult respondent or spouse/partner
○ Employment status of adult respondent or spouse/partner
○ Presence of own children in household
○ Age of youngest own child in household
○ Age of oldest own child in household
○ Existence of own children who have left home
○ Intention to have (more) children in future

Family Functioning
○ Family activities or time use
○ Community involvement (civic, religious, recreational)
○ Family communication patterns
○ Family decision-making
○ Marital conflict
○ Marital happiness/satisfaction
○ Parent-child conflict
○ History of marital separations
● History of family violence
○ History of marital counselling

CHARACTERISTICS OF ADULT FAMILY MEMBERS
Sample size: 85,300

Adult Respondent or Reference Person	Current Spouse in HH	Current or Former Spouse Not in HH	
●	●	○	Age
●	●	○	Gender
●	●	○	Race
●	●	○	Hispanic origin
○	○	○	Other origin/ethnicity
○	○	○	Religious affiliation
○	○	○	Religious participation
○	○	○	Country of birth
○	○	○	Immigrant status
○	○	○	English fluency
●	●	○	Current marital status
○	○	○	Marital history
○	○	○	Cohabitation status
○	○	○	Cohabitation history
○	○	○	Parental status
○	○	○	Number children ever born/sired
○	○	○	Age at first birth
○	○	○	Age of youngest child
○	○	○	Children living elsewhere
●	●	○	Duration at current address
●	●	○	Residential mobility
●	●	○	Educational attainment
○	○	○	Degrees attained
○	○	○	GED or regular HS diploma
○	○	○	Current enrollment
●	●	○	Current employment status
○	○	○	Hours usually worked (ft/pt)
○	○	○	Weeks worked
○	○	○	Annual employment pattern
○	○	○	Main occupation
○	○	○	Earnings
○	○	○	Wage rate
○	○	○	Payment of child support
○	○	○	Aptitude or achievement score
○	○	○	Health/disability status
○	○	○	Self-esteem
○	○	○	Locus of control or efficacy
○	○	○	Depression or subjective well-being
○	○	○	Work-related attitudes

CHARACTERISTICS OF CHILD FAMILY MEMBERS
Sample size: 9,400 children aged 12 and over

Reference Child or Youth Respondent	Other Children (in HH)	
O	●	Age
O	O	Month and year of birth
O	●	Gender
O	●	Race
O	●	Hispanic origin
O	O	Other origin/ethnicity
O	O	Religious affiliation
O	O	Religious participation
O	O	Country of birth
O	O	Immigrant status
O	O	English fluency
O	●	Exact relationship to adult family members
O	O	Exact relationship to other children in HH
O	●	Marital status/history
O	O	Parental status/history
O	O	Current enrollment in regular school
O	O	Current enrollment in preschool/daycare
O	●	Highest grade completed
O	O	Grade now enrolled
O	●	Employment status/history
O	O	Health status
O	O	Handicapping conditions
O	O	Grade repetition
O	O	Aptitude or achievement score
O	O	Pregnancy/birth history
O	O	Psychological well-being
O	O	Delinquency

NOTES
1. Asked only of those household members requiring medical care after an attack. There is no distinction made between private health insurance and Medicaid.

High School and Beyond

PURPOSE High School and Beyond is one of a series of longitudinal studies conducted by National Center for Education Statistics at the U.S. Department of Education (see also write-ups on the National Education Longitudinal Survey of 1988 and the National Longitudinal Study of 1972). High School and Beyond is a study of the transition from secondary school to early adulthood. It includes data on high school experiences as well as events in the years following high school graduation: post-secondary education, marriage, work, and family formation.

SPONSORSHIP High School and Beyond (HS&B) was sponsored by the National Center for Education Statistics (NCES). Within the Department of Education, the Office for Bilingual Education and Minority Language Affairs and the Office of Civil Rights funded an oversample of Hispanics. The Department of Defense funded a sampling of students enrolled in Department of Defense Dependents Schools located overseas, but these students were not part of the main probability sample and are not included in data tapes distributed by NCES. The data were collected by the National Opinion Research Center (NORC).

DESIGN The study is based on a national probability sample of high school sophomores and seniors enrolled in public and private schools in the fall of 1980. Students were selected through a two-stage stratified sampling plan. In the first stage, schools were stratified by type and several strata were oversampled. These were: alternative, Hispanic, high-performance private, other non-Catholic private, and black Catholic schools. Catholic and public schools were in regular strata which were not oversampled. With the exception of oversampled strata, schools were selected with probability proportional to estimated enrollment. Within each school 36 seniors and 36 sophomores were randomly selected. (In schools with fewer than these numbers, all were selected into the sample.) The base year sample consisted of 30,030 sophomores and 28,240 seniors enrolled in 1,015 schools, reflecting an 84% completion rate for students, after a 91% school participation rate.

Weights have been developed to account for the oversampled strata and differential cooperation rates at the school and student level, as well as other minor sources of sampling error. Weights lead to approximate unbiased estimates of the population of tenth and twelfth grade students in U.S. schools in the spring of 1980.

Base year data, and data for the first followup of sophomores, were collected directly from the students in their schools using self- administered questionnaires. Students also completed cognitive tests in school. Later followups were conducted primarily through the mail, with some telephone interviewing. The principal of each school completed a questionnaire providing information about the school. Teachers filled out forms concerning their knowledge about and evaluations of students in the sample. A subsample of about 2,500 parents of students in each cohort provided information in the base year.

The subsample to be followed up consisted of approximately 14,994 1980 sophomores and 11,995 1980 seniors. It retained the multi-stage, stratified, and clustered design of the base year sample. The followup sample included 495 1980 seniors who had been selected for the base year sample but had not participated. Subsample rates were adjusted to include in the followup sufficient numbers of students with characteristics necessary for educational policy research.

HS&B was designed to build on the National Longitudinal Study of 1972 (NLS 72) in three ways. First, the HS&B 1980 senior cohort is directly comparable with the NLS 72 senior cohort, and replication of selected questionnaire and test items make it possible to relate changes in the two cohorts to federal educational policies and programs. Second, the addition of the sophomore cohort to HS&B provides further data on the secondary school experience and its impact on students. Finally, HS&B expanded the focus of NLS 72 by collecting information on a range of life cycle factors such as family formation and intellectual development.

PERIODICITY High School and Beyond is a longitudinal study for which the first wave of data was collected in the spring of

109

1980. Followups have been conducted in 1982, 1984, and 1986. The 1980 sophomore followup sample consisted of approximately 30,000 in 1982, 13,682 in 1984, and 13,429 in 1986. The 1980 senior followup sample consisted of 11,227 in 1982, 10,925 in 1984, and 10,564 in 1986. A fourth followup of 1,300 1980 sophomores was conducted in the spring of 1992, and transcripts from their post-secondary institutions are being collected in 1992-93.

CONTENT The student questionnaires focus primarily on educational topics but also contain questions on social and demographic characteristics, personality characteristics, political and social attitudes, family environment, and physical disabilities. Educational topics include coursework; performance (including test scores); plans and aspirations for college; the influence of peers, parents, and teachers on educational goals; school-related activities; and attitudes toward school. Some retrospective information was gathered about students' grade school experiences. About three-fourths of the items in the sophomore and senior questionnaires were identical in the base year, and the third followup questionnaires were identical.

Data collected at the first followup from 1980 sophomores utilized four separate student questionnaires: for in-school students, students not currently in school (dropouts), transfer students, and early graduates. Cognitive tests were also conducted. At every other time, all students completed the same questionnaire.

School questionnaires, completed by an official of each participating school, provided information about enrollment, staff, programs, facilities and services, dropout rates, and special programs. The teacher comment checklists provided teacher observations on participating students. The parent questionnaire elicited information about how family attitudes and financial planning affected post-secondary educational goals.

A number of different files from HS&B are available for secondary analysis. These are described below.

Base Year Files:

Language File. The Language File contains information on each student who reported some non-English language experience either during childhood or at the time of the survey.

Parent File. The Parent File contains responses from the parents of 3,367 sophomores and 3,197 seniors who are on the Student File. Data on this file include parents' educational attainment, employment patterns, family income, assets and expenses, and parents' aspirations and plans for their children's post-secondary education and family formation.

Twin and Sibling File. Special efforts were made in the base year to identify sampled students who were twins or triplets so their twins or co-triplets could be invited to participate in the study. The Twin and Sibling File contains responses from sampled twins and triplets; augmented data on twins and triplets of sample members; and data from siblings in the sample. This file includes all of the variables that are on the student file, plus two additional variables (family identification and type of twin or sibling).

Teachers' Comments File. This file included data from 14,103 teachers of 18,291 sophomores from 616 schools, and 13,683 teachers of 17,056 seniors from 611 schools. All teachers who had taught a sample student in the 1979-1980 academic year had the opportunity to answer questions about the student. Questions involve students' traits and behaviors, popularity, probability of going to college, discussions with teacher about school work or plans, and physical or emotional handicaps that affect school work. The typical student in the sample was rated by an average of four different teachers.

Friends' File. The Friends' File contains identification numbers of students in the sample who were named as friends of other sampled students. Each student's record contains up to three friends. Linkages among friends can be used to investigate the sociometry of friendship structures, including reciprocity of choices among students in the sample, and for tracing friendship networks.

Merged Base Year and Followup Files:

Sophomore File. The Sophomore File includes base year data and data from the first, second, and third followups, as well as some composite variables constructed by NCES. This file includes information on high school and post-secondary educational experiences, job training and employment history, educational and occupational aspirations, personal attitudes and beliefs, financial status, demographics, military service, unemployment, income, voting and television habits, computer literacy, interest in graduate education, and alcohol consumption. It includes data on marital history and children. Data on employment and education are arranged in event history format. The file includes scores on base year cognitive tests (vocabulary, reading, mathematics, science, writing, and civic education).

Senior File. The Senior File includes base year data and data from the first, second, and third followups, as well as some composite variables constructed by NCES. Data contained in the senior file are overall very similar to the sophomore data. However, due to the two-year difference between the two cohorts, the sophomore data provides more extensive information on secondary school experience, and the senior file provides more information on employment experience. The file includes scores on senior base year cognitive tests (vocabulary, reading, mathematics, picture number, mosaic comparisons, and visualization).

Other HS&B Files:

School File. The School File contains base year school questionnaire data provided by administrators in 988 public, Catholic, and other private schools. The questionnaire focused on a number of school characteristics, including: type and organization, enrollment, proportion of students and faculty belonging to policy-relevant groups, instructional programs, course offerings, specialized programs, participation in Federal programs, faculty characteristics, per pupil expenditures, funding sources, discipline problems, teacher organizations (e.g., unions), and grading systems. A followup questionnaire in 1982 gathered data from those schools whose 1980 sophomores were still enrolled.

Offerings and Enrollments File. This file contains data from 957 schools on course offerings, duration and timing of courses, credits given, and number of students enrolled in 1981-1982 academic year.

Administrator and Teacher Survey. This school-based survey resurveyed 457 original schools in 1984 to assess school goals, guidance service use, work loads, staff attitudes, and other school-based issues. The ATS was designed to explore findings from research on effective schools (those in which students perform at higher levels than their backgrounds would predict). Responses from 10,370 teachers and 402 principals and heads of guidance and vocational education programs are included.

Local Labor Market Indicators. Data on wage rates, employment, and personal income in 1980, 1981, and 1982 are provided for the unidentified county or SMSA and state of the 1,015 schools, with linking school identification code.

High School Transcript File. Complete high school transcripts (9th-12th grade) were collected in 1982 for a subsample (12,116 usable transcripts) of the sophomore cohort. In addition to grades and courses taken, this file contains data on absences, suspensions, and, for students who left school, when and why they left. Scores on standardized tests taken by the subsampled students are also included.

Post-Secondary Education Transcript File: Contains data on dates of attendance, fields of study, degrees received, and title, grades, and credits of every course attempted, for all members of the 1980 senior cohort who reported attending post-secondary school in the first or second followup.

Senior Financial Aid File: Contains financial aid records from post-secondary institutions that respondents reported attending, and federal records of the Guaranteed Student Loan and Pell Grant programs.

HS&B HEGIS and PSVD File: Contains post-secondary school codes for schools respondents reported attending in first and second followups. This file permits linkage of HS&B questionnaire data to data on post-secondary institution characteristics.

LIMITATIONS Only limited family demographic data are available for students' family of origin, and parent questionnaires are available for only about 10% of the HS&B sample. Furthermore, family background data provided by students (such as family income, and parent education and occupation) have been found to be subject to some error when compared with the same information provided by the parents themselves. In addition, in 1980 many of the demographic variables were located near the end of the student questionnaires. Slow students who were unable to complete the questionnaires in the allotted time were thus unable to provide this basic descriptive information. The senior sample, based as it was on in-school students, did not cover students who had already dropped out or graduated in 1980. Therefore, it is somewhat less generalizable to the overall population of youth aged 17-18. This is much less of a problem for the sophomore cohort.

Despite these limitations, the fact that most sample members lived with their family of origin in the base year but were often married and/or had children in later years allows for interesting analyses of family transitions among young adults. The efforts to complement and build on NLS 72 are a distinct advantage of the HS&B data, as is the construction by NCES of several different data files.

AVAILABILITY The documentation and data tapes for the 1980, 1982, 1984, and 1986 waves of the survey are available directly from NCES. Compact disks are available from the Government Printing Office. NCES has produced a number of contractor reports and topical tabulations, some of which are listed below, as well as a detailed bibliography of studies using HS&B data. Contact:

> Dennis Carroll
> National Center for Education Statistics
> U.S. Department of Education
> 555 New Jersey Ave., N.W., Room 310-F
> Washington, DC 20208-5652
> 202/219-1774
>
> Oliver Moles
> (for Administrator and Teacher Survey)
> Office of Educational Research
> and Improvement
> U.S. Department of Education
> 555 New Jersey Ave., N.W.
> Washington, DC 20208-5649
> 202/219-1207

Data files are also available through:

Inter-University Consortium
for Political and Social Research
P.O. Box 1248
Ann Arbor, MI 48106-1248
313/763-5010

PUBLICATIONS

Baldwin, B. (1984). *A causal model of the effects of maternal employment on adolescent achievement*. New Orleans: American Educational Research Association.

Brown, G.H. (1985). *The relationship of parental involvement to high school grades*. NCES Bulletin, Washington, DC: NCES.

Hanson, S.L., Morrison, D.R., & Ginsburg, A. (1989). The antecedents of teenage fatherhood. *Demography, 26*(4), 579-596.

Milne, A.M., Myers, D.E., Rosenthal, A.S., & Ginsburg, A. (1986). Single parents, working mothers, and the educational achievements of school children. *Sociology of Education, 59*, 125-139.

Peterson, J.L., & Zill, N. (1984). *American Jewish high school students: A national profile*. New York: The American Jewish Council.

High School and Beyond
Years of Questionnaire: 1980, 1982, 1984, 1986, 1992
Sample size: 58,270
FAMILY-LEVEL CHARACTERISTICS
Sample size: 58,270

Family Composition
O Full roster of household members (first name, age, sex, and relationship to reference person of each member)
● Partial roster of household members
● Number of adults in household
● Number of children in household
● Approximate relationship of family members to householder, child, or one another
O Exact relationship of family members to householder, child, or one another
O Information about part-time household member
● Information about family members no longer living in household
O Information about relatives who live nearby but not in household

Socioeconomic
● Total family income
● Number of persons who depend on family income
● Sources of income
● Income amounts identified separately by source
O Poverty status
● Welfare status
O Food Stamps receipt
● Child support receipt
O Medicaid coverage
O Private health insurance
● Home ownership/renters
● Assets (other than home ownership)
O Public housing status
O Telephone in household
● Language other than English spoken in home

Geographic/Community Variables[1]
● Region of country
O State of residence
O County/city/MSA of residence
● Size/type of community
O Zip code
O Telephone area code
● Metropolitan residence
O Neighborhood quality
● Local labor market

Stage in Family Life Cycle
● Age of adult respondent or spouse/partner
● Marital status of adult respondent or spouse/partner
● Employment status of adult respondent or spouse/partner
● Presence of own children in household
O Age of youngest own child in household
O Age of oldest own child in household
O Existence of own children who have left home
O Intention to have (more) children in future

116

Family Functioning
○ Family activities or time use
○ Community involvement (civic, religious, recreational)
○ Family communication patterns
● Family decision-making
○ Marital conflict
○ Marital happiness/satisfaction
○ Parent-child conflict
○ History of marital separations
○ History of family violence
○ History of marital counselling

CHARACTERISTICS OF ADULT FAMILY MEMBERS
Sample size: 6,564 parents[2]

Adult Respondent or Reference Person	Current Spouse in HH	Current or Former Spouse Not in HH	
●	●	○	Age
●	○	○	Gender
●	○	○	Race
●	○	○	Hispanic origin
●	○	○	Other origin/ethnicity
○	○	○	Religious affiliation
○	○	○	Religious participation
○	○	○	Country of birth
○	○	○	Immigrant status
○	○	○	English fluency
●	●	○	Current marital status
○	○	○	Marital history
○	○	○	Cohabitation status
○	○	○	Cohabitation history
●	○	○	Parental status
●	○	○	Number children ever born/sired
○	○	○	Age at first birth
○	○	○	Age of youngest child
○	○	○	Children living elsewhere
○	○	○	Duration at current address
○	○	○	Residential mobility
●	●	○	Educational attainment
●	●	○	Degrees attained
○	○	○	GED or regular HS diploma
●	●	○	Current enrollment
●	●	○	Current employment status
●	●	○	Hours usually worked (ft/pt)
○	○	○	Weeks worked
●	●	○	Annual employment pattern
●	●	○	Main occupation
●	●	○	Earnings
○	○	○	Wage rate
○	○	○	Payment of child support
○	○	○	Aptitude or achievement score
○	○	○	Health/disability status
○	○	○	Self-esteem
○	○	○	Locus of control or efficacy
○	○	○	Depression or subjective well-being
●	○	○	Work-related attitudes

CHARACTERISTICS OF CHILD FAMILY MEMBERS
Sample size: 58,270 high school students

Reference Child or Youth Respondent	Other Children (in HH)	
●	O	Age
●	O	Month and year of birth
●	O	Gender
●	O	Race
●	O	Hispanic origin
●	O	Other origin/ethnicity
●	O	Religious affiliation
●	O	Religious participation
●	O	Country of birth
O	O	Immigrant status
●	O	English fluency
O	O	Exact relationship to adult family members
O	O	Exact relationship to other children in HH
●	O	Marital status/history
●	O	Parental status/history
●	O	Current enrollment in regular school
O	O	Current enrollment in preschool/daycare
●	O	Highest grade completed
●	O	Grade now enrolled
●	O	Employment status/history
●	O	Health status
●	O	Handicapping conditions
O	O	Grade repetition
●	O	Aptitude or achievement score
O	O	Pregnancy/birth history
●	O	Psychological well-being
●	O	Delinquency

NOTES
1. Community variables reflect community in which high school, not necessarily family, was located.
2. Sample size for adult family members reflects the number of parents who completed parent questionnaires. However, some data on parents were provided by students.

National Educational Longitudinal Survey of 1988

PURPOSE The National Educational Longitudinal Survey of 1988 (NELS:88) is the most recent in a series of longitudinal studies conducted by the National Center for Education Statistics at the U.S. Department of Education (see also write-ups on the National Longitudinal Study of 1972 and High School and Beyond). The NELS:88 is designed to assess trends in secondary school education, focusing on the transition into and progress through high school, and the transition into post-secondary school and the world of work. Data from this study can be used to examine educational issues such as tracking, cognitive growth, and dropping out of school.

SPONSORSHIP The survey is sponsored by the National Center for Education Statistics (NCES). The National Science Foundation co-funded a teacher study and funded the math and science items on the student, parent and school questionnaires. The National Endowment for the Humanities sponsored questions about the humanities and history in the student, parent, teacher and school questionnaires. Within the Department of Education, the Office of Planning, Budget, and Evaluation sponsored questions about gifted and talented programs, and the Office of Bilingual Education and Minority Language Affairs funded an oversampling of Asian and Hispanic students. Gallaudet University sponsored the collection of audiological data about hearing impairments for sampled students enrolled in Individual Education Programs. Data collection was conducted by the National Opinion Research Center (NORC).

DESIGN The NELS:88 is a longitudinal study of a national probability sample of eighth graders. The base year student population excluded students with severe mental handicaps, students whose command of the English language was insufficient to understand survey materials, and students with physical or emotional problems that would limit their participation. A subsample

119

of these excluded students were added back into the study during the first followup.

The survey used a two-stage stratified, clustered sample design. The first stage, selection of schools, was accomplished by a complex design involving two sister pools of schools. (Further details on school selection are available in NCES reports.) The second stage included selection of about 24 students per school. At the second stage, 93% of 26,435 selected students agreed to participate. Weights for school administrators and students were adjusted to compensate for non-response.

Data were collected via questionnaires from 24,599 students from 1,057 public, private and church-affiliated schools from all 50 states and the District of Columbia in the base year. Most questionnaires were administered in the schools and returned by mail to NORC. Eighth graders participated in group sessions at their schools where they completed student questionnaires and cognitive tests. School administrator data were collected from the senior school administrator (usually the principal or head-master). For base year teacher data, each school was randomly assigned two of four subject areas of interest (English, math, science, social studies) and teachers were chosen who could provide data for each student respondent in these two subjects. Parent data were obtained through the mail from the (parent-identified) "parent or guardian who is most familiar with the student's school situation and educational plans."

For the first (1990) followup, all students were surveyed in schools containing ten or more eligible NELS:88 respondents. Only a sub-sample of students were surveyed in schools with fewer than ten students. Because 90% of students changed schools between eighth and tenth grade, it was necessary to sub-sample schools in this way. Weights have been developed to adjust for this differential sampling probability. The 1990 sample size was approximately 20,000 students, and the 1992 sample size is anticipated to be about the same.

The sample was freshened in 1990 and 1992 to give 1990 tenth graders and 1992 twelfth graders who were not in the eighth grade in 1988 some chance of selection into the NELS:88 followup. Such students included primarily those who had skipped or repeated a grade between 1988 and the followup year, and those who had moved to the U.S. after 1988. This freshening was conducted so that the first and second followup samples were representative of U.S. tenth graders in 1990 and U.S. twelfth graders in 1992, respectively.

PERIODICITY Base year data were collected in 1988 and included questionnaires from students, school administrators, and parents; teacher ratings of students; and students' achievement test scores.

The first followup of the NELS:88 sample was conducted in 1990. At this time, data included a student questionnaire (including a brief new student questionnaire for new students who were brought into the sample to preserve representativeness), an out-of-school questionnaire (of base-year respondents who had since left school), student achievement test scores, a teacher questionnaire, and a school administrator questionnaire.

A second followup was conducted in 1992. Data include student (original, new, and former) questionnaires, student achievement test scores, school administrator and teacher questionnaires, and a parent questionnaire focusing on the financing of post-secondary education. In the second followup, only math and science teachers for each student were surveyed. Academic transcripts were collected for each student. Additional followups will occur every two years.

CONTENT

School administrator questionnaire: school, student and teaching staff characteristics, school policies and practices (e.g. admissions, discipline, grading and testing structure), school governance and climate, and school problems.

Teacher questionnaire: impressions of the student, student's school behavior and academic performance, curriculum and classroom instructional practices, school climate and policies, and teacher background and activities. The teacher questionnaire for the second followup was only given to math and science teachers, who were asked to rate students' performance and to describe the content of their course, the school climate, and their own professional qualifications and preparation.

Student questionnaire: family background and characteristics (including household composition, ethnicity, parental education, economic status), relationship with parents, unsupervised time at home, language use, opinions about self, attitudes, values, educational and career plans, jobs and chores, school life (including problems in school, discipline, peer relations, school climate), school work (homework, course enrollment, attitudes toward school, grade repetition, absenteeism), and extracurricular activities. First followup included similar content, as well as information about significant life events, family decision making, and substance abuse. The second followup contained similar material, as well as plans for the future, money and work, and an early graduate supplement which contained items about reasons for graduating early and current employment and enrollment.

Parent questionnaire: marital status, household composition, employment, ethnicity, religion, child's school experiences and attendance, child's family life (activities, rules and regulations) and friends, opinion about and contact with child's school, child's disabilities, educational expectations for child, financial information, and educational expenditures. The second followup questionnaire included additional brief questions about neighborhood quality and some supplemental questions for parents new to NELS:88.

Student achievement tests: reading, math, science, and history/citizenship tests were administered in all waves.

New Student Supplement: provides brief information about language, ethnicity, objects in the home, parents' employment, and grade repetition.

Not Currently in School Questionnaire: reasons for leaving school, school attitudes and experiences, current activities (employment and education), family background, future plans, self-opinion and attitudes, substance abuse, money and work, family composition and events, and language use.

Because questionnaires were not identical at each wave, all the information described above and indicated in the checklist are not available for every wave.

LIMITATIONS The base year survey is limited to a specific cohort of children, those in the eighth grade in the spring of 1988. The sample excludes several potentially interesting subgroups of students: those with severe mental handicaps, insufficient command of the English language, limiting physical or emotional conditions, and students who had dropped out of school or were chronically absent as of the eighth grade. Base year ineligible students were subsampled in the first followup data collection.

All sources of data are not available for every student, although the completion rate for each of the four questionnaires in the base year was over 90%. Parents were not surveyed at the first followup, so detailed data on family circumstances are not available for that time period. Overall, however, the NELS:88 family related data are quite comprehensive and are well suited for analyses relating students' family background to their educational experiences.

AVAILABILITY Data tapes for the base year and first followup (combined) are available from NCES; separate tapes are available for student, parent, teacher and school administrator data. Copies of the data collection instruments; a description of the data collection, preparation, and processing procedures; and a guide to the data files and code-book, are contained in four Data File Users' Manuals (student, parent, teacher, and school administrator). Data from the second followup will become available in 1993, and in 1994 all three waves will be merged on a CD-ROM, making longitudinal analyses easier. Contact:

> Jeffrey Owings
> National Center for Education Statistics
> U.S. Department of Education
> 555 New Jersey Avenue NW
> Room 310C
> Washington, D.C.
> 202/219-1737 or Peggy Quinn, 202/219-1743

PUBLICATIONS NCES has produced a number of special publications, technical reports, and statistical analysis reports using the NELS:88 data, some of which are listed below:

Hafner, A., Ingels, S., Schneider, B., Stevenson, D. 1990. *A profile of the American Eighth Grader: NELS:88 Student Descriptive Data.* National Center for Education Statistics.

Office of Educational Research and Improvement. (1990). Parental involvement in education. *Issues in Education* (August). Washington, DC: U.S. Department of Education.

Rasinski, K. and West, J. (1990). *Eighth Graders' Reports of Courses Taken During the 1988 Academic Year by Selected Student Characteristics*. National Center for Education Statistics.

Rock D., Pollock J., & Hafner, A. (1991). *The tested achievement of the NELS:88 eighth grade class*. National Center for Education Statistics.

Spencer, D., Frankel, M., Ingels, S., Rasinski, K. and Tourangeau, R. (1990). *NELS:88 Base Year Sample Design Report*. National Center for Education Statistics.

National Educational Longitudinal Study of 1988
Years of Questionnaire: 1988, 1990, 1992
Sample size: base year: 24,599; and 1992: approx. 20,000
FAMILY-LEVEL CHARACTERISTICS
Sample size: 24,599

Family Composition
○ Full roster of household members (first name, age, sex, and relationship to reference person of each member)
● Partial roster of household members
● Number of adults in household
● Number of children in household
● Approximate relationship of family members to householder, child, or one another
○ Exact relationship of family members to householder, child, or one another
○ Information about part-time household member
○ Information about family members no longer living in household
○ Information about relatives who live nearby but not in household

Socioeconomic
● Total family income
● Number of persons who depend on family income
○ Sources of income
○ Income amounts identified separately by source
○ Poverty status
○ Welfare status
○ Food Stamps receipt
○ Child support receipt
○ Medicaid coverage
○ Private health insurance
○ Home ownership/renters
● Assets (other than home ownership)[1]
○ Public housing status
○ Telephone in household
● Language other than English spoken in home

Geographic/Community Variables[2]
● Region of country
○ State of residence
○ County/city/MSA of residence
● Size/type of community
○ Zip code
○ Telephone area code
● Metropolitan residence
● Neighborhood quality
○ Local labor market

Stage in Family Life Cycle
● Age of adult respondent or spouse/partner
● Marital status of adult respondent or spouse/partner
● Employment status of adult respondent or spouse/partner
● Presence of own children in household
○ Age of youngest own child in household
○ Age of oldest own child in household
○ Existence of own children who have left home
○ Intention to have (more) children in future

Family Functioning
- ● Family activities or time use
- ● Community involvement (civic, religious, recreational)[2]
- ○ Family communication patterns
- ● Family decision-making
- ○ Marital conflict
- ○ Marital happiness/satisfaction
- ○ Parent-child conflict
- ○ History of marital separations
- ○ History of family violence
- ○ History of marital counselling

CHARACTERISTICS OF ADULT FAMILY MEMBERS
Sample size: 22,651

Adult Respondent or Reference Person	Current Spouse in HH	Current or Former Spouse Not in HH	
●	●	○	Age
●	●	○	Gender
●	○	○	Race
●	○	○	Hispanic origin
●	○	○	Other origin/ethnicity
●	○	○	Religious affiliation
○	○	○	Religious participation
●	○	○	Country of birth
○	○	○	Immigrant status
●	○	○	English fluency
●	○	○	Current marital status
○	○	○	Marital history
○	○	○	Cohabitation status
○	○	○	Cohabitation history
●	○	○	Parental status
○	○	○	Number children ever born/sired
○	○	○	Age at first birth
○	○	○	Age of youngest child
○	○	○	Children living elsewhere
●	○	○	Duration at current address
○	○	○	Residential mobility
●	●	○	Educational attainment
●	●	○	Degrees attained
●	●	○	GED or regular HS diploma
●	●	○	Current enrollment
●	●	○	Current employment status
●	●	○	Hours usually worked (ft/pt)
○	○	○	Weeks worked
○	○	○	Annual employment pattern
●	●	○	Main occupation
○	○	○	Earnings
○	○	○	Wage rate
○	○	○	Payment of child support
○	○	○	Aptitude or achievement score
○	○	○	Health/disability status
○	○	○	Self-esteem
○	○	○	Locus of control or efficacy
○	○	○	Depression or subjective well-being
○	○	○	Work-related attitudes

CHARACTERISTICS OF CHILD FAMILY MEMBERS
Sample size: 24,599

Reference Child or Youth Respondent	Other Children (in HH)	
●	○	Age
●	○	Month and year of birth
●	○	Gender
●	○	Race
●	○	Hispanic origin
●	○	Other origin/ethnicity
●	○	Religious affiliation
●	○	Religious participation
●	○	Country of birth
○	○	Immigrant status
●	○	English fluency
●	○	Exact relationship to adult family members
●	○	Exact relationship to other children in HH
●	○	Marital status/history
●	○	Parental status/history
●	●	Current enrollment in regular school
○	○	Current enrollment in preschool/daycare
●	○	Highest grade completed
●	○	Grade now enrolled
●	○	Employment status/history
○	○	Health status
●	○	Handicapping conditions
●	○	Grade repetition
●	○	Aptitude or achievement score
○	○	Pregnancy/birth history
●	○	Psychological well-being
●	○	Delinquency

NOTES
1. Assets to be used for educational expenditures only.
2. Community variables refer to community in which school, not necessarily household, is located.

National Longitudinal Study of the High School Class of 1972

PURPOSE The National Longitudinal Study of the High School Class of 1972 (NLS 72) was designed to provide information on a national sample of students as they move out of the American high school system into early adulthood. The study was designed to inform planning, implementation, and evaluation of Federal policies and programs designed to enhance educational opportunity and achievement and to improve occupational attainments and career outcomes.

SPONSORSHIP NLS 72 is the first in a series of longitudinal studies sponsored by the National Center for Education Statistics (NCES), Office of the Assistant Secretary for Educational Research and Improvement, U.S. Department of Education. In 1970 NCES convened a panel of educational researchers and administrators, as well as representatives of other Department of Education agencies, to provide guidance in planning and implementing the survey. A variety of government agencies and private foundations provided funding for different waves and sections of NLS 72. In addition, the National Science Foundation provided funding for a separate Teaching Supplement conducted in 1986.

Base year data were collected by the Educational Testing Service (ETS). Research Triangle Institute carried out the first through fourth followup surveys, and NORC conducted the fifth in conjunction with the third followup of High School and Beyond (see separate write-up).

DESIGN NLS 72 used a deeply stratified two-stage national probability sample of students from all schools, public and private, in the 50 states and Washington, D.C. which contained twelfth graders during the 1971-1972 school year. The sample excluded students from schools for the physically or mentally handicapped, those for legally confined students, and those in special situations (e.g. area vocational schools) where students were also enrolled in other high schools in the sampling frame. Early graduates and students attending adult education classes were excluded from the sampling.

In the first stage of sample selection, two schools were sampled without replacement from 600 strata. Strata were based upon type of control, geographic region, size of grade twelve enrollment, proximity to institutions of higher learning, percent minority enrollment, income level of community, and degree of urbanization. Schools in low-income areas and schools with a high proportion of minority students were oversampled at twice the rate of other schools in order to obtain more disadvantaged students in the sample. The primary sample consisted of 1,200 high schools. The second stage consisted of drawing a simple random sample of 18 students per school (or all if fewer than 18 were available). The oversampling of schools led to an oversampling of low-income and minority students.

Some base year data were collected for a total of 19,001 students from 1,061 schools; of these, 16,683 completed the student questionnaire (a 71% response rate for the student survey). Students were given the option of completing the student questionnaire either during group administration in school, or at home with parental assistance.

Follow-up data collection was conducted by mail, telephone, and personal interview. At the first followup, 4,450 1972 high school seniors from 257 schools were added to the sample to compensate for base-year non-participation. These respondents provided retrospective data on some base-year variables. All sample members (including those added in the first followup) were eligible to participate in the first through fourth followup student questionnaires. Response rates in these followups ranged from 92% to 79%.

Only sample members who had participated in at least one of these waves were eligible for the fifth followup sample. Those belonging to groups of special policy interest (Hispanics, teachers and potential teachers, college graduates, and never-married or no longer married persons) were retained with certainty, while all other sample members were subsampled. The response rate for the fifth followup was 89%.

A subsample of 1,016 respondents were selected in 1979 for retesting with a portion of the original test battery. In 1986, sample persons who had teaching experience or training were sent a Teaching Supplement.

Thus far, the longitudinal studies program of the National Center for Education Statistics consists of three studies, all of which are described in this guide: NLS 72, High School and Beyond, and the National Education Longitudinal Study of 1988. The three studies have been designed so that data can be compared in a number of ways. First, the three cohorts can be compared in a time-lag basis (e.g. to compare changes over time in the high school experience of 1972, 1980 and 1992 seniors). Second, the data for each cohort can be viewed as a cross-sectional study (e.g. one can compare employment rates for two cohorts in 1986). Finally, within-cohort, longitudinal analyses can be undertaken. The time of data collection, and content of the questionnaires, have been closely coordinated across studies.

PERIODICITY Base year data were collected in spring 1972. Followups occurred in the spring of 1973; the fall and winter of 1974, 1976, 1979; and the spring and summer of 1986. Sample sizes in the first through fourth followups varied from 21,350 in 1973 to 18,630 in 1979. The sample size for the fifth followup was 12,841. A Postsecondary Education Transcript Study was conducted in 1984, and a Teaching Supplement was conducted in 1986.

CONTENT Base year data consist of a test battery, a school record information form, and a student questionnaire. Subsequent followups consisted of student questionnaires only, with the addition of the Postsecondary Transcript data and the Teaching Supplement.

Student Questionnaire: The base year questionnaires included items on education and work experiences and plans, students' family background, aspirations, attitudes, and opinions. Followup questionnaires asked about students' work, educational, and military experiences since leaving high school; earnings; family status; job supervision; sex-role orientation and sex and race biases; a subjective rating of high school experiences; future educational and career plans (including graduate school entry);

opinions and attitudes; and aspirations and expectations. While earlier questionnaires asked questions about respondents' family of origin, later questionnaires focused on respondents' own family (i.e. spouse and children). Many questions were identical in every student questionnaire.

The fifth followup questionnaire contained many of the same items in the fourth followup and the High School and Beyond third followup. An event history format was used to obtain information about jobs held, schools attended, periods of unemployment, and marriage and divorce patterns. Questions on sample persons' family formation and dissolution were far more detailed in the fifth followup than in earlier surveys. Additional questions were added about applying to and enrolling in graduate school (particularly graduate management programs), and about incentives and disincentives to entering the teaching profession and perceptions of teacher quality and shortages.

Test Battery: The base year test battery consisted of six tests: vocabulary, picture number (memory), reading, letter groups (nonverbal reasoning), mathematics, and mosaic comparisons (perceptual speed and accuracy). A subgroup of 2,648 sample members were retested during the fourth followup on a subset of the base year test battery (vocabulary and mathematics items).

School Record Information Form: Sampled schools provided base-year data on students' high school curricula, grade point average, credit hours in major courses, and (if applicable) students' positions in ability groupings, remedial instruction record, involvement in federally supported programs, and standardized test scores.

Activity State Questionnaire: Used in the second follow-up to collect retrospective data about key activities from 3,088 (of 3,904 targeted) respondents who had not provided this information previously. This data collection was undertaken because it appeared that low SES and low aptitude respondents were particularly likely to have unclassifiable activity status, thereby introducing potential bias.

Supplemental Questionnaire: In the fourth followup 5,548 respondents completed this questionnaire in order to collect key work and educational history data that had been requested but not obtained in earlier follow ups. The supplemental questionnaire consisted of 11 brief sections. Respondents were administered from two to four of the possible questions, specifically tailored to that person's missing data.

Postsecondary Education Transcripts: Transcripts were collected from academic and vocational postsecondary education institutions that respondents had reported attending. Schools provided information on sample members' course-taking patterns, and grades, credits, and credentials earned.

Teaching Supplement: This questionnaire was mailed in 1986 to all persons who had teaching experience or had been trained for teaching. Information was gathered about teachers' qualifications, teaching experience, educational background, satisfaction with career, and plans for remaining in the teaching profession. Those who had left teaching provided information about the jobs and activities they had pursued afterwards .

LIMITATIONS Because the initial sample was drawn from current students, students who had already dropped out of school or graduated by spring 1972 are not represented. Also, schools for mentally or physically handicapped students, schools for legally confined students, and supplementary schools (e.g. vocational) were excluded from the sample, so students in such schools are not represented.

Students provided all information about their families. Therefore, data on students' family of origin and household composition are quite limited, and some information, particularly about income, may not be accurate. Information on adult respondents' own family procreation is more detailed, particularly due to NICHD-funded items in the fifth followup, and allows for examination of how education and employment patterns relate to family formation and dissolution.

AVAILABILITY Magnetic computer tapes are available that contain merged data from the base year and first through fourth followups. Data from the fifth followup are available on a separate data file, but can be easily merged with earlier data.

The Teaching Supplement and the Postsecondary Education Transcript file are each available on separate data files from NCES.

Contact:

> Dr. Dennis Carroll
> National Center for Education Statistics
> 555 New Jersey Ave. NW, Room 310-F
> Washington, DC 20208-5652
> 202/219-1774

PUBLICATIONS

Eagle, E., Fitzgerald, R., Gifford, A., and Tuma, J. (1988). *A Descriptive Summary of 1972 High School Seniors: Fourteen Years Later* (Report No. CS 88-406). Washington, D.C.: Center for Education Statistics, U.S. Department of Education.

Riccobono, J., Henderson, L.B., Burkheimer, G.J., Place, G., and Levinsohn, J.R. (1981). *National Longitudinal Study: Base Year (1972) through Fourth Follow-up (1979) Data File Users' Manual*, Vols. 1, 2, and 3 (Contract No. OEC-0-73-6666). Washington, D.C.: Center for Education Statistics, U.S. Department of Education.

Tourangeau, R., Sebring, P., Campbell, B., Glusberg, M., Spencer, B., and Singleton, M. (1987). *The National Longitudinal Study of the High School Class of 1972 (NLS-72) Fifth Follow-up (1986) Data File User's Manual* (Contract No. 300-84-0169). Washington, D.C.: Center for Education Statistics, U.S. Department of Education.

133

National Longitudinal Study of the High School Class of 1972 (respondent as child)

Years of Questionnaire: 1972, 73, 74, 76, 79, 86 Sample size: Base year: 19,001 students; 1986: 12,841

FAMILY-LEVEL CHARACTERISTICS

Family Composition

○ Full roster of household members (first name, age, sex, and relationship to reference person of each member)
● Partial roster of household members
○ Number of adults in household
○ Number of children in household
● Approximate relationship of family members to householder, child, or one another
○ Exact relationship of family members to householder, child, or one another
○ Information about part-time household member
○ Information about family members no longer living in household
○ Information about relatives who live nearby but not in household

Socioeconomic

● Total family income
● Number of persons who depend on family income
○ Sources of income
○ Income amounts identified separately by source
○ Poverty status
○ Welfare status
○ Food Stamps receipt
○ Child support receipt
○ Medicaid coverage
○ Private health insurance
○ Home ownership/renters
○ Assets (other than home ownership)
○ Public housing status
○ Telephone in household
● Language other than English spoken in home

Geographic/Community Variables

● Region of country[1]
● State of residence[1]
○ County/city/MSA of residence
● Size/type of community
○ Zip code
○ Telephone area code
○ Metropolitan residence
○ Neighborhood quality
○ Local labor market

Stage in Family Life Cycle

○ Age of adult respondent or spouse/partner
○ Marital status of adult respondent or spouse/partner
○ Employment status of adult respondent or spouse/partner
○ Presence of own children in household
○ Age of youngest own child in household
○ Age of oldest own child in household
○ Existence of own children who have left home
○ Intention to have (more) children in future

134

Family Functioning
○ Family activities or time use
○ Community involvement (civic, religious, recreational)
○ Family communication patterns
● Family decision-making[2]
○ Marital conflict
○ Marital happiness/satisfaction
○ Parent-child conflict
○ History of marital separations
○ History of family violence
○ History of marital counselling

CHARACTERISTICS OF ADULT FAMILY MEMBERS

Adult Respondent or Reference Person[3]	Current Spouse in HH[4]	Current or Former Spouse Not in HH	
●	●	○	Age
●	●	○	Gender
○	○	○	Race
○	○	○	Hispanic origin
○	○	○	Other origin/ethnicity
○	○	○	Religious affiliation
○	○	○	Religious participation
○	○	○	Country of birth
○	○	○	Immigrant status
○	○	○	English fluency
○	○	○	Current marital status
○	○	○	Marital history
○	○	○	Cohabitation status
○	○	○	Cohabitation history
○	○	○	Parental status
○	○	○	Number children ever born/sired
○	○	○	Age at first birth
○	○	○	Age of youngest child
○	○	○	Children living elsewhere
○	○	○	Duration at current address
○	○	○	Residential mobility
●	●	○	Educational attainment
●	●	○	Degrees attained
○	○	○	GED or regular HS diploma
○	○	○	Current enrollment
○	○	○	Current employment status
○	○	○	Hours usually worked (ft/pt)
○	○	○	Weeks worked
●	○	○	Annual employment pattern
●	●	○	Main occupation
○	○	○	Earnings
○	○	○	Wage rate
○	○	○	Payment of child support
○	○	○	Aptitude or achievement score
○	○	○	Health/disability status
○	○	○	Self-esteem
○	○	○	Locus of control or efficacy
○	○	○	Depression or subjective well-being
○	○	○	Work-related attitudes

CHARACTERISTICS OF CHILD FAMILY MEMBERS

Reference Child or Youth Respondent	Other Children (in HH)	
●	O	Age
●	O	Month and year of birth
●	O	Gender
●	O	Race
●	O	Hispanic origin
O	O	Other origin/ethnicity
●	O	Religious affiliation
O	O	Religious participation
O	O	Country of birth
O	O	Immigrant status
O	O	English fluency
O	O	Exact relationship to adult family members
O	O	Exact relationship to other children in HH
●	O	Marital status/history
●	O	Parental status/history
●	O	Current enrollment in regular school
O	O	Current enrollment in preschool/daycare
●	O	Highest grade completed
●	O	Grade now enrolled
●	O	Employment status/history
O	O	Health status
●	O	Handicapping conditions
O	O	Grade repetition
●	O	Aptitude or achievement score
O	O	Pregnancy/birth history
●	O	Psychological well-being
O	O	Delinquency

NOTES

1. Reflects community in which high school, not necessarily family, is located.
2. Regarding educational decisions only.
3. Student's mother/female guardian; information provided by student.
4. Student's father/male guardian; information provided by student.

National Longitudinal Study of the High School Class of 1972 (respondent as adult)

Years of Questionnaire: 1972, 73, 74, 76, 79, 86 Sample size: Base year: 16,683 students; 1986: 12,841

FAMILY-LEVEL CHARACTERISTICS

Family Composition

○ Full roster of household members (first name, age, sex, and relationship to reference person of each member)
● Partial roster of household members
○ Number of adults in household
● Number of children in household
● Approximate relationship of family members to householder, child, or one another
○ Exact relationship of family members to householder, child, or one another
○ Information about part-time household member
● Information about family members no longer living in household
○ Information about relatives who live nearby but not in household

Socioeconomic

● Total family income
○ Number of persons who depend on family income
● Sources of income
● Income amounts identified separately by source
○ Poverty status
● Welfare status
○ Food Stamps receipt
● Child support receipt
○ Medicaid coverage
○ Private health insurance
○ Home ownership/renters
● Assets (other than home ownership)[1]
○ Public housing status
○ Telephone in household
○ Language other than English spoken in home

Geographic/Community Variables

● Region of country[2]
● State of residence[2]
○ County/city/MSA of residence
● Size/type of community
○ Zip code
○ Telephone area code
○ Metropolitan residence
○ Neighborhood quality
○ Local labor market

Stage in Family Life Cycle

● Age of adult respondent or spouse/partner
● Marital status of adult respondent or spouse/partner
● Employment status of adult respondent or spouse/partner
● Presence of own children in household
○ Age of youngest own child in household
○ Age of oldest own child in household
● Existence of own children who have left home
● Intention to have (more) children in future

Family Functioning

- ○ Family activities or time use
- ● Community involvement (civic, religious, recreational)
- ○ Family communication patterns
- ● Family decision-making
- ○ Marital conflict
- ● Marital happiness/satisfaction
- ○ Parent-child conflict
- ○ History of marital separations
- ○ History of family violence
- ○ History of marital counselling

CHARACTERISTICS OF ADULT FAMILY MEMBERS

Adult Respondent or Reference Person	Current Spouse in HH	Current or Former Spouse Not in HH	
●	○	○	Age
●	●	○	Gender
●	○	○	Race
●	○	○	Hispanic origin
○	○	○	Other origin/ethnicity
●	●	○	Religious affiliation
○	○	○	Religious participation
○	○	○	Country of birth
○	○	○	Immigrant status
○	○	○	English fluency
●	●	○	Current marital status
●	○	○	Marital history
○	○	○	Cohabitation status
○	○	○	Cohabitation history
●	●	●	Parental status
●	●	●	Number children ever born/sired
●	○	○	Age at first birth
●	○	○	Age of youngest child
●	○	○	Children living elsewhere
○	○	○	Duration at current address
○	○	○	Residential mobility
●	●	●	Educational attainment
●	●	●	Degrees attained
●	●	○	GED or regular HS diploma
●	●	○	Current enrollment
●	●	○	Current employment status
●	○	○	Hours usually worked (ft/pt)
●	○	○	Weeks worked
●	○	○	Annual employment pattern
●	●	○	Main occupation
●	●	○	Earnings
●	○	○	Wage rate
●	○	○	Payment of child support
●	○	○	Aptitude or achievement score
●	○	○	Health/disability status
●	○	○	Self-esteem
○	○	○	Locus of control or efficacy
●	○	○	Depression or subjective well-being
●	○	○	Work-related attitudes

138

CHARACTERISTICS OF CHILD FAMILY MEMBERS

Reference Child or Youth Respondent	Other Children (in HH)[3]	
O	●	Age
O	●	Month and year of birth
O	●	Gender
O	O	Race
O	O	Hispanic origin
O	O	Other origin/ethnicity
O	O	Religious affiliation
O	O	Religious participation
O	O	Country of birth
O	O	Immigrant status
O	O	English fluency
O	O	Exact relationship to adult family members
O	O	Exact relationship to other children in HH
O	O	Marital status/history
O	O	Parental status/history
O	O	Current enrollment in regular school
O	O	Current enrollment in preschool/daycare
O	O	Highest grade completed
O	O	Grade now enrolled
O	O	Employment status/history
O	O	Health status
O	O	Handicapping conditions
O	O	Grade repetition
O	O	Aptitude or achievement score
O	O	Pregnancy/birth history
O	O	Psychological well-being
O	O	Delinquency

NOTES
1. Assets intended for financing own children's education only.
2. Community in which high school, not necessarily family, is located. Not updated if respondent has moved.
3. Respondent's first four children.

National Family Violence Surveys

PURPOSE The main purpose of these studies is to measure the incidence of family violence nationally over a ten year period and to look at the underlying social causes of family violence. The study set out to ascertain methods of conflict resolution within the family, specifically those tactics used to resolve conflicts between spouses, between children, and between parents and children. One goal was to measure the means employed in conflict resolution via a "Conflict Tactics Scale" (Straus, 1988). This scale defines a continuum from the use of reasoning and rational discussion at one end, to violence and the use of physical force at the other.

SPONSORSHIP The first survey was conducted in 1975 at the University of New Hampshire by Murray A. Straus and Richard Gelles, under a grant from the National Institutes on Mental Health (NIMH). It was partially replicated in 1985 by Straus and Gelles. Followup interviews with the 1985 sample were conducted in 1986 and 1987 by Williams and Straus under a grant from the National Science Foundation.

DESIGN The first survey was conducted in 1975 using a national probability sample of 2,143 currently married or cohabiting persons between the ages of 18 and 70. The sample was stratified by geographic region, type of community, and other population characteristics; a random half of the respondents were male, half female. If there were children in the household between the ages of 3 and 17, a referent child was randomly selected. The interviews were conducted face to face in 1975, and there was a 65% completion rate.

The 1985 Resurvey was conducted over the telephone on a national probability sample of 4,032 U.S. households; in addition they oversampled for blacks, Hispanics, and states, for a total sample of 6,002 households. For the national probability sample, telephone numbers were selected using random digit dialing, stratifying the United States into four regions (East, South, Midwest, and West) and three community types (urban, suburban, and rural areas defined by population size). The response rate was 84%. To be included in this study, a household had to have: (1) a male and female 18 years of age or older who were presently married or presently cohabiting, or (2) one adult 18 years of age or older who was either divorced or separated within the last two years or a single parent living with a child under the age of 18. When more than one adult was eligible in the household, a respondent was randomly selected. As in 1975, the referent child (if relevant) was also randomly selected.

Longitudinal followups were done in 1986 and 1987 on a subsample of those interviewed in 1985; the followup questions only concerned couple violence, no data were collected on parent-child violence.

PERIODICITY This study was conducted in 1975, and large parts of the study were replicated in 1985. The investigators are planning another cycle of this survey, pending funding.

CONTENT Questions were asked to assess the use of reasoning, verbal aggression, and physical violence in resolution of conflicts between spouses, between children, and between parents and children, including information on the development of conflicts resulting in violence; the type and frequency of conflicts; resolution of conflicts in respondent's childhood family; family power structure and power norms; marital closeness and stability; and personality and stress factors. The Conflict Tactics Scale, developed by Murray Straus, is composed of 19 items designed to measure the means employed in resolving conflicts. Three factors are encompassed and measured by this scale: 1) reasoning-rational discussion, 2) verbal aggression-insults or threats, and 3) a violence sub-scale containing eight items ranging from "pushed, grabbed, or shoved the other one" to "used a knife or gun."

LIMITATIONS The 1975 and 1985 surveys utilize different samples, although both are national probability samples. The 1985 survey was a thirty-five-minute telephone interview, whereas the 1975 survey lasted approximately an hour and was done in person.

In 1985, the survey does not ask if the spouse or partner of the respondent abuses the referent child. In addition, in 1985 it does not ask about the child's abuse of parents, although this was asked in 1975.

The Severe Violence Index (which is computed based on responses to the Conflict Tactics Scale) is held to be an indicator of physical abuse. Although the questions used to measure use of reasoning, verbal aggression, and physical violence are highly specific, they are based on self reports of sensitive and personal phenomena, and may therefore be subject to underreporting or other biases.

AVAILABILITY Data files are available from the Inter-University Consortium for Political and Social Research in two formats: card image and OSIRIS. The Consortium has also published a document that briefly describes the study and presents the codebook with marginal totals. This document is available through:

> Inter-University Consortium for
> Political and Social Research
> P.O. Box 1248
> Ann Arbor, MI 48106-1248
> 313/763-5010

For more detailed information on both the 1975 and 1985 surveys and a complete list of related publications, contact:

> Dr. Murray A. Straus
> Family Research Laboratory
> University of New Hampshire
> Durham, NH 03824-3586
> 603/862-1888

PUBLICATIONS

Gelles, R.J. (1989). Child abuse and violence in single-parent families: Parent absence and economic deprivation. *American Journal of Orthopsychiatry, 59*(4), 492-501.

Gelles, R.J. & Straus, M.A. (1988). *Intimate violence*. New York: Simon.

Straus, M.A. (1988). *Measuring psychological and physical abuse of children with the Conflict Tactics Scale*. (available from author).

Straus, M.A. & Gelles, R.J. (1990). *Physical violence in American families: Risk factors and adaptations to violence in 8,145 families*. New Jersey: Transaction.

Straus, M.A. et al. (1980). *Behind closed doors: Violence in the American family*. Garden City, NJ: Doubleday, Anchor Press.

National Family Violence Survey
Year of Questionnaire: 1985 Sample size: 6,002 households
FAMILY-LEVEL CHARACTERISTICS

Family Composition
O Full roster of household members (first name, age, sex, and relationship to reference person of each member)
● Partial roster of household members
● Number of adults in household
● Number of children in household
● Approximate relationship of family members to householder, child, or one another
O Exact relationship of family members to householder, child, or one another
O Information about part-time household member
O Information about family members no longer living in household
O Information about relatives who live nearby but not in household

Socioeconomic
● Total family income
O Number of persons who depend on family income
O Sources of income
O Income amounts identified separately by source
O Poverty status
O Welfare status
O Food Stamps receipt
O Child support receipt
O Medicaid coverage
O Private health insurance
O Home ownership/renters
O Assets (other than home ownership)
O Public housing status
● Telephone in household
O Language other than English spoken in home

Geographic/Community Variables
O Region of country
● State of residence
O County/city/MSA of residence
O Size/type of community
O Zip code
O Telephone area code
● Metropolitan residence
O Neighborhood quality
O Local labor market

Stage in Family Life Cycle
● Age of adult respondent or spouse/partner
● Marital status of adult respondent or spouse/partner
● Employment status of adult respondent or spouse/partner
● Presence of own children in household
● Age of youngest own child in household
● Age of oldest own child in household
● Existence of own children who have left home
O Intention to have (more) children in future

Family Functioning

○ Family activities or time use
○ Community involvement (civic, religious, recreational)
○ Family communication patterns
○ Family decision-making
● Marital conflict
● Marital happiness/satisfaction
● Parent-child conflict
○ History of marital separations
● History of family violence
○ History of marital counselling

CHARACTERISTICS OF ADULT FAMILY MEMBERS

Adult Respondent or Reference Person	Current Spouse in HH	Current or Former Spouse Not in HH	
●	○	○	Age
●	●	●	Gender
●	○	○	Race
●	○	○	Hispanic origin
○	○	○	Other origin/ethnicity
●	●	●	Religious affiliation[1]
○	○	○	Religious participation
○	○	○	Country of birth
○	○	○	Immigrant status
○	○	○	English fluency
●	●	○	Current marital status
●	●	○	Marital history[1]
●	●	○	Cohabitation status[1]
●	●	○	Cohabitation history[1]
●	○	○	Parental status
●	●	○	Number children ever born/sired[1,2]
○	○	○	Age at first birth
●	●	○	Age of youngest child[1,3]
●	○	○	Children living elsewhere
●	○	○	Duration at current address[4]
○	○	○	Residential mobility
●	●	●	Educational attainment[1]
●	●	●	Degrees attained[1]
○	○	○	GED or regular HS diploma
○	○	○	Current enrollment
●	●	○	Current employment status[1]
●	●	●	Hours usually worked (ft/pt)[1]
○	○	○	Weeks worked
○	○	○	Annual employment pattern
●	●	●	Main occupation[1]
○	○	○	Earnings
○	○	○	Wage rate
○	○	○	Payment of child support
○	○	○	Aptitude or achievement score
●	○	○	Health/disability status
○	○	○	Self-esteem
○	○	○	Locus of control or efficacy
●	○	○	Depression or subjective well-being
○	○	○	Work-related attitudes

CHARACTERISTICS OF CHILD FAMILY MEMBERS
Sample Size: 3,232 children

Reference Child or Youth Respondent	Other Children (in HH)	
●	●	Age
○	○	Month and year of birth
●	●	Gender
○	○	Race
○	○	Hispanic origin
○	○	Other origin/ethnicity
○	○	Religious affiliation
○	○	Religious participation
○	○	Country of birth
○	○	Immigrant status
○	○	English fluency
●	●	Exact relationship to adult family members
●	●	Exact relationship to other children in HH
○	○	Marital status/history
○	○	Parental status/history
○	○	Current enrollment in regular school
○	○	Current enrollment in preschool/daycare
○	○	Highest grade completed
○	○	Grade now enrolled
○	○	Employment status/history
○	○	Health status
○	○	Handicapping conditions
○	○	Grade repetition
○	○	Aptitude or achievement score
○	○	Pregnancy/birth history
○	○	Psychological well-being
●	○	Delinquency

NOTES
1. This information is also available for a cohabiting partner.
2. This information is only available for the current spouse if the children are living in the household.
3. Only if living in household.
4. Asks duration in current community.

National Health and Nutrition Examination Survey

PURPOSE The National Health and Nutrition Examination Survey (NHANES), like its predecessor program, the Health Examination Survey, is a vehicle for collecting and disseminating medical and biometric data on the U.S. civilian noninstitutional population, data of the sort that can best be obtained by direct physical examination, clinical and laboratory tests, and related measurement procedures. The types of information collected include:

- objectively measured data on the prevalence of specific diseases or pathological conditions;
- normative data that show the distribution of the population with respect to particular parameters such as height, weight, blood pressure, visual acuity, or serum cholesterol;
- data on the interrelationships among biometric and physiological variables in the general population, such as the relationship of height and weight to blood pressure; and
- data on the relationships of demographic and socioeconomic variables to health conditions.

The examination surveys have sometimes included measures of intellectual functioning and emotional well-being as well as physical health. Since 1970, the program has also been designed to measure the nutritional status and dietary intake of the population and to monitor changes in that status over time.

SPONSORSHIP The survey program is designed and sponsored by the National Center for Health Statistics (NCHS), with other federal agencies often sharing in the sponsorship of the survey. In past cycles of the survey, initial household interviewing was done by Census interviewers. Since 1982, the interviewing, as well as history taking, examining, testing, and measuring of survey respondents, has been done by contractors.

DESIGN Probability samples of the population are made and interviewers are provided with randomized selection criteria for specific household members at each address. Several members of a single family may all be included in the sample, with each one having a known relationship to a household reference person. First, respondents are interviewed at home, then they are examined, tested, and interviewed further in mobile examination centers, where examination procedures can be carried out under uniform and controlled conditions. The examination centers are moved about the country along with data collection teams consisting of interviewers, medical examiners, dentists, technicians, dietary interviewers, and laboratory personnel. The general pattern of data collection and limitations in the number of persons who can be examined in a given time span have meant that each cycle of the survey has required three to four years to complete.

The samples for all of the cycles of the survey have been multi-stage, highly clustered probability samples, stratified by geographic region and population density. Persons residing in institutions are not included in the samples. The age range covered by the survey has varied across cycles. During the 1960s, three cycles of the Health Examination Survey (HES) were carried out that focused on specific age groups, namely adults, children, and adolescents. The most recent national survey, NHANES III, covers the non-institutionalized population aged 2 months and older. NHANES I and NHANES II covered ages from 1 through 74 years and 6 months through 74 years, respectively. (Only persons aged 25-74 were given the detailed physical examination in NHANES I, however.)

The size of the survey sample has varied. In each of the three cycles of the HES done in the 1960s, the sample size was approximately 7,500 and the response rate was high (87% for the adult cycle, 96% for the children's examinations, and 90% for the youth examinations). For the two NHANES cycles done in the 1970s, the samples selected for the major nutrition components of the examination contained approximately 28,000 people and yielded about 21,000 examined persons. Response rates for the household interviews were extremely high (91%). Completion rates for the physical examination components were lower (74% for the nutrition component of NHANES I, and 70% for the detailed health examination; 73% overall for the examination component of NHANES II). A policy of remunerating examined persons was introduced to maintain response levels.

Young people were oversampled in NHANES II and are over-sampled again in NHANES III. The total number of young people examined in NHANES II was 9,605: 4,118 children aged 6 months to 5 years; 1,725 children aged 6-11 years; and 1,975 adolescents aged 12-17 years. The NHANES III sample will include approximately 14,000-15,000 young people, aged 2 months to 19 years.

The basic design of the examination program is that of the repeated cross-sectional survey. There have been three instances of longitudinal followups to the examination surveys, however. In the 1960s, the same sampling areas were used for the youth examination survey as had been used for the children's examination survey. Hence, about 2,200 of the same children were examined in both cycles. More recently, there has been a longitudinal followup of the adults examined in NHANES I and a mortality-only followup of adults in NHANES II. All NHANES III respondents will be followed up using the National Death Index.

PERIODICITY The dates of the completed Health Examination Surveys and Health and Nutrition Examination Surveys are shown below.

Survey	*Age Range Covered*	*Years Conducted*
HES, Cycle I	18-79	1959-62
HES, Cycle II	6-11	1963-65
HES, Cycle III	12-17	1966-70
NHANES I	1-74	1971-74
NHANES I (Augmentation)	25-74	1974-75
NHANES II	6 mos.-74	1976-80

Survey	Age Range Covered	Years Conducted
HHANES	6 mos.-74	1982-84
NHANES III (currently in the field)	2 mos.+	1988-94

The last examination program (in operation in 1982-84) was Hispanic HANES, a study of the health and nutritional status and medical care utilization patterns of the Mexican American population in the Southwest, the Cuban population in Dade County, Florida, and the Puerto Rican population in and around New York City. The current national survey (the third NHANES) began in 1988 and will conclude in 1994.

CONTENT A family questionnaire precedes the other instruments during the data collection process. For NHANES III, the information on the head of the family (not necessarily a sampled respondent) includes school attainment, ethnic origin, age, sex, race, marital status, employer, industry, and occupation. Family housing characteristics are ascertained (type of heat, water softening, ventilation, type of cooking fuel). All household members who smoke are identified. Family insurance coverage data and Social Security, Food Stamps, and WIC benefits receipts are provided.

The kinds of information on individual family members that have been collected in the HES and NHANES have varied across the different surveys. The data have been put to important practical as well as scientific uses. For example, the body measurement data developed through the examination surveys form the basis for the growth charts that may be found in every pediatrician's office. Data on blood lead levels and pesticide residues in the population have figured in major policy decisions of the Environmental Protection Agency. And data based on the dental examinations that are performed in the survey have been used to estimate what it would cost to provide dental coverage under various national health insurance schemes. The following paragraphs present a sampling of the data that have been collected in the program.

Information about nutritional status collected in NHANES has included: data on nutritional intake and eating habits based on twenty-four-hour recall interviews and food frequency questionnaires; a sizable battery of hematological and biochemical tests based on blood and urine specimens; and careful body measurements of height, weight, and skinfolds.

Information about dental health collected in the survey has included: counts of the number of decayed, missing, and filled teeth; and data on the presence of malocclusion and periodontal disease.

Information about sensory functioning and communication disorders has included: tests of visual acuity in children and adults; tests of hearing acuity in children and adolescents; and evaluations of speech pathology in young children.

Information about pulmonary and cardiovascular health has included: measurements of lung function (spirometry); x-rays; measurements of blood pressure, EKG, and serum cholesterol; and data on clinical signs of respiratory or cardiovascular disease.

Information about environmental effects on health collected in NHANES has included: the amounts of carbon monoxide present in the blood (carboxyhemoglobin); blood lead levels; the presence of pesticide residues and certain trace elements in the blood; and medical history and allergen skin tests.

Cycles II and III of the Health Examination Survey included a battery of psychological tests administered to the children and adolescents examined. The tests included parts of the Wechsler Intelligence Scale for Children (WISC) and the Wide Range Achievement Test (WRAT); and the Goodenough-Harris Draw-A-Person Test. NHANES III includes parts of the WISC and the WRAT for children and youth aged 6-16.

Ratings of the behavior of children and adolescents by their parents and teachers were collected in Cycles II and III of the Health Examination Survey. Questionnaire data on the emotional well-being of adults were collected in Cycle I of the Health Examination Survey and in NHANES I and NHANES III. NHANES II contained a questionnaire for adults dealing with "Type A" behavior, which is thought to relate to the incidence of cardiovascular disease.

Each cycle of the survey has collected an extensive set of background data on the examined persons (and, in the case of children, on their parents) including age, sex, race and Hispanic origin, educational attainment, occupation, employment status, family income, and poverty status. For NHANES III, at 10 years of age and older, pregnancy and menstruation histories are obtained from females. Questions are asked regarding alcohol and drug use of respondents 12 and over, and questions on physical activities and tobacco use are asked of respondents who are at least eight years old. Also in NHANES III, households provide information on whether they have any pets and what kind.

LIMITATIONS The Health and Nutrition Examination Survey program has several important advantages as a source of data on the health of U.S. family members. It is the only nationwide data program that provides estimates of the health status of the population based on direct examination and testing.

Everyone is given a standard examination, and the estimates of disease/condition prevalence are not as dependent on the knowledge and reporting of a parent or a physician, as is the case in other health surveys. Nor are the estimates limited to selected population groups, as is often the case with studies based on screening programs or clinic records. The quality of the data collected is generally very high. Adolescents aged 12 and over respond for themselves concerning matters such as their food consumption and recent bodily symptoms. Children of 8 and over are asked about smoking and tobacco; girls of 10 and over respond about their menstrual histories. (In Hispanic HANES, children as young as 6 years of age were asked a short series of questions about possible vision and hearing problems in school.) In addition, questionnaires concerning diet, medication, and behavior are administered in the privacy of the examination trailers. This may produce more candid reporting, especially on the part of adolescents, who could be reluctant to disclose information about certain aspects of their behavior if the interview were conducted at home or in school. The examination surveys also afford the opportunity to compare interview and questionnaire responses with the results of examination and testing procedures, thus providing "calibration" data on the significance of different types of responses, the overall validity of respondent reporting, and differential bias or distortion in reports concerning certain groups of children.

Unfortunately, the HANES program also has several drawbacks as a source of social indicator data on families. To begin with, the long intervals between completed surveys make the program of little use for tracking short term changes in child health or for assessing the impact of cutbacks in public health programs. The number of specific components in any cycle is limited and the same components are not repeated in all cycles. There is, moreover, a good deal of variation in the wording of survey questionnaires from cycle to cycle, even when the same topics are being covered.

Another limitation of the HANES data sets is the lack of a summary evaluation by a physician of each person's overall health status, based on the full battery of tests and examinations administered. There is a summary rating by the person of his or her own health (or, in the case of children under 12, a rating by the parent respondent). This rating is, by design, nearly the same as that collected in the National Health Interview Survey.

The estimates of disease prevalence produced by HANES are not dependent on the respondent's ability to remember and report clinical information, as is the case for the Health Interview Survey. The physician takes blood pressure and conducts a limited exam; conditions such as diabetes, osteoporosis, gallbladder and dental disease, retinopathy, etc., are diagnosed by examination. However, some other conditions require self report, and some biases associated with the respondent's education level, race, and prior exposure to medical terminology may enter into the HANES data as well.

The institutionalized population is excluded from HANES, as it is from the National Health Interview Survey, the CPS, and the NSFG, among others.

AVAILABILITY Public use data tapes are available for all completed cycles of HES, NHANES, and HHANES. Beginning with NHANES 1, the tapes have been released to both in-house analysts and the public as soon as final editing has been performed and the necessary documentation prepared. There is an

NHANES Data Users' Group that meets regularly in Washington. Tapes can be obtained from:

National Technical Information Service
5285 Port Royal Road
Springfield, VA 22161
703/487-4650

Magnetic tapes of NHANES II are available from:

Inter-University Consortium
for Political and Social Research
P.O. Box 1248
Ann Arbor, MI 48106-1248
313/763-5010

Descriptions of the sample design and collection procedures for each cycle of the survey and copies of all data collection forms may be found in the following numbers of Series I of Vital and Health Statistics: Number 4 (Cycle I of HES); 5 (Cycle II); 8 (Cycle III); 10a & b and 14 (NHANES I); 15 (NHANES II); and 19 (HHANES). A forthcoming number will describe NHANES III.

For substantive questions, contact:

Wilbur Hadden, M.S. 301/436-7068
Christopher Sempos, Ph.D. 301/436-7485
Ronette Briefel, Dr.P.H. 301/436-3473
Division of Health Examination Statistics
National Center for Health Statistics
6525 Belcrest Road, Room 900
Hyattsville, MD 20782

PUBLICATIONS Findings from the Health Examination Surveys and the National Health and Nutrition Examination Surveys are presented in Series 11 of the Vital and Health Statistics publication series. Published reports are not issued on a set frequency, but rather made available as completed. The reports are generally organized on a topical basis with the earlier numbers from a survey being descriptive whereas the later numbers are more analytic. Results are also published in articles such as:

Dorbusch, S.M., Gross, R.T., Duncan, P.D., & Ritter, P.L. (1987). Stanford studies of adolescence using the National Health Examination Survey. In R.M Lerner & T.T. Foch (Eds.), *Biological-psychosocial interaction in early adolescence* (pp. 189-205). Hillsdale, NJ: Earlbaum.

Oliver, L.I. (1974). *Parent ratings of behavioral patterns of youths 12-17 years: United States.* Vital and Health Statistics, Series 11, No. 137. Rockville, MD: National Center for Health Statistics.

Roberts, J. & Engel, A. (1974). *Family background, early development, and intelligence of children 6-11 years: United States.* Vital and Health Statistics, Series 11, No. 142. Rockville, MD: National Center for Health Statistics.

Vogt, D.K. (1973). *Literacy among youths 12-17 years: United States.* Vital and Health Statistics, Series 11, No. 131. Rockville, MD: National Center for Health Statistics.

National Health and Nutrition Examination Survey
Years of Questionnaire: 1988-1994[1]
FAMILY-LEVEL CHARACTERISTICS
Sample size: about 15,000

Family Composition
- ● Full roster of household members (first name, age, sex, and relationship to reference person of each member)
- ○ Partial roster of household members
- ● Number of adults in household
- ● Number of children in household
- ● Approximate relationship of family members to householder, child, or one another
- ○ Exact relationship of family members to householder, child, or one another
- ○ Information about part-time household member
- ○ Information about family members no longer living in household
- ● Information about relatives who live nearby but not in household

Socioeconomic
- ● Total family income
- ○ Number of persons who depend on family income
- ○ Sources of income
- ○ Income amounts identified separately by source
- ● Poverty status
- ● Welfare status
- ● Food Stamps receipt
- ○ Child support receipt
- ● Medicaid coverage
- ● Private health insurance
- ● Home ownership/renters
- ○ Assets (other than home ownership)
- ○ Public housing status
- ● Telephone in household
- ● Language other than English spoken in home

Geographic/Community Variables
- ● Region of country
- ● State of residence
- ● County/city/MSA of residence
- ○ Size/type of community
- ○ Zip code
- ○ Telephone area code
- ○ Metropolitan residence
- ○ Neighborhood quality
- ○ Local labor market

Stage in Family Life Cycle
- ● Age of adult respondent or spouse/partner
- ● Marital status of adult respondent or spouse/partner
- ● Employment status of adult respondent or spouse/partner
- ● Presence of own children in household
- ● Age of youngest own child in household
- ● Age of oldest own child in household
- ○ Existence of own children who have left home
- ○ Intention to have (more) children in future

Family Functioning

- ○ Family activities or time use
- ○ Community involvement (civic, religious, recreational)
- ○ Family communication patterns
- ○ Family decision-making
- ○ Marital conflict
- ○ Marital happiness/satisfaction
- ○ Parent-child conflict
- ○ History of marital separations
- ○ History of family violence
- ○ History of marital counselling

CHARACTERISTICS OF ADULT FAMILY MEMBERS
Sample size: about 26,000

Adult Respondent or Reference Person	Current Spouse in HH	Current or Former Spouse Not in HH	
●	○	○	Age
●	○	○	Gender
●	○	○	Race
●	○	○	Hispanic origin
●	○	○	Other origin/ethnicity
○	○	○	Religious affiliation
○	○	○	Religious participation
●	○	○	Country of birth
○	○	○	Immigrant status
○	○	○	English fluency
●	○	○	Current marital status
●	○	○	Marital history
○	○	○	Cohabitation status
○	○	○	Cohabitation history
●	○	○	Parental status
●	○	○	Number children ever born/sired[2]
●	○	○	Age at first birth
●	○	○	Age of youngest child
○	○	○	Children living elsewhere
●	○	○	Duration at current address
●	○	○	Residential mobility
●	○	○	Educational attainment
○	○	○	Degrees attained
○	○	○	GED or regular HS diploma
○	○	○	Current enrollment
●	○	○	Current employment status
○	○	○	Hours usually worked (ft/pt)
○	○	○	Weeks worked
○	○	○	Annual employment pattern
●	○	○	Main occupation
●	○	○	Earnings
○	○	○	Wage rate
○	○	○	Payment of child support
○	○	○	Aptitude or achievement score
●	○	○	Health/disability status
○	○	○	Self-esteem
○	○	○	Locus of control or efficacy
●	○	○	Depression or subjective well-being
○	○	○	Work-related attitudes

CHARACTERISTICS OF CHILD FAMILY MEMBERS
Sample size: about 14,000

Reference Child or Youth Respondent	Other Children (in HH)	
●	○	Age
●	○	Month and year of birth
●	○	Gender
●	○	Race
●	○	Hispanic origin
●	○	Other origin/ethnicity
○	○	Religious affiliation
○	○	Religious participation
●	○	Country of birth
●	○	Immigrant status
●	○	English fluency
●	○	Exact relationship to adult family members
○	○	Exact relationship to other children in HH
●	○	Marital status/history
○	○	Parental status/history
●	○	Current enrollment in regular school
●	○	Current enrollment in preschool/daycare[3]
●	○	Highest grade completed
●	○	Grade now enrolled
●	○	Employment status/history
●	○	Health status
●	○	Handicapping conditions
●	○	Grade repetition
●	○	Aptitude or achievement score
●	○	Pregnancy/birth history[4]
●	○	Psychological well-being
○	○	Delinquency

NOTES
1. Current cycle now being conducted.
2. Children ever born, only.
3. History of preschool/daycare enrollment.
4. Asked of female respondents twelve and over.

National Health Interview Survey

PURPOSE The National Health Interview Survey (NHIS) is intended to provide a continuing picture of the health status of the U.S. population based on people's reports of their own health-related experiences and attributes. The survey collects national data on the incidence of acute illness and accidental injuries, the prevalence of chronic conditions and impairments, the extent of disability, the utilization of health care services, and other related topics. These health characteristics are determined and displayed for the population as a whole and for a number of demographic and socioeconomic subgroups.

SPONSORSHIP The Survey is designed by the National Center for Health Statistics (NCHS) and consists of the basic health and demographic questionnaire and additional questionnaires on special health topics of current interest. These annual current topics are funded by NCHS and other agencies. Survey interviewing is performed by a permanent staff of trained interviewers and supervisors employed by the U.S. Bureau of the Census. The sample is designed by the Bureau of the Census.

DESIGN The National Health Interview Survey is a cross-sectional household interview survey. It covers the civilian, noninstitutional population of the 50 states and the District of Columbia. The sampling plan follows a multi-stage probability design that permits the continuous sampling of households. The overall sample is designed so that tabulations can be provided for each of the four major geographic regions. In-person interviews are conducted each week throughout the year. Each week's sample is representative of the target population and weekly samples are additive over time. Data collected over the period of a year form the basis for the development of annual estimates of the health characteristics of the population and for the analysis of trends in those characteristics.

Several new sample design features were added in 1985, although conceptually the sampling plan remained the same. The major changes included reducing the number of primary sampling locations from 376 to 198; oversampling the black population; dividing the sample into four separate representative panels to facilitate linkage to other NCHS surveys; and using an all-area frame not based on the decennial census. In 1985 through 1994, data will be collected annually on about 127,000 persons in approximately 49,000 households.

The annual response rate of the NHIS is over 90% of the eligible households in the sample. All adult members of the household 17 years of age and over who are at home at the time of the interview are invited to participate and to respond for themselves. Between 60% and 65% of the adults 17 years or over are self-respondents. Approximately 28% of the persons sampled are children under the age of 18. The mother is usually the respondent for children.

The NHIS sample provided the sampling frame for the 1988 National Survey of Family Growth of women ages 15-44, and will provide the sampling frame for the 1994 NSFG (see separate write-up on that survey). Data from the two surveys are also now explicitly linked, making analyses of the combined files possible.

A redesign of the NHIS is scheduled to be fielded in 1995. The new NHIS will consist of three types of questionnaires: basic module, periodic module, and topical module. The basic module will be fielded every year and will collect basic sociodemographic information and a few health measures for all family members, and a few more health measures for a self-responding sample person. There will probably be three periodic modules, one of which will be fielded each year: health status, health behavior, and health care. There will be one or more topical modules each year on topics of current interest. The basic and periodic modules will be funded by NCHS, and the topical modules by other sources. A working group is underway to investigate the potential for improving the family-level data (e.g., family configuration, marital history) obtained by the NHIS.

PERIODICITY The National Health Interview Survey has been conducted annually since 1957. Over that period, many changes have occurred in the format, content, and administration of the core questionnaire (see Vital and Health Statistics, Series 1, No. 11, "Health Interview Survey Procedure, 1957-74," and Series 1, No. 18, "The National Health Interview Survey Design, 1973-84, and Procedures, 1975-83"). The basic procedures used for measuring the incidence of acute illness and injuries, the prevalence of chronic conditions, the extent of disability, and the use of health-care services have remained fairly consistent between the late 1960s or early 1970s and 1990; however each person is now given only one of six condition lists.

The most recent major changes in the basic health and demographic questionnaire took place in 1982. Changes were made in the format and order of questions on limitations of activity, disability days, doctor visits, hospital stays, and overall health status, and questions on the receipt of dental care were moved from the basic health and demographic questionnaire to a periodic special health topic. These changes require that caution be used when comparing pre- and post-1982 data. Major redesign changes are usually implemented in 10 year intervals.

The questionnaires on special health topics change in response to current interests. The content of some recent and planned supplements is described below. There has also been some variation in background items from year to year.

CONTENT The basic health and demographic questionnaire provides for the following types of data:

- Basic demographic characteristics of household members, including age, sex, marital status, race and Hispanic origin, education, occupation of adults, and family income.
- Disability days, including restricted activity and bed days, and work and school loss days occurring during the two week period prior to the week of the interview; and disability days during the preceding 12 months.
- Acute and chronic conditions responsible for these disability days and for doctor visits.
- Physician visits occurring during the two weeks prior to the interview.
- Long-term limitation of activity (three months or more) resulting from chronic disease or impairment and the conditions associated with the limitation.
- Hospitalization data, including the number of persons with hospital episodes during the past year and the number of discharges and days from hospitals.

- Indicators of the health status and health care use of each household member, including number of bed days and doctor visits in the past 12 months, interval since the last doctor visit, incidence of accidents and injuries in the two weeks prior to the interview, and an overall assessment of each family member's health from excellent to poor by the family respondent.

The basic health and demographic questionnaire also includes six lists of chronic conditions. Each list concentrates on a group of chronic conditions involving a specific system of the body (e.g., digestive, circulatory, respiratory). Respondents are asked whether anyone in the family has had each condition on the list. Since 1978, each of six representative subsamples has been asked the questions in one of the six lists. In this way, national prevalence estimates on all conditions are obtained during the same interview year.

In recent years, supplemental questionnaires on current topics have dealt with the following areas:

Topic	Year
Eye care; immunization; smoking	1979
Home health care; residential mobility; retirement income; smoking	1979, 1980
Health insurance (includes section in 1983 and 1984 on loss of insurance coverage due to losing or being laid off from a job)	1980, 1982, 1983 , 1984
The health of children and youth (0-17 years) (see separate write-ups)	1981, 1988
Preventive health care	1982
Doctor services; dental care; alcohol/ health practices (including smoking cessation)	1983
The health of the elderly (55 years and older)	1984

Topics	Year
Health promotion and disease prevention (see separate write-up)	1985, 1990, 1991
Dental care; functional limitation; longest job worked; and vitamin and mineral intake	1986
Adoption (see separate write-up)	1987
Cancer control and epidemiology	1987, 1992
Knowledge and attitudes on AIDS	1987 thru 1993
Medical device implants; occupational health (includes smoking); alcohol	1988
Health insurance; immunization; mental health; dental care; diabetes screening and risk factors; orofacial pain; digestive disorders	1989
Assistive devices; hearing; podiatry; detailed income and federal program participation	1990
Year 2000 Objectives (health promotion and disease prevention); drug use; detailed income; youth risk behaviors	1991

The AIDS supplement which began in 1987 will be continued indefinitely. The detailed income and federal program participation supplement, which began in 1990 and greatly improves the quality of economic data collected, is expected to be included every year. That supplement is administered to every family in the sample.

LIMITATIONS The National Health Interview Survey does not cover some of the least healthy segments of the population in that adults and children in long-term hospitals, prisons, and other residential institutions are excluded from the sample. The illness experience and use of medical care by persons who die during the course of a year are also under-represented in the survey data.

Only persons aged 17 and older can be respondents and one adult aged 19 or older can respond for everyone in the family. Children and even teenagers as old as 16 are not permitted to respond for themselves.

Data on acute and chronic conditions are only as good as the respondent's ability to report them. Subclinical or symptom- free illnesses are generally not reported. Diagnostic categories are probably not well defined and the household respondent can usually only pass on the diagnostic information that a physician has given to the family. For conditions not medically attended, diagnostic information is often no more than a description of symptoms. Persons with more education or more exposure to medical services tend to be more familiar with the diagnostic terms used in the survey than persons with less education or less exposure to physicians. Changes over time in the reported prevalence of a given condition may reflect increased public familiarity with a diagnostic label rather than (or as well as) an increase in the actual prevalence of the condition.

Because six different lists of chronic conditions are used in the Health Interview Survey, the prevalence of a given chronic condition is obtained on only one-sixth of the sample. Inasmuch as the prevalence of chronic conditions is low in children, too few cases may be available for meaningful analysis of particular childhood conditions. Moreover, counts of the number of children with certain chronic conditions (e.g., mental retardation) are much lower when based on parent reporting than when based on teacher reporting or clinical evaluations.

Acute conditions or injuries are counted in the NHIS only if they result in medical consultation or one or more days of restricted activity. Incidence data are collected by two week recall and summed over the survey year. This gives a valid estimate of the total volume of events in the course of a year, and the mean number of events per person per year, but not the distribution of persons by events experienced (i.e., how many persons experienced no events, one event, two events, etc., over the course of the year).

Some twelve-month estimates of disability days and use of medical care are obtained directly from respondents, but these estimates tend to be lower than estimates based on shorter recall periods.

Data on the impact of illness (e.g., the number of disability days caused by a given condition) are probably obtained more accurately from family members than from any other source. However, survey data such as these are not simply measures of the severity of an illness; they reflect personal preferences and external constraints as well as medical need. For example, given two children with the same set of respiratory symptoms, one family may keep their child home from school whereas the other family may choose to send the child to school.

There appear to be persistent racial discrepancies in the NHIS data (and other survey data as well) that are due to differences in recall or reporting styles rather than to differences in experience with an illness. Black adults generally use less positive terms than white adults do when rating their own health or the health of their children, and black mortality rates are generally higher than white rates. Yet blacks report fewer episodes of illness-related disability and medical care than do white persons, even when the two week recall periods are used and adjustments are made for racial differences in education levels.

No information is collected on family dynamics, such as level of marital conflict. Thus, it is not possible to examine the link between the health of individual family members and how the family is functioning. It is expected that the redesigned NHIS will allow more family level analyses.

AVAILABILITY Basic descriptive statistical reports based on NHIS data appear in Series 10 of the *Vital and Health Statistics* publication series. The first report of a year's basic health and demographic data, which is typically published in October of the following year, is the "Current Estimates" report (e.g., for 1990, Series 10, No. 181). This report also provides comparison figures from the previous two years for major health characteristics, as well as a copy of the core and supplemental questionnaires for that year. Three to five Series 10 reports and several additional reports on each year's data are also prepared, covering specific core topics, such as "Acute Conditions" or "Physician Visits," but most cover data from the year's special health topics. Special analyses involving more detailed tabulations appear in the NCHS Advance Data series. Recent publications on family related topics are now available.

In addition to the data tables that appear in the Series 10 publications and *Health, United States,* many unpublished tabulations of the NHIS data are routinely generated by NCHS and made available upon request. These include more detailed breakdowns of health data on the population under 18, including tabulations by age, sex, race, family income, and education level of the head of the family. Public use tapes covering both basic health and demographic and special health topic data are released about one year after the completion of data collection. The data tapes for the basic health and demographic survey are available back to the 1969 survey year from the National Technical Information Service, Springfield, Virginia 22761 (703/487- 4780). For substantive questions, contact:

> Gerry E. Hendershot, Ph.D.
> Chief, Illness and Disability Statistics Branch
> Division of Health Interview Statistics/NCHS
> 6525 Belcrest Road, Room 850
> Hyattsville, MD 20782
> 301/436-7089

PUBLICATIONS

Adams, P.F. & Benson, V. (1991). Current estimates from the National Health Interview Survey. National Center for Health Statistics. *Vital and Health Statistics, 10*(181).

Dawson, D.A. (1991). Family structure and children's health: United States, 1988. National Center for Health Statistics. *Vital and Health Statistics, 10*(178).

LeClere, F.B. & Hendershot, G. (1992). *The timing of marital dissolution and the utilization of health care services.* Paper presented at the Population Association of America meetings, Denver, CO.

Reis, P.W. (1991). Educational differences in health status and health care. National Center for Health Statistics. *Vital and Health Statistics, 10*(179).

Schoenborn, C.A. (1991). Exposure to alcoholism in the family: United States, 1988. *Advance Data from Vital and Health Statistics, 205.*

Schoenborn, C.A. & Wilson, B.F. (1988). *Are married people healthier? Health characteristics of married and unmarried U.S. men and women.* Paper presented at the American Public Health Association meetings, Boston, MA.

National Health Interview Survey
Year of Questionnaire: 1990
Sample size: 119,631 people
FAMILY LEVEL CHARACTERISTICS
Sample size: 46,476 families

Family Composition
- Full roster of household members (first name, age, sex, and relationship to reference person of each member)
○ Partial roster of household members
- Number of adults in household
- Number of children in household
○ Approximate relationship of family members to householder, child, or one another
- Exact relationship of family members to householder, child, or one another
- Information about part-time household member
○ Information about family members no longer living in household
○ Information about relatives who live nearby but not in household

Socioeconomic
- Total family income
○ Number of persons who depend on family income
- Sources of income
- Income amounts identified separately by source
- Poverty status
- Welfare status
- Food Stamps receipt
○ Child support receipt
- Medicaid coverage
- Private health insurance
○ Home ownership/renters
- Assets (other than home ownership)
○ Public housing status
- Telephone in household
○ Language other than English spoken in home

Geographic/Community Variables
- Region of country
- State of residence
- County/city/MSA of residence
- Size/type of community
- Zip code
- Telephone area code
- Metropolitan residence
○ Neighborhood quality
○ Local labor market

Stage in Family Life Cycle
- Age of adult respondent or spouse/partner
- Marital status of adult respondent or spouse/partner
- Employment status of adult respondent or spouse/partner
- Presence of own children in household
- Age of youngest own child in household
- Age of oldest own child in household
○ Existence of own children who have left home
○ Intention to have (more) children in future

Family Functioning
- ○ Family activities or time use
- ○ Community involvement (civic, religious, recreational)
- ○ Family communication patterns
- ○ Family decision-making
- ○ Marital conflict
- ○ Marital happiness/satisfaction
- ○ Parent-child conflict
- ○ History of marital separations
- ○ History of family violence
- ○ History of marital counselling

CHARACTERISTICS OF ADULT FAMILY MEMBERS
Sample size: 86,388

Adult Respondent or Reference Person	Current Spouse in HH	Current or Former Spouse Not in HH	
●	○	○	Age
●	○	○	Gender
●	○	○	Race
●	○	○	Hispanic origin
○	○	○	Other origin/ethnicity
○	○	○	Religious affiliation
○	○	○	Religious participation
●	○	○	Country of birth
○	○	○	Immigrant status
○	○	○	English fluency
●	○	○	Current marital status
○	○	○	Marital history
○	○	○	Cohabitation status
○	○	○	Cohabitation history
●	○	○	Parental status[1]
○	○	○	Number children ever born/sired
○	○	○	Age at first birth
●	○	○	Age of youngest child[1]
○	○	○	Children living elsewhere
○	○	○	Duration at current address
●	○	○	Residential mobility
●	○	○	Educational attainment
○	○	○	Degrees attained
○	○	○	GED or regular HS diploma
●	○	○	Current enrollment
●	○	○	Current employment status
●	○	○	Hours usually worked (ft/pt)
○	○	○	Weeks worked
●	○	○	Annual employment pattern
●	○	○	Main occupation
●	○	○	Earnings
○	○	○	Wage rate
○	○	○	Payment of child support
○	○	○	Aptitude or achievement score
●	○	○	Health/disability status
○	○	○	Self-esteem
○	○	○	Locus of control or efficacy
○	○	○	Depression or subjective well-being
○	○	○	Work-related attitudes

CHARACTERISTICS OF CHILD FAMILY MEMBERS
Sample size: 33,243

Reference Child or Youth Respondent	All Children (in HH)	
O	●	Age
O	●	Month and year of birth
O	●	Gender
O	●	Race
O	●	Hispanic origin
O	O	Other origin/ethnicity
O	O	Religious affiliation
O	O	Religious participation
O	●	Country of birth
O	O	Immigrant status
O	O	English fluency
O	O	Exact relationship to adult family members
O	O	Exact relationship to other children in HH
O	O	Marital status/history
O	O	Parental status/history
O	●	Current enrollment in regular school
O	O	Current enrollment in preschool/daycare
O	●	Highest grade completed
O	O	Grade now enrolled
O	O	Employment status/history
O	●	Health status
O	●	Handicapping conditions
O	O	Grade repetition
O	O	Aptitude or achievement score
O	O	Pregnancy/birth history
O	O	Psychological well-being
O	O	Delinquency

NOTES
1. Only if children usually live in household.

NHIS—1987 Adoption Supplement

PURPOSE The National Health Interview Survey (NHIS) fielded in 1987 contained adoption questions in an effort to gain information on the prevalence of adoption and on the characteristics of adoptive mothers and children. A comparable set of questions was asked of more than 8,400 women 15-44 years of age in the 1988 National Survey of Family Growth, which used the same sampling frame as the NHIS.

SPONSORSHIP This supplement was sponsored by the National Center for Health Statistics. The U.S. Bureau of the Census designed the sample and conducted the interviews.

DESIGN The Adoption Supplement was a part of the cross-sectional household NHIS. This supplement, however, was limited to females aged 20 to 54 in the interviewed household, of which there were 31,124. The respondent was shown a card, M, and asked to respond yes (there had been an adoption) or no (none). If no person under 18 was present in the household, the respondent was asked, "Has anyone in the family ever adopted any children?" If yes, "Who is this?" and "Anyone else?" (The names of the adopters).

PERIODICITY There are no current plans for repetition of this supplement.

CONTENT Variables include the relationship, if any, of the two most recently adopted children to the adoptive mother before the adoption(s), whether the adoptive child was born in the United States or a foreign country, the month, date, and year of the adoptive child's birth and the month and year that the adoptive child began living with the adoptive mother. The survey also includes whether the adoption was arranged through a public agency, a private agency, or some other way. Other information included in the supplement is the health status of the mothers and those adoptive children still living in the home, including limitation of activity, bed days, doctor visits, and information on living quarters, family income, education, occupation and industry, height, weight, race, and Hispanic origin.

LIMITATIONS Adoptions during any year by women who were older than age 55 in 1987 are not included. Thus, women who adopted at ages 40 and over in 1972 will be too old to be included in the sample. Adoptions by anyone other than an interviewable female 20-54 are not included; therefore, the situation where a stepfather adopts his wife's child is not represented. Limiting the sample to women thus introduces a greater bias for related adoptions than for unrelated adoptions.

The number of women adopting a child (566) is fairly small, even given such a large sample size. The total non-interview rate was 4.7 percent, and information on relationship is missing for 7.4 percent of adopted children, with about 3 percent missing information on year and type of adoption arrangement.

AVAILABILITY For those with access to a CD-ROM reader, this data set may be purchased for a very low cost from the Government Printing Office as NCHS CD-ROM Series 10, No. 1, which includes the entire 1987 survey with over 300,000 records, 5 core files and 4 supplemental files. Data are also available on tape.

> National Technical Information Service
> 5285 Port Royal Road
> Springfield, VA 22161
> (703)487-4650
> Order Number: PB91-505073BCP

> Government Printing Office
> (202)783-3238
> Order Number: 017-022-01117-4

For technical questions, contact:
> Nelma Keen
> Chief, Systems and Programming Branch
> 6525 Belcrest Road, Room 850
> Hyattsville, MD 20782
> 301/436-7087

For questions on the Health Interview Survey:

Patricia F. Adams
National Center for Health Statistics
Hyattsville, MD 20782
301/436-7089

PUBLICATIONS

Bachrach, C.A., Adams, P.F., Sambrano, S., & London, K.A. (1990). Adoption in the 1980s. *Advance Data from Vital and Health Statistics* (Report No. 181). Hyattsville, Maryland: National Center for Health Statistics.

NHIS-Adoption Supplement

Year of Questionnaire: 1987 Sample size: 31,124 women aged 20-54[1]

FAMILY LEVEL CHARACTERISTICS

Family Composition

O Full roster of household members (first name, age, sex, and relationship to reference person of each member)
● Partial roster of household members
● Number of adults in household
● Number of children in household
● Approximate relationship of family members to householder, child, or one another
O Exact relationship of family members to householder, child, or one another
O Information about part-time household member
O Information about family members no longer living in household
O Information about relatives who live nearby but not in household

Socioeconomic

● Total family income
O Number of persons who depend on family income
O Sources of income
O Income amounts identified separately by source
● Poverty status
O Welfare status
O Food Stamps receipt
O Child support receipt
O Medicaid coverage
O Private health insurance
O Home ownership/renters
O Assets (other than home ownership)
O Public housing status
● Telephone in household
O Language other than English spoken in home

Geographic/Community Variables

● Region of country
O State of residence
O County/city/MSA of residence
● Size/type of community
O Zip code
O Telephone area code
● Metropolitan residence
O Neighborhood quality
O Local labor market

Stage in Family Life Cycle

● Age of adult respondent or spouse/partner
● Marital status of adult respondent or spouse/partner
● Employment status of adult respondent or spouse/partner
O Presence of own children in household
O Age of youngest own child in household
O Age of oldest own child in household
● Existence of own children who have left home[2]
O Intention to have (more) children in future

Family Functioning
- ○ Family activities or time use
- ○ Community involvement (civic, religious, recreational)
- ○ Family communication patterns
- ○ Family decision-making
- ○ Marital conflict
- ○ Marital happiness/satisfaction
- ○ Parent-child conflict
- ○ History of marital separations
- ○ History of family violence
- ○ History of marital counselling

CHARACTERISTICS OF ADULT FAMILY MEMBERS

Adult Respondent or Reference Person	Current Spouse in HH	Current or Former Spouse Not in HH	
●	○	○	Age
●	○	○	Gender
●	○	○	Race
●	○	○	Hispanic origin
○	○	○	Other origin/ethnicity
○	○	○	Religious affiliation
○	○	○	Religious participation
○	○	○	Country of birth
○	○	○	Immigrant status
○	○	○	English fluency
●	○	○	Current marital status
○	○	○	Marital history
○	○	○	Cohabitation status
○	○	○	Cohabitation history
●	○	○	Parental status
●	○	○	Number children ever born/sired
○	○	○	Age at first birth
○	○	○	Age of youngest child
○	○	○	Children living elsewhere
○	○	○	Duration at current address
○	○	○	Residential mobility
●	○	○	Educational attainment
○	○	○	Degrees attained
○	○	○	GED or regular HS diploma
○	○	○	Current enrollment
●	○	○	Current employment status
○	○	○	Hours usually worked (ft/pt)
○	○	○	Weeks worked
○	○	○	Annual employment pattern
●	○	○	Main occupation
○	○	○	Earnings
○	○	○	Wage rate
○	○	○	Payment of child support
○	○	○	Aptitude or achievement score
●	○	○	Health/disability status
○	○	○	Self-esteem
○	○	○	Locus of control or efficacy
○	○	○	Depression or subjective well-being
○	○	○	Work-related attitudes

175

CHARACTERISTICS OF CHILD FAMILY MEMBERS
Sample size: 766 adopted children[3]

Reference Child or Youth Respondent	Other Children (in HH)	
O	O	Age
●	O	Month and year of birth
O	O	Gender
O	O	Race
O	O	Hispanic origin
O	O	Other origin/ethnicity
O	O	Religious affiliation
O	O	Religious participation
O	O	Country of birth
●	O	Immigrant status
O	O	English fluency
●	O	Exact relationship to adult family members
O	O	Exact relationship to other children in HH
O	O	Marital status/history
O	O	Parental status/history
O	O	Current enrollment in regular school
O	O	Current enrollment in preschool/daycare
O	O	Highest grade completed
O	O	Grade now enrolled
O	O	Employment status/history
●	O	Health status
●	O	Handicapping conditions
O	O	Grade repetition
O	O	Aptitude or achievement score
O	O	Pregnancy/birth history
O	O	Psychological well-being
O	O	Delinquency

NOTES
1. Only 566 of the surveyed women aged 20-54 had ever adopted one or more children.
2. Existence of adopted children who left home.
3. "Child" may be older than 18 by the 1987 survey date. While 566 women had adopted a child, information was obtained on 766 adopted children.

NHIS—1981 Child Health Supplement

PURPOSE The 1981 Child Health Supplement (CHS) to the National Health Interview Survey (NHIS) was designed to provide more detailed information on the physical and mental health, school performance, and behavior of children than provided in the core survey. In particular, it covered topics of special relevance to children, such as prenatal care, social and motor development, and behavior problems.

SPONSORSHIP The 1981 CHS was designed and funded by the National Center for Health Statistics. Advice on questionnaire content was obtained from other health agencies and from a panel of nongovernment researchers convened by the National Institute of Child Health and Human Development (NICHD). Interviewing was conducted by the same permanent staff of trained interviewers and supervisors employed by the Bureau of the Census for the core NHIS.

DESIGN The Child Health Supplement is a component of the National Health Interview Survey, the design for which is described in a separate write-up. For the CHS, additional information was gathered for one child aged 0-17 in each family having such a child. In families having more than one eligible child, one was selected at random. A knowledgeable adult member of the household, usually the biological mother, served as a proxy respondent for each selected child. As with the core survey, interviewing was conducted continually throughout the year. Altogether, 15,416 children were included in the 1981 CHS.

PERIODICITY The first Child Health Supplement was conducted in 1981. Related earlier surveys providing some comparable data are Cycle II and Cycle III of the National Health and Nutrition Examination Surveys. A second Child Health Supplement was conducted in 1988.

CONTENT The 1981 CHS covered the following topics: the exact relationship between the child and each other household member; child care arrangements; contact with biological parents who live outside the household; the biological mother's marital history; residential mobility; motor and social development; circumstances surrounding birth; health conditions at birth; prenatal care; breastfeeding; hospitalizations and surgery; health condition history; height and weight; use of medications; progress and behavior in school; need for or use of psychological counseling; behavior problems; social effects of ill health; and sleep and seat belt habits. CHS data are linked to data from the core NHIS survey, so that additional individual data on the children as well as background data on the family are available.

LIMITATIONS The information in the 1981 CHS was provided by the biological parent or the adult in the household most knowledgeable about the health of the child. While such a respondent may be most appropriate for some topics and for all younger children, older children may be better able to provide some information on their own account. Only one child is selected in each family to be the subject of the CHS interview. This situation precludes analyses of intra-familial variations in the physical and mental health of children, or of the relationship between the health of one child and that of other children in the household. Moreover, no information is collected on family dynamics (such as levels of conflict or stress). Thus, although researchers are beginning to recognize the role that families play in the health of individual members, such results cannot be studied with the CHS. In addition, many of the limitations described in the write-up on the National Health Interview Survey apply to these data as well, for example the difficulty of recalling illness over the past year, and reporting biases associated with race or familiarity with diagnostic labels. Overall, the sample of children covered in the Supplement is relatively large. However, many questions are relevant for only certain age ranges. For such questions, the sample size is more modest (just under 900 per year of age).

AVAILABILITY A working paper by Gail Poe describing the design and procedures of the 1981 CHS is available from the

National Center for Health Statistics. The questionnaire has been published in *Vital and Health Statistics*, Series 10, No. 141. A public use tape is available from:

>Division of Health Interview Statistics
>National Center for Health Statistics
>6525 Belcrest Road
>Hyattsville, MD 20782
>301/436-7089

Contact:

>Gerry E. Hendershot, Ph.D.
>Chief, Illness and Disability Statistics Branch
>Division of Health Interview Statistics/NCHS
>6525 Belcrest Road, Rm. 850
>Hyattsville, MD 20782
>301/436-7089

PUBLICATIONS

Gortmacher, S.L., Walker, D.K., Weitzman, M., & Sobal, A.M. (1990). Chronic conditions, socioeconomic risks, and behavioral problems in children and adolescents. *Pediatrics, 85,* 267-276.

Poe, G.S. (1986). *Design and procedures for the 1981 Child Health Supplement to the National Health Interview Survey* (Working paper series). Hyattsville, MD: National Center for Health Statistics.

Zill, N. (1988). Behavior, achievement, and health problems among children in stepfamilies: Findings from a national survey of child health. In E.M. Hetherington & J. Arasteh (Eds.), *The impact of divorce, single parenting, and step-parenting on children* (pp. 325-368). Hillsdale, NJ: Lawrence Erlbaum.

NHIS-1981 Child Health Supplement
Year of Questionnaire: 1981
Sample size: 15,416 children aged 0-17
FAMILY LEVEL CHARACTERISTICS

Family Composition
- Full roster of household members (first name, age, sex, and relationship to reference person of each member)
○ Partial roster of household members
- Number of adults in household
- Number of children in household
○ Approximate relationship of family members to householder, child, or one another
- Exact relationship of family members to householder, child, or one another
○ Information about part-time household member
○ Information about family members no longer living in household
○ Information about relatives who live nearby but not in household

Socioeconomic
- Total family income
- Number of persons who depend on family income
○ Sources of income
○ Income amounts identified separately by source
○ Poverty status
- Welfare status
○ Food Stamps receipt
○ Child support receipt
- Medicaid coverage
○ Private health insurance
○ Home ownership/renters
○ Assets (other than home ownership)
○ Public housing status
- Telephone in household
○ Language other than English spoken in home

Geographic/Community Variables
- Region of country
○ State of residence
- County/city/MSA of residence
- Size/type of community
○ Zip code
○ Telephone area code
- Metropolitan residence
○ Neighborhood quality
○ Local labor market

Stage in Family Life Cycle
- Age of adult respondent or spouse/partner
- Marital status of adult respondent or spouse/partner
- Employment status of adult respondent or spouse/partner
○ Presence of own children in household
○ Age of youngest own child in household
○ Age of oldest own child in household
○ Existence of own children who have left home
○ Intention to have (more) children in future

180

familiarity with diagnostic labels. Overall, the sample of children covered in the CHS is relatively large. However, many questions are relevant for only certain age ranges. For such questions, the sample size is more modest (about 1,000 per single year of age).

AVAILABILITY Data from the National Health Interview Survey, including its special health topics, are published by the National Center for Health Statistics in Vital and Health Statistics, Series 10. Public use tapes for the special health topics are available from the Systems and Programming Branch, Division of Health Interview Statistics, NCHS

Contact:

>Gerry E. Hendershot, Ph.D.
>Illness and Disability Statistics Branch
>Division of Health Interview Statistics
>National Center for Health Statistics
>6525 Belcrest Rd., Room 850
>Hyattsville, MD 20782
>301/436-7089

The data are also available from:

>Inter-University Consortium for Political
> and Social Research
>Institute for Social Research
>P.O. Box 1248
>Ann Arbor, MI 48106-1248
>313/763-5010

PUBLICATIONS

Dawson, D.A. (1991). Family structure and children's health and well-being: Data from the 1988 National Health Interview Survey on Child Health. *Journal of Marriage and the Family, 53,* 573-584.

Dawson, D.A., & Cain, V.S. (1990). Childcare arrangements: Health of our nation's children, United States, 1988. *Advance Data from Vital and Health Statistics, 187.*

Hardy, A. (1991). Incidence and impact of selected infectious diseases in childhood. *Vital and Health Statistics, 10*(180).

Overpeck, M., & Moss, A.J. (1991). Children's exposure to environmental cigarette smoke before and after birth: Health of our nation's children, United States, 1988. *Advance Data from Vital and Health Statistics, 202.*

Zill, N., & Schoenborn, C.A. (1990). Health of our nation's children: Developmental, learning, and emotional problems, United States, 1988. *Advance Data from Vital and Health Statistics, 190.*

NHIS—1988 Child Health Supplement
Year of Questionnaire: 1988
Sample size: 17,110 children aged 0-17
FAMILY LEVEL CHARACTERISTICS

Family Composition
- ● Full roster of household members (first name, age, sex, and relationship to reference person of each member)
- ○ Partial roster of household members
- ● Number of adults in household
- ● Number of children in household
- ○ Approximate relationship of family members to householder, child, or one another
- ● Exact relationship of family members to householder, child, or one another
- ● Information about part-time household member[1]
- ○ Information about family members no longer living in household
- ○ Information about relatives who live nearby but not in household

Socioeconomic
- ● Total family income
- ○ Number of persons who depend on family income
- ○ Sources of income
- ○ Income amounts identified separately by source
- ● Poverty status
- ● Welfare status
- ○ Food Stamps receipt
- ○ Child support receipt
- ● Medicaid coverage
- ● Private health insurance
- ○ Home ownership/renters
- ○ Assets (other than home ownership)
- ○ Public housing status
- ● Telephone in household
- ○ Language other than English spoken in home

Geographic/Community Variables
- ● Region of country
- ○ State of residence
- ○ County/city/MSA of residence
- ● Size/type of community
- ○ Zip code
- ○ Telephone area code
- ● Metropolitan residence
- ○ Neighborhood quality
- ○ Local labor market

Stage in Family Life Cycle
- ● Age of adult respondent or spouse/partner
- ● Marital status of adult respondent or spouse/partner
- ● Employment status of adult respondent or spouse/partner
- ● Presence of own children in household[2]
- ● Age of youngest own child in household[2]
- ● Age of oldest own child in household[2]
- ● Existence of own children who have left home
- ○ Intention to have (more) children in future

Family Functioning
○ Family activities or time use
○ Community involvement (civic, religious, recreational)
○ Family communication patterns
○ Family decision-making
○ Marital conflict
○ Marital happiness/satisfaction
○ Parent-child conflict
○ History of marital separations
○ History of family violence
○ History of marital counselling

CHARACTERISTICS OF ADULT FAMILY MEMBERS

Adult Respondent or Reference Person	Current Spouse in HH	Current or Former Spouse Not in HH	
●	●	○	Age
●	●	●	Gender
●	●	○	Race
●	●	○	Hispanic origin
○	○	○	Other origin/ethnicity
○	○	○	Religious affiliation
○	○	○	Religious participation
○	○	○	Country of birth
○	○	○	Immigrant status
○	○	○	English fluency
●	●	○	Current marital status
●	○	○	Marital history[2]
○	○	○	Cohabitation status
○	○	○	Cohabitation history
●	●	●	Parental status[3]
●	○	○	Number children ever born/sired[3]
●	○	○	Age at first birth[3]
●	○	○	Age of youngest child
●	○	○	Children living elsewhere
○	○	○	Duration at current address
○	○	○	Residential mobility
●	●	○	Educational attainment
○	○	○	Degrees attained
○	○	○	GED or regular HS diploma
●	●	○	Current enrollment
●	●	○	Current employment status
●	○	○	Hours usually worked (ft/pt)[3]
○	○	○	Weeks worked
○	○	○	Annual employment pattern
●	●	○	Main occupation
○	○	○	Earnings
○	○	○	Wage rate
○	○	○	Payment of child support
○	○	○	Aptitude or achievement score
●	●	○	Health/disability status
○	○	○	Self-esteem
○	○	○	Locus of control or efficacy
○	○	○	Depression or subjective well-being
○	○	○	Work-related attitudes

CHARACTERISTICS OF CHILD FAMILY MEMBERS

Reference Child or Youth Respondent	Other Children (in HH)	
●	●	Age
●	●	Month and year of birth
●	●	Gender
●	●	Race
●	●	Hispanic origin
○	○	Other origin/ethnicity
○	○	Religious affiliation
○	○	Religious participation
○	○	Country of birth
○	○	Immigrant status
○	○	English fluency
●	○	Exact relationship to adult family members
●	○	Exact relationship to other children in HH
●	●	Marital status/history
○	○	Parental status/history
●	●	Current enrollment in regular school
●	○	Current enrollment in preschool/daycare
●	●	Highest grade completed
●	○	Grade now enrolled
○	○	Employment status/history
●	●	Health status
●	●	Handicapping conditions
●	○	Grade repetition
○	○	Aptitude or achievement score
●	○	Pregnancy/birth history
●	○	Psychological well-being
○	○	Delinquency

NOTES
1. Armed Services members.
2. Available if adult respondent is child's parent.
3. Available if adult respondent is child's mother.

NHIS—Health Promotion and Disease Prevention Supplements

PURPOSE The Health Promotion and Disease Prevention (HPDP) Supplements to the National Health Interview Survey (NHIS) were designed to track the nation's progress toward several of the health objectives established by the U.S. Public Health Service in its 1980 report *Promoting Health, Preventing Disease: Objectives for the Nation*. The HPDP provides national estimates of people's understanding and practice of a variety of health-related behaviors. In 1991 the HPDP supplement was revised to reflect the new national goals outlined in the Public Health Service's 1990 report, *Healthy People 2000*.

SPONSORSHIP Several federal agencies provided partial funding for or participated in the planning and development of the 1990 HPDP. Data were collected as a supplement to the NHIS (see separate write-up), a continuous, nationwide, household interview survey of the civilian non-institutionalized population of the United States. The NHIS and supplements are conducted for the National Center for Health Statistics by the interviewing staff of the U.S. Bureau of the Census.

DESIGN The HPDP Supplement is a component of the NHIS, the design for which is described in the write-up for that survey. For the HPDP, additional information was gathered from one randomly selected adult (18 years or older) per family in the 1990 NHIS sample. The sample person provided information about him/herself for the bulk of the supplement, and provided injury control and child health and safety data about every child in the household. Information about smoking during pregnancy was collected from every woman in the household aged 18-44 who had given birth in the last five years or was currently pregnant. As with the core survey, interviewing was conducted continually throughout the year. Questionnaires were completed by 41,104 people, an estimated 83.4% of eligible respondents.

PERIODICITY Health Promotion and Disease Promotion supplements are added to the NHIS periodically but not regularly. The first HPDP was conducted in 1985 and repeated in 1990. The HPDP was redesigned in 1991.

CONTENT The 1990 HPDP asked about behaviors and opinions related to the following topics: general health habits, mammography, radon, cardiovascular disease, stress, exercise, smoking, alcohol use, and dental care. In addition, the sample person was asked to identify all women aged 18-44 in the household who were currently pregnant or had given birth within the past five years. All such identified house-hold members were administered the questions on pregnancy and smoking. Furthermore, information on injury control and child health and safety was obtained from the sample person about every child in the household. For each question concerning children, the exact relationship between the child and the HPDP respondent was obtained. For 82% of the children, data were based on parental report. Content of the 1985 HPDP was similar but not identical to the 1990 HPDP.

The 1991 HPDP contained questions about unintentional injuries, pregnancy and smoking, child health, environmental health, tobacco, nutrition, immunization and infectious diseases, occupational safety and health, heart disease and stroke, other chronic and disabling conditions, clinical and preventive services, physical activity and fitness, alcohol, oral health, and mental health.

Each record in the HPDP data file also contains the NHIS person record from the core survey, so health promotion and disease prevention information can be linked to socio-demographic characteristics of the respondent and other household members.

LIMITATIONS The fact that data on most HPDP topics are collected about one household member only (the sample person) precludes analyses of intra-familial variations in health promotion and disease prevention behaviors and knowledge. However, some family-level description is possible by linking HPDP data to data from the core survey. Data on injury control and child health and safety is provided by the sample respondent, who is usually the child's parent. While such a respondent may be most appropriate for some topics and for all younger children, older children may be better able to provide some information on their own. Furthermore, data obtained from respondents who are not the child's parent may be less accurate than for other children.

AVAILABILITY The data are distributed on three separate tapes, one each for the sample person survey, the child health and safety survey, and the smoking and pregnancy survey. The questionnaire has been published in Vital and Health Statistics, Series 10, No. 181. A Series 10 report tabulating the 1990 HPDP data will be available in March 1993. An *Advance Data* report showing marginals for every HPDP variable by age, sex, and race will be available around December 1993. Public use tapes for the 1990 HPDP and for the 1990 core NHIS are available from:

> National Center for Health Statistics
> Division of Health Interview Statistics
> Systems and Programming Branch
> 6525 Belcrest Road, Rm. 850
> Hyattsville, MD 20782
> 301/436-7087

[Data from the 1991 Year 2000 Objectives supplement to the NHIS are also available on public use tapes. This supplement contains many comparable items to HPDP, and files can be combined to increase sample size.]

Contact:

> Gerry E. Hendershot, Ph.D.
> Chief, Illness and Disability Statistics Branch
> Division of Health Interview Statistics/NCHS
> 6525 Belcrest Road, Room 850
> Hyattsville, MD 20782
> 301/436-7089

NHIS—Health Promotion and Disease Prevention Supplement

Year of Questionnaire: 1990
Sample size: 41,104 persons aged 18 and older

FAMILY-LEVEL CHARACTERISTICS

Family Composition[1]

- ○ Full roster of household members (first name, age, sex, and relationship to reference person of each member)
- ○ Partial roster of household members
- ○ Number of adults in household
- ● Number of children in household[2]
- ○ Approximate relationship of family members to householder, child, or one another
- ○ Exact relationship of family members to householder, child, or one another
- ○ Information about part-time household member
- ○ Information about family members no longer living in household
- ○ Information about relatives who live nearby but not in household

Socioeconomic

- ● Total family income
- ○ Number of persons who depend on family income
- ○ Sources of income
- ○ Income amounts identified separately by source
- ● Poverty status
- ○ Welfare status
- ○ Food Stamps receipt
- ○ Child support receipt
- ○ Medicaid coverage
- ○ Private health insurance
- ○ Home ownership/renters
- ○ Assets (other than home ownership)
- ○ Public housing status
- ● Telephone in household
- ○ Language other than English spoken in home

Geographic/Community Variables

- ● Region of country
- ○ State of residence
- ○ County/city/MSA of residence
- ● Size/type of community
- ○ Zip code
- ○ Telephone area code
- ● Metropolitan residence
- ○ Neighborhood quality
- ○ Local labor market

Stage in Family Life Cycle

- ● Age of adult respondent or spouse/partner
- ● Marital status of adult respondent or spouse/partner
- ● Employment status of adult respondent or spouse/partner
- ● Presence of own children in household
- ● Age of youngest own child in household
- ● Age of oldest own child in household
- ○ Existence of own children who have left home
- ○ Intention to have (more) children in future

193

Family Functioning
○ Family activities or time use
○ Community involvement (civic, religious, recreational)
○ Family communication patterns
○ Family decision-making
○ Marital conflict
○ Marital happiness/satisfaction
○ Parent-child conflict
○ History of marital separations
○ History of family violence
○ History of marital counselling

CHARACTERISTICS OF ADULT FAMILY MEMBERS
Sample size: 41,104[3]

Adult Respondent or Reference Person	Current Spouse in HH	Current or Former Spouse Not in HH	
●	○	○	Age
●	○	○	Gender
●	○	○	Race
●	○	○	Hispanic origin
○	○	○	Other origin/ethnicity
○	○	○	Religious affiliation
○	○	○	Religious participation
○	○	○	Country of birth
○	○	○	Immigrant status
○	○	○	English fluency
●	○	○	Current marital status
○	○	○	Marital history
○	○	○	Cohabitation status
○	○	○	Cohabitation history
○	○	○	Parental status
○	○	○	Number children ever born/sired
○	○	○	Age at first birth
○	○	○	Age of youngest child
○	○	○	Children living elsewhere
○	○	○	Duration at current address
○	○	○	Residential mobility
●	○	○	Educational attainment
○	○	○	Degrees attained
○	○	○	GED or regular HS diploma
●	○	○	Current enrollment
●	○	○	Current employment status
○	○	○	Hours usually worked
○	○	○	Weeks worked
○	○	○	Annual employment pattern
●	○	○	Main occupation
○	○	○	Earnings
○	○	○	Wage rate
○	○	○	Payment of child support
○	○	○	Aptitude or achievement score
●	○	○	Health/disability status
○	○	○	Self-esteem
○	○	○	Locus of control or efficacy
○	○	○	Depression or subjective well-being
○	○	○	Work-related attitudes

CHARACTERISTICS OF CHILD FAMILY MEMBERS
Sample size: 33,243

Reference Child or Youth Respondent	Other Children (in HH)	
O	●	Age
O	●	Month and year of birth
O	●	Gender
O	●	Race
O	●	Hispanic origin
O	O	Other origin/ethnicity
O	O	Religious affiliation
O	O	Religious participation
O	O	Country of birth
O	O	Immigrant status
O	O	English fluency
O	O	Exact relationship to adult family members
O	O	Exact relationship to other children in HH
O	●	Marital status/history
O	O	Parental status/history
O	O	Current enrollment in regular school
O	O	Current enrollment in preschool/daycare
O	●	Highest grade completed
O	O	Grade now enrolled
O	O	Employment status/history
O	●	Health status
O	●	Handicapping conditions
O	O	Grade repetition
O	O	Aptitude or achievement score
O	O	Pregnancy/birth history
O	O	Psychological well-being
O	O	Delinquency

NOTES

1. Family characteristics are available by linking HPDP data to NHIS core survey data.

2. Available on child safety and health file.

3. For pregnancy and smoking section, N=25,839 women.

National Hospital Discharge Survey

PURPOSE The National Hospital Discharge Survey (NHDS) is designed to provide national estimates of the inpatient utilization of non-federal short-stay hospitals in the United States. The survey focuses on describing characteristics of patients, their diagnoses and surgical procedures, lengths of stay, as well as information on the types of hospitals in which they are treated.

SPONSORSHIP The survey is designed and funded by The National Center for Health Statistics (NCHS). The U.S. Bureau of the Census provides assistance in survey development and data collection.

DESIGN The survey is based on a multi-stage stratified probability sample of patient discharges from non-federal short-stay hospitals (length of stay less than 30 days) in the 50 states and the District of Columbia. All military and veteran's hospitals and hospital units within existing health institutions are excluded from the sampling frame. The original NHDS sample included 6,695 short-stay hospitals listed in the 1963 National Master Facility Inventory developed by NCHS. The Inventory is a list of all institutions in the United States established to provide medical, nursing, or personal care to individuals. Hospitals that opened after 1963 were sampled periodically from lists of hospitals provided by the American Hospital Association and added to the original NHDS sample

In 1988 the NHDS was redesigned to enhance the efficiency of data collection by linking it with other NCHS surveys. The sampling frame consisted of hospitals contained in the April 1987 National Health Interview Survey (NHIS) sampling frame. The definition of a hospital was also modified slightly to include general medical, surgical, and children's hospitals, regardless of average length of stay. The 1988 NHDS sample included with certainty all hospitals with 1,000 or more beds or 40,000 or more discharges per year. Hospitals with fewer beds or discharges were sampled via a three-stage stratified design. In the first stage, a subsample of PSUs from the NHIS was selected based on population size and geographic location. In the second stage, hospitals were stratified by region, PSU, and level of data automation.

Next, within each participating hospital, a systematic sample of daily discharges was selected. All discharges, irrespective of patient age or any other specific characteristic, were sampled. The records were then abstracted by trained representatives of the NCHS. The final sample was weighted to produce national and regional estimates. Prior to 1980 this weight was computed using the noninstitutionalized civilian sample. After 1980 the civilian resident population was used. This change primarily affects rates for persons 65 or older and has minimal effects on any estimates for children. In 1989 a total of 408 hospitals participated in the NHDS, representing 233,000 hospital discharges.

PERIODICITY The survey has been conducted continuously (except for 1969) since 1965. Published estimates are available through 1990.

CONTENT Information about the patient's personal characteristics and each episode of hospitalization are collected. Patient data include birth date, sex, race, ethnicity (since 1979), residence (using zip code) and marital status. Data concerning hospitalizations cover dates of stay, diagnoses, surgical and diagnostic procedures, expected sources of payment for each hospitalization, and disposition of the patient at discharge. The same data are collected on all patients, regardless of age or race/ethnicity. The name of the hospital, medical record number and zip code are not available for public use to preserve anonymity.

LIMITATIONS As noted in the corresponding checklist, the number of family level indicators collected is limited. The data available on these items can only imply family level information. Furthermore, while the NHDS shares the same sampling frame as the NHIS, information in the NHIS relevant to family health cannot be linked with hospital discharge information on the NHDS. Thus, family history concerning utilization of hospital-based services or health status based on conditions requiring hospitalization cannot be determined. Also, the unit of analysis is the hospital discharge. Thus, a respondent with multiple admissions may be represented several times within the data set, and data cannot be collapsed to calculate person level estimates.

Although race/ethnicity is collected, it is not consistently present on discharge abstracts across all hospitals sampled. Thus, analyses by race are limited. Information on newborns has been collected since the late 1960s, although data were not published until 1981. The published tabulations that are available, however, have limited age breaks for children. Calculations using more detailed age breaks are available from unpublished tables and from public data tapes that could be made available upon request.

Changes made to the sampling frame in 1988 may affect trend analyses that may be conducted using these data.

AVAILABILITY Data from the survey are published in Series 13 of the *Vital and Health Statistics* publication series from NCHS. (Example: *Detailed Diagnoses and Procedures, National Hospital Discharge Survey*, 1989, Series 13, No. 108.)

Machine-readable data files of the survey are available for individual years from the National Technical Information Service and from the National Center for Health Statistics. The latest year currently available is 1990. Unpublished data in tabular form is also available for a fee conditional upon the type of information and the format requested. Data are available on diskette and magnetic tape.

Contact:

Robert Pokras, Chief
Hospital Care Statistics Branch
National Center for Health Statistics
6525 Belcrest Road, Rm. 952
Hyattsville, Maryland 20782
301/436-7125

PUBLICATIONS

Haupt, B.J., & Kozak, L.J. (1992). Estimates from two survey designs. *Vital and Health Statistics, 13*(111). Hyattsville, MD: National Center for Health Statistics.

National Center for Health Statistics. (1990). National Hospital Discharge Survey: 1988 summary. *Advance Data from Vital and Health Statistics, 185.*

Pokras, R., Kozak, L.J., McCarthy, E., & Graves, E.J. (1990). Trends in hospital utilization, 1965-1986. *American Journal of Public Health, 80*(4), 488-490.

National Hospital Discharge Survey
Year of Questionnaire: 1989   Sample size: 408 hospitals/233,000 discharges
FAMILY-LEVEL CHARACTERISTICS

Family Composition
○ Full roster of household members (first name, age, sex, and relationship to reference person of each member)
○ Partial roster of household members
○ Number of adults in household
○ Number of children in household
○ Approximate relationship of family members to householder, child, or one another
○ Exact relationship of family members to householder, child, or one another
○ Information about part-time household member
○ Information about family members no longer living in household
○ Information about relatives who live nearby but not in household

Socioeconomic
○ Total family income
○ Number of persons who depend on family income
○ Sources of income
○ Income amounts identified separately by source
○ Poverty status
○ Welfare status
○ Food Stamps receipt
○ Child support receipt
● Medicaid coverage[1]
● Private health insurance[1]
○ Home ownership/renters
○ Assets (other than home ownership)
○ Public housing status
○ Telephone in household
○ Language other than English spoken in home

Geographic/Community Variables
● Region of country[2]
○ State of residence
○ County/city/MSA of residence
○ Size/type of community
○ Zip code
○ Telephone area code
○ Metropolitan residence
○ Neighborhood quality
○ Local labor market

Stage in Family Life Cycle
○ Age of adult respondent or spouse/partner
○ Marital status of adult respondent or spouse/partner
○ Employment status of adult respondent or spouse/partner
○ Presence of own children in household
○ Age of youngest own child in household
○ Age of oldest own child in household
○ Existence of own children who have left home
○ Intention to have (more) children in future

200

Family Functioning
- ○ Family activities or time use
- ○ Community involvement (civic, religious, recreational)
- ○ Family communication patterns
- ○ Family decision-making
- ○ Marital conflict
- ○ Marital happiness/satisfaction
- ○ Parent-child conflict
- ○ History of marital separations
- ○ History of family violence
- ○ History of marital counselling

CHARACTERISTICS OF ADULT FAMILY MEMBERS

Adult Respondent or Reference Person	Current Spouse in HH	Current or Former Spouse Not in HH	
●	○	○	Age
●	○	○	Gender
●	○	○	Race
●	○	○	Hispanic origin
○	○	○	Other origin/ethnicity
○	○	○	Religious affiliation
○	○	○	Religious participation
○	○	○	Country of birth
○	○	○	Immigrant status
○	○	○	English fluency
●	○	○	Current marital status
○	○	○	Marital history
○	○	○	Cohabitation status
○	○	○	Cohabitation history
○	○	○	Parental status
○	○	○	Number children ever born/sired
○	○	○	Age at first birth
○	○	○	Age of youngest child
○	○	○	Children living elsewhere
○	○	○	Duration at current address
○	○	○	Residential mobility
○	○	○	Educational attainment
○	○	○	Degrees attained
○	○	○	GED or regular HS diploma
○	○	○	Current enrollment
○	○	○	Current employment status
○	○	○	Hours usually worked (ft/pt)
○	○	○	Weeks worked
○	○	○	Annual employment pattern
○	○	○	Main occupation
○	○	○	Earnings
○	○	○	Wage rate
○	○	○	Payment of child support
○	○	○	Aptitude or achievement score
●	○	○	Health/disability status[3]
○	○	○	Self-esteem
○	○	○	Locus of control or efficacy
○	○	○	Depression or subjective well-being
○	○	○	Work-related attitudes

CHARACTERISTICS OF CHILD FAMILY MEMBERS

Reference Child or Youth Respondent	Other Children (in HH)	
●	○	Age
●	○	Month and year of birth
●	○	Gender
●	○	Race
●	○	Hispanic origin
○	○	Other origin/ethnicity
○	○	Religious affiliation
○	○	Religious participation
○	○	Country of birth
○	○	Immigrant status
○	○	English fluency
○	○	Exact relationship to adult family members
○	○	Exact relationship to other children in HH
●	○	Marital status/history
○	○	Parental status/history
○	○	Current enrollment in regular school
○	○	Current enrollment in preschool/daycare
○	○	Highest grade completed
○	○	Grade now enrolled
○	○	Employment status/history
○	○	Health status
○	○	Handicapping conditions
○	○	Grade repetition
○	○	Aptitude or achievement score
○	○	Pregnancy/birth history
○	○	Psychological well-being
○	○	Delinquency

NOTES
1. Expected sources of payment for hospitalization.
2. Region of country where hospital is located.
3. Conditions diagnosed requiring hospitalization.

National Household Education Survey

PURPOSE The National Household Education Survey (NHES) is a data collection system designed to provide information on education-related issues that are best addressed through contacts with households rather than with schools or other educational institutions. The survey monitors participation in adult education and the care arrangements and educational experiences of young children. Other topics the survey has or will cover are school safety and discipline, parental involvement in their children's schooling, and measures of citizenship and civic participation in children and adults. The survey collects information about family characteristics to relate these characteristics to data on the program participation and school performance of family members.

SPONSORSHIP The NHES is sponsored by the National Center for Education Statistics (NCES) of the U.S. Department of Education. The survey is conducted by Westat, Inc. under contract to NCES.

DESIGN The NHES is a telephone survey of the non-institutionalized civilian population of the U.S. The data are weighted to permit estimates that apply to the entire population, including persons living in households without a telephone. Households are selected using random digit dialing (RDD) methods. Data are collected using computer assisted telephone interviewing (CATI) procedures. These procedures permit more complex interviews to be conducted and enable survey results to be made available shortly after completion of fieldwork.

Between 60,000 and 75,000 households are screened for the annual surveys. Based on information gathered in the screening interviews, one or more household members may be selected to complete more extended interviews on specific topics that vary from year to year. In the 1991 NHES, for example, parents or guardians of 14,000 3- to 8-year-old children were questioned about their children's early educational and nonparental care experiences. In the same year, 9,800 persons aged 16 years and older who were identified as having participated in an adult education activity in the previous 12 months were questioned about their courses. Another 2,800 nonparticipants were questioned about barriers to participation. Extended interviews typically run 15-20 minutes. Within several weeks of the original survey, partial reinterviews are conducted with a subsample of respondents to gather information on overall data quality and the stability of specific responses.

Response rates are well above those typically achieved in commercial polls, but somewhat lower than those obtained in household surveys conducted by the Census Bureau. In the NHES:91, for example, the screener response rate was 81%. Ninety-five percent of those screened and found eligible completed the early childhood extended interview; 85% of those eligible for the adult education component completed that interview. Thus, the composite coverage rates were 77% for the early childhood survey and 69% for the adult education component.

PERIODICITY The NHES was first implemented in the spring of 1991. Beginning in 1993, it will be conducted annually with a rotating topical focus. In 1993, the early childhood component focuses on school readiness, while families with children in the third through twelfth grades are being interviewed about school safety and discipline. NHES:94 will be similar to the 1991 survey, covering participation in early childhood programs and adult education. In 1995, the early childhood component will explore parental involvement, while measures of citizenship and civic participation will be gathered for older students and adults. NHES:96 will have modules similar to those in the 1993 survey.

CONTENT The NHES is designed to provide a current cross-section of the population rather than an in-depth research data base. However, the large sample sizes and fairly extensive set of household and respondent descriptors permit a range of family-related issues to be addressed. For example, family characteristics can be used to predict adults' participation in continuing education programs or preschoolers' participation in early childhood programs. Family attributes can be related to indicators of the child's school performance and behavior, such as current grade placement, the parent's estimate of the child's standing in class, the occurrence of learning or conduct problems that resulted in the parent being called in for a conference, the child having had to repeat a grade, and the child being suspended or expelled from school. Family characteristics can also be correlated with educational activities in the home, such as reading, playing games, or doing household chores or errands with the child, regulating the child's television watching, and taking the child on outings to libraries, museums, or shows.

In the school safety and discipline component of the NHES:93, both parents and students are asked for their perceptions of discipline and safety problems at the youth's school, their aspirations for the youth's education, their satisfaction with various aspects of the youth's current schooling, and parental standards with regard to matters such as the youth's smoking and drinking. Thus, the degree of agreement between parent and youth, as well as their separate views and feelings, can be analyzed as a function of family attributes.

Family descriptors available in the NHES include the race and Hispanic origin of each parent, their education levels and employment patterns, family income, whether both birth parents, a single parent, or a parent and stepparent are present in the household, and whether the parent's first language was a language other than English. The specific respondent and family characteristics provided vary from year to year and from component to component within a given year. In the NHES:93 early childhood component, the exact relationship of the subject child to other family members is specified, and retrospective data are furnished on the mother's employment history and welfare dependence during the child's early years.

LIMITATIONS Because most of the data collected in the NHES are cross-sectional in nature, causal links are more difficult to establish than with longitudinal studies. Retrospectively collected data are subject to recall biases. Some responses about parent involvement and educational activities in the home may be biased in socially desirable directions because respondents are told that the data are being collected for the Department of Education. Information about the child's program participation and school performance are provided by the parent, who may not be well informed about program characteristics or may take an unduly positive view of the child's academic accomplishments. Although the data have been weighted to compensate for families who do not have telephones, the weights may not be fully effective when the focus is on low-income or minority subpopulations with high proportions of households without a telephone.

AVAILABILITY Public use files for each year's NHES are available within a year from the end of data collection, from:

> Data Systems Branch
> Office of Educational Research and Improvement
> U.S.Department of Education
> 555 New Jersey Avenue, NW
> Washington, DC 20208-5725
> 202/219-1847

For substantive questions, contact:

> Kathryn A. Chandler, NHES Project Officer
> National Center for Education Statistics
> 555 New Jersey Avenue, NW
> Washington, DC 20208-5651
> 202/219-1767

PUBLICATIONS

Brick, M.J., Chandler, K., Collins, M.A., Celebuski, C.A., Ha, P.C., Hausken, E.G., Nolin, M.J., Owings, J., Squadere, T.A., & Wernimont, J. (1992). *National Household Education Survey of 1991: Preprimary and primary data files user's manual* (NCES 92-057). Washington, DC: U.S. Department of Education, National Center for Education Statistics.

Brick, M.J., Chandler, K., Collins, M.A., Celebuski, C.A., Ha, P.C., Hausken, E.G., Nolin, M.J., Owings, J., Squadere, T.A., & Wernimont, J. (1991). *1991 National Household Education Survey: Methodology report*. Washington, DC: U.S. Department of Education, National Center for Education Statistics.

Collins, M. (1991). *Early childhood experiences of 1- to 8-year-olds.* Report prepared for U.S. Department of Education, National Center for Education Statistics, Washington, DC.

Collins, M. & Brick, J.M. (1993). *Parent reports on children's academic progress and school adjustment in the National Household Education Survey.* Presented at the 1993 Mid-Winter Meetings of the American Statistical Association, Ft. Lauderdale, FL.

Korb, R. (1991). Adult education profile for 1990-91. *Statistics in Brief* (September, NCES 91-00007). Washington, DC: U.S. Department of Education, Office of Educational Research and Improvement.

West, J., Hausken, E.G., Chandler, K., & Collins, M. (1992). Experiences in child care and early childhood programs of first and second graders. *Statistics in Brief* (January, NCES 92-005). Washington, DC: U.S. Department of Education, Office of Educational Research and Improvement.

West, J., Hausken, E.G., Chandler, K., & Collins, M. (1992). Home activities of 3- to 8-year-olds. *Statistics in Brief* (January, NCES 92-004). Washington, DC: U.S. Department of Education, Office of Educational Research and Improvement.

National Household Education Survey
School Readiness Component
Year of Questionnaire: 1993   Sample size: 12,500 children aged 3-8
FAMILY-LEVEL CHARACTERISTICS
Sample size: 9,600 families

Family Composition
- ● Full roster of household members (first name, age, sex, and relationship to reference person of each member)
- ○ Partial roster of household members
- ● Number of adults in household
- ● Number of children in household
- ○ Approximate relationship of family members to householder, child, or one another
- ● Exact relationship of family members to householder, child, or one another
- ○ Information about part-time household member
- ○ Information about family members no longer living in household
- ○ Information about relatives who live nearby but not in household

Socioeconomic
- ● Total family income
- ○ Number of persons who depend on family income
- ○ Sources of income
- ○ Income amounts identified separately by source
- ○ Poverty status
- ● Welfare status
- ● Food Stamps receipt
- ○ Child support receipt
- ○ Medicaid coverage
- ○ Private health insurance
- ● Home ownership/renters
- ○ Assets (other than home ownership)
- ○ Public housing status
- ● Telephone in household
- ● Language other than English spoken in home

Geographic/Community Variables
- ● Region of country
- ● State of residence
- ○ County/city/MSA of residence
- ● Size/type of community
- ○ Zip code
- ○ Telephone area code
- ● Metropolitan residence
- ○ Neighborhood quality
- ○ Local labor market

Stage in Family Life Cycle
- ● Age of adult respondent or spouse/partner
- ● Marital status of adult respondent or spouse/partner
- ● Employment status of adult respondent or spouse/partner
- ● Presence of own children in household
- ● Age of youngest own child in household
- ● Age of oldest own child in household
- ○ Existence of own children who have left home
- ○ Intention to have (more) children in future

Family Functioning

- ● Family activities or time use
- ○ Community involvement (civic, religious, recreational)
- ○ Family communication patterns
- ○ Family decision-making
- ○ Marital conflict
- ○ Marital happiness/satisfaction
- ○ Parent-child conflict
- ○ History of marital separations
- ○ History of family violence
- ○ History of marital counselling

CHARACTERISTICS OF ADULT FAMILY MEMBERS
Sample size: 10,400 parent respondents

Adult Respondent or Reference Person	Current Spouse in HH	Current or Former Spouse Not in HH	
●	●	○	Age
●	●	○	Gender
●	●	○	Race
●	●	○	Hispanic origin
○	○	○	Other origin/ethnicity
○	○	○	Religious affiliation
○	○	○	Religious participation
○	○	○	Country of birth
○	○	○	Immigrant status
○	○	○	English fluency
●	●	○	Current marital status
●	○	○	Marital history
●	●	○	Cohabitation status
○	○	○	Cohabitation history
●	●	○	Parental status
○	○	○	Number children ever born/sired
○	○	○	Age at first birth
●	○	○	Age of youngest child
○	○	○	Children living elsewhere
○	○	○	Duration at current address
●	○	○	Residential mobility
●	●	○	Educational attainment
○	○	○	Degrees attained
○	○	○	GED or regular HS diploma
●	●	○	Current enrollment
●	●	○	Current employment status
●	●	○	Hours usually worked (ft/pt)
●	○	○	Weeks worked
●	○	○	Annual employment pattern
○	○	○	Main occupation
○	○	○	Earnings
○	○	○	Wage rate
○	○	○	Payment of child support
○	○	○	Aptitude or achievement score
○	○	○	Health/disability status
○	○	○	Self-esteem
○	○	○	Locus of control or efficacy
○	○	○	Depression or subjective well-being
○	○	○	Work-related attitudes

CHARACTERISTICS OF CHILD FAMILY MEMBERS
Sample size: 12,500 children

Reference Child or Youth Respondent	Other Children (in HH)	
●	●	Age
●	○	Month and year of birth
●	●	Gender
●	○	Race
●	○	Hispanic origin
○	○	Other origin/ethnicity
○	○	Religious affiliation
○	○	Religious participation
○	○	Country of birth
○	○	Immigrant status
○	○	English fluency
●	○	Exact relationship to adult family members
●	○	Exact relationship to other children in HH
○	○	Marital status/history
○	○	Parental status/history
●	○	Current enrollment in regular school
●	○	Current enrollment in preschool/daycare
○	○	Highest grade completed
●	○	Grade now enrolled
○	○	Employment status/history
●	○	Health status
●	○	Handicapping conditions
●	○	Grade repetition
○	○	Aptitude or achievement score
○	○	Pregnancy/birth history
●	○	Psychological well-being
○	○	Delinquency

210

National Household Survey on Drug Abuse

PURPOSE The National Household Survey on Drug Abuse (NHSDA) is a series of surveys designed to provide estimates of the prevalence of illicit drug use over time. Use of a number of drugs is estimated for individuals of different ages. Since the questions and how they are worded have been reasonably comparable across successive waves of the study, this series of surveys provides information on trends in illicit drug use over more than a decade.

SPONSORSHIP The NHSDA is sponsored by the National Institute on Drug Abuse (NIDA) of the National Institutes of Health. The Division of Epidemiology and Statistical Analysis within NIDA has oversight.

DESIGN The NHSDA is a national probability sample of households in the United States (Alaska and Hawaii since 1991). The present sample is representative of virtually the entire population; major exceptions being prisoners and military personnel on active duty. The survey samples individuals age 12 and over. Youths aged 12-17 are sampled independently of adults and are over-sampled. Among adults, those aged 18-25 are over-sampled. Since 1985, blacks and Hispanics have been over-sampled. The District of Columbia metropolitan statistical area was also over-sampled in 1990. In 1991, the District of Columbia and five additional cities (New York, Chicago, Denver, Miami, and Los Angeles) were over-sampled. The response rate in 1988 was 74.3%

The surveys are administered in person. For sensitive questions, the respondent fills out confidential answer sheets to reduce the tendency to underreport. This is a cross-sectional survey; no respondents are followed over time.

PERIODICITY Surveys were conducted in 1971, 1972, 1974, 1976, 1977, 1979, 1982, 1985, 1988, and 1990. Surveys have been

211

conducted in 1991 and 1992 but the data are not yet available. A survey is planned for 1993.

CONTENT The survey gathers information on lifetime, past year and current use, as well as frequency of use of several illicit drugs including marijuana, cocaine (including crack), inhalants, hallucinogens, PCP, heroin, nonmedical use of stimulants, sedatives, tranquilizers, analgesics, cigarettes and smokeless tobacco, and alcohol. Core questions have remained the same over the series of surveys; in addition, specific topics are sometimes looked at in depth in different years.

LIMITATIONS People in group quarters (such as military installations, correctional institutions, dormitories) and those people who have no permanent residence (such as the homeless) are not included in the sample.

There are no questions pertaining to a young person's victimization status or to offenses other than drug use. They only ask the respondent for their own earnings; family income cannot be determined. Often the respondent is under 17 so there is no income information on the major wage earner in the family.

AVAILABILITY Information about the survey can be obtained from:

> Joe Gfroerer, Project Officer
> National Institute on Drug Abuse, Division
> of Epidemiology and Prevention Research
> Rockwall II, Suite 615
> 5600 Fishers Lane
> Rockville, Maryland 20857
> 301/443-7980

A data tape is available for the 1988 survey from:

> Inter-University Consortium for
> Political and Social Research
> P.O Box 1248
> Ann Arbor, MI 48106-1248
> 313/763-5010

PUBLICATIONS

U.S. Department of Health and Human Services. (1990). *National Household Survey on Drug Abuse: Main findings 1988* (DHHS Pub. No. (ADM)90-1682). Washington, DC: GPO.

U.S. Department of Health and Human Services. (1990). *National Household Survey on Drug Abuse: Highlights 1988*. Washington, DC: GPO.

U.S. Department of Health and Human Services. (1990). *National Household Survey on Drug Abuse: Population estimates 1988*. Washington, DC: GPO.

National Household Survey on Drug Abuse

Year of Questionnaire: 1988
Sample size: 8,814
FAMILY LEVEL CHARACTERISTICS
Sample size: 8,814

Family Composition

○ Full roster of household members (first name, age, sex, and relationship to reference person of each member)
● Partial roster of household members
● Number of adults in household
● Number of children in household
○ Approximate relationship of family members to householder, child, or one another
● Exact relationship of family members to householder, child, or one another
○ Information about part-time household member
● Information about family members no longer living in household
○ Information about relatives who live nearby but not in household

Socioeconomic

○ Total family income
○ Number of persons who depend on family income
○ Sources of income
○ Income amounts identified separately by source
○ Poverty status
○ Welfare status
○ Food Stamps receipt
○ Child support receipt
○ Medicaid coverage
○ Private health insurance
○ Home ownership/renters
○ Assets (other than home ownership)
○ Public housing status
● Telephone in household
○ Language other than English spoken in home

Geographic/Community Variables

● Region of country
○ State of residence
○ County/city/MSA of residence
○ Size/type of community
○ Zip code
○ Telephone area code
● Metropolitan residence
○ Neighborhood quality
○ Local labor market

Stage in Family Life Cycle

● Age of adult respondent or spouse/partner
● Marital status of adult respondent or spouse/partner
● Employment status of adult respondent or spouse/partner
● Presence of own children in household
○ Age of youngest own child in household
○ Age of oldest own child in household
○ Existence of own children who have left home
○ Intention to have (more) children in future

214

Family Functioning
- ○ Family activities or time use
- ○ Community involvement (civic, religious, recreational)
- ○ Family communication patterns
- ○ Family decision-making
- ○ Marital conflict
- ○ Marital happiness/satisfaction
- ○ Parent-child conflict
- ○ History of marital separations
- ○ History of family violence
- ○ History of marital counselling

CHARACTERISTICS OF ADULT FAMILY MEMBERS
Sample Size: 5,719

Adult Respondent or Reference Person	Current Spouse in HH	Current or Former Spouse Not in HH	
●	○	○	Age
●	○	○	Gender
●	○	○	Race
●	○	○	Hispanic origin
○	○	○	Other origin/ethnicity
○	○	○	Religious affiliation
○	○	○	Religious participation
○	○	○	Country of birth
○	○	○	Immigrant status
○	○	○	English fluency
●	○	○	Current marital status
●	○	○	Marital history[1]
○	○	○	Cohabitation status
○	○	○	Cohabitation history
○	○	○	Parental status
●	○	○	Number children ever born/sired
○	○	○	Age at first birth
○	○	○	Age of youngest child
●	○	○	Children living elsewhere[2]
●	○	○	Duration at current address
●	○	○	Residential mobility
●	○	○	Educational attainment
○	○	○	Degrees attained
○	○	○	GED or regular HS diploma
●	○	○	Current enrollment
●	●	○	Current employment status[3]
●	○	○	Hours usually worked (ft/pt)[3]
○	○	○	Weeks worked
●	○	○	Annual employment pattern[4]
●	●	○	Main occupation[3]
●	○	○	Earnings
○	○	○	Wage rate
○	○	○	Payment of child support
○	○	○	Aptitude or achievement score
●	○	○	Health/disability status
○	○	○	Self-esteem
○	○	○	Locus of control or efficacy
○	○	○	Depression or subjective well-being
○	○	○	Work-related attitudes

CHARACTERISTICS OF CHILD FAMILY MEMBERS
Sample size: 3,095 children aged 12-17

Reference Child or Youth Respondent	Other Children (in HH)	
●	○	Age
○	○	Month and year of birth
●	○	Gender
●	○	Race
●	○	Hispanic origin
○	○	Other origin/ethnicity
○	○	Religious affiliation
○	○	Religious participation
○	○	Country of birth
○	○	Immigrant status
○	○	English fluency
●	○	Exact relationship to adult family members
●	○	Exact relationship to other children in HH
●	○	Marital status/history[5]
○	○	Parental status/history
●	○	Current enrollment in regular school
○	○	Current enrollment in preschool/daycare
●	○	Highest grade completed
○	○	Grade now enrolled
○	○	Employment status/history
○	○	Health status
○	○	Handicapping conditions
○	○	Grade repetition
○	○	Aptitude or achievement score
●	○	Pregnancy/birth history[5]
○	○	Psychological well-being
●	○	Delinquency

NOTES
1. Number of times R has been married.
2. Unless their children are no longer living at the time of the survey.
3. Spouse is identified only if "chief wage earner."
4. Asks number of jobs R has had in past five years.
5. If R is 15 years or younger.

216

National Integrated Quality Control System

PURPOSE The federal government provides substantial assistance to states through three assistance programs: Aid to Families with Dependent Children (AFDC), Medicaid, and Food Stamps (FS). To be eligible to receive funds, state agencies are required to perform quality control reviews for each of these programs to ensure that ineligible persons are not receiving benefits and that the benefit amounts received are correct. The data obtained are also used for research purposes.

SPONSORSHIP The National Integrated Quality Control System (NIQCS) is sponsored by the Administration for Children and Families and the Health Care Financing Administration within the Department of Health and Human Services and by the Food and Nutrition Service within the Department of Agriculture.

DESIGN Prior to 1983, separate quality control reviews were conducted for the three programs. Not infrequently families would be visited two or more times by reviewers from the different systems. It was recognized that substantial savings could be gained if families receiving more than one benefit were interviewed only once about all the benefits they received.

The quality control review period is the entire fiscal year from October through September of the following year. Each month, states select probability samples of cases receiving a payment of at least $10 for review. The minimum required sample size depends on the caseload of the state. It ranges from about 300 to about 2400 cases over the twelve month period. State data are weighted to obtain national estimates. Approximately 60,000 cases are reviewed across the nation every year.

Within each state, a quality control unit evaluates the eligibility of each selected case based on information from several sources such as home visits, bank reports, landlords, and from other collateral sources as needed. These data are collected on a worksheet and the information is used to determine whether an eligibility or payment error exists.

Characteristics data along with eligibility data are entered into a national database. To ensure that states are correctly applying error definitions, an independent subsample is drawn from the database by federal staff working at the regional level. Approximately 9,000 records across the nation are pulled and the data are independently verified. A regression methodology is used to adjust the error rate, based on the relationship between federal and state findings. Differences can be appealed.

PERIODICITY The NIQCS began in 1981 on a trial basis. It replaced the three separate quality control review systems in 1983 and has been conducted annually since that time.

CONTENT Because the main function of NIQCS is to determine errors in eligibility or payment within each program, a substantial amount of information is generated regarding error rates. This information, however, is not available in the public use files. In addition, information is collected about characteristics of recipients such as their age, sex, race/ethnicity, education, income, and employment, about other household members, and about significant persons not living in the home such as absent fathers.

LIMITATIONS The range of data available are relatively narrow given the limited purpose of the data collection effort. Moreover, the data only represent the population receiving income transfers. However, this population is of considerable interest to researchers and policymakers.

AVAILABILITY The NIQCS is state operated. Each of the sponsoring agencies has access to data pertaining to its own program. A national data file with state level data on characteristics of AFDC recipients is compiled and used by the Administration for Children and Families. Information from this file is summarized in an annual report on recipient characteristics (see publications below) and is available from the National Technical Information

Service (NTIS). Public use files are available for each year and can be obtained through NTIS as well.

> National Technical Information Service
> 5285 Port Royal Road
> Springfield, VA 22161
> 703/487-4650

For substantive questions about the AFDC component of the NIQCS, contact:

> Gerald A. Joireman
> Administration for Children
> and Families, OFA/DPE
> 370 L'Enfant Promenade, SW
> Washington, DC 20447-0001
> 202/401-5097

or

> Muriel Feshbach
> Administration for Children
> and Families, OFA/DPE
> 370 L'Enfant Promenade, SW
> Washington, DC 20447-0001
> 202/401-5052

PUBLICATIONS

Administration for Children and Families (undated). *Characteristics of State Plans for Aid to Families with Dependent Children: 1990-91 Edition.* Washington, DC: Department of Health and Human Services.

Administration for Children and Families (undated). *Characteristics and Financial Circumstances of AFDC Recipients: FY 1990.* Washington, DC: Department of Health and Human Services.

Family Support Administration (now the Administration for Children and Families) (undated). *Characteristics and Financial Circumstances of AFDC Recipients: FY 1989.* Washington, DC: Department of Health and Human Services.

National Integrated Quality Control System
Years of Questionnaire: Conducted annually
Sample size: Varies year to year. Approximately 60,000 cases in 1991
FAMILY LEVEL CHARACTERISTICS

Family Composition
- Full roster of household members (first name, age, sex, and relationship to reference person of each member)[1]
- ○ Partial roster of household members
- Number of adults in household[2]
- Number of children in household[2]
- Approximate relationship of family members to householder, child, or one another
- ○ Exact relationship of family members to householder, child, or one another
- ○ Information about part-time household member
- ○ Information about family members no longer living in household
- ○ Information about relatives who live nearby but not in household

Socioeconomic
- Total family income
- ○ Number of persons who depend on family income
- ○ Sources of income
- ○ Income amounts identified separately by source
- ○ Poverty status
- Welfare status
- Food Stamps receipt
- ○ Child support receipt
- Medicaid coverage
- ○ Private health insurance
- Home ownership/renters
- Assets (other than home ownership)
- Public housing status
- ○ Telephone in household
- ○ Language other than English spoken in home

Geographic/Community Variables
- ○ Region of country
- State of residence
- ○ County/city/MSA of residence
- ○ Size/type of community
- ○ Zip code
- ○ Telephone area code
- ○ Metropolitan residence
- ○ Neighborhood quality
- ○ Local labor market

Stage in Family Life Cycle
- Age of adult respondent or spouse/partner
- ○ Marital status of adult respondent or spouse/partner
- Employment status of adult respondent or spouse/partner
- ○ Presence of own children in household
- ○ Age of youngest own child in household
- ○ Age of oldest own child in household
- ○ Existence of own children who have left home
- ○ Intention to have (more) children in future

Family Functioning
○ Family activities or time use
○ Community involvement (civic, religious, recreational)
○ Family communication patterns
○ Family decision-making
○ Marital conflict
○ Marital happiness/satisfaction
○ Parent-child conflict
○ History of marital separations
○ History of family violence
○ History of marital counselling

CHARACTERISTICS OF ADULT FAMILY MEMBERS

Adult Respondent or Reference Person	Current Spouse in HH	Current or Former Spouse Not in HH	
●	●	○	Age
●	●	○	Gender
●	●	○	Race
●	●	○	Hispanic origin
●	●	○	Other origin/ethnicity
○	○	○	Religious affiliation
○	○	○	Religious participation
○	○	○	Country of birth
●	●	○	Immigrant status
○	○	○	English fluency
○	○	○	Current marital status
○	○	○	Marital history
○	○	○	Cohabitation status
○	○	○	Cohabitation history
○	○	○	Parental status
○	○	○	Number children ever born/sired
○	○	○	Age at first birth
○	○	○	Age of youngest child
○	○	○	Children living elsewhere
○	○	○	Duration at current address
○	○	○	Residential mobility
●	●	○	Educational attainment
○	○	○	Degrees attained
○	○	○	GED or regular HS diploma
○	○	○	Current enrollment
●	●	○	Current employment status
●	●	○	Hours usually worked (ft/pt)
○	○	○	Weeks worked
○	○	○	Annual employment pattern
○	○	○	Main occupation
●	●	○	Earnings
○	○	○	Wage rate
●	●	○	Payment of child support [3]
○	○	○	Aptitude or achievement score
●	●	○	Health/disability status
○	○	○	Self-esteem
○	○	○	Locus of control or efficacy
○	○	○	Depression or subjective well-being
○	○	○	Work-related attitudes

CHARACTERISTICS OF CHILD FAMILY MEMBERS

Reference Child or Youth Respondent	Other Children (in HH)	
O	●	Age
O	O	Month and year of birth
O	●	Gender
O	●	Race
O	●	Hispanic origin
O	●	Other origin/ethnicity
O	O	Religious affiliation
O	O	Religious participation
O	O	Country of birth
O	●	Immigrant status
O	O	English fluency
O	O	Exact relationship to adult family members
O	O	Exact relationship to other children in HH
O	O	Marital status/history
O	O	Parental status/history
O	O	Current enrollment in regular school
O	O	Current enrollment in preschool/daycare
O	●	Highest grade completed
O	O	Grade now enrolled
O	O	Employment status/history
O	O	Health status
O	O	Handicapping conditions
O	O	Grade repetition
O	O	Aptitude or achievement score
O	O	Pregnancy/birth history
O	O	Psychological well-being
O	O	Delinquency

NOTES
1. Household roster covers up to 16 individuals.
2. Can be calculated.
3. Child support payment to agency.

National Longitudinal Surveys of Labor Market Experience

PURPOSE The National Longitudinal Surveys of Labor Market Experience (NLS) are longitudinal surveys initiated to explore the labor market experiences over time of four cohorts facing employment problems of particular concern to policymakers. These cohorts were: Young Men ages 14-24 in 1966; Young Women ages 14-24 in 1968; Older Men ages 45-59 in 1966; and Mature Women ages 30-44 in 1967.

Issues of concern for the Young Men and Young Women cohorts included the school-to-work transition, initial occupational choice, adaptation to the world of work, the work-family interface, and attainment of stable employment. For Young Men, information on service in the military and union membership was also obtained. Information on Young Women included fertility, child care, responsibility for household tasks, attitude toward women working, and perceived job discrimination.

For the Older Men cohort, issues of declining health, unemployment, the obsolescence of skills, and age discrimination were of concern. In the Mature Women cohort, the key issue initially was labor force re-entry for women as their children became older. Subsequently, issues associated with women's retirement became important.

Following these cohorts over time enables analysts to describe the situations of different population groups, to understand the factors that are antecedents and consequences of their behaviors, and to study the interrelationships among factors ranging from education and employment, to marriage and family, to economic status.

SPONSORSHIP The NLS was initiated by the Office of Manpower Policy Evaluation of the Department of Labor. Currently, ultimate responsibility for the project resides with the Bureau of Labor Statistics (BLS) of the U.S. Department of Labor. Administration of the project has been shared by three separate

223

organizations: The Center for Human Resource Research (CHRR) at the Ohio State University, the National Opinion Research Center (NORC) at the University of Chicago, and the U.S. Bureau of the Census. The specific tasks of these agencies has varied over the lifetime of the project; however, CHRR has maintained primary responsibility for design of survey instruments, data analysis, and dissemination of project reports. Sample design and field work for the older cohorts have been the responsibility of the Bureau of the Census, with NORC performing similar tasks for the younger cohorts.

DESIGN Each of the four cohorts are represented by a multi-stage probability sample of the civilian non-institutionalized population, with a total of 235 sample areas representing 485 counties and independent cities covering every state and the District of Columbia. Households in enumeration districts that were primarily black were sampled at a rate between three and four times that of other households to provide separate and reliable statistics for blacks. From over 35,000 housing units available for interview, 5,020 older men 45-49, 5,225 young men 14-24, 5,083 mature women 30-44, and 5,159 young women 14-24 were interviewed. Over 90% of all individuals designated for interview within each age-sex cohort responded to the survey during the first year.

Although the base year survey for each cohort was conducted in person, followup surveys have alternated between personal and telephone interviews.

Data were weighted to correct for oversampling and attrition, and are nationally representative when weighted. Retention rates for each cohort after the 15-year followup period were 52% for Older Men, 64% for Mature Women, 65% for Young Men, and 68% for Young Women.

PERIODICITY Older Men were interviewed annually between 1966 and 1969, and in 1971, 1973, 1975, 1976, 1978, 1980, 1981, and 1983. In 1990 there was a resurvey of either the surviving sample member or their widow or, in the absence of a living spouse, next of kin. The 2,092 surviving men and 1,341 widows and 865 next of kin of the decedents were interviewed for a total data collection completion rate of 86% of the original sample.

Mature Women were interviewed annually between 1967-1969, and in 1971, 1972, 1974, 1976, 1977, 1979, 1982, 1984, 1986, 1987, 1989, and 1992.

Young Men were interviewed annually between 1966 and 1971, and in 1973, 1975, 1976, 1978, 1980, and 1981. No further interviews are planned for this cohort.

Young Women were interviewed annually between 1968 and 1973, and in 1975, 1977, 1978, 1980, 1982, 1983, 1985, 1987, 1988, 1991, and 1993.

CONTENT In keeping with the primary orientation of the surveys toward labor force issues, numerous questions focus on employment experience, unemployment, income, and training. The range of questions included for each cohort are to some degree dependent upon the life stage of the cohort and their attachment to the labor force (i.e., retirement planning for Older Men and Mature Women, transition from school to work for Young Men and Young Women).

A core set of topics for each survey instrument include employment, education, training, work experience, income, marital status, health, attitudes toward work, occupation and geographic mobility, and family and household structure.

Subtopics for each cohort include:

Older Men: plans for retirement, pensions, and health.

Mature Women: volunteer work, household activities, retirement, child care, and care of parents and other elderly relatives.

Young Men: educational goals, high school and college experience, school characteristics, military service, union membership, and job plans.

Young Women: educational goals, high school and college completion, school characteristics, job plans, fertility, child care, and attitudes toward women working.

Numerous background and household characteristics such as parental education and educational attainment of other family members were collected. In the Young Men and Young Women cohorts, considerable information concerning the respondent's family background at age 14 is available.

LIMITATIONS From the perspective of families and children, the NLS has limited information about the respondent's childhood. Available background information includes education of the respondent's parents and who the respondent lived with at age 14. From a family perspective, the family structure can be described. Changes in family composition and patterns of type of living quarters over time can be constructed through household questions that are asked every year. The consequences of the labor force and education decisions the respondents make can be studied. However, no information is collected on how the families formed by the respondents are functioning. The sampling design used by the Census Bureau to select respondents for these four cohorts often generated more than one respondent for the same household. Variables are provided within each data set which link respondents who shared the same household at the time of screening, such as husband-wife, brother-sister, and mother-child.

AVAILABILITY Magnetic data tapes and cartridges, CD-ROM, and file documentation are available from the Center for Human Resource Research at the Ohio State University. Handbooks describing the NLS, references, and publications are also available. Also available free of charge is a practical, how-to guide for those researchers working with one or more of the NLS data sets. Contact:

> NLS User Services
> The Center for Human Resource Research
> The Ohio State University
> 921 Chatham Lane, Suite 200
> Columbus, OH 43221-2418
> 614/442-7366

For substantive questions, contact:

> Steve McClaskie
> The Center for Human Resource Research
> The Ohio State University
> 921 Chatham Lane, Suite 200
> Columbus, OH 43221-2418
> 614/442-7366

PUBLICATIONS

NLS User's Guide 1992. (1992). Columbus, OH: Center for Human Resource Research, The Ohio State University.

NLS Handbook 1992. (1992). Columbus, OH: Center for Human Resource Research, The Ohio State University.

Beck, S.H. (1983). The role of other family members in inter-generational occupational mobility. *Sociological Quarterly*, 24(Spring), 273-285.

Constantine, J.A. & Bahr, S.J. (1980). Locus of control and marital stability: A longitudinal study. *Journal of Divorce*, 4(1), 11-22.

Fleisher, B.M. (1977). Mother's home time and the production of child quality. *Demography*, 14(May), 197-212.

Neilsen, J.M. & Endo, R. (1983). Marital status and socioeconomic status: The case of female-headed families. *International Journal of Women's Studies*, 6(2), 130-147.

Shapiro, D. & Mott, F.L. (1979). Labor supply behavior of prospective and new mothers. *Demography*, 16(May), 199-208.

Shaw, L.B. (1982). *Effects of low income and living with a single parent on high school completion for young women.* Columbus, OH: Center for Human Resource Research, The Ohio State University.

NLS-Young Men
Year of Questionnaire: 1966-1981
Sample size: 5,225 young men aged 14-24 in 1966
FAMILY-LEVEL CHARACTERISTICS

Family Composition
● Full roster of household members (first name, age, sex, and relationship to reference person of each member)
○ Partial roster of household members
● Number of adults in household
● Number of children in household
○ Approximate relationship of family members to householder, child, or one another
● Exact relationship of family members to householder, child, or one another
○ Information about part-time household member
○ Information about family members no longer living in household
○ Information about relatives who live nearby but not in household

Socioeconomic
● Total family income
● Number of persons who depend on family income
● Sources of income
● Income amounts identified separately by source
● Poverty status[1]
● Welfare status
● Food Stamps receipt
● Child support receipt
○ Medicaid coverage
○ Private health insurance
● Home ownership/renters
● Assets (other than home ownership)
○ Public housing status
○ Telephone in household
● Language other than English spoken in home[2]

Geographic/Community Variables
● Region of country
○ State of residence
○ County/city/MSA of residence
● Size/type of community
○ Zip code
○ Telephone area code
● Metropolitan residence
○ Neighborhood quality
● Local labor market

Stage in Family Life Cycle
● Age of adult respondent or spouse/partner
● Marital status of adult respondent or spouse/partner
● Employment status of adult respondent or spouse/partner
● Presence of own children in household
● Age of youngest own child in household[3]
● Age of oldest own child in household[3]
○ Existence of own children who have left home
● Intention to have (more) children in future

228

Family Functioning

- ● Family activities or time use[4]
- ○ Community involvement (civic, religious, recreational)
- ○ Family communication patterns
- ○ Family decision-making
- ○ Marital conflict
- ○ Marital happiness/satisfaction
- ○ Parent-child conflict
- ○ History of marital separations
- ○ History of family violence
- ○ History of marital counselling

CHARACTERISTICS OF ADULT FAMILY MEMBERS

Sample size: 3,373 young men aged 18-24 in 1966

Adult Respondent or Reference Person	Current Spouse in HH	Current or Former Spouse Not in HH	
●	●	○	Age
●	●	○	Gender
●	○	○	Race
○	○	○	Hispanic origin
○	○	○	Other origin/ethnicity
○	○	○	Religious affiliation
○	○	○	Religious participation
○	○	○	Country of birth
○	○	○	Immigrant status
○	○	○	English fluency
●	○	○	Current marital status
●	○	○	Marital history
○	○	○	Cohabitation status
○	○	○	Cohabitation history
●	○	○	Parental status
●	○	○	Number children ever born/sired
●	○	○	Age at first birth
●	○	○	Age of youngest child
●	○	○	Children living elsewhere
●	○	○	Duration at current address
●	○	○	Residential mobility
●	●	○	Educational attainment
●	○	○	Degrees attained
○	○	○	GED or regular HS diploma
●	●	○	Current enrollment
●	●	○	Current employment status
●	●	○	Hours usually worked (ft/pt)
●	●	○	Weeks worked
●	○	○	Annual employment pattern
●	●	○	Main occupation
●	●	○	Earnings
●	●	○	Wage rate
●	○	○	Payment of child support[5]
●	○	○	Aptitude or achievement score
●	●	○	Health/disability status[6]
○	○	○	Self-esteem
●	○	○	Locus of control or efficacy
○	○	○	Depression or subjective well-being
●	○	○	Work-related attitudes

CHARACTERISTICS OF CHILD FAMILY MEMBERS
Sample size: 2,294 young men aged 14–17 in 1966

Reference Child or Youth Respondent	Other Children (in HH)	
●	○	Age
●	●	Month and year of birth
●	●	Gender
●	○	Race
○	○	Hispanic origin
○	○	Other origin/ethnicity
○	○	Religious affiliation
○	○	Religious participation
○	○	Country of birth
○	○	Immigrant status
○	○	English fluency
●	○	Exact relationship to adult family members
●	○	Exact relationship to other children in HH
●	○	Marital status/history
●	○	Parental status/history
●	●	Current enrollment in regular school
○	●	Current enrollment in preschool/daycare
●	●	Highest grade completed
●	●	Grade now enrolled
●	○	Employment status/history
●	○	Health status[6]
○	○	Handicapping conditions
○	○	Grade repetition
●	○	Aptitude or achievement score
●	○	Pregnancy/birth history
○	○	Psychological well-being
●	○	Delinquency

NOTES
1. Can be computed using income and household rosters.
2. When respondent was a child.
3. Age of youngest and oldest child in categories under 3 and over 5.
4. Respondent's household activities.
5. Payment of child support *and* alimony are grouped together. Receipt of child support is also asked.
6. Health condition limits school or work.

NLS - Young Women

Years of Questionnaire: 1968-1988
Sample size: 5,159 young women aged 14-24 in 1968
FAMILY-LEVEL CHARACTERISTICS

Family Composition

- Full roster of household members (first name, age, sex, and relationship to reference person of each member)
- Partial roster of household members
- Number of adults in household
- Number of children in household
- Approximate relationship of family members to householder, child, or one another
- Exact relationship of family members to householder, child, or one another
- Information about part-time household member
- Information about family members no longer living in household
- Information about relatives who live nearby but not in household

Socioeconomic

- Total family income
- Number of persons who depend on family income
- Sources of income
- Income amounts identified separately by source
- Poverty status
- Welfare status
- Food Stamps receipt
- Child support receipt
- Medicaid coverage
- Private health insurance
- Home ownership/renters
- Assets (other than home ownership)
- Public housing status
- Telephone in household
- Language other than English spoken in home[1]

Geographic/Community Variables

- Region of country
- State of residence
- County/city/MSA of residence
- Size/type of community
- Zip code
- Telephone area code
- Metropolitan residence
- Neighborhood quality
- Local labor market

Stage in Family Life Cycle

- Age of adult respondent or spouse/partner
- Marital status of adult respondent or spouse/partner
- Employment status of adult respondent or spouse/partner
- Presence of own children in household
- Age of youngest own child in household
- Age of oldest own child in household
- Existence of own children who have left home
- Intention to have (more) children in future

231

Family Functioning

- ● Family activities or time use[2]
- ○ Community involvement (civic, religious, recreational)
- ○ Family communication patterns
- ○ Family decision-making
- ○ Marital conflict
- ○ Marital happiness/satisfaction
- ○ Parent-child conflict
- ○ History of marital separations
- ○ History of family violence
- ○ History of marital counselling

CHARACTERISTICS OF ADULT FAMILY MEMBERS
Sample size: 3,310 young women aged 18-24 in 1968

Adult Respondent or Reference Person	Current Spouse in HH	Current or Former Spouse Not in HH	
●	●	○	Age
●	●	○	Gender
●	○	○	Race
○	○	○	Hispanic origin
○	○	○	Other origin/ethnicity
○	○	○	Religious affiliation
○	○	○	Religious participation
○	○	○	Country of birth
○	○	○	Immigrant status
○	○	○	English fluency
●	○	○	Current marital status
●	○	○	Marital history
○	○	○	Cohabitation status
○	○	○	Cohabitation history
●	○	○	Parental status
●	○	○	Number children ever born/sired
●	○	○	Age at first birth
●	○	○	Age of youngest child
○	○	○	Children living elsewhere
●	○	○	Duration at current address
●	○	○	Residential mobility
●	●	○	Educational attainment
●	○	○	Degrees attained
●	○	○	GED or regular HS diploma
●	●	○	Current enrollment
●	●	○	Current employment status
●	●	○	Hours usually worked (ft/pt)
●	●	○	Weeks worked
●	○	○	Annual employment pattern
●	●	○	Main occupation
●	●	○	Earnings
●	○	○	Wage rate
○	○	○	Payment of child support
●	○	○	Aptitude or achievement score
●	●	○	Health/disability status
○	○	○	Self-esteem
●	○	○	Locus of control or efficacy
●	○	○	Depression or subjective well-being
●	○	○	Work-related attitudes

CHARACTERISTICS OF CHILD FAMILY MEMBERS
Sample size: 2,029 young women aged 14-17 in 1968

Reference Child or Youth Respondent	Other Children (in HH)	
●	○	Age
●	●	Month and year of birth
●	●	Gender
●	○	Race
○	○	Hispanic origin
○	○	Other origin/ethnicity
○	○	Religious affiliation
○	○	Religious participation
○	○	Country of birth
○	○	Immigrant status
○	○	English fluency
●	○	Exact relationship to adult family members
●	○	Exact relationship to other children in HH
●	○	Marital status/history
●	○	Parental status/history
●	●	Current enrollment in regular school
○	●	Current enrollment in preschool/daycare
●	●	Highest grade completed
●	●	Grade now enrolled
●	○	Employment status/history
●	○	Health status[3]
○	○	Handicapping conditions
○	○	Grade repetition
●	○	Aptitude or achievement score
●	○	Pregnancy/birth history
●	○	Psychological well-being
●	○	Delinquency

NOTES
1. When respondent was a child.
2. Respondent's household activities.
3. Health limits school work.

NLS - Mature Women
Year of Questionnaire: Every year or two since 1967
Sample size: 5,083 women aged 30-44 in 1967
FAMILY-LEVEL CHARACTERISTICS

Family Composition
- Full roster of household members (first name, age, sex, and relationship to reference person of each member)
○ Partial roster of household members
- Number of adults in household
- Number of children in household
○ Approximate relationship of family members to householder, child, or one another
- Exact relationship of family members to householder, child, or one another
○ Information about part-time household member
○ Information about family members no longer living in household
○ Information about relatives who live nearby but not in household

Socioeconomic
- Total family income
- Number of persons who depend on family income
- Sources of income
- Income amounts identified separately by source
○ Poverty status
- Welfare status
- Food Stamps receipt
- Child support receipt
- Medicaid coverage
- Private health insurance
- Home ownership/renters
- Assets (other than home ownership)
○ Public housing status
○ Telephone in household
- Language other than English spoken in home

Geographic/Community Variables
- Region of country
○ State of residence
○ County/city/MSA of residence
- Size/type of community
○ Zip code
○ Telephone area code
- Metropolitan residence
○ Neighborhood quality
- Local labor market

Stage in Family Life Cycle
- Age of adult respondent or spouse/partner
- Marital status of adult respondent or spouse/partner
- Employment status of adult respondent or spouse/partner
- Presence of own children in household
- Age of youngest own child in household
- Age of oldest own child in household
- Existence of own children who have left home
- Intention to have (more) children in future

Family Functioning

- ● Family activities or time use
- ● Community involvement (civic, religious, recreational)
- ○ Family communication patterns
- ○ Family decision-making
- ○ Marital conflict
- ○ Marital happiness/satisfaction
- ○ Parent-child conflict
- ○ History of marital separations
- ○ History of family violence
- ○ History of marital counselling

CHARACTERISTICS OF ADULT FAMILY MEMBERS

Adult Respondent or Reference Person	Current Spouse in HH	Current or Former Spouse Not in HH	
●	●	○	Age
●	●	○	Gender
●	○	○	Race
○	○	○	Hispanic origin
○	○	○	Other origin/ethnicity
○	○	○	Religious affiliation
○	○	○	Religious participation
●	○	○	Country of birth
○	○	○	Immigrant status
○	○	○	English fluency
●	○	○	Current marital status
●	○	○	Marital history
○	○	○	Cohabitation status
○	○	○	Cohabitation history
●	○	○	Parental status
●	○	○	Number children ever born/sired
●	○	○	Age at first birth
●	○	○	Age of youngest child
●	○	○	Children living elsewhere
○	○	○	Duration at current address
●	○	○	Residential mobility
●	●	○	Educational attainment
●	○	○	Degrees attained
●	○	○	GED or regular HS diploma
●	●	○	Current enrollment
●	●	○	Current employment status
●	●	○	Hours usually worked (ft/pt)
●	●	○	Weeks worked
○	●	○	Annual employment pattern
●	●	○	Main occupation
●	●	○	Earnings
●	●	○	Wage rate
●	●	○	Payment of child support
○	○	○	Aptitude or achievement score
●	●	○	Health/disability status
○	○	○	Self-esteem
●	○	○	Locus of control or efficacy
●	○	○	Depression or subjective well-being
●	○	○	Work-related attitudes

CHARACTERISTICS OF CHILD FAMILY MEMBERS

Reference Child or Youth Respondent	Other Children (in HH)	
O	O	Age
O	●	Month and year of birth
O	●	Gender
O	O	Race
O	O	Hispanic origin
O	O	Other origin/ethnicity
O	O	Religious affiliation
O	O	Religious participation
O	O	Country of birth
O	O	Immigrant status
O	O	English fluency
O	O	Exact relationship to adult family members
O	O	Exact relationship to other children in HH
O	O	Marital status/history
O	O	Parental status/history
O	●	Current enrollment in regular school
O	●	Current enrollment in preschool/daycare
O	●	Highest grade completed
O	●	Grade now enrolled
O	O	Employment status/history
O	O	Health status
O	O	Handicapping conditions
O	O	Grade repetition
O	O	Aptitude or achievement score
O	O	Pregnancy/birth history
O	O	Psychological well-being
O	O	Delinquency

NLS - Older Men

Year of Questionnaire: Every year or two between 1966 and 1983
Sample size: 5,020 men aged 45-59 years in 1966

FAMILY-LEVEL CHARACTERISTICS

Family Composition

- Full roster of household members (first name, age, sex, and relationship to reference person of each member)
- ○ Partial roster of household members
- Number of adults in household
- Number of children in household
- ○ Approximate relationship of family members to householder, child, or one another
- Exact relationship of family members to householder, child, or one another
- ○ Information about part-time household member
- ○ Information about family members no longer living in household
- ○ Information about relatives who live nearby but not in household

Socioeconomic

- Total family income
- Number of persons who depend on family income
- Sources of income
- Income amounts identified separately by source
- ○ Poverty status
- Welfare status
- Food Stamps receipt
- ○ Child support receipt
- ○ Medicaid coverage
- Private health insurance
- Home ownership/renters
- Assets (other than home ownership)
- Public housing status
- ○ Telephone in household
- ○ Language other than English spoken in home

Geographic/Community Variables

- Region of country
- ○ State of residence
- ○ County/city/MSA of residence
- Size/type of community
- ○ Zip code
- ○ Telephone area code
- Metropolitan residence
- ○ Neighborhood quality
- Local labor market

Stage in Family Life Cycle

- Age of adult respondent or spouse/partner
- Marital status of adult respondent or spouse/partner
- Employment status of adult respondent or spouse/partner
- Presence of own children in household
- Age of youngest own child in household
- Age of oldest own child in household
- Existence of own children who have left home
- ○ Intention to have (more) children in future

237

Family Functioning
○ Family activities or time use
○ Community involvement (civic, religious, recreational)
○ Family communication patterns
○ Family decision-making
○ Marital conflict
○ Marital happiness/satisfaction
○ Parent-child conflict
○ History of marital separations
○ History of family violence
○ History of marital counselling

CHARACTERISTICS OF ADULT FAMILY MEMBERS

Adult Respondent or Reference Person	Current Spouse in HH	Current or Former Spouse Not in HH	
●	●	○	Age
●	●	○	Gender
●	○	○	Race
○	○	○	Hispanic origin
○	○	○	Other origin/ethnicity
○	○	○	Religious affiliation
○	○	○	Religious participation
●	○	○	Country of birth
○	○	○	Immigrant status
○	○	○	English fluency
●	○	○	Current marital status
●	○	○	Marital history
○	○	○	Cohabitation status
○	○	○	Cohabitation history
○	○	○	Parental status
○	○	○	Number children ever born/sired
○	○	○	Age at first birth
○	○	○	Age of youngest child
○	○	○	Children living elsewhere
●	○	○	Duration at current address
●	○	○	Residential mobility
●	●	○	Educational attainment
●	●	○	Degrees attained
○	○	○	GED or regular HS diploma
○	●	○	Current enrollment
●	●	○	Current employment status
●	●	○	Hours usually worked (ft/pt)
●	●	○	Weeks worked
○	○	○	Annual employment pattern
●	●	○	Main occupation
●	●	○	Earnings
●	○	○	Wage rate
○	○	○	Payment of child support
○	○	○	Aptitude or achievement score
●	●	○	Health/disability status
○	○	○	Self-esteem
●	○	○	Locus of control or efficacy
○	○	○	Depression or subjective well-being
●	○	○	Work-related attitudes

CHARACTERISTICS OF CHILD FAMILY MEMBERS

Reference Child or Youth Respondent	Other Children (in HH)	
O	●	Age
O	O	Month and year of birth
O	●	Gender
O	O	Race
O	O	Hispanic origin
O	O	Other origin/ethnicity
O	O	Religious affiliation
O	O	Religious participation
O	O	Country of birth
O	O	Immigrant status
O	O	English fluency
O	O	Exact relationship to adult family members
O	O	Exact relationship to other children in HH
O	O	Marital status/history
O	O	Parental status/history
O	●	Current enrollment in regular school
O	●	Current enrollment in preschool/daycare
O	●	Highest grade completed
O	●	Grade now enrolled
O	O	Employment status/history
O	O	Health status
O	O	Handicapping conditions
O	O	Grade repetition
O	O	Aptitude or achievement score
O	O	Pregnancy/birth history
O	O	Psychological well-being
O	O	Delinquency

National Longitudinal Survey of Youth

PURPOSE The primary purpose of the National Longitudinal Survey of Youth (NLSY) is to replicate and enhance data collected in the original four cohorts of the National Longitudinal Surveys (see separate write-up). It was anticipated that this additional cohort would add to the discussion of labor force participation and transition to work from school, and also enable an evaluation of expanded employment and training programs for youth established in the 1977 amendments to the Comprehensive Employment Training Act (CETA). A supplemental sample of youth enlisted in the Armed Forces permitted review of the recruitment and service experience of youth in the military; however, this military sample was discontinued after the 1984 interview. The supplemental sample of poor white youth was discontinued after the 1990 interview.

SPONSORSHIP While the Department of Labor initiated the NLSY, as it did the original four cohorts, other agencies have been actively involved with the development of the youth data. The National Institute of Child Health and Human Development (NICHD), the National Institute on Drug Abuse, the National Institute on Alcohol and Alcohol Abuse, and the Department of Defense all sponsored portions of the youth surveys. Data were collected by the National Opinion Research Center (NORC).

DESIGN The Youth cohort is a multi-stage probability sample of a nationally representative sample of about 11,400 non-institutionalized men and women who were between the ages of 14 and 21 as of January 1, 1979. An additional 1,280 young people serving in the Armed Forces supplemented the civilian cohort. Blacks, Hispanics, and poor whites were oversampled to facilitate analysis of these subgroups. The civilian population was selected via a screening interview administered in approximately 75,000 dwellings and group quarters in 202 primary sampling units. Military respondents were sampled from rosters provided by the Department of Defense of members on active military duty as of September 30, 1978. A sample of 200 "military units" was selected based on probabilities proportional to the number of persons aged 17-21 within the unit, from which persons 17-21 were subsampled. Women were oversampled at a rate approximately six times that of males to obtain approximately equal numbers of men and women. The military sample was interviewed between 1979 and 1984. Approximately 200 respondents were retained for post-1984 followup surveys.

As of the completion of the 13th (1991) interview wave, 90% (9,018 of the original 11,406 civilian respondents) were still eligible for interview.

PERIODICITY Interviews on the Youth sample have been conducted annually since 1979. All surveys, with the exception of the 1987 telephone interview, were conducted in person.

CONTENT As the focus of the NLSY was to determine variation of labor force participation and experience of a recent cohort of young men and women, the content, as with the original four cohorts of the NLS, is slanted toward preparation for labor force entry and work experience. A good deal of information on education, income, family background, marriage, fertility and family planning, child care, and maternal and child health was also collected.

LIMITATIONS Most background information is in reference to when the respondent was age 14. Information concerning childhood experiences are not collected, although experiences as a young adult are documented extensively. However, as the youngest are roughly 24 to 25 years of age by 1989, their experiences may not necessarily be comparable to those of contemporary youth. In 1988, a childhood residence history collected information from birth to age 18.

Detailed lists of family and household structure are available, with the capability of constructing patterns of family/household change over time and determining any subsequent effect on a variety of respondent outcomes. Factors affecting the family or household unit and/or functioning cannot be assessed.

AVAILABILITY Magnetic data tapes or cartridges, CD-ROM, file documentation, handbooks describing the NLS, references, and publications are all available from:

> NLS User Services
> Center for Human Resource Research
> The Ohio State University
> 921 Chatham Lane, Suite 200
> Columbus, OH 43221-2418
> 614/442-7366

For substantive questions, contact:

> Steve McClaskie
> The Center for Human Resource Research
> The Ohio State University
> 921 Chatham Lane, Suite 200
> Columbus, OH 43221-2418
> 614/442-7366

PUBLICATIONS Details of sampling procedures can be found in:

National Longitudinal Survey of Labor Force Behavior, Youth Survey (NLS): Technical Sampling Report and the *Household Screening: Interviewer's Reference Manual*, available from the Center for Human Resource Research.

Recent examples of papers that have examined child outcomes in the NLSY from the perspective of the family include:

Desai, S., Chase-Lansdale, P.L., & Michael, R.T. (1989). Mother or market? Effects of maternal employment on the intellectual ability of 4-year-old children. *Demography, 16*(4), 545-561.

Haurin, R.J., & Mott, F.L. (1990). Adolescent sexual activity in the family context: The impact of older siblings. *Demography, 27*(4), 537-557.

Upchurch, D., & McCarthy, J. (1990). The effects of the timing of a first birth on high school completion. *American Sociological Review, 55*(2), 224-234.

National Longitudinal Survey of Youth
Years of Questionnaire: 1979-1991
Sample size: 12,686 persons aged 14-21 as of January 1, 1979
FAMILY-LEVEL CHARACTERISTICS

Family Composition
- ● Full roster of household members (first name, age, sex, and relationship to reference person of each member)
- ○ Partial roster of household members
- ● Number of adults in household
- ● Number of children in household
- ○ Approximate relationship of family members to householder, child, or one another
- ● Exact relationship of family members to householder, child, or one another
- ○ Information about part-time household member
- ○ Information about family members no longer living in household
- ○ Information about relatives who live nearby but not in household

Socioeconomic
- ● Total family income
- ● Number of persons who depend on family income
- ● Sources of income
- ● Income amounts identified separately by source
- ● Poverty status
- ● Welfare status
- ● Food Stamps receipt
- ● Child support receipt
- ● Medicaid coverage
- ● Private health insurance
- ● Home ownership/renters
- ● Assets (other than home ownership)
- ● Public housing status
- ○ Telephone in household
- ● Language other than English spoken in home

Geographic/Community Variables
- ● Region of country
- ● State of residence
- ● County/city/MSA of residence
- ● Size/type of community
- ○ Zip code
- ○ Telephone area code
- ● Metropolitan residence
- ● Neighborhood quality
- ● Local labor market

Stage in Family Life Cycle
- ● Age of adult respondent or spouse/partner
- ● Marital status of adult respondent or spouse/partner
- ● Employment status of adult respondent or spouse/partner
- ● Presence of own children in household
- ● Age of youngest own child in household
- ● Age of oldest own child in household
- ● Existence of own children who have left home
- ● Intention to have (more) children in future

Family Functioning

- ● Family activities or time use
- ○ Community involvement (civic, religious, recreational)
- ○ Family communication patterns
- ○ Family decision-making
- ○ Marital conflict
- ● Marital happiness/satisfaction
- ○ Parent-child conflict
- ● History of marital separations
- ○ History of family violence
- ○ History of marital counselling

CHARACTERISTICS OF ADULT FAMILY MEMBERS

Adult Respondent or Reference Person	Current Spouse in HH	Current or Former Spouse Not in HH	
●	●	○	Age
●	●	○	Gender
●	●	○	Race
●	●	○	Hispanic origin
●	●	○	Other origin/ethnicity
●	●	●	Religious affiliation
●	●	●	Religious participation
●	○	○	Country of birth
●	○	○	Immigrant status
●	○	○	English fluency
●	○	○	Current marital status
●	●	○	Marital history[1]
●	○	○	Cohabitation status
●	○	○	Cohabitation history
●	○	○	Parental status
●	○	○	Number children ever born/sired
●	○	○	Age at first birth
●	○	○	Age of youngest child
●	○	○	Children living elsewhere
●	○	○	Duration at current address
●	○	○	Residential mobility
●	●	○	Educational attainment
●	○	○	Degrees attained
●	○	○	GED or regular HS diploma
●	●	●	Current enrollment
●	●	●	Current employment status
●	●	●	Hours usually worked (ft/pt)
●	●	●	Weeks worked
●	○	○	Annual employment pattern
●	●	●	Main occupation
●	●	●	Earnings
●	○	○	Wage rate
●	●	○	Payment of child support
●	○	○	Aptitude or achievement score
●	○	○	Health/disability status
●	○	○	Self-esteem
●	○	○	Locus of control or efficacy
○	○	○	Depression or subjective well-being
●	○	○	Work-related attitudes

CHARACTERISTICS OF CHILD FAMILY MEMBERS

Reference Child or Youth Respondent	Other Children (in HH)	
●	●	Age
●	●	Month and year of birth
●	●	Gender
●	●	Race
●	●	Hispanic origin
●	○	Other origin/ethnicity
●	○	Religious affiliation
●	○	Religious participation
●	○	Country of birth
○	○	Immigrant status
●	○	English fluency
●	○	Exact relationship to adult family members
○	○	Exact relationship to other children in HH
●	○	Marital status/history
●	○	Parental status/history
●	○	Current enrollment in regular school
○	○	Current enrollment in preschool/daycare
●	●	Highest grade completed
●	○	Grade now enrolled
●	○	Employment status/history
●	○	Health status[2]
○	○	Handicapping conditions
●	○	Grade repetition
●	○	Aptitude or achievement score
●	○	Pregnancy/birth history
○	○	Psychological well-being
●	○	Delinquency

NOTES
1. Total number of marriages only, 1982 survey.
2. Limiting conditions.

National Longitudinal Survey of Youth Child-Mother Data

PURPOSE Child development data were collected on the children born to female respondents in the National Longitudinal Survey of Youth (NLSY) to create a large, national data resource for the study of child outcomes. The child assessment measures can be linked to rich data on the education, training, family, employment, and related behaviors and attitudes of the NLSY respondents from 1979 through the present. These merged mother-child data represent an unprecedented opportunity to study the dynamics of family transitions and their implications for the well-being and development of children.

SPONSORSHIP The National Longitudinal Survey of Youth was initiated by the Department of Labor, which continues to provide funding for the survey. Since the first survey in 1979, a number of other government agencies have also provided support for data collection on topics of interest to them, including the National Institute of Child Health and Human Development (NICHD), the National Institute on Drug Abuse, the National Institute on Alcohol and Alcohol Abuse, and the Department of Defense. Funding for the Child Supplement to the regular interview is provided by NICHD. Data are collected by the National Opinion Research Center (NORC), Chicago, Illinois.

DESIGN The NLSY child data were collected and merged with NLS Youth main file data to permit explorations of the ways in which families, particularly mothers, affect the early social, emotional, cognitive, and physiological development of their children. The NLS Youth data set contains an over-sample of economically disadvantaged whites (until 1992), Hispanics, and blacks. More than one child from the same family are included. In choosing child assessment measures for the children of NLSY females, the goals were to select a set that would tap a range of child characteristics, could be administered by interviewers without training in child development, would not require expensive or bulky equipment, would be acceptable to parents, would not be exorbitantly expensive to administer to a large sample, and would be valid across a sample varying in social and economic characteristics and age. The intent was to select existing measures that were known to work well, and to modify their length or manner of administration when necessary to accommodate the survey setting.

The Center for Human Resource Research (CHRR) assumed overall responsibility for selection, design and adaptation of the child assessments. Development of the 1986 child assessment began in the summer of 1985. CHRR staff work in collaboration with NORC on such issues as placement and formatting of questions, survey timing, and special data collection considerations such as confidentiality, child interview rapport, and testing conditions. NICHD staff also provides input into the process on a continuing basis. Center staff seeks advice on question inclusion and a review of the draft survey instrument from the various funding agencies, a technical advisory board, and the designers of the original instruments.

The Foundation for Child Development provided funding to convene a panel of experts to make recommendations for appropriate assessment measures. The panel was drawn from the fields of psychology, child development, medicine, and child assessment. Two pre-tests of the draft child instrument were conducted in Chicago at NORC in August of 1985. Pre-test results were used to analyze response frequencies for selected questions and to identify problems encountered by both respondents and interviewers. Based on the results of the pre-tests, modifications to the instruments and administrative procedures were made by NORC and forwarded to CHRR for review.

PERIODICITY The initial wave of interviews was completed in 1986. Second and third waves were conducted in 1988 and 1990, respectively, and a 1992 wave was recently administered. Children previously studied received modules appropriate to their current ages. New children born were added to the sample and given age-appropriate modules.

CONTENT A Mother Supplement (i.e., questions addressed to the mother about the child) was designed to be completed by the mother or guardian for each child prior to or during the administration of the Child Supplement. Certain modules differ according to the age of the child, for example, the items on the HOME scale. The Mother Supplement contains the four following assessments:

HOME —Items adapted from the Home Observation for Measurement of the Environment (HOME) Inventory for children of all ages.

How My Child Usually Acts—Maternal report of temperament or behavioral style over the past two weeks for children under seven.

Motor and Social Development—Motor-social-cognitive development for children under age four.

Behavior Problems Index— Mother ratings of children ages four or older in areas of problem behavior such as hyperactivity, anxiety, depression, dependency, and aggressiveness.

The 1990 and 1992 waves ask mothers additional questions related to child up-bringing, for example, their perceived level of difficulty in raising the child, their familiarity with the child's friends, and the child's frequency of religious attendance.

The Child Supplement collects general and health-related background information from the mother of each child, responses from the children to items from additional assessment instruments, interviewer evaluations of the testing conditions, and interviewer evaluations of the child's home environment.

While assessments are administered to only age-eligible children each time, not all children are re-administered each assessment in subsequent surveys, even if they remain age-eligible. The content of the Child Supplement varies across the three waves of child data collection. The original Child Supplement contained the following sections:

Child Background Section—Identifying information (age, sex, grade in school, etc.) from the mother of the child. Questions on Head Start participation were added in 1988.

Child Health Section—Maternal reports of the child's health limitations, illnesses, medical treatment, health insurance coverage, and height and weight at time of interview. Incidence of accidents and injuries were measured starting in 1988.

248

Parts of the Body Scale (not available after 1988)
The Peabody Picture Vocabulary Test - Revised (PPVT-R)
The Memory for Location Task (not available after 1988)
The McCarthy Scale of Children's Abilities:
Verbal Memory Subscales A-C (Part C not available after 1988)
What I Am Like
Memory for Digit Span
Peabody Individual Achievement Test (PIAT):
Math Subscale
Reading Recognition Subscale
Reading Comprehension Subscale

In addition to these assessments, information gathered on the child's mother and her family as part of the NLSY main files can be merged with the child data including information about employment, education, job training, fertility, child care, income and assets. The 1990 and 1992 waves include additional detail about children's television viewing as well as how the older children spend their time after school. The 1992 instrument introduces an abbreviated birth history for children age 13 and older. Detailed information on pre- and post-natal behaviors and practices will be limited in 1992 to pregnancies resulting in live births.

LIMITATIONS The NLSY-Child -Mother data is an increasingly used data set, utilized by sociologists, economists, developmental psychologists, and demographers interested in the family and family processes. Because of the availability of longitudinal data on both mothers and their children it allows for life-course approaches to the effects of family factors on child development. Researchers are able to interweave information about family structure, income, ethnicity, aspirations, and attainment into their examinations of child well-being. The presence of child assessments across the cognitive and socioemotional domains is another key strength of these data. Finally, the availability of the data on a menu-driven CD make the files extremely accessible to users.

Despite its considerable strengths, the Child-Mother data do have several limitations that bear mention. Since the sample of children about whom data are collected are those born to an age cohort of young parents, they are not currently a nationally representative sample of all youth. The 1990 panel (the most recent available) represents approximately the first 65% of the children that this age cohort can be expected to bear. Consequently, the sample includes disproportionate numbers of children born to young parents. However, as additional waves of interviews are conducted, the sample becomes increasingly representative of all offspring born to a cohort of American females.

Another limitation is that only female respondents from the main survey and their children are included in the child-mother survey; male respondents and their children are not covered. In addition, no direct information is obtained from the child's father, although this can be inferred for over 90% of the children. Prior to 1984, items were not included to identify whether the mother's spouse was the child's biological father. This limitation was corrected in later rounds of the survey. The 1990 and 1992 interviews gather information about the child's relationship with a father figure as well as with the biological father. The exact relationship of the father figure to both the mother and the child is also ascertained.

Researchers examining specific topics such as child care may encounter gaps in data availability, for example some of the information collected about child care experiences is retrospective. However, the Center's Handbook serves as a helpful tool for laying out an analysis plan. Additionally, most of the developmental measures selected for the initial assessment were oriented toward young children since a majority of the children born to women in NLSY by 1986 were quite young (70% were age 5 or younger). One of the challenges facing the CHRR is to develop appropriate assessments for examining the older children as they near adulthood.

Finally, children whose mothers were part of the over-sample of economically disadvantaged whites were not administered assessments after 1988.

AVAILABILITY A merged mother-child data tape and CD covering the 1986, 1988, and 1990 waves are currently available. Users can also obtain a user's guide, copies of instruments, a substantial codebook with numeric listings of all variables, and a handbook describing the child assessments in some detail. A detailed data file containing raw data from the child interviews is also available from CHRR. These data files can be obtained from:

NLS User Services
The Center for Human Resource Research
The Ohio State University
921 Chatham Lane, Suite 200
Columbus, OH 43221-2418
614/442-7366

Substantive questions related to the NLSY-Child Supplement can be directed to:

Steve McClaskie
The Center for Human Resource Research
The Ohio State University
921 Chatham Lane, Suite 200
Columbus, OH 43221-2418
614/442-7366

PUBLICATIONS

CHRR publishes NLSUPDATE, a quarterly newsletter that details progress related to the NLS, reports data and documentation corrections and lists in-progress research using the NLS surveys.

CHRR keeps track of the hundreds of publications based on analyses of NLS data that appear in scholarly journals. A bibliography of studies based on the NLS is currently available for 1968-1989, as is an annotated bibliographic supplement containing a coded index for and abstracts of post-1989 publications. CHRR also makes available the following guide books:

Baker, P.C., & Mott, F.L. (1989). *NLSY Child Handbook 1989: A Guide and Resource Document for the National Longitudinal Survey of Youth 1986 Child Data.*

Mott, F.L. & Quinlan, S. (1991). *Children of the NLSY: 1988 Tabulations and Summary Discussion.*

Researchers who are considering using the NLSY-CS may also find helpful:

Chase-Lansdale, P.L., Mott,F.L., Brooks-Gunn, J., & Phillips, D. (1991). Children of the national longitudinal survey of youth: A unique research opportunity. *Developmental Psychology*, 22(6), 918-931.

Recent examples of papers that have examined child outcomes from the NLSY-CS from the perspective of the family include:

Desai, S., Chase-Lansdale, P.L., & Michael, R.T. (1989). Mother or market? Effects of maternal employment on the intellectual ability of four-year-old children. *Demography*, 26(4), 545-561.

Menaghan, E.G., & Parcel, T.L. (1991). Determining children's home environments: The impact of maternal characteristics and current occupational and family conditions. *Journal of Marriage and the Family*, 53(2), 417-431.

Moore, K.A., & Snyder, N.O. (1991). Cognitive attainment among first born children of adolescent mothers. *American Sociological Review*, 56, 612-624.

NLSY—Child-Mother Data
Years of Questionnaire: 1986, 1988, 1990
Sample size: 7,346 children ages 0-18 in 1988
FAMILY-LEVEL CHARACTERISTICS

Family Composition
O Full roster of household members (first name, age, sex, and relationship to reference person of each member)
● Partial roster of household members
● Number of adults in household
● Number of children in household
● Approximate relationship of family members to householder, child, or one another
O Exact relationship of family members to householder, child, or one another
O Information about part-time household member
O Information about family members no longer living in household
O Information about relatives who live nearby but not in household

Socioeconomic
● Total family income
O Number of persons who depend on family income
● Sources of income
● Income amounts identified separately by source
● Poverty status
● Welfare status
● Food Stamps receipt
● Child support receipt
O Medicaid coverage
● Private health insurance
● Home ownership/renters
● Assets (other than home ownership)
O Public housing status
O Telephone in household
O Language other than English spoken in home

Geographic/Community Variables
● Region of country
● State of residence
● County/city/MSA of residence
● Size/type of community
O Zip code
O Telephone area code
● Metropolitan residence
O Neighborhood quality
O Local labor market

Stage in Family Life Cycle
● Age of adult respondent or spouse/partner
● Marital status of adult respondent or spouse/partner
● Employment status of adult respondent or spouse/partner
● Presence of own children in household
● Age of youngest own child in household
● Age of oldest own child in household
● Existence of own children who have left home
O Intention to have (more) children in future

253

Family Functioning
○ Family activities or time use
○ Community involvement (civic, religious, recreational)
○ Family communication patterns
○ Family decision-making
○ Marital conflict
○ Marital happiness/satisfaction
○ Parent-child conflict
● History of marital separations
○ History of family violence
○ History of marital counselling

CHARACTERISTICS OF ADULT FAMILY MEMBERS

Adult Respondent or Reference Person	Current Spouse in HH	Current or Former Spouse Not in HH	
●	●	○	Age
●	●	○	Gender
●	○	○	Race
●	○	○	Hispanic origin
○	○	○	Other origin/ethnicity
●	○	○	Religious affiliation
●	○	○	Religious participation
○	○	○	Country of birth
○	○	○	Immigrant status
○	○	○	English fluency
●	○	○	Current marital status
●	○	○	Marital history
●	○	○	Cohabitation status
●	○	○	Cohabitation history[1]
●	○	○	Parental status
●	○	○	Number children ever born/sired
●	○	○	Age at first birth
●	○	○	Age of youngest child
○	○	○	Children living elsewhere
○	○	○	Duration at current address
○	○	○	Residential mobility
●	●	○	Educational attainment
○	○	○	Degrees attained
●	○	○	GED or regular HS diploma
●	●	○	Current enrollment
●	●	○	Current employment status
●	●	○	Hours usually worked (ft/pt)
●	●	○	Weeks worked
●	○	○	Annual employment pattern
●	●	○	Main occupation
●	●	○	Earnings
●	●	○	Wage rate
○	○	○	Payment of child support
●	○	○	Aptitude or achievement score
●	○	○	Health/Disability status
●	○	○	Self-esteem
○	○	○	Locus of control or efficacy
○	○	○	Depression or subjective well-being
●	○	○	Work-related attitudes

CHARACTERISTICS OF CHILD FAMILY MEMBERS

Reference Child or Youth Respondent	Other Children (in HH)	
●	○	Age
●	○	Month and Year of Birth
●	○	Gender
●	○	Race[2]
●	○	Hispanic origin[2]
○	○	Other origin/ethnicity
○	○	Religious affiliation
○	○	Religious participation
○	○	Country of birth
○	○	Immigrant status
○	○	English fluency
○	○	Exact relationship to adult family members
○	○	Exact relationship to other children in HH
○	○	Marital status/history
○	○	Parental status/history
●	○	Current enrollment in regular school
●	○	Current enrollment in preschool/daycare
○	○	Highest grade completed
●	○	Grade now enrolled
○	○	Employment status/history
●	○	Health status[3]
●	○	Handicapping conditions
○	○	Grade repetition
●	○	Aptitude or achievement score
○	○	Pregnancy/birth history
●	○	Psychological well-being
○	○	Delinquency

NOTES
1. Presence of male partner can be established from household record for each year.
2. Ascertained from mother's race/ethnicity in 1979.
3. Pre/postnatal behaviors and practices are also available.

1988 National Maternal and Infant Health Survey and 1991 Longitudinal Followup

PURPOSE The 1988 National Maternal and Infant Health Survey (NMIHS) was conducted to study factors related to poor pregnancy outcome, such as adequacy of prenatal care; inadequate and excessive weight gain during pregnancy; maternal smoking, drinking, and drug use; and pregnancy and delivery complications. The Longitudinal Followup (LF) conducted in 1991 provides information on the health and development of low- and very low-birthweight babies, child care and safety, maternal health, maternal depression, and plans for adoption and foster care.

SPONSORSHIP The NMIHS and the LF were conducted by the National Center for Health Statistics/Centers for Disease Control in collaboration with the Agency for Toxic Substances and Disease Registry; the Center for Prevention Services, the Division of Diabetes Translation, and the Office of Minority Health, of the Centers for Disease Control; the Center for Devices and Radiological Health and the Center for Food Safety and Applied Nutrition of the Food and Drug Administration; the Health Care Financing Administration; the Maternal and Child Health Bureau of the Health Resources and Services Administration; the Indian Health Service; the Office of Minority Health of the Public Health Service; the National Institute on Alcoholism and Alcohol Abuse; the National Institute of Child Health and Human Development; the National Institute on Drug Abuse; the National Institute of Mental Health; the Food and Nutrition Service of the U.S. Department of Agriculture; the Texas Department of Health; and the National Center for Health Statistics.

DESIGN The 1988 NMIHS is the equivalent of a combined National Natality, National Fetal Mortality, and National Infant Mortality Survey. Vital records were sampled throughout 1988. The survey is a nationally representative sample of 9,953 women who had live births, 3,309 who had late fetal deaths, and 5,332 who had infant deaths in 1988. Blacks were oversampled so that they comprised half of each subsample. In addition, low birth-weight babies were oversampled so that among the live births traced, 15% of the births had a birth weight of under 1,500 grams, 15% had a birth weight of 1,500 to 2,499 grams, and the remaining 70% had a birth weight of 2,500 grams or more.

Data were obtained by mailed questionnaires and/or telephone interviews with mothers, with hospitals where births and infant deaths occurred, and with providers of prenatal care. The survey data were linked with vital records information. Unlike earlier followback surveys, unmarried as well as married women were asked to participate in the survey.

To obtain as high a response rate as possible, non-respondents were re-contacted by telephone. In addition, for the hospital portion of the survey, hospitals that did not respond within the given time period were sent a second questionnaire and received a telephone reminder. If they still did not fill out the questionnaire, a representative of the American Medical Record Association called them to encourage them to comply.

The Longitudinal Followup survey of the mothers in the 1988 NMIHS was conducted in 1991. About 9,400 mothers whose infants were living at the time of the NMIHS interview were re-contacted, and telephone or personal interviews were conducted. Pediatricians and hospitals were asked to complete questionnaires. Also re-interviewed were 1,000 respondents who had infant deaths in 1988 and 1,000 respondents who had stillbirths in 1988.

PERIODICITY This is the first time that the three types of followback surveys have been combined. The National Center for Health Statistics conducted Followback National Natality Surveys in 1963, 1964-66, 1967-69, 1972, and 1980. The 1980 Natality Survey was linked to the National Death Index to locate infants in the survey who had died during the 12 months after birth. National Fetal Mortality Surveys have been conducted in 1964-66 and in 1980.

CONTENT A great deal of information on health and health care was collected in the NMIHS. Mothers were asked about prenatal care; sources of payment for prenatal care; their smoking, drinking, and marijuana use; WIC use patterns; work patterns before and after delivery; infant feeding practices; infant health and medical care up to 6 months; and sociodemographic characteristics.

Hospitals were asked to provide information on such topics as maternal hospitalizations (prenatal and up to six months postpartum), maternal and infant diagnoses, charges for care, Cesarean delivery and trial of labor, fetal monitoring, medical devices such as apnea monitors and respirators, infant resuscitation and neonatal intensive care, and infant hospitalizations up to six months.

Prenatal care providers were asked about the women's weight, blood pressure, hematocrit, urine glucose, urine protein, and hemoglobin at each prenatal visit. In addition, they were asked about such topics as patient education, advice, and referral; testing for AIDS and other sexually-transmitted diseases; use of sonograms and X-rays; prescribed medications and vitamins; amniocentesis and chorionic villi sampling; and charges for care.

Information collected in the 1991 Longitudinal Followup includes child development and behavior up to three years of age; child care; WIC food use; child immunizations and injuries; parental smoking, drinking and drug use; stress and social support; subsequent fertility; and occupational information.

LIMITATIONS Illegal drug use may be under-reported. In addition, the sample size limits certain types of analyses.

AVAILABILITY Public use data tapes are available from:

> National Technical Information Service
> 5285 Port Royal Road
> Springfield, VA 22161
> 703/487-4650

For substantive questions about the 1988 NMIHS and the 1991 Followback, contact:

Paul J. Placek, Ph.D., Chief
Followback Survey Branch
Division of Vital Statistics/NCHS
6525 Belcrest Rd., Room 840
Hyattsville, MD 20782
301/436-7464

PUBLICATIONS

Hoffman, J., Overpeck, M., Berendes, H., Gupta, S., & Krauss, N. (1991, November). *The influence of social factors on birth weight in the United States: Results from the 1988 National Maternal and Infant Health Survey.* Presented at the American Public Health Association meetings, Atlanta, GA.

Kogan, M., Simpson, G., Keppel, K., & Placek, P. (1988, October). *Demographic aspects of the 1990 Longitudinal Followup of Mothers in the 1988 National Maternal and Infant Health Survey.* Presented at the Southern Demographic Association meetings, San Antonio, TX.

Kogan, M., & Simpson, G. (1988, September). *Survey methods for the 1990 Longitudinal Followup of the NMIHS.* Washington, DC: NCHS.

Krulewitch, C. (1991, November). *The 1988 National Maternal and Infant Health Survey: A unique dataset to analyze perinatal problems.* Presented at the National Perinatal Association meetings, Boston, MA.

Sanderson, M., Placek, P., & Keppel, K. (1991). The 1988 National Maternal and Infant Health Survey: Design, content, and data availability. *Birth, 18*(1), 26-32.

Teitelbaum, M., Bourdon, K., & Locke, B. (1991, November). *Depression in women after an adverse birth outcome: 1988 National Maternal and Infant Health Survey.* Presented at the American Public Health Association meetings, Atlanta, GA.

National Maternal and Infant Health Survey and 1991 Longitudinal Followup

Year of Questionnaire: 1988

Sample size: 9,953 live births; 3,309 late fetal deaths; 5,332 infant deaths

FAMILY LEVEL CHARACTERISTICS

Family Composition

- ○ Full roster of household members (first name, age, sex, and relationship to reference person of each member)
- ● Partial roster of household members
- ● Number of adults in household
- ● Number of children in household
- ● Approximate relationship of family members to householder, child, or one another
- ● Exact relationship of family members to householder, child, or one another
- ○ Information about part-time household member
- ● Information about family members no longer living in household
- ○ Information about relatives who live nearby but not in household

Socioeconomic

- ● Total family income
- ○ Number of persons who depend on family income
- ● Sources of income
- ● Income amounts identified separately by source
- ● Poverty status
- ● Welfare status
- ● Food Stamps receipt
- ● Child support receipt
- ● Medicaid coverage
- ● Private health insurance
- ● Home ownership/renters
- ○ Assets (other than home ownership)
- ● Public housing status
- ● Telephone in household
- ○ Language other than English spoken in home

Geographic/Community Variables

- ● Region of country
- ● State of residence
- ○ County/city/MSA of residence
- ○ Size/type of community
- ○ Zip code
- ○ Telephone area code
- ○ Metropolitan residence
- ○ Neighborhood quality
- ○ Local labor market

Stage in Family Life Cycle

- ● Age of adult respondent or spouse/partner
- ● Marital status of adult respondent or spouse/partner
- ● Employment status of adult respondent or spouse/partner
- ● Presence of own children in household
- ● Age of youngest own child in household
- ○ Age of oldest own child in household
- ○ Existence of own children who have left home
- ● Intention to have (more) children in future

Family Functioning

- ● Family activities or time use
- ○ Community involvement (civic, religious, recreational)
- ○ Family communication patterns
- ○ Family decision-making
- ○ Marital conflict
- ○ Marital happiness/satisfaction
- ○ Parent-child conflict
- ○ History of marital separations
- ○ History of family violence
- ○ History of marital counselling

CHARACTERISTICS OF ADULT FAMILY MEMBERS

Mother	Husband or Male Partner	Current or Former Spouse Not in HH	
●	●	○	Age
●	●	○	Gender
●	●	○	Race
●	●	○	Hispanic origin
●	●	○	Other origin/ethnicity
○	○	○	Religious affiliation
○	○	○	Religious participation
●	●	○	Country of birth
○	○	○	Immigrant status
○	○	○	English fluency
●	●	○	Current marital status
●	○	○	Marital history
○	○	○	Cohabitation status
○	○	○	Cohabitation history
●	○	○	Parental status
●	○	○	Number children ever born/sired
○	○	○	Age at first birth
○	○	○	Age of youngest child
●	○	○	Children living elsewhere
○	○	○	Duration at current address
●	○	○	Residential mobility
●	●	○	Educational attainment
○	○	○	Degrees attained
○	○	○	GED or regular HS diploma
●	●	○	Current enrollment
●	●	○	Current employment status
●	●	○	Hours usually worked (ft/pt)
●	●	○	Weeks worked
●	●	○	Annual employment pattern
●	●	○	Main occupation
●	●	○	Earnings
●	●	○	Wage rate
●	●	○	Payment of child support
○	○	○	Aptitude or achievement score
●	○	○	Health/disability status
●	○	○	Self-esteem
●	○	○	Locus of control or efficacy
●	○	○	Depression or subjective well-being
●	○	○	Work-related attitudes

CHARACTERISTICS OF CHILD FAMILY MEMBERS

Reference Child or Youth Respondent	Other Children (in HH)	
●	○	Age
●	○	Month and year of birth
●	○	Gender
●	○	Race
●	○	Hispanic origin
○	○	Other origin/ethnicity
○	○	Religious affiliation
○	○	Religious participation
●	○	Country of birth
○	○	Immigrant status
○	○	English fluency
●	○	Exact relationship to adult family members
○	○	Exact relationship to other children in HH
○	○	Marital status/history
○	○	Parental status/history
●	○	Current enrollment in regular school
●	○	Current enrollment in preschool/daycare
○	○	Highest grade completed
○	○	Grade now enrolled
○	○	Employment status/history
●	○	Health status
●	○	Handicapping conditions
○	○	Grade repetition
○	○	Aptitude or achievement score
○	○	Pregnancy/birth history
●	○	Psychological well-being
○	○	Delinquency

National Medical Expenditure Survey

PURPOSE The primary goal of the National Medical Expenditure Survey (NMES) is to document how Americans use health care services and to determine the amount and pattern of health expenditures. Data cover a one year period. The NMES provides the most comprehensive statistical picture to date of how health services are used and financed in the United States.

SPONSORSHIP The first and second rounds of the NMES (I and II) were conducted by the Agency for Health Care Policy and Research (formerly the National Center for Health Services Research and Technology Assessment), Center for General Health Services Intramural Research, U.S. Department of Health and Human Services. The Center documents current publications from NMES and houses public user data files for individuals interested in conducting secondary analyses from NMES data.

Numerous agencies played a role in the development, collection and maintenance of the component surveys of NMES II. The Indian Health Service supported the Survey of American Indians and Alaskan Natives, while HCFA, NCHS and the Office of the Assistant Secretary for Planning and Evaluation provided technical assistance on the survey design and the development of all survey instruments. Interviews were conducted by independent contractors, including Westat, Inc., National Opinion Research Center, and The Council of Energy Resource Tribes.

DESIGN NMES includes three primary components: The Household Survey (which included two supplemental surveys, the Medical Provider Survey and the Health Insurance-Employer Survey), the Survey of American Indians and Alaska Natives, and the Survey in Institutions. All components of NMES were designed to provide unbiased national estimates of health status, health service utilization, insurance coverage, health expenditures, and sources of payment of health services for the civilian population of the United States in the year in which the survey was conducted: January 1 to December 31, 1977, for NMES I, and January 1 to December 31, 1987 for NMES II.

The NMES I was collected in 1977 and completed in 1979. Data covered a wide variety of issues including the number and characteristics of the uninsured and underinsured, tax implications of excluding employer-paid premiums for health insurance from employee income, and differences in health service utilization by demographic and socioeconomic characteristics. Respondents were the non-institutionalized population.

The NMES II was initiated in the 1980s with the primary data collection in 1987. Although the NMES II included the non-institutionalized population as well, it also covered extensive information on populations residing in or admitted to nursing homes and facilities for the mentally ill.

The Household Survey - This is a national probability sample of the civilian, non-institutionalized population, with an oversampling of poor and low income families, the elderly, the functionally impaired, and black and Hispanic minorities. A total sample of 35,000 individuals in 14,000 households who completed all five rounds of data collection make up the Household Survey sample. A sub-sample of respondents employed (excluding self-employed respondents) any time during the 1987 calendar year was used to conduct the Medical Provider Survey and the Health Insurance-Employer Survey.

Medical Provider Survey and Health Insurance-Employer Survey — Permission for the supplemental surveys was carried out in two stages. In the second round of the Household Survey, a 25% sample of respondents reporting any group insurance was asked to sign a form authorizing use of a questionnaire to obtain verification of coverage, benefits, and premium information from medical providers and third party payers. Ninety percent of respondents with insurance provided permission. Approximately 16,000 permission forms were mailed, with a response rate of 85%.

The Survey of American Indians and Alaska Natives (SAIAN) - This survey queried American Indians and Alaska natives eligible to receive care through the Indian Health Service (IHS). SAIAN adopted a probability sample design using an IHS-constructed sampling frame of counties with eligible individuals living on or near federally recognized reservations or in Alaska. Initial screening was completed in approximately 13,700 dwelling units, of which 6,500 respondents were interviewed. Data from the SAIAN can be compared to the general U.S. population regarding health status, health service utilization, and access to care.

Survey in Institutions (SII) - SII sampled persons residing in or admitted to nursing and personal care homes and facilities for the mentally ill. A three stage probability sample design was employed to select facilities (Stages I and II) and to further sample health providers who were available to deliver care on January 1, 1987. A sample of admissions from each facility between January 1 and December 31, 1987 was also selected. A total of 1,500 facilities, 7,000 current health residents and 3,500 new admissions were selected.

Data collected in each component were weighted to correct for oversampling and differential rates of non-response.

PERIODICITY The NMES is conducted every ten years to estimate the health care utilization and expenditures during the past calendar year of the year of interview. NMES I was conducted in 1977 and completed in 1979. NMES II was conducted in 1987 and completed in 1989. NMES III is planned for 1996. Data for each ten year panel is collected through a series of five rounds of core and supplementary interviews.

Families participating in the Household Survey were interviewed five times (rounds) over a period of 16 months to ascertain data concerning the family's health and patterns of health care during the 1987 calendar year.

CONTENT *Household Survey* — Baseline data included information on household composition, employment and insurance, illnesses, use of health services, and health expenditures for each family member. Employment and insurance information was updated at each round.

Rounds one through four included a core survey plus a series of supplemental questions covering different health related topics.

Rounds one and four included a supplement on use of long term care to estimate the number of persons with functional disabilities and the formal use of long-term care facilities or home care provided by family or friends.

Round two added questions on giving and receiving care, with round three as a supplement addressing access to care.

Round five collected information only on tax filing and medical deductions for each household.

A self-administered questionnaire was conducted between the first and second rounds to both the Household and SAIAN samples to ascertain health status, attitudes about health and health behaviors. Questionnaires were given to both adults and children (ages 0-4 and 5-17).

Two additional components of the Household Survey include:

Medical Provider Survey — which obtained information from physicians, hospitals, outpatient clinics, emergency rooms, and home health agencies used by respondents in the Household sample. *Health Insurance-Employer Survey* — which covered information on private insurance of persons in the Household Survey, including premiums paid by all sources, and provisions of health coverage. A substudy, the Employer Health Insurance Cost Survey, incorporated a combination of telephone and mail surveys of employers of working persons in the Household Survey. Data concerning employee wages, the number of employees covered by group health plans, the total amount of employer payments for employee health insurance, and the premiums paid by the employee were collected.

The Survey of American Indians and Alaska Natives — Data collection instruments and interview procedures used in the Household Survey were also used in the SAIAN and thus provides a basis for comparing health service utilization of American Indians and Alaska Natives to the general population. Data focused on access to care, sources of payment for care provided by sources other than the Indian Health Service, and use of traditional medical care.

Survey in Institutions (SII) - This component obtained extensive information on demographics, health and functional status, living arrangements, and insurance coverage at time of admission. Data were obtained from two sources. Characteristics of the facilities and associated charges were obtained from facility administrators, and the financial status, insurance coverage, and personal history of the institutionalized person were obtained from the next of kin.

Information from all components are currently person- and family-based level data. Data are available to conduct event estimates (total hospitalizations, bouts of illness, etc.) and perform event-level analyses.

NMES II data, unlike information from program or provider surveys, can be used to estimate all public and private sources of coverage for health services as well as out-of-pocket payments by individuals and families. Comprehensive analyses of health expenditures and utilization patterns of families may be conducted as well.

LIMITATIONS Information on health care utilization is for a one year period, with latest information for the 1987 calendar year. Analysis of trends in the use of health services over time can only be done over roughly ten year segments. Important information concerning health services that may have occurred during the time prior to the one year in question cannot be investigated.

AVAILABILITY Data are available to the public on magnetic tape and may be purchased through the National Technical Information Service (see below). Although a total of 40 NMES tapes are planned for release, 14 are currently available. Each tape contains data from various components of the total NMES. File descriptions and coding documentation accompany each tape.

To purchase data tapes, contact:

> National Technical Information Service
> 5285 Port Royal Road
> Springfield, VA 22161
> 703/487-4780

To obtain information concerning availability and content of data sets, contact:

> Deb Potter
> Public Use Data Tapes
> Agency for Health Care Policy
> and Research/DHHS
> Rockville, MD 20852
> 301/227-8406

To obtain additional information on NMES II, contact:

Daniel C. Walden, Ph.D., Director
Division of Medical Expenditure Studies
Agency for Health Care Policy
  and Research/DHHS
Executive Office Center, Suite 500
2101 East Jefferson Street
Rockville, MD 20852
301/227-8400

PUBLICATIONS

Cafferata, G. (1986). *Poor health and the American family.* Annual meeting of the Eastern Sociological Society.

Cohen, S. (1982). *Family unit analysis in the National Medical Expenditure Survey.* Proceedings of the Survey Research Section, American Statistical Association.

Cohen, S. (1990). *Estimation concerns for family level analysis in national panel surveys.* Paper presented at the annual meeting of the American Statistical Association.

Cohen, S., DiGaetano, R. & Waksberg, J. (1987). *Sample design of the National Medical Expenditure Survey - Household Component.* Proceedings of the Survey Research Methods Section, American Statistical Association.

Cunningham, P. (1990). Medical care and expenditures for children across stages of the family life cycle. *Journal of Marriage and the Family, 52*(1), 197-207.

Kasper, J., Rossiter, L. & Wilson, R. (1987). *A summary of expenditures and sources of payment for personal health services from the National Medical Care Expenditure Survey.* NHCES Data Preview Series, No. 24 (DHHS Pub. No. (PHS)87-3411). Washington, DC: GPO.

National Medical Expenditure Survey
Year of Questionnaire: 1987
Sample size: 12,104 (Household) & 2,019 (SAIAN)
FAMILY LEVEL CHARACTERISTICS

Family Composition
- ● Full roster of household members (first name, age, sex, and relationship to reference person of each member)
- ○ Partial roster of household members
- ● Number of adults in household
- ● Number of children in household
- ○ Approximate relationship of family members to householder, child, or one another
- ● Exact relationship of family members to householder, child, or one another
- ○ Information about part-time household member
- ○ Information about family members no longer living in household
- ○ Information about relatives who live nearby but not in household

Socioeconomic
- ● Total family income
- ○ Number of persons who depend on family income
- ● Sources of income
- ● Income amounts identified separately by source
- ○ Poverty status
- ● Welfare status
- ● Food Stamps receipt
- ● Child support receipt
- ● Medicaid coverage
- ● Private health insurance
- ● Home ownership/renters
- ● Assets (other than home ownership)
- ○ Public housing status
- ● Telephone in household
- ○ Language other than English spoken in home

Geographic/Community Variables
- ● Region of country
- ● State of residence
- ● County/city/MSA of residence
- ○ Size/type of community
- ● Zip code
- ● Telephone area code
- ○ Metropolitan residence
- ○ Neighborhood quality
- ○ Local labor market

Stage in Family Life Cycle
- ● Age of adult respondent or spouse/partner
- ● Marital status of adult respondent or spouse/partner
- ● Employment status of adult respondent or spouse/partner
- ○ Presence of own children in household
- ● Age of youngest own child in household
- ○ Age of oldest own child in household
- ● Existence of own children who have left home
- ○ Intention to have (more) children in future

Family Functioning

○ Family activities or time use
○ Community involvement (civic, religious, recreational)
○ Family communication patterns
○ Family decision-making
○ Marital conflict
○ Marital happiness/satisfaction
○ Parent-child conflict
○ History of marital separations
○ History of family violence
○ History of marital counselling

CHARACTERISTICS OF ADULT FAMILY MEMBERS

Adult Respondent or Reference Person	Current Spouse in HH	Current or Former Spouse Not in HH	
●	●	○	Age
●	●	○	Gender
●	●	○	Race
●	●	○	Hispanic origin
○	○	○	Other origin/ethnicity
○	○	○	Religious affiliation
○	○	○	Religious participation
○	○	○	Country of birth
○	○	○	Immigrant status
○	○	○	English fluency
●	○	○	Current marital status
○	○	○	Marital history
○	○	○	Cohabitation status
○	○	○	Cohabitation history
○	○	○	Parental status
○	○	○	Number children ever born/sired
○	○	○	Age at first birth
○	○	○	Age of youngest child
○	○	○	Children living elsewhere
○	○	○	Duration at current address
○	○	○	Residential mobility
●	○	○	Educational attainment
○	○	○	Degrees attained
○	○	○	GED or regular HS diploma
●	○	○	Current enrollment
●	●	○	Current employment status
●	○	○	Hours usually worked (ft/pt)
●	○	○	Weeks worked
○	○	○	Annual employment pattern
●	○	○	Main occupation
○	○	○	Earnings
●	○	○	Wage rate
○	○	○	Payment of child support
○	○	○	Aptitude or achievement score
●	○	○	Health/disability status
○	○	○	Self-esteem
○	○	○	Locus of control or efficacy
●	●	○	Depression or subjective well-being
○	○	○	Work-related attitudes

CHARACTERISTICS OF CHILD FAMILY MEMBERS

Reference Child or Youth Respondent	Other Children (in HH)	
○	●	Age
○	●	Month and year of birth
○	●	Gender
○	○	Race
○	○	Hispanic origin
○	○	Other origin/ethnicity
○	○	Religious affiliation
○	○	Religious participation
○	○	Country of birth
○	○	Immigrant status
○	○	English fluency
○	●	Exact relationship to adult family members[2]
○	○	Exact relationship to other children in HH
○	○	Marital status/history
○	○	Parental status/history
○	○	Current enrollment in regular school
○	○	Current enrollment in preschool/daycare
○	○	Highest grade completed
○	○	Grade now enrolled
○	○	Employment status/history
○	●	Health status
○	●	Handicapping conditions
○	○	Grade repetition
○	○	Aptitude or achievement score
○	○	Pregnancy/birth history
○	●	Psychological well-being
○	○	Delinquency

NOTES
1. Medicare coverage also available.
2. Exact relationship to adult respondent only.

National Mortality Followback Survey

PURPOSE The National Mortality Followback Survey (NMFS) supplements information from death certificates with data on important characteristics of the deceased in order to identify and address pressing future health issues. Data include use of health services prior to death, socioeconomic status, and lifestyle and health behaviors. Data are obtained from informants and hospitals or institutions identified on the death certificate. Data from NMFS extend beyond the range of items normally included on the death certificate, permitting epidemiological and statistical analyses of mortality not possible using data solely contained in vital records. National estimates can be calculated and used to assess the reliability of data reported on the vital record.

SPONSORSHIP The NMFS is sponsored by the Division of Vital Statistics, National Center for Health Statistics, U.S. Department of Health and Human Services.

DESIGN Information from the death certificate is coupled with data obtained from the next of kin or informant who provided the information concerning the deceased on the death certificate, and from hospital, hospice, or nursing home facilities in which the deceased was admitted during the last year of life. Surveys of informants are conducted both by telephone and in person. Information obtained from next of kin is then corroborated through followup questionnaires to health facilities. A sample of about 20,000 deaths from all certificates filed in state and independent registration areas is taken, from which followup questionnaires are sent. The 1986 sample was nationally representative of all deaths of persons aged 25 and older. The 1993 NMFS will be a nationally representative sample of adults and adolescents 15 years of age or older who died in 1993. The 1993 NMFS sampling frame will comprise death certificates selected from the Current Mortality Sample (CMS) of 1993, a ten percent sample of the states' death certificates received by the National Center for Health Statistics. Approximately 20,000 deaths will be examined, with an oversampling of deaths due to AIDS, substance abuse, cancer, heart and lung disease, accidents, homicides and suicides, and deaths among minorities.

PERIODICITY Surveys were conducted in 1961, 1962-63, 1964-65, 1966-68, and 1986. The 1993 NMFS will be conducted during 1993-1994.

CONTENT Questions on the 1986 NMFS included health care services provided in the last year of life, sources of payment of health services, and lifestyle, health, personal, and background characteristics. The 1993 NMFS will closely follow that of the 1986 survey; in addition, information on HIV/AIDS, substance abuse, accidents, homicides, suicides, the elderly, mortality among minorities, and chronic disease and disease prevention will be collected.

LIMITATIONS In 1966-68, death certificates were sampled only for those 35-84. In 1986, the sample was limited to those aged 25 and older. The 1993 sample will include adults and adolescents aged 15 or older. Information pertaining to deceased children or their families, however, was not obtained in either the 1966-1968 or 1986 surveys, and will not be collected in the 1993 NMFS. While the NMFS allows for identification and planning for future health issues, death registration systems can vary from state to state in terms of the consistency, completeness, and accuracy of recorded information, particularly with respect to cause of death. Therefore, the comparability of information on death certificates across states may be limited. In addition, the next of kin or informant may not know or may have to estimate specific details concerning the deceased (for example, year of birth or social security number), especially if the deceased is elderly. These items may be important to accurately link the death certificate with other health records.

AVAILABILITY Division of Vital Statistics tapes can be purchased from:

National Technical Information Service
5285 Port Royal Road
Springfield, VA 22161
703/487-4780

For information on tape specification, price, and stock numbers, contact:

> Division of Vital Statistics
> Scientific and Technical Information Branch
> 6525 Belcrest Road
> Hyattsville, MD 20782
> 301/436-8500

For information on tape content, methodology and procedures, contact:

> Joe Fred Gonzalez
> Mathematical Statistician
> Office of Research and Methodology
> National Center for Health Statistics
> 6525 Belcrest Rd., Rm. 915
> Hyattsville, MD 20782
> 301/436-7022

For information specifically on the 1986 or 1993 National Mortality Followback Survey, contact:

> Dr. Paul J. Placek
> Chief, Followback Survey Branch
> Division of Vital Statistics/NCHS
> 6525 Belcrest Road, Rm. 1070
> Hyattsville, MD 20782
> 301/436-7032

PUBLICATIONS

Centers for Disease Control. (1989). National Mortality Followback Survey: Characteristics of persons who died from diseases of the heart, United States, 1986. *Morbidity and Mortality Weekly Reports, 38*
(34), 597-600.

Kapantais, G., and Powell-Griner, E. (1989). Characteristics of persons dying from AIDS: Preliminary data from the 1989

National Mortality Followback Survey. *Advance Data from Vital and Health Statistics, 173*. Hyattsville, MD: National Center for Health Statistics.

Seeman, I. (1992). National Mortality Followback Survey: 1986 Summary, United States. *Vital and Health Statistics, 20*(19). Hyattsville, MD: National Center for Health Statistics.

Seeman, I., Poe, G.S., & McLaughlin, J.K. (1989). Design of the 1986 National Mortality Followback Survey: Considerations on collecting data on decedents. *Public Health Report, 104*(2), 183-188.

National Mortality Followback Survey
Year of Questionnaire: 1986
Sample size: 20,000 deaths of persons 25 and older[1]
FAMILY LEVEL CHARACTERISTICS

Family Composition
- ○ Full roster of household members (first name, age, sex, and relationship to reference person of each member)
- ○ Partial roster of household members
- ● Number of adults in household[2]
- ● Number of children in household[2]
- ○ Approximate relationship of family members to householder, child, or one another
- ○ Exact relationship of family members to householder, child, or one another
- ○ Information about part-time household member
- ○ Information about family members no longer living in household
- ○ Information about relatives who live nearby but not in household

Socioeconomic
- ● Total family income
- ○ Number of persons who depend on family income
- ○ Sources of income
- ○ Income amounts identified separately by source
- ○ Poverty status
- ○ Welfare status
- ○ Food Stamps receipt
- ○ Child support receipt
- ● Medicaid coverage[3]
- ● Private health insurance[3]
- ○ Home ownership/renters
- ○ Assets (other than home ownership)
- ○ Public housing status
- ○ Telephone in household
- ○ Language other than English spoken in home

Geographic/Community Variables
- ● Region of country
- ● State of residence
- ● County/city/MSA of residence
- ○ Size/type of community
- ● Zip code
- ○ Telephone area code
- ○ Metropolitan residence
- ○ Neighborhood quality
- ○ Local labor market

Stage in Family Life Cycle
- ○ Age of adult respondent or spouse/partner
- ○ Marital status of adult respondent or spouse/partner
- ○ Employment status of adult respondent or spouse/partner
- ○ Presence of own children in household
- ○ Age of youngest own child in household
- ○ Age of oldest own child in household
- ○ Existence of own children who have left home
- ○ Intention to have (more) children in future

Family Functioning

- Family activities or time use
- Community involvement (civic, religious, recreational)
- Family communication patterns
- Family decision-making
- Marital conflict
- Marital happiness/satisfaction
- Parent-child conflict
- History of marital separations
- History of family violence
- History of marital counselling

CHARACTERISTICS OF ADULT FAMILY MEMBERS

Adult Respondent or Reference Person	Current Spouse in HH	Current or Former Spouse Not in HH	
●	○	○	Age
●	○	○	Gender
●	○	○	Race
●	○	○	Hispanic origin
○	○	○	Other origin/ethnicity
○	○	○	Religious affiliation
○	○	○	Religious participation
○	○	○	Country of birth
○	○	○	Immigrant status
○	○	○	English fluency
●	○	○	Current marital status
●	○	○	Marital history
○	○	○	Cohabitation status
○	○	○	Cohabitation history
○	○	○	Parental status
○	○	○	Number children ever born/sired
○	○	○	Age at first birth
○	○	○	Age of youngest child
○	○	○	Children living elsewhere
○	○	○	Duration at current address
○	○	○	Residential mobility
●	●	○	Educational attainment
○	○	○	Degrees attained
○	○	○	GED or regular HS diploma
○	○	○	Current enrollment
●	●	○	Current employment status
○	○	○	Hours usually worked (ft/pt)
○	○	○	Weeks worked
○	○	○	Annual employment pattern
●	●	○	Main occupation
○	○	○	Earnings
○	○	○	Wage rate
○	○	○	Payment of child support
○	○	○	Aptitude or achievement score
●	○	○	Health/disability status[5]
○	○	○	Self-esteem
○	○	○	Locus of control or efficacy
○	○	○	Depression or subjective well-being
○	○	○	Work-related attitudes

CHARACTERISTICS OF CHILD FAMILY MEMBERS[4]

Reference Child or Youth Respondent	Other Children (in HH)	
●	○	Age
●	○	Month and year of birth
●	○	Gender
●	○	Race
●	○	Hispanic origin
○	○	Other origin/ethnicity
○	○	Religious affiliation
○	○	Religious participation
○	○	Country of birth
○	○	Immigrant status
○	○	English fluency
○	○	Exact relationship to adult family members
○	○	Exact relationship to other children in HH
○	○	Marital status/history
○	○	Parental status/history
○	○	Current enrollment in regular school
○	○	Current enrollment in preschool/daycare
●	○	Highest grade completed
○	○	Grade now enrolled
○	○	Employment status/history
●	○	Health status[5]
○	○	Handicapping conditions
○	○	Grade repetition
○	○	Aptitude or achievement score
○	○	Pregnancy/birth history
○	○	Psychological well-being
○	○	Delinquency

NOTES

1. Information refers to period surrounding the deceased's last year of life, or at least the time of death.
2. Total family size only.
3. Identifies sources used to pay for health care, including Medicare.
4. Items represent information to be collected on persons 15-17 who will die in 1993.
5. Varying details concerning limiting, chronic conditions, diet, and general health behavior.

278

National Survey of Black Americans

PURPOSE The National Survey of Black Americans (NSBA) is one of eight surveys conducted under the Program for Research on Black Americans (PRBA) at the Institute for Social Research at the University of Michigan. The PRBA was formed in 1976 by social scientists and students at the University of Michigan to collect and analyze information on national and international studies of African Americans and peoples of African descent.

While information concerning the African American adult population has been collected as part of surveys of the general adult population, the concepts, measures, and theoretical premises underlying such studies typically have been designed to capture issues most relevant to the life of white Americans. The NSBA was specifically developed for two purposes: 1) to address the cultural context of black life in America and to document issues most salient to the lives of black Americans, and 2) to provide research and training opportunities for black social scientists and students interested in the social, economic, and psychological issues pertinent to the lives of black Americans.

SPONSORSHIP The NSBA was initiated in 1977 through funding from the National Institute of Mental Health. Data were originally collected by James S. Jackson and Gerald Gurin. Sampling methodology, survey development, staff training, and data collection and analysis were made possible in part by the Survey Research Center, Institute for Social Research, University of Michigan.

DESIGN The NSBA is a multi-stage national probability sample based on the 1970 Census, incorporating census updates of the black population. The selection of the sample came from 76 certainty and non-certainty areas (areas predetermined to contain or not to contain a minimum number of black households). A total of 2,107 adults 18 years of age and older were interviewed over a seven month period between 1979 and 1980, representing an overall response rate of 67%.

Two distinct screening methods were employed to identify households for subsequent participation in the study. One was the Standard Listing and Screening Procedures (SLASP). SLASP was applied to mixed and mostly black areas and provided, along with a listing of every household in the designated sampling area, a subset of households which served as references for race identification and selection purposes. The other method was the Wide Area Screening Procedure (WASP), which employed white interviewers in areas where few or no black households were suspected. WASP interviewers questioned the reference households about black households or black families in their area, and then listed only the identified black housing units for screening. This process minimized the cost and time involved in locating and listing black housing units in areas where few black households were identified.

PERIODICITY The first survey was conducted between 1979 and 1980 over a seven month period. Two followup interviews of the original cohort were conducted. The first followup, between 1987 and 1988, included a total of 935 respondents from the original 1979 cohort. The second followup was carried out between 1988 and 1989 on 782 respondents. Members of the original cohort who were also from a three generation family were reinterviewed between 1980 and 1981 as part of PRBA's National Three Generation Study.

CONTENT The NSBA covers eight general areas:
- Neighborhood - general life satisfaction, and community involvement;
- Religion - religious affiliation and the role of the church;
- Health and problems - health status, health service utilization, and satisfaction with services, locus of control, and self esteem;
- Employment status - type of work and work history, barriers to employment, racial discrimination and composition of work force;
- Family and friends - general support from family and friends, importance of relationships;
- Use of help resources - mental health and help seeking behavior;

- Group and personal identity - racial identity, attitudes and group affiliations; and
- Personal data - background characteristics, family and household structure.

LIMITATIONS Although the NSBA covers general questions on the background and socioeconomic status of adult black respondents, the detail of many of those questions is less than that provided by most surveys of the general adult population. However, the range of content areas allows for more analyses regarding the life situation of black Americans that have not been adequately examined using other national data sets.

As the survey is limited to the adult population, only the effects of various factors on adult outcomes and functioning can be investigated. No specific or detailed information on children is collected, with the exception of the household roster, where age and relation of children in the home to the respondent are identified. However, profiles of adults living in different family circumstances (such as married-couple or single-parent households) can be made.

AVAILABILITY The NSBA is available from the Inter-University Consortium for Political and Social Research (ICPSR) in two formats: card image and OSIRIS. The card image file contains several decks per case. The OSIRIS dictionary provides the format and coding information for each variable contained on the data file. A single logical record is constructed for each case, with 1,451 variables and 2,107 records. Data can be obtained from:

> Inter-University Consortium
>   for Political and Social Research
> P.O. Box 1248
> Ann Arbor, MI 48106-1248
> 313/763-5010

For substantive questions, contact:

> Dr. James S. Jackson or Sally E. Oswald
> Program for Research on Black Americans
> University of Michigan
> 5118 Institute for Social Research
> Ann Arbor, Michigan 48106-1248
> 313/763-0045

PUBLICATIONS

Jackson, J.S. (Ed.). (1991). *Life in black America*. Newbury Park, CA: Sage.

Bowman, P.J. (1987). Post-industrial displacement and family role strains: Challenges to the black family. In P. Voydanoff & L.C. Majka (Eds.), *Families and economic distress*. Beverly Hills, CA: Sage.

Bowman, P.J. (1985). Black fathers and the provider role: Role strain, informal coping resources and life happiness. In A.W. Boykin (Ed.), *Empirical research in black psychology*. Rockville, MD: National Institute of Mental Health.

Bowman, P.J. & Howard, C.S. (1985). Race-related socialization, motivation, and academic achievement: A study of black youth in three-generation families. *Journal of the American Academy of Child Psychiatry, 24*(2): 134-141.

Chatters, L.M. (1990). The family life of older black adults: Stressors and resources. *Journal of Health and Social Policy, 1*(4), 45-53.

Gibson, R.C. (1986). Perspectives on the black family. In A. Pifer & D.L. Bronte (Eds.), *Our aging society: Paradox and promise*. New York: W.W. Norton.

Hatchett, S.J. & Jackson, J.S. (in press). An assessment of African-American extended kin systems: Data from a national survey of black Americans. In H.P. McAdoo (Ed.), *Family ethnicity: Strengths in diversity*. Newbury Park, CA: Sage.

Taylor, R.J. (1986). Receipt and support from family among black Americans: Demographic and familial differences. *Journal of Marriage and the Family, 48*, 67-77.

National Survey of Black Americans
Year of Questionnaire: 1979-1980
Sample size: 2,107
FAMILY LEVEL CHARACTERISTICS

Family Composition
- Full roster of household members (first name, age, sex, and relationship to reference person of each member)
- ○ Partial roster of household members
- Number of adults in household
- Number of children in household
- Approximate relationship of family members to householder, child, or one another
- ○ Exact relationship of family members to householder, child, or one another
- ○ Information about part-time household member
- ○ Information about family members no longer living in household
- Information about relatives who live nearby but not in household

Socioeconomic
- Total family income
- ○ Number of persons who depend on family income
- ○ Sources of income
- ○ Income amounts identified separately by source
- ○ Poverty status
- Welfare status
- ○ Food Stamps receipt
- ○ Child support receipt
- ○ Medicaid coverage[1]
- Private health insurance[1]
- Home ownership/renters
- ○ Assets (other than home ownership)
- ○ Public housing status
- ○ Telephone in household
- ○ Language other than English spoken in home

Geographic/Community Variables
- Region of country
- State of residence
- County/city/MSA of residence
- ○ Size/type of community
- ○ Zip code
- ○ Telephone area code
- Metropolitan residence
- ○ Neighborhood quality
- ○ Local labor market

Stage in Family Life Cycle
- Age of adult respondent or spouse/partner
- Marital status of adult respondent or spouse/partner
- Employment status of adult respondent or spouse/partner
- Presence of own children in household
- Age of youngest own child in household
- Age of oldest own child in household
- Existence of own children who have left home
- ○ Intention to have (more) children in future

Family Functioning

○ Family activities or time use
● Community involvement (civic, religious, recreational)
○ Family communication patterns
○ Family decision-making
○ Marital conflict
● Marital happiness/satisfaction[2]
● Parent-child conflict
○ History of marital separations
○ History of family violence
○ History of marital counselling

CHARACTERISTICS OF ADULT FAMILY MEMBERS

Adult Respondent or Reference Mother	Current Father in HH	Current or Former Spouse Not in HH	
●	○	○	Age
●	○	○	Gender
●	○	○	Race
○	○	○	Hispanic origin
○	○	○	Other origin/ethnicity
●	○	○	Religious affiliation
●	○	○	Religious participation
●	○	○	Country of birth
○	○	○	Immigrant status
○	○	○	English fluency
●	○	○	Current marital status
○	○	○	Marital history
●	○	○	Cohabitation status
○	○	○	Cohabitation history
●	○	○	Parental status
●	○	○	Number children ever born/sired
○	○	○	Age at first birth
●	○	○	Age of youngest child
●	○	○	Children living elsewhere[3]
●	○	○	Duration at current address[4]
●	○	○	Residential mobility
●	●	○	Educational attainment
●	●	○	Degrees attained
●	●	○	GED or regular HS diploma
○	○	○	Current enrollment
●	●	○	Current employment status
●	○	○	Hours usually worked (ft/pt)
●	○	○	Weeks worked
○	○	○	Annual employment pattern
●	●	○	Main occupation
●	○	○	Earnings
●	○	○	Wage rate
○	○	○	Payment of child support
○	○	○	Aptitude or achievement score
●	○	○	Health/disability status
●	○	○	Self-esteem
●	○	○	Locus of control or efficacy
●	○	○	Depression or subjective well-being
●	○	○	Work-related attitudes

CHARACTERISTICS OF CHILD FAMILY MEMBERS

Reference Child or Youth Respondent	Other Children (in HH)	
O	●	Age
O	O	Month and year of birth
O	●	Gender
O	O	Race
O	O	Hispanic origin
O	O	Other origin/ethnicity
O	O	Religious affiliation
O	O	Religious participation
O	O	Country of birth
O	O	Immigrant status
O	O	English fluency
O	●	Exact relationship to adult family members[5]
O	O	Exact relationship to other children in HH
O	O	Marital status/history
O	O	Parental status/history
O	O	Current enrollment in regular school
O	O	Current enrollment in preschool/daycare
O	O	Highest grade completed
O	O	Grade now enrolled
O	O	Employment status/history
O	O	Health status
O	O	Handicapping conditions
O	O	Grade repetition
O	O	Aptitude or achievement score
O	O	Pregnancy/birth history
O	O	Psychological well-being
O	O	Delinquency

NOTES

1. No distinction between private or public health insurance is made.
2. General satisfaction with family life.
3. Can verify by using household roster and vital status of children ever born.
4. Can be approximated using date of last move and date of interview. Only year of last move is available.
5. Exact relationship to adult respondent.

National Survey of Children

PURPOSE First fielded in 1976, the National Survey of Children (NSC) was designed to provide a broad profile of the physical health, emotional well-being, and social development of U.S. children of elementary-school age, and an assessment of the family and neighborhood circumstances in which they were growing up. In a second wave of interviews conducted in 1981, these goals were augmented by a focus on the effects of marital conflict and disruption on children. In a third wave of interviews conducted in 1987, additional information was collected on welfare dependence and early sexual and fertility behavior as well as various measures of youth development and well-being in young adulthood.

SPONSORSHIP Funding for the initial survey (Wave I) was provided by the Foundation for Child Development. Data collection activities in 1981 (Wave II) were jointly sponsored by the Foundation for Child Development and the National Institute of Mental Health. The third wave (Wave III) of data collection was funded by the Center for Population Research of the National Institute of Child Health and Human Development, the Office of the Assistant Secretary for Planning and Evaluation of the Department of Health and Human Services, the Robert Wood Johnson Foundation, and the Ford Foundation. Field work for all three waves was conducted by the Institute for Survey Research at Temple University.

DESIGN The original 1976 sample was a multi-stage stratified probability sample of households containing children aged 7 to 11 (i.e., born between the years 1965 and 1970). Up to two children per household were eligible to be in the survey. Data were collected on 2,301 children in 1,747 households, for an 80% completion rate. Personal interviews were conducted with the children themselves and the parent most knowledgeable about the child (usually the mother). Self-administered questionnaires were completed by the teachers of 1,682 (74%) of the children. Black households were oversampled to produce approximately 500 black children. The data were weighted to correct for this over-sampling and other minor differences between sample and census estimates by age, sex, and place of residence.

The second wave was conducted in 1981, when the children were 12-16 years of age. Because of funding limitations, a subset of 1,749 children was selected for restudy, and telephone rather than in-person interviews were conducted. As before, data were collected from the child, a parent, and a teacher. All children from disrupted or high-conflict families were followed, as was a subsample of the rest. Data were gathered on 1,423 children, or 79% of the chosen subset. Weights were developed to adjust for differential subsampling and completion rates.

In 1987, respondent youths were 18 to 22 years of age. Telephone interviews were completed with 1,147 youth, or nearly 81% of eligible respondents. Interviews were conducted with the young person and with the most knowledgeable parent or parent substitute.

Overall attrition from the initial completed set of cases to Wave III was 36%; although substantial, attrition was not disproportionately high among children whose parents divorced or were in high-conflict marriages at the first wave. (Tables showing analyses of NSC attrition patterns are available from Child Trends, Inc.). The final set of weights adjusts for the differential attrition, as well as the oversampling of black children and undersampling of children from large families in Wave I, and the oversampling of youth from disrupted or high-conflict families in Wave II. Estimates derived from the weighted sample should be representative of all youth in the U.S. in the eligible age range.

PERIODICITY No additional data collection is planned, though location information has been obtained to make such data collection feasible.

CONTENT The main goal of the 1976 survey was to learn about the perceptions and feelings of elementary schoolchildren, and to assess their health, development, and well-being. In addition, the NSC collected a wealth of information about the families in which the children were being raised. The first wave is especially rich in data on parental backgrounds, including the national origins of their ancestors, religions in which the parents were raised, types of places in which they grew up, educational attainments, occupations, and detailed marital and parenting histories. This information was collected not only about parents currently in the household, but for those living elsewhere because of a separation or divorce that had occurred within the last five years.

The interviewer inquired about the functioning and well-being of the parent respondent (usually the mother), asking about such things as time pressures, money worries, feelings of tension, depression, and exhaustion with parental responsibilities, physical health, and overall life satisfaction. The parent was also asked to report on neighborhood characteristics, childrearing goals, children's time use, family activities, and areas of conflict with the other parent.

The Wave I interview with the child included questions about rules at home and how the child was rewarded and punished by each parent, as well as feelings of neglect and fears and worries about the family. However, children's responses are more mercurial than those of adults (though often less guarded and more candid as well). Thus, scales based on child interviews tend to be less reliable than those social researchers are used to dealing with. Despite this limitation, meaningful relationships between family characteristics and parenting variables based on children's reports have been found.

The Wave II survey contains the richest information about family processes, including questions to both parent and adolescent respondents about family activities, family decision-making, husband-wife and parent-child communication, and family climate. Items on marital satisfaction and marital conflict from Wave I are repeated and expanded upon, supplemented by information about physical abuse and marital separations. The focus on divorce and its sequelae leads to questions about child support, custody arrangements, and post-divorce cooperation and conflict.

Multi-item scales with good psychometric properties index the quality of the teen's relationship with each parent, including absent biological parents or resident stepparents, where relevant. Questions on family-related attitudes are also put to parent and child respondents. Because the youth respondents are teenagers in Wave II, their responses are generally more reliable than those given by the children in Wave I.

Wave III contains information describing the young people in the survey as they embark on the developmental challenges of young adulthood. These include the initiation of higher education or the conclusion of formal schooling, early employment, the start of adult love relationships, and for some, early parenthood. Many questions asked of the youths replicate items asked in the second wave, including questions on family relationships and contact with any parents living outside the home, school progress, educational aspirations, delinquent behavior, and substance abuse. There are some new measures as well, such as scales on depression and locus of control. Teenage mothers are asked about their relationships with their child or children.

Parents in Wave III provide retrospective information on maternal employment and welfare receipt while the child was growing up, as well as data on whether and when the youth ever lived away from home, such as in foster care. Parents also give a current assessment of the youth's problem behavior and communication with the family, as well as reports on marital conflict, family violence, and adult functioning similar to those gathered in Waves I and II.

Thus, the longitudinal component makes it possible to relate family variables from the first waves to adolescent and young adult outcomes. Also possible are studies correlating earlier family characteristics with measures of adult well-being and family functioning at the third wave. Before embarking on the latter type of study, one should recognize that some high-risk families had already been disrupted by Wave I, and that the units for whom family-level measures are available from all three waves are only a subset of American families with children.

The NSC is unusual for a national survey in the wealth of information that is collected about family life and about the attitudes and behaviors of young people as they grow from early childhood to adulthood. The fact that information is collected from children as well as parents makes it well suited for studying family dynamics and the implication of family behaviors for children's development and well-being.

The richness of the NSC files will be further enhanced by a current effort at Child Trends to append state and zip-code level policy variables to the data set. An example of a state-level variable is the AFDC benefit level, while examples of zip-code level measures include the local unemployment rate, percent of families headed by single parents, and percent of families in poverty. The addition of these measures should make the NSC useful for studying the influence of public policy on family life.

LIMITATIONS The relatively modest size of the sample (1,147 youths and just under 900 parents in 1987) limits the analytical uses of the data, especially with regard to relatively rare family forms, such as adoptive families, or extreme behaviors, such as serious delinquency. There is also evidence of underreporting of delinquency and substance abuse, especially by African American youth. Although the response rate for each of the waves approximated 80 percent, the cumulative attrition means that longitudinal data are available for only 64 percent of the subset selected for follow up. Attrition was more severe for black families and those who were informally separated or never married than for white families and those who remained married or were legally divorced.

AVAILABILITY
Data from all three waves are available from:

Inter-University Consortium for
 Political and Social Research
P.O. Box 1248
Ann Arbor, MI 48106-1248
313/763-5010

Data Archive on Adolescent Pregnancy
 and Pregnancy Prevention
Sociometrics Corporation
170 State St., Suite 260
Los Altos, CA 94022-2812
800/846-3475

For substantive questions, contact:

Nicholas Zill, Ph.D.
Westat, Inc.
1650 Research Blvd.
Rockville, MD 20850-3129
301/294-4448

PUBLICATIONS

Allison, P.D. & Furstenberg, F.F., Jr. (1989). How marital dissolution affects children: Variations by age and sex. *Developmental Psychology, 25,* 540-549.

Baydar, N. (1988). Effects of parental separation and re-entry into union on the emotional well-being of children. *Journal of Marriage and the Family, 50,* 967-981.

Cherlin, A.J., Furstenberg, F.F., Jr., Chase-Lansdale, P.L., Kiernan, K.E., Robins, P.K., Morrison, D.R., & Tietler, J.O. (1991). Longitudinal studies of the effects of divorce on children in Great Britain and the United States. *Science, 252,* 1386-1389.

Furstenberg, F.F., Jr. (1987). The new extended family: The experience of parents and children after remarriage. In K. Pasley & M. Ihinger-Tollman (Eds.), *Remarriage and stepparenting today* (pp. 42-61). New York: Guilford.

Furstenberg, F.F., Jr., & Nord, C.W. (1985). Parenting apart: Patterns of childrearing after marital dissolution. *Journal of Marriage and the Family, 47*(4), 893-904.

Furstenberg, F.F., Jr., Nord, C.W., Peterson, J.L., & Zill, N. (1983). The life course of children of divorce: Marital disruption and parental conflict. *American Sociological Review, 48*(5), 656-666.

Harris, K.M., & Morgan, S.P. (1991). Fathers, sons, and daughters: Differential paternal involvement in parenting. *Journal of Marriage and the Family, 53*(3), 531-544.

Moore, K. A., Peterson, J.L., & Furstenberg, F.F., Jr. (1986). Parental attitudes and the occurrence of early sexual activity. *Journal of Marriage and the Family, 48*(4), 777-782.

Moore, K.A., & Stief, T. (1991). Changes in marriage and fertility behavior: Behavior versus attitudes of young adults. *Youth and Society, 22*(3), 362-386.

Peterson, J.L., & Zill, N. (1986). Marital disruption, parent-child relationships, and behavioral problems in children. *Journal of Marriage and the Family, 48*(2), 295-307.

Zill, N., Morrison, D.R., & Coiro, M.J. (forthcoming). Long-term effects of parental divorce on parent-child relationships, adjustment, and achievement in adulthood. *Journal of Family Psychology.*

Zill, N., & Peterson, J.L. (1982). Learning to do things without help. In L.M. Laosa & I.E. Sigal (Eds.), *Families as learning environments for children.* New York: Plenum.

Zill, N., & Rhoads, A. (1991). *Assessing family strengths in a national sample of families with adolescent children.* Washington, DC: Child Trends.

National Survey of Children
Years of Questionnaire: 1976, 1981, 1987
Sample size: 2,301 children aged 7-11 in 1976[1]
FAMILY-LEVEL CHARACTERISTICS
Sample size: 1,747 families (Wave I)

Family Composition
- ● Full roster of household members (first name, age, sex, and relationship to reference person of each member)
- ○ Partial roster of household members
- ● Number of adults in household
- ● Number of children in household
- ○ Approximate relationship of family members to householder, child, or one another
- ● Exact relationship of family members to householder, child, or one another
- ○ Information about part-time household member
- ● Information about family members no longer living in household
- ● Information about relatives who live nearby but not in household

Socioeconomic
- ● Total family income
- ● Number of persons who depend on family income
- ● Sources of income
- ○ Income amounts identified separately by source
- ○ Poverty status
- ● Welfare status
- ● Food Stamps receipt
- ● Child support receipt
- ○ Medicaid coverage
- ○ Private health insurance
- ● Home ownership/renters
- ○ Assets (other than home ownership)
- ○ Public housing status
- ○ Telephone in household
- ● Language other than English spoken in home

Geographic/Community Variables
- ● Region of country
- ○ State of residence
- ○ County/city/MSA of residence
- ● Size/type of community
- ● Zip code
- ○ Telephone area code
- ● Metropolitan residence
- ● Neighborhood quality
- ○ Local labor market

Stage in Family Life Cycle
- ● Age of adult respondent or spouse/partner
- ● Marital status of adult respondent or spouse/partner
- ● Employment status of adult respondent or spouse/partner
- ● Presence of own children in household
- ● Age of youngest own child in household
- ● Age of oldest own child in household
- ● Existence of own children who have left home
- ○ Intention to have (more) children in future

293

Family Functioning
- Family activities or time use
- Community involvement (civic, religious, recreational)
- Family communication patterns
- Family decision-making
- Marital conflict
- Marital happiness/satisfaction
- Parent-child conflict
- History of marital separations
- History of family violence
○ History of marital counselling

CHARACTERISTICS OF ADULT FAMILY MEMBERS
Sample size: 1,747 parent respondents (Wave I)[2]

Adult Respondent or Reference Person	Current Spouse in HH	Current or Former Spouse Not in HH	
●	●	●	Age
●	●	●	Gender
●	●	●	Race
●	●	●	Hispanic origin
●	●	●	Other origin/ethnicity
●	●	●	Religious affiliation
●	○	○	Religious participation
●	●	●	Country of birth
○	○	○	Immigrant status
○	○	○	English fluency
●	●	●	Current marital status
●	●	●	Marital history
●	●	●	Cohabitation status
○	○	○	Cohabitation history
●	●	○	Parental status
●	●	●	Number children ever born/sired
●	●	○	Age at first birth
●	●	○	Age of youngest child
●	●	○	Children living elsewhere
●	●	○	Duration at current address
●	●	○	Residential mobility
●	●	●	Educational attainment
●	●	●	Degrees attained
○	○	○	GED or regular HS diploma
●	●	○	Current enrollment
●	●	○	Current employment status
○	○	○	Hours usually worked (ft/pt)
○	○	○	Weeks worked
○	○	○	Annual employment pattern
●	●	●	Main occupation
○	○	○	Earnings
○	○	○	Wage rate
●	●	●	Payment of child support
○	○	○	Aptitude or achievement score
●	●	●	Health/disability status
○	○	○	Self-esteem
○	○	○	Locus of control or efficacy
●	●	○	Depression or subjective well-being
○	○	○	Work-related attitudes

CHARACTERISTICS OF CHILD FAMILY MEMBERS
Sample size: 2,279 children with parent and child data (Wave I)[3]

Reference Child or Youth Respondent	Other Children (in HH)	
●	●	Age
●	●	Month and year of birth
●	●	Gender
●	●	Race
●	●	Hispanic origin
●	●	Other origin/ethnicity
●	●	Religious affiliation
●	●	Religious participation
○	○	Country of birth
○	○	Immigrant status
○	○	English fluency
●	○	Exact relationship to adult family members
○	○	Exact relationship to other children in HH
●	○	Marital status/history
●	○	Parental status/history
●	○	Current enrollment in regular school
○	○	Current enrollment in preschool/daycare
●	○	Highest grade completed
●	○	Grade now enrolled
●	○	Employment status/history
●	○	Health status
●	○	Handicapping conditions
●	○	Grade repetition
●	○	Aptitude or achievement score
●	○	Pregnancy/birth history
●	○	Psychological well-being
●	○	Delinquency

NOTES
1. 1,794 children selected for restudy in subsequent waves.
2. 894 parents with data from all three waves.
3. 1,143 youth with data from all three waves.

National Survey of Families and Households

PURPOSE Major changes in patterns of fertility, marriage, mortality, migration, family composition, and household structure have occurred over the past several decades in the United States. The National Survey of Families and Households (NSFH) was developed to gain more information on the causes and consequences of the changes in American families.

SPONSORSHIP The Center for Population Research of the National Institute of Child Health and Human Development funded the survey and the five-year followup, both of which were developed and conducted by the University of Wisconsin.

DESIGN This is a cross-sectional survey of approximately 13,000 households. The overall sample includes a main sample of 9,643 households, plus a double sampling of black and Hispanic households, single-parent families, families with stepchildren, cohabiting couples, and recently married couples. Personal interviews were conducted with the primary respondent, although information on sensitive topics was obtained using self-administered forms.

One adult per household was randomly selected as the primary respondent. Spouses and cohabiting partners of this person were given a shorter self-administered questionnaire. One of the unique and potentially useful features of this survey is the fact that many identical questions were asked independently of the respondent and his or her spouse.

The cross-sectional design enables researchers to describe current living arrangements of American households in great detail. Retrospective information was also obtained on selected topics. Detailed life history information was collected on the living arrangements of adults when they were children, on their experiences leaving home, on cohabitation and marital experience, as well as on educational and employment experiences. The inclusion of this historical information supports research on the consequences of varied living patterns for current well-being.

The substantive focus of the survey is intentionally broad to facilitate examination of how household and family factors affect a wide variety of outcomes, including marital and parenting relationships, contact with kin, economic status, and psychological well-being.

A five year followup survey began in the fall of 1992. This is virtually a complete replication of the first survey, with the exception of a few measures which did not perform well. There are some additional psychological measures added as well for the focal children. The following persons are being interviewed in the followup survey: all original respondents; spouses, current and ex, of the respondent; all focal children who were ages five through eighteen at the time of the first survey; all deceased respondents (a relative will be interviewed); and a randomly selected parent of all respondents, if the parent is age 60 or older.

PERIODICITY Data collection took place during the summer and fall of 1987. The followup survey, described above, began in the fall of 1992.

CONTENT Given the central focus of the survey on family and household structure, numerous questions were asked regarding household composition, both currently and historically. For example, occasional residents of the household were identified. Questions were also asked about periods when the respondent lived apart from his/her parents as a child, as well as periods when the parents lived with the adult respondent. In addition, the existence of kin outside the household and the frequency of contact with such kin was ascertained. For example, children born to the respondent and/or to their spouse who do not live in the household were identified and information about contact with these children was obtained.

A complete fertility history was obtained for the primary respondent, as was information about the respondent's fertility plans.

Some information was obtained about each of the children in the household, and additional information obtained about a selected "focal child." For all of the children, questions were asked about school attendance, grade repetition, behavior pro-blems requiring a meeting, school suspension or expulsion, emotional problems, trouble with the police, running away, and whether the child was seen as difficult or as easy to raise. Additional questions asked about the focal child include educational expectations, whether the parent and child had ever been separated for six months or longer, enjoyable and difficult times during the past 30 days, behavior problems, and whether the amount or the type of television viewed by the child is restricted by the parent. These questions vary somewhat according to the age of the focal child.

Additional questions were asked about focal children aged 4 and younger, including whether and the hours the child attended nursery or preschool; whether and how often the child was spanked; whether the child seemed fast, slow or on time in developing; the hours the parent spent caring for the child's physical needs on a typical day; and how frequently the parent read to the child.

For all focal children aged 11 and younger, several additional questions were asked, including whether and how frequently the child was spanked; the child's usual bedtime; and how frequently the child stayed up late. For children aged 5 through 11, parents were asked to assess their child's class ranking (e.g., one of the best, above the middle, middle, below the middle, or near the bottom).

For all focal children aged 5 to 18, questions were asked about times when the child was left alone (such as before school, all day, and overnight); whether the child had regular chores to do; whether they had to be reminded to do chores; whether chores had to be done before TV or play; and how frequently chores got done. Respondents were also asked whether these children get an allowance and the amount; whether the allowance was paid for work; whether any work was done for pay; and how much was paid for such work around the house in a typical month. Parents were also asked whether the child was supposed to let them know their whereabouts when the young person is away from home.

For focal children aged 12 to 18, further questions appropriate for older youth were asked, such as how frequently the adolescent dated; whether the young person had a steady boyfriend or girlfriend; and whether the young person had a car, motorcycle, or moped, and if so, who purchased it and who paid the costs for maintenance and insurance. The frequency of disagreements with parents about friends, sex, money, school, and other topics was ascertained, as was the time the youth was expected to be home on school nights and weekend nights. Regarding homework, parents were asked if the child had regular homework; how often they had to remind the child to do it; whether the child had to do homework before other activities; and how often the child got it done. In addition, parents were asked what sort of grades their child received. The money earned by these older children from occasional or regular jobs was also ascertained, as were the hours worked by the young person and parental expectations for how the child should spend his or her earnings.

If the child had an non-residential parent, the respondent was asked about visitation and contact with that parent by phone or letter. Information on the type and content of agreements about custody and child support and about the regularity of payments was obtained. The respondent was asked about the location and the marital status of the non-residential parent, and whether the non-residential parent had had additional children. A similar set of questions was asked about children of the respondent or the respondent's spouse who lived outside of the respondent's household. Information about children living away at school and children over age 19 who live elsewhere was also obtained.

Background information was obtained on the respondent's education, religion, military experience, employment and income, assets and debts, work schedule, and child care arrangements for children through age 11, as well as parent education and parental employment. Questions were also asked about gifts and payments both to and from persons within and outside of the household.

Questions that were completed by the respondent using the self-administered questionnaire included items on psychological well-being; satisfaction with work, marriage, and parenthood; alcohol and drug problems; health; availability and receipt of help; social activities; assistance given to or received from adult children; information from adult children who lived with parents about their living arrangements and plans; feelings about living with a partner among those having such a partner; feelings about their marriage among married respondents; considerations in having a child; family activities; relationship with each child; relationship and contact with own parents, with any stepparent(s), with sibling(s), and with parents of partner or spouse, if any; attitudes about marriage and family; reports of family violence; thoughts concerning divorce; and methods of conflict resolution.

A relatively short self-administered interview was also conducted with spouses or cohabiting partners. This interview provides information on this person's contact and relationships with parents, spouse's parents, siblings, and children; marriage and fertility history; marital disagreements and satisfaction; considerations in having a child; relationship with each child; family activities; attitudes about marriage and family; contact with and support of children who live elsewhere; relationships with adult children who live in the household; health, drinking and drug problems; religion; education; parent education; military experience; work history; income; work schedule; child care; and time spent on household tasks.

LIMITATIONS The coverage of topics in this survey is very complete, and there are innumerable analysis possibilities. The quality of the data obtained is very good, although a few measures did not work well and will not be used in the followup study. The interview schedule was demanding for both interviewer and respondent, so data completeness may be a concern. The completion of the five-year follow up will greatly expand the capacity of the data to document transitions and support causal analyses.

AVAILABILITY A public use data tape and codebooks for the first survey are available. Contact:

> National Survey of Families and Households
> Center for Demography and Ecology
> University of Wisconsin-Madison
> 4412 Social Science Building,
> 1180 Observatory Drive
> Madison, WI 53706-1393
> 608/262-2182

PUBLICATIONS The project keeps a current list of papers available for distribution. Some of these papers cover aspects of the survey and the data set. Most of them report research which has been done using the data. This list can be ordered by calling the number above or by writing to "Publications" at the above address.

Bumpass, L., & Sweet, J. (1991). *The effect of marital disruption on intergenerational relationships*. National Survey of Families and Households Working Paper Series No. 40.

Thomson, E., Hanson, T., & McLanahan, S. (1990). *Family structure, socialization, and child well-being*. National Survey of Families and Households Working Paper Series No. 29.

Wu, L., & Martinson, B. (1991). *Family structure and the risk of premarital birth*. National Survey of Families and Households Working Paper Series No. 45.

National Survey of Families and Households

Year of Questionnaire: 1987
Sample size: 13,017 households
FAMILY-LEVEL CHARACTERISTICS
Sample size: 13,017

Family Composition

- ● Full roster of household members (first name, age, sex, and relationship to reference person of each member)
- ○ Partial roster of household members
- ● Number of adults in household
- ● Number of children in household
- ○ Approximate relationship of family members to householder, child, or one another
- ● Exact relationship of family members to householder, child, or one another
- ● Information about part-time household member
- ● Information about family members no longer living in household
- ● Information about relatives who live nearby but not in household

Socioeconomic

- ● Total family income
- ● Number of persons who depend on family income
- ● Sources of income
- ● Income amounts identified separately by source
- ● Poverty status
- ● Welfare status
- ● Food Stamps receipt[1]
- ● Child support receipt
- ○ Medicaid coverage
- ○ Private health insurance
- ● Home ownership/renters
- ● Assets (other than home ownership)
- ○ Public housing status
- ○ Telephone in household
- ○ Language other than English spoken in home

Geographic/Community Variables

- ● Region of country
- ○ State of residence
- ● County/city/MSA of residence[2]
- ● Size/type of community
- ○ Zip code
- ○ Telephone area code
- ● Metropolitan residence
- ○ Neighborhood quality
- ○ Local labor market

Stage in Family Life Cycle

- ● Age of adult respondent or spouse/partner
- ● Marital status of adult respondent or spouse/partner
- ● Employment status of adult respondent or spouse/partner
- ● Presence of own children in household
- ● Age of youngest own child in household
- ● Age of oldest own child in household
- ● Existence of own children who have left home
- ● Intention to have (more) children in future

Family Functioning
- Family activities or time use
- Community involvement (civic, religious, recreational)
- Family communication patterns
- Family decision-making
- Marital conflict
- Marital happiness/satisfaction
- Parent-child conflict
- History of marital separations
- History of family violence
- ○ History of marital counselling

CHARACTERISTICS OF ADULT FAMILY MEMBERS
Sample size: 13,017 adults

Adult Respondent or Reference Person	Current in HH	Current or Former Not in HH	
●	●	●	Age
●	●	●	Gender
●	●	○	Race
●	●	○	Hispanic origin
○	○	○	Other origin/ethnicity
●	●	●	Religious affiliation
●	●	○	Religious participation
●	○	○	Country of birth
●	●	○	Immigrant status
○	○	○	English fluency
●	●	●	Current marital status
●	●	●	Marital history
●	●	○	Cohabitation status
●	●	○	Cohabitation history
●	●	○	Parental status
●	●	○	Number of children born/sired
●	●	○	Age at first birth
●	●	○	Age of youngest child
●	●	○	Children living elsewhere
●	○	○	Duration at current address
●	○	○	Residential mobility
●	●	●	Educational attainment
●	●	○	Degrees attained
●	●	○	GED or regular HS diploma
●	●	○	Current enrollment
●	●	○	Current employment status
●	●	○	Hours usually worked (ft/pt)
●	●	○	Weeks worked
○	○	○	Annual employment pattern
●	●	○	Main occupation
●	●	○	Earnings
●	●	○	Wage rate
●	●	●	Payment of child support
○	○	○	Aptitude or achievement score
●	●	○	Health/Disability status
○	○	○	Self-esteem
○	○	○	Locus of control or efficacy
●	○	○	Depression or subjective well-being
○	○	○	Work-related attitudes

CHARACTERISTICS OF CHILD FAMILY MEMBERS
Sample size: 7,926 reference children

Reference Child or Youth Respondent	Other Children (in HH)	
●	●	Age
●	●	Month and year of birth
●	●	Gender
○	○	Race
○	○	Hispanic origin
○	○	Other origin/ethnicity
○	○	Religious affiliation
○	○	Religious participation
○	○	Country of birth
○	○	Immigrant status
○	○	English fluency
●	●	Exact relationship to adult family members
●	●	Exact relationship to other children in HH
●	○	Marital status/history
○	○	Parental status/history
●	●	Current enrollment in regular school
●	○	Current enrollment in preschool/daycare
●	○	Highest grade completed
●	○	Grade now enrolled
●	○	Employment status/history[3]
○	○	Health status
○	○	Handicapping conditions
●	●	Grade repetition
○	○	Aptitude or achievement score
○	○	Pregnancy/birth history
●	●	Psychological well-being
●	●	Delinquency

NOTES
1. Not indentified separately from other forms of public assistance.
2. County characteristics are identified. Individual counties are not identified by name.
3. Asked only of children ages 12 and older.

National Survey of Family Growth

PURPOSE The National Survey of Family Growth (NSFG) is designed to provide current information on childbearing, factors affecting childbearing, and related aspects of maternal and child health. It is a primary source of data on U.S. fertility patterns, infertility, reproductive health, contraception, sterilization, and fertility intentions. In addition, the survey obtains information on such topics as unwanted childbearing, adoption, adolescent pregnancy and unwed motherhood, prenatal care, postnatal care, and infant and maternal health. Because the NSFG represents the continuation of a line of fertility surveys extending back to 1955, it is possible to use the data to continue a set of time-series statistics on family building, contraceptive use, and reproductive health that has covered a period of dramatic change in U.S. family patterns. Data are used by health care providers and researchers, demographers and other social scientists, and by policy makers at both the federal and local level.

SPONSORSHIP The survey is sponsored by the National Center for Health Statistics, Division of Vital Statistics, Family Growth Survey Branch. Funding for the 1988 survey was provided by the Center for Population Research, National Institute of Child Health and Human Development; the Office of Population Affairs, Office of the Assistant Secretary for Health ; the National Center for Health Statistics, Centers for Disease Control; and the Administration for Children, Youth, and Families, all within the Department of Health and Human Services.

DESIGN Cycle IV of the National Survey of Family Growth, conducted in 1988, interviewed women aged 15 to 44 of all marital statuses. African American women were oversampled. The 8,450 women who were interviewed came from households in which someone had been interviewed for the National Health Interview Survey (NHIS) between October 1985 and March 1987. The use of the NHIS sampling frame allowed women to be selected from a larger number of primary sampling units (PSUs) than had been true in previous cycles of the NSFG. Cycle IV, for example, drew women from 156 PSUs compared to 79 for Cycle III. By drawing women from more PSUs, sampling errors were reduced which, in turn, increases the precision of estimates. Moreover the use of the same sampling frame allows analysts to link persons interviewed in both the NSFG and the NHIS (see for example, LeClere and Hendershot, 1992). No more than one woman from each household was selected. If a woman had moved, she was tracked to her new place of residence whenever possible.

Cycles I and II represented the civilian household population of women 15-44 years old who lived in the contiguous United States and who were currently or previously married or, if never married, had a child of their own living with them. Cycle III was expanded to include women of all marital statuses and women living in group quarters. Cycle IV was further expanded to include women living in Alaska and Hawaii, although no one was interviewed in Alaska. All cycles have consisted of in-person interviews. The first three lasted approximately one hour. Cycle IV lasted approximately 70 minutes. Cycle V will be conducted using a computer assisted personal interview system (CATI).

PERIODICITY The NSFG provides data that continue a statistical time series on American fertility patterns that was initiated during the early years of the "baby boom." The Growth of American Families surveys took place in 1955 and 1960 and were continued by the National Fertility Studies of 1965 and 1970. Cycles I, II, III, and IV of the NSFG were fielded in 1973, 1976, 1982, and 1988, respectively. Planning is currently underway for Cycle V which is expected to be fielded in 1994.

CONTENT The National Survey of Family Growth gathers detailed histories on contraceptive use, pregnancies, and live births. As part of the pregnancy history, for all pregnancies ending January 1984 or later, women are asked about whether they received any prenatal care, where such care was received, and how often they visited a doctor, midwife or clinic for prenatal care. They are also asked how many different places they visited for prenatal care and how their medical bills were paid. If a doctor had ever told them to remain in bed for one or more weeks because of a pregnancy related problem, they are asked what conditions were the reasons for the bed rest. They are also asked how each pregnancy ended and how many weeks pregnant they were when the pregnancy ended.

As part of the birth history, women are asked whether the child had to remain in the hospital for medical reasons after the respondent was released, how old the child was when the respondent first took him or her to a doctor or clinic for a well-baby or routine checkup, and whether and how long they breast fed the child.

Women are also asked about difficulties in becoming pregnant, whether pregnancies were wanted when they occurred, and plans for future pregnancies. Other topics covered include adoption, sex education, sexually transmitted diseases including AIDS, chlamydia, and genital herpes, and questions about child care arrangements.

The National Survey of Family Growth also contains a limited number of family background questions including with whom the women lived at age 14, how strict were the family rules about dating, staying out late, and alcohol use when they were 14, whether their mother worked when they were between the ages of 5 and 15, and their mother's age at first birth. They are also asked about their own educational attainment, whether they received a regular high school diploma or a GED, dates of the beginning and ending of their first, second, and most recent marriages, and whether they are currently employed. They are also asked about whether and for how long they cohabited with their current spouse before marriage, whether they had cohabited with previous spouses, and whether they had ever cohabited with anyone. They are also asked a limited set of questions about their current spouse or partner including his educational attainment, religious affiliation, ethnic background, current employment status, and income.

LIMITATIONS Since the focus of the survey is on fertility, the range of information on families is quite limited. Because a relatively complete marital history is obtained, however, it is possible to examine issues related to marital dissolution including links between difficulties with pregnancies and marital dissolution. It also possible to look at the intergenerational transmission of teenage pregnancy.

AVAILABILITY Public use data tapes are available for the entire series of national surveys from the National Technical Information Service. Contact the following telephone numbers for the services identified:

> Customer Services: 703/487-4660
> Computer Products: 703/487-4763
> General Information: 703/487-4600
> Document Rush Order: 1-800-336-4700

For substantive questions about the National Survey of Family Growth, contact:

> Kathryn London
> Family Growth Survey Branch
> National Center for Health Statistics
> 6525 Belcrest Road, Room 840
> Hyattsville, MD 20782
> 301/436-8731

PUBLICATIONS

Bachrach, C.A. & Horn M.C. (1987). Married and unmarried couples: United States, 1982. *Vital and Health Statistics* Series 23, No. 15. Public Health Service. Washington, DC: GPO.

Forrest, J. & Singh, S. (1990). The sexual and reproductive behavior of American women 1982-1988. *Family Planning Perspectives* 22(5): 206-214.

Judkins, D.R., Mosher, W.D., & Botman, S. (1991). National Survey of Family Growth: Design, estimation, and inference. *Vital and Health Statistics* Series 2, No. 109. Public Health Service. Washington, DC: GPO.

LeClere, F.B. & Hendershot, G.E. (1992). The timing of marital dissolution and the utilization of health care services. Paper presented at the 1992 annual meetings of the Population Association of America. Denver, Colorado.

London, K. (1990). Cohabitation, marriage, marital dissolution, and remarriage: United States, 1988. *Advance Data from Vital and Health Statistics* No. 192. Washington, DC: National Center for Health Statistics.

Mosher, W.D. & Pratt, W.F. (1990). Use of contraception and family planning services in the United States, 1988. *American Journal of Public Health 90*(9): 1132-1133.

Williams, L.B. & Pratt, W.F. (1990). Wanted and unwanted childbearing in the United States: 1973-1988. *Advance Data from Vital and Health Statistics* No. 189. Washington, DC: National Center for Health Statistics.

National Survey of Family Growth
Years of Questionnaire: Cycle IV (1988)
Sample size: 8,450 women aged 15-44
FAMILY LEVEL CHARACTERISTICS

Family Composition
○ Full roster of household members (first name, age, sex, and relationship to reference person of each member)
○ Partial roster of household members
● Number of adults in household
● Number of children in household
○ Approximate relationship of family members to householder, child, or one another
○ Exact relationship of family members to householder, child, or one another
○ Information about part-time household member
○ Information about family members no longer living in household
○ Information about relatives who live nearby but not in household

Socioeconomic
● Total family income
○ Number of persons who depend on family income
● Sources of income
○ Income amounts identified separately by source
● Poverty status
● Welfare status
● Food Stamps receipt
● Child support receipt
○ Medicaid coverage
○ Private health insurance
○ Home ownership/renters
○ Assets (other than home ownership)
○ Public housing status
○ Telephone in household
○ Language other than English spoken in home

Geographic/Community Variables
● Region of country
○ State of residence
○ County/city/MSA of residence
○ Size/type of community
○ Zip code
○ Telephone area code
● Metropolitan residence
○ Neighborhood quality
○ Local labor market

Stage in Family Life Cycle
● Age of adult respondent or spouse/partner
● Marital status of adult respondent or spouse/partner
● Employment status of adult respondent or spouse/partner
● Presence of own children in household
● Age of youngest own child in household
● Age of oldest own child in household
● Existence of own children who have left home
● Intention to have (more) children in future

310

Family Functioning

- Family activities or time use
- Community involvement (civic, religious, recreational)
- Family communication patterns
- Family decision-making
- Marital conflict
- Marital happiness/satisfaction
- Parent-child conflict
- History of marital separations
- History of family violence
- History of marital counselling

CHARACTERISTICS OF ADULT FAMILY MEMBERS
Sample Size: 7,716 women aged 18 years and older

Adult Respondent or Reference Person	Current Spouse in HH	Current or Former Spouse Not in HH	
●	●	●	Age
●	●	●	Gender
●	●	●	Race
●	●	●	Hispanic origin
●	●	●	Other origin/ethnicity
●	●	●	Religious affiliation
●	○	○	Religious participation
○	○	○	Country of birth
○	○	○	Immigrant status
○	○	○	English fluency
●	●	○	Current marital status
●	●	○	Marital history
●	○	○	Cohabitation status
●	○	○	Cohabitation history
●	●	○	Parental status
●	○	○	Number children ever born/sired
●	○	○	Age at first birth
●	○	○	Age of youngest child
●	●	○	Children living elsewhere
●	○	○	Duration at current address
○	○	○	Residential mobility
●	●	●	Educational attainment
○	○	○	Degrees attained
●	○	○	GED or regular HS diploma
●	○	○	Current enrollment
●	●	○	Current employment status
●	●	○	Hours usually worked (ft/pt)
●	○	○	Weeks worked
○	○	○	Annual employment pattern
●	●	○	Main occupation
●	●	○	Earnings
○	○	○	Wage rate
○	●	○	Payment of child support
○	○	○	Aptitude or achievement score
○	○	○	Health/disability status
○	○	○	Self-esteem
○	○	○	Locus of control or efficacy
○	○	○	Depression or subjective well-being
○	○	○	Work-related attitudes

CHARACTERISTICS OF CHILD FAMILY MEMBERS
Sample Size: 734 women aged 15-17

Reference Child or Youth Respondent	Other Children (in HH)	
O	●	Age
O	●	Month and year of birth
O	●	Gender
O	●	Race
O	●	Hispanic origin
O	●	Other origin/ethnicity
O	●	Religious affiliation
O	●	Religious participation
O	O	Country of birth
O	O	Immigrant status
O	O	English fluency
O	O	Exact relationship to adult family members
O	O	Exact relationship to other children in HH
O	●	Marital status/history
O	●	Parental status/history
O	●	Current enrollment in regular school
O	●	Current enrollment in preschool/daycare[1]
O	●	Highest grade completed
O	O	Grade now enrolled
O	●	Employment status/history
O	O	Health status
O	O	Handicapping conditions
O	O	Grade repetition
O	O	Aptitude or achievement score
O	●	Pregnancy/birth history
O	O	Psychological well-being
O	O	Delinquency

NOTES
1. Mothers who were working or in school were asked how their children under 13 were cared for while they were at work or school.

Noncustodial Parents Survey: Parents Without Children

PURPOSE The study was designed to test a theoretically based (social exchange) model of noncustodial parenting.

SPONSORSHIP The survey was sponsored by the National Institute of Child Health and Human Development.

DESIGN The sample included at least one member of 372 divorcing families. The sample was randomly selected from all families with children under age 15 in the Phoenix, Arizona, metropolitan area, and appears to be representative of the divorcing population in the area (Braver and Bay, 1992). In all cases, both parents were contacted and asked to participate in the survey. In over 200 cases, both were interviewed; the sole consenting subject was interviewed in the remaining cases. About 80 children from participating families (between the ages of 8 and 18) were also interviewed.

All interviews took place in the respondents' homes and lasted about 1.5 hours. Interviews with out-of-state respondents were conducted over the telephone.

PERIODICITY The study followed a sample of divorcing families from petitioning for divorce until 3 years post-petitioning (about 2.5 years post-divorce). Data were collected at three times: immediately after petition (1986), one year after petition (1987), and three years after petition (1989).

CONTENT The survey assessed a mixture of economic and psychological constructs of interest to the principal investigators. Measures of visitation and child support payments were collected to serve as dependent variables. Measures of various affective, material, and symbolic rewards and costs associated with parenting were collected to served as predictors (See Braver, Wolchik, Sandler and Sheets, 1992).

Additional data were collected to assess social, psychological, and economic outcomes that might result from, or moderate the

313

effects of, divorce. These included job and educational status changes, psychopathology, social support networks, romantic relationships, and settlement and custody decision-making.

LIMITATIONS The data set is rich in psychological measures of the noncustodial parent-child relationship and child well-being. An additional strength is that analysts can use information from multiple respondents from the same family. In exchange for its depth, however, the data set is limited by its relatively small sample size (compared to national social science data sets) and its complexity of organization.

AVAILABILITY For substantive information regarding the data sets, contact:

> Dr. Sanford Braver
> Program for Prevention Research
> Community Services Bldg.
> Arizona State University
> Tempe, AZ 85287-1108
> 602/965-5405

PUBLICATIONS

Braver, S.L., & Bay, R.C. (1992). Assessing and compensating for self-selection bias of the family research sample. Submitted for publication.

Braver, S.L., Wolchik, S., Sandler, I., & Sheets, V. (1992). A social exchange model of nonresidential parental involvement. In C. Depner & J.H. Bray (Eds.), *Nonresidential parenting: New vistas in family living*. Newbury Park, CA: Sage.

Braver, S.L., Wolchik, S., Sandler, I., Fogas, B.S. & Zvetina, D. (1991). Frequency of visitation by divorced fathers: Differences in reports by fathers and mothers. *American Journal of Orthopsychiatry, 61*, 448-454.

Braver, S.L., Fitzpatrick, P., & Bay, R.C. (1991). Noncustodial parents' reports of child-support payments. *Family Relations, 40,* 180-185.

Bay, R.C. & Braver, S.L. (1990). Perceived control of the divorce settlement process and interpersonal conflict. *Family Relations, 39,* 382-387.

Fogas, B.S., Wolchik, S.A., Braver, S.L., Freedom, D.S., & Bay, R.C. (1992). Locus of control as a mediator of negative divorce-related events and adjustment problems in children. *American Journal of Orthopsychiatry* 62(4), 589-598.

Noncustodial Parents: Parents Without Children
Years of Questionnaire: 1986, 1987, 1989
Sample size: 201 - 321 noncustodial parents
FAMILY-LEVEL CHARACTERISTICS
Sample size: 125 - 216 families (using both custodial and noncustodial reports)

Family Composition
- Full roster of household members (first name, age, sex, and relationship to reference person of each member)
- ○ Partial roster of household members
- Number of adults in household
- Number of children in household
- ○ Approximate relationship of family members to householder, child, or one another
- Exact relationship of family members to householder, child, or one another
- ○ Information about part-time household member
- Information about family members no longer living in household
- ○ Information about relatives who live nearby but not in household

Socioeconomic
- Total family income
- ○ Number of persons who depend on family income
- Sources of income
- ○ Income amounts identified separately by source
- ○ Poverty status
- Welfare status
- Food Stamps receipt
- Child support receipt
- Medicaid coverage
- ○ Private health insurance
- Home ownership/renters
- Assets (other than home ownership)
- ○ Public housing status
- ○ Telephone in household
- ○ Language other than English spoken in home

Geographic/Community Variables
- Region of country
- State of residence
- County/city/MSA of residence
- ○ Size/type of community
- ○ Zip code
- ○ Telephone area code
- ○ Metropolitan residence
- ○ Neighborhood quality
- ○ Local labor market

Stage in Family Life Cycle
- Age of adult respondent or spouse/partner
- Marital status of adult respondent or spouse/partner
- Employment status of adult respondent or spouse/partner
- Presence of own children in household
- Age of youngest own child in household
- Age of oldest own child in household
- ○ Existence of own children who have left home
- ○ Intention to have (more) children in future

316

Family Functioning
- ● Family activities or time use
- ○ Community involvement (civic, religious, recreational)
- ○ Family communication patterns
- ● Family decision-making
- ● Marital conflict
- ○ Marital happiness/satisfaction
- ○ Parent-child conflict
- ● History of marital separations
- ● History of family violence
- ● History of marital counselling

CHARACTERISTICS OF ADULT FAMILY MEMBERS
Sample size: 201 - 321 noncustodial parents   170-257 custodial parents

Adult Respondent or Reference Mother	Current Father in HH	Current or Former Spouse Not in HH	
●	○	○	Age
●	○	○	Gender
○	○	●	Race
●	○	●	Hispanic origin
●	○	●	Other origin/ethnicity
●	○	●	Religious affiliation
●	○	○	Religious participation
○	○	○	Country of birth
○	○	○	Immigrant status
○	○	○	English fluency
●	○	○	Current marital status
●	○	○	Marital history
○	○	○	Cohabitation status
○	○	○	Cohabitation history
○	○	○	Parental status
○	○	○	Number children ever born/sired
○	○	○	Age at first birth
○	○	○	Age of youngest child
○	○	○	Children living elsewhere
○	○	○	Duration at current address
○	○	○	Residential mobility
●	○	●	Educational attainment
○	○	○	Degrees attained
○	○	○	GED or regular HS diploma
○	○	○	Current enrollment
●	○	●	Current employment status
●	○	●	Hours usually worked (ft/pt)
○	○	○	Weeks worked
○	○	○	Annual employment pattern
●	○	●	Main occupation
●	○	○	Earnings
●	○	○	Wage rate
○	○	○	Payment of child support
○	○	○	Aptitude or achievement score
○	○	○	Health/disability status
○	○	○	Self-esteem
●	○	○	Locus of control or efficacy
●	○	○	Depression or subjective well-being
○	○	○	Work-related attitudes

CHARACTERISTICS OF CHILD FAMILY MEMBERS
Sample size: 35 - 85 children

Reference Child or Youth Respondent	Other Children (in HH)	
●	○	Age
●	○	Month and year of birth
●	○	Gender
○	○	Race
○	○	Hispanic origin
○	○	Other origin/ethnicity
○	○	Religious affiliation
○	○	Religious participation
○	○	Country of birth
○	○	Immigrant status
○	○	English fluency
○	○	Exact relationship to adult family members
○	○	Exact relationship to other children in HH
○	○	Marital status/history
○	○	Parental status/history
○	○	Current enrollment in regular school
○	○	Current enrollment in preschool/daycare
○	○	Highest grade completed
○	○	Grade now enrolled
○	○	Employment status/history
○	○	Health status
○	○	Handicapping conditions
○	○	Grade repetition
●	○	Aptitude or achievement score
○	○	Pregnancy/birth history
●	○	Psychological well-being
●	○	Delinquency

318

Panel Study of Income Dynamics

PURPOSE The Panel Study of Income Dynamics (PSID) is designed to study the determinants of changes in the economic well-being of families and individuals across time and across generations, and to see whether any factors subject to change through public policy or personal effort make a difference in changing economic fortunes. The effects of environmental, behavioral, and attitudinal variables on the changing economic status of families are also studied. The study is designed to supplement and complement the regular assessments of poverty conducted by the U.S. Bureau of the Census. The study has followed the same sample of families and their descendants over an extended period of time and collected a rich mixture of demographic, economic, behavioral, and some attitudinal information.

SPONSORSHIP The study was initially funded by the U.S. Office of Economic Opportunity. Major funding for the study shifted to the Department of Health, Education, and Welfare (now the Department of Health and Human Services (DHHS)) in 1972. Since 1983, the National Science Foundation has been the principal sponsor, with substantial continuing support from the Office of the Assistant Secretary for Planning and Evaluation (ASPE) of DHHS. The Ford, Sloan, and Rockefeller foundations have provided important supplementary grants to the PSID. The National Institute of Child Health and Human Development, the National Institute on Aging, and the Departments of Labor and of Agriculture have also provided support to the study. Data have been collected, processed, analyzed, and disseminated to the research community by the Institute for Social Research of the University of Michigan. Since 1982, the study has had an advisory board of overseers, made up of scholars, researchers, and policymakers.

DESIGN The PSID is based on a probability sample of about 4,800 U.S. households first interviewed in 1968. Interviews have been fielded annually since then. The rules for following household members are designed to maintain a representative sample of families at any point in time as well as across time. Thus, the PSID tracks members of the 1968 households, including all those leaving to establish separate family units. All direct descendants of original sample members (e.g., children, grandchildren, great grandchildren) are classified as sample members and are eligible for tracking as separate family units when they set up their own households. Ex-spouses and other adult sample members who move out of PSID family units are tracked to their new family units, as well.

The PSID sample is a combination of a cross-section of about 3,000 families selected from the Survey Research Center's master sampling frame and a subsample of about 2,000 families from the Census Bureau's Survey of Economic Opportunity. The families from the Census Bureau study were selected from those with incomes less than twice the official poverty line who had also been willing to sign a release form. Although the original design oversampled lower income and minority households, the sample also included a complete representative sample of families at all income levels. Thus, when appropriately weighted, the combined sample is representative of all U.S. families, except for families of immigrants arriving in the U.S. since 1968. To correct for these omissions, a representative sample of 2,043 Latino (Mexican, Cuban, and Puerto Rican) households was added in 1990.

The study was originally planned to last for five years, but in 1973 it was decided to extend the survey to measure outcome variables — employment, earnings, income, housing, and family change — over a longer period of time. Telephone interviews were used wherever possible to keep survey costs down, and the questionnaire was reduced to a third of its original size.

Most of the data collected in the PSID are organized around the concept of a family, defined somewhat differently from the standard Census definition. In addition to the normative nuclear family, a family unit can consist of a single person either living alone or with other unrelated individuals. Family members can also be household members related only by economic interdependence and not by blood, marriage, or adoption. When multiple families reside in the same household, this fact is recorded, and interviews are taken with each family containing a sample member. Additionally, some panel family members may be temporarily residing in institutions. Interviews are usually conducted with one adult per family, usually the head of the family unit, defined as the husband in married couple families. Couples not married but living together for two consecutive interviews are treated as though they are married.

In each year, information is collected about families containing a member or a descendant of one of the original families. The study follows families interviewed the prior wave, as well as members who "split-off." Split-off families are formed when children leave home, when couples divorce, and when more complicated changes break families apart.

Natural demographic processes at work in the population produce a changing sample of families each year, as some families split into two or more families and other families die out. The panel represents these changes in the population. The inclusion of newly formed families has caused the total sample to grow gradually, despite attrition among original sample families due to death or nonresponse. As of 1988 the sample consisted of some 7,100 families (37,500 individuals).

Since the first two years of the PSID, losses to the sample have been small, and checks against other data indicate no appreciable sample biases. The sample is weighted to take into account initial variations in sampling rates, variations in non-response rates, and other complexities of the survey design (for example, potential overlap of the two samples and marriage to non-sample members). After some initial sample losses, the annual response rate of the panel has been very high. Respondents were paid from the second interview forward and for sending in an annual address correction postcard, both of which clearly helped in keeping in touch with respondents. Since 1975, most interviews have been conducted by telephone and, occasionally, by mail or in person.

PERIODICITY The PSID is an ongoing study initially conducted in 1968. Interviews are conducted over a 6-month period in the spring through summer, and reports on flows of income, consumption, and work hours refer to the previous calendar year. The status reports on family composition are measured as of the time of the interview and changes are also recorded. Each family has been interviewed annually since first constituted as a separate household. Various supplements have been included, with a birth, adoption, substitute parenting, and marital history supplement in 1985, updating of births, adoptions, and marriages since then, a kinship supplement in 1988, and health supplements in 1990 and 1991.

CONTENT The PSID investigates the effects of demographic, environmental, and institutional variables on the economic well-being of families, as well as the effects of attitudes and behavior patterns. In each year, the survey measures money and some non-money components of family income; behavior in crucial areas such as labor force participation, family formation and dissolution, living arrangements, and public program participation; and some relevant attitudes. Family background questions (age, race, sex, education) were asked in the first two interviews, and then whenever a new family head or wife appears. In the 1972 survey, a short series of questions on day care for children of working parents was added. A unique aspect of this study is the combination of standard background variables with measures of the attitudes and behavior patterns which might be expected to affect the economic progress of families. Additionally, an advantage of the PSID is that re-interviewing the same families and individuals over an extended period of time provides a more accurate measurement of change.

The core content of the survey comes from a series of questions covering employment, income, housing, food expenditures, education, disability, and family background. Questions are asked about income sources and amounts during the previous calendar year, including transfer income; family composition; detailed employment information about female heads and male heads of the family unit and wives, with less detailed employment information obtained about other family members; earnings of all family members; hours spent working and performing housework; food expenditures; housing; and geographic mobility. Although there have been changes in the survey over time, most of these variables are comparable from year to year.

An extensive set of background data are collected the first time an individual appears in the study as a *head* (a single primary adult, usually the male adult) or *wife* (or cohabitor, referred to as

322

"wife"). The county and state of residence of the respondents are also coded. To supplement information obtained in the interview, in many waves questionnaires asking about local wage and employment conditions were sent to each county where there were respondents. Census data were accessed in some waves to obtain information such as public school expenditures.

Since the PSID follows all individuals in sample households, a number of different levels of analysis are possible; analyses can be performed on household, families, individuals, or particular subgroups of individuals. The PSID is particularly advantageous for studying children and their families. The study follows children, even when only one parent is a sample member. PSID also obtains greater precision in studying new young families than a simple probability sample and, furthermore, subfamilies can be identified. In addition, the PSID provides extensive past and current information on the parental family and siblings. The longitudinal nature of the panel study makes it an important vehicle for understanding underlying causes and short- and long-run consequences of family formation, dissolution, and other demographic changes.

Various family topics have been included intermittently in the PSID interview. Fertility and family planning were asked in 1968-1972, 1976, and 1985. Questions about child care costs were asked in 1970-1972, 1976, 1977, 1979, 1985, and 1988. The mode of child care was asked in the surveys of 1968, 1973, 1974, 1976, 1977, 1979, 1980, and 1985. In 1988, questions were asked about the health, living arrangements, and wealth of parents and about assistance flows in the form of money or time with family and friends. In 1990 a special supplement on health was asked. Persons 65 and older who received Medicare were asked permission to access their Medicare records between 1984 and 1990. When combined with the health questionnaire items and the long time-series of core PSID items, the resulting data should be very useful in studying the health and well-being of the elderly. Moreover, in 1991, adult male and female household heads and the wives of male household heads were asked a lengthy questionnaire about the health of their parents including items on actual conditions their parents have, the ability of their parents to take care of themselves, and rehabilitation hospital or residential care facilities in which their parents may have stayed.

The 1985 wave was the first to obtain a complete birth and adoption history from all heads and spouses. Respondents included all heads, whether single or married, and spouses. Retrospective marital histories and details about children who they helped raise but did not give birth to or adopt were also obtained. Respondents answered questions about their own experience in both the fertility and marital history portions of the supplement. Birth and marriage histories were also collected about any person aged 12 to 44 in the family unit. Special emphasis was given to the dating of events, for both births and marital events. Births of children, and marriages, divorces, and separations are dated by the month and year in which they occurred. The data can be used to link children in the sample with their natural or adoptive parents or with stepparents, and to sort out many of the complicated family composition changes that have occurred during the panel period. In addition, as the survey tracks split-off families, one can determine the ability of absent fathers to provide child support. The birth, marriage, and adoption histories have been collected afresh each wave since 1985 for new members of PSID families and updated for past members.

LIMITATIONS Since the most detailed information is collected about the head and spouse, longitudinal analysis of individuals who change from a status such as child to head or spouse is more difficult. The sample is relatively small compared with other major surveys, as the entire age range is covered. Information on children is somewhat limited, though information on families is rich. The central focus of the data is economic and demographic. Thus, there is substantial information on income sources and amounts, employment, family composition changes, and residential location. Although there is information on attitudes and other topics of a more sociological or psychological nature in some of the early waves, it is more limited. In the birth, adoption, and marital history data, some error in recall can be expected, as is true for all retrospective histories.

AVAILABILITY Data are available in several forms: computer tape with merged data from all the annual interviews for each of the survey families (cross-year family file); tapes containing the record for each individual in a responding family in the most recent wave, including all the information about the families in which he or she has lived (cross-year family-individual response file); tapes containing the record for each individual ever in a responding family but not in a responding family in the most recent wave (cross-year family-individual non-response file), and a CD-ROM version containing the family-individual response and non-response files. Each wave of data is merged with all prior waves' data. Files on special topics are also available. These include a marital history file, the childbirth and adoption history file, a work history file, the 1990 Health Supplement file, and others.

Each year the updated cross-year files are made available to outside users within a month after they have been cleaned and checked for inconsistencies. The cross-year family-individual file is usually available roughly 18 months after interviewing is completed. Extensive documentation is printed annually, giving tape codes, variable distributions, editing methods, and an alphabetical index of variables and a concordance which facilitates location of the same variable in successive years.

Public data tapes can be obtained from:

> Janet Vavra
> Inter-University Consortium of
> Political and Social Research
> University of Michigan
> P.O. Box 1248
> Ann Arbor, MI 48106
> 313/763-5010

For substantive questions, contact:

> Martha Hill, Ph.D.
> Survey Research Center
> Institute for Social Research
> University of Michigan
> P.O. Box 1248
> Ann Arbor, MI 48106
> 313/763-5131

PUBLICATIONS

Morgan, J.N., & the staff of the Economic Behavior Program. Annual. *Five thousand American families: Patterns of economic progress*. Ann Arbor, MI: Institute for Social Research.

Duncan, G.J. (1984). *Years of poverty, years of plenty*. Ann Arbor, MI: Institute for Social Research.

Duncan, G.J., & S.D. Hoffman. (1985). A reconsideration of the economic consequences of marital dissolution. *Demography* 22(4), 485-497.

Ellwood, D. (1988). *Poor support: Poverty and the American family*. New York: Basic Books.

Hill, M.S. (1983). Trends in the economic situation of U.S. families and children: 1970-1980. In *The high costs of living: economic and demographic conditions of American families*. Washington, DC: National Academy of Sciences.

Hill, M.S. (1992). *The Panel Study of Income Dynamics*. Newbury Park, CA: Sage.

Hill, M.S. (1992). The role of economic resources and remarriage in financial assistance to children of divorce. *Journal of Family Issues* 13(2), 158-178.

McLanahan, S.S. (1988). Family structure and dependency: Early transitions to female household headship. *Demography* 25(1), 1-16.

Rexroat, C., & Shehan, C. (1987). The Family Life Cycle and Spouses' Time in Housework. *Journal of Marriage and the Family* 49(4), 737-750.

Survey Research Center, Institute for Social Research. (1991). *Publications, working papers and government reports based on the Panel Study of Income Dynamics*. Ann Arbor, MI: University of Michigan.

Panel Study of Income Dynamics
Years of Questionnaire: 1968 through the present
Sample size: 7,200 households
FAMILY LEVEL CHARACTERISTICS

Family Composition
- ● Full roster of household members (first name, age, sex, and relationship to reference person of each member)
- ○ Partial roster of household members
- ● Number of adults in household
- ● Number of children in household
- ○ Approximate relationship of family members to householder, child, or one another
- ● Exact relationship of family members to householder, child, or one another
- ● Information about part-time household member
- ● Information about family members no longer living in household
- ○ Information about relatives who live nearby but not in household

Socioeconomic
- ● Total family income
- ○ Number of persons who depend on family income
- ● Sources of income
- ● Income amounts identified separately by source
- ● Poverty status
- ● Welfare status
- ● Food Stamps receipt
- ● Child support receipt
- ● Medicaid coverage
- ○ Private health insurance
- ● Home ownership/renters
- ● Assets (other than home ownership)
- ● Public housing status
- ○ Telephone in household
- ○ Language other than English spoken in home

Geographic/Community Variables
- ● Region of country
- ● State of residence
- ● County/city/MSA of residence
- ○ Size/type of community
- ○ Zip code
- ○ Telephone area code
- ● Metropolitan residence
- ○ Neighborhood quality
- ○ Local labor market

Stage in Family Life Cycle
- ● Age of adult respondent or spouse/partner
- ● Marital status of adult respondent or spouse/partner
- ● Employment status of adult respondent or spouse/partner
- ● Presence of own children in household
- ● Age of youngest own child in household
- ● Age of oldest own child in household
- ● Existence of own children who have left home
- ● Intention to have (more) children in future

327

Family Functioning
○ Family activities or time use
○ Community involvement (civic, religious, recreational)
○ Family communication patterns
○ Family decision-making
○ Marital conflict
○ Marital happiness/satisfaction
○ Parent-child conflict
● History of marital separations
○ History of family violence
○ History of marital counselling

CHARACTERISTICS OF ADULT FAMILY MEMBERS

Adult Respondent or Reference Person	Current Spouse in HH	Current or Former Spouse Not in HH[1]	
●	●	●	Age
●	●	●	Gender
●	●	●	Race
●	●	●	Hispanic origin
●	●	●	Other origin/ethnicity
●	○	○	Religious affiliation
○	○	○	Religious participation
●	●	●	Country of birth
○	○	○	Immigrant status
○	○	○	English fluency
●	●	●	Current marital status
●	●	●	Marital history[2]
●	●	●	Cohabitation status
●	●	●	Cohabitation history
●	●	●	Parental status
●	●	●	Number children ever born/sired
●	●	●	Age at first birth
●	●	●	Age of youngest child
●	●	●	Children living elsewhere
●	●	●	Duration at current address
●	●	●	Residential mobility
●	●	●	Educational attainment
●	●	●	Degrees attained
●	●	●	GED or regular HS diploma
○	○	○	Current enrollment
●	●	●	Current employment status
●	●	●	Hours usually worked (ft/pt)
●	●	●	Weeks worked
●	●	●	Annual employment pattern
●	●	●	Main occupation
●	●	●	Earnings
●	●	●	Wage rate
●	●	●	Payment of child support
○	○	○	Aptitude or achievement score
●	●	●	Health/disability status
○	○	○	Self-esteem
○	○	○	Locus of control or efficacy
○	○	○	Depression or subjective well-being
○	○	○	Work-related attitudes

CHARACTERISTICS OF CHILD FAMILY MEMBERS

Reference Child or Youth Respondent	Children (in HH)	
O	●	Age
O	●	Month and year of birth
O	●	Gender
O	●	Race
O	●	Hispanic origin
O	●	Other origin/ethnicity
O	O	Religious affiliation
O	O	Religious participation
O	O	Country of birth
O	O	Immigrant status
O	O	English fluency
O	●	Exact relationship to adult family members
O	●	Exact relationship to other children in HH
O	●	Marital status/history³
O	●	Parental status/history³
O	●	Current enrollment in regular school
O	O	Current enrollment in preschool/daycare
O	●	Highest grade completed
O	O	Grade now enrolled
O	●	Employment status/history
O	●	Health status
O	O	Handicapping conditions
O	O	Grade repetition
O	O	Aptitude or achievement score
O	●	Pregnancy/birth history³
O	O	Psychological well-being
O	O	Delinquency

NOTES

1. Information is available for those who are the head or spouse in a new household that has "split-off" from one of the original households surveyed.

2. Detailed fertility and marital histories were obtained in 1985. These have been updated in subsequent years.

3. If a youth has been married or has had a child, that information is recorded.

The Public Opinion Location Library

PURPOSE The Public Opinion Location Library (POLL) is a service provided by the Roper Center for Public Opinion Research that gives researchers access to an archive of public opinion survey data. As of January of 1992 POLL contained about 170,000 questions from various surveys and opinion polls, such as the Gallup Organization, the National Opinion Research Center, and various news station and newspaper polls that were conducted in the United States.

CONTENT POLL contains a large variety of questions, most of which concern opinions and attitudes. The types of topics include beliefs and opinions about the types of family structure; attitudes towards various government programs; attitudes about marriage, divorce, and sexuality; and many others. For each question contained in the database, POLL stores the following information for researchers' retrieval: the exact wording of the item, the response categories used with the percent of the sample falling into each category, the polling organization that sponsored the research or survey, the dates the survey was conducted, the interview method (i.e., telephone, mail), the target population (i.e., registered voters, all Americans, adults only), sample size, and the subject or subjects the question is about. Some questions also indicate subpopulations that may have answered that specific question.

The coverage of questions in POLL is extensive, from 1960 to the present, although not exhaustive of every polling question asked. In addition to constantly updating this database with new survey questions as they come out, the Roper Center is also continually working on increasing its coverage of past questions. Some questions from surveys as early as 1950 are available.

LIMITATIONS Many of the poll and survey questions archived at the Roper Center use small sample sizes. These small samples may not allow, for example, sufficient numbers of parents of young children to be looked at separately. The polling organizations do not always use real probability sampling; they sometimes use quota sampling instead at the last stages.

AVAILABILITY POLL is available to researchers in the United States as well as those outside the U.S. Through a mainframe computer, users can locate questions asked nationally in the U.S. on whatever subject they are examining. Users have the ability to search for questions on specific subjects, to view those questions and information pertaining to them on their computer screen, and to print out whatever information interests them. Researchers can conduct searches by subject, by polling organizations, by a specified time span, or by other specifications. After identifying questions of interest, a researcher may be interested in seeing how the responses broke down by sex or race. The Roper Center can *sometimes* do runs of this sort for a charge that varies greatly depending on the request.

For information on POLL, contact:

> Roper Center for Public Opinion Research
> P.O. Box 440
> Storrs, CT 06268
> 203/486-4440

PUBLICATIONS A number of publications have pulled together responses from a variety of polls on family issues, enhancing their usefulness by allowing comparisons to be made among them and observing trends or discrepancies. Some of these include:

Komarnicki, M. (1991, June). *Public attitudes toward the American family: An overview of survey responses covering 1963-1991* (Working Paper WP9). Washington, DC: Institute for American Values.

Smith, T.W. (1990). The polls - A report: The sexual revolution? *Public Opinion Quarterly, 54,* 415-435.

Thornton, A. (1988). *Changing attitudes towards family issues in the United States.* Ann Arbor: Institute for Social Research.

(There is no checklist with this description.)

331

RAND Survey of Prison Inmates

PURPOSE In July and August of 1976 the RAND Corporation conducted surveys in five California prisons among 624 male inmates to gain detailed information about individual patterns of criminal behavior, prior juvenile criminal activity, the use of illegal drugs as a juvenile and as an adult, and the effectiveness of prison treatment programs. Commitment to criminality as a way of life was investigated as well.

DESIGN Researchers selected institutions felt to be most representative of the California male prison population in terms of age, race, and prior record. At each institution the California Department of Corrections drew a 20% random sample using computerized files. The sample lists were sent to prison authorities; corrected lists indicated inmates no longer there or unavailable due to protective or high-security housing arrangements. The remaining inmates were scheduled for group survey administration. Response rates are based on this latter group and include failures to report, choosing not to participate after the introduction, and the provision of an illegible survey questionnaire. The institutions, number of respondents, and response rate for each are as follows:

California Correctional Institute at Tehachapi	91	56%
Deuel Vocational Institute at Tracy	109	58%
California Institute for Men at Chino	121	55%
California Training Facility at Soledad	125	63%
San Quentin Penitentiary	178	55%
Total:	624	57%

CONTENT The instrument was a 24-page self-administered questionnaire. The data file contains 378 variables for 624 cases (inmates). Variables include prior criminal histories, social and demographic descriptors, psychological characteristics, varieties of criminal behavior, and different types of prison treatment programs.

PERIODICITY What began as a one-state study became a three-state study. The researchers conducted a much larger survey of men in 12 prisons and 14 county jails in California, Michigan, and Texas in late 1978 to early 1979. A purposive sample was again made of the jail and prison institutions. Since then, it has been administered in a few other states.

LIMITATIONS First, veracity is a problem inherent in self-reports of crime. Both overreporting and underreporting are found. A more subtle limitation of these data is sampling bias: a statistically significant difference in prior records was found between the sample and the population from which it was drawn. This is because inmates with longer prior records were more likely to be in the sample, as they were more likely to be institutionalized for a longer period of time. The sampling technique allowed those with no prior records to be somewhat more likely to be released before the date of the survey.

Another possible source of confusion is that inmates are only a subset of the total criminal population. First, criminals must be apprehended, then convicted, and finally sentenced. Obviously, an inmate survey provides no information on criminals who do not get caught. Also, sentencing practices make some types of criminals more likely to receive prison terms. Burglars with few prior convictions, for example, are unlikely to serve time. Thus a survey of this type overrepresents the types of criminals who are sentenced to long terms in prison. Also, there are no control groups of noncriminals or of unincarcerated offenders.

There are no questions on family composition, other than marriage or the presence of a girlfriend. There are no sociodemographic data or family functioning variables.

Finally, researcher decisions about interpretations of ambiguous responses affect the rates at which individual offenders are found to commit crimes (c.f. Visher).

AVAILABILITY The National Criminal Justice Reference Service at 301/251-5500 is the repository of materials associated with this survey.

333

The 1978 three-state survey is available on magnetic tape with SAS control cards from:

> Inter-University Consortium for Political
> and Social Research
> P. O. Box 1248
> Ann Arbor, MI 48106-1248
> 313/763-5010

For substantive questions, contact:

> Mark A. Peterson
> RAND Corporation
> 310/393-0411

PUBLICATIONS

Peterson, M.A., & Braiker, H.B. (1980). *Doing crime: A Survey of California Prison Inmates*. (Report No. R-2200-DOJ.) Santa Monica, CA: RAND.

Peterson, M.A., & Braiker, H.B., with Polich, S. (1981). *Who commits crimes: A survey of prison inmates*. Cambridge, MA: Oelgeschlager, Gunn & Hain. [This book is based on the original California survey, and it includes the survey instrument.]

Peterson, M.A., Chaiken, J., & Ebener, P. (1983). *Survey of Jail and Prison Inmates, 1978: California, Michigan, and Texas* (Report No. 83-IJ-CX-0006) Santa Monica, CA: RAND

Peterson, M.A., Chaiken, J., Ebener, P. & Honig, P. (1982). *Survey of Prison and Jail Inmates: Background and methods*. A Rand Note. Santa Monica, CA: RAND.

For a description of this and several similar surveys, see:

J. Cohen (1986). Research on Criminal Careers: Individual Frequency Rates and Offense Seriousness. Pp. 292-418 in A. Blumstein, J. Cohen, J.A. Roth, & C.A. Visher (Eds.), *Criminal careers and 'career criminals'* (vol. 1). Washington, DC: National Academy of Sciences Press.

For a reanalysis of these data, see:

Visher, C.A. (1986). The RAND Inmate Survey: a Reanalysis. Pp. 161-211 in A. Blumstein, J. Cohen, J.A. Roth, & C.A. Visher (Eds.), *Criminal careers and 'career criminals'* (vol. 2). Washington, DC: National Academy of Sciences Press.

RAND Survey of Prison Inmates

Year of Questionnaire: 1976
Sample size: 624 male inmates

FAMILY-LEVEL CHARACTERISTICS

Family Composition

O Full roster of household members (first name, age, sex, and relationship to reference person of each member)
O Partial roster of household members
O Number of adults in household
O Number of children in household
O Approximate relationship of family members to householder, child, or one another
O Exact relationship of family members to householder, child, or one another
O Information about part-time household member
O Information about family members no longer living in household
O Information about relatives who live nearby but not in household

Socioeconomic

O Total family income
O Number of persons who depend on family income
O Sources of income
O Income amounts identified separately by source
O Poverty status
O Welfare status
O Food Stamps receipt
O Child support receipt
O Medicaid coverage
O Private health insurance
O Home ownership/renters
O Assets (other than home ownership)
O Public housing status
O Telephone in household
O Language other than English spoken in home

Geographic/Community Variables

● Region of country
● State of residence
O County/city/MSA of residence
O Size/type of community
O Zip code
O Telephone area code
O Metropolitan residence
O Neighborhood quality
O Local labor market

Stage in Family Life Cycle

● Age of adult respondent or spouse/partner
● Marital status of adult respondent or spouse/partner
● Employment status of adult respondent or spouse/partner
O Presence of own children in household
O Age of youngest own child in household
O Age of oldest own child in household
O Existence of own children who have left home
O Intention to have (more) children in future

Family Functioning

- Family activities or time use
- Community involvement (civic, religious, recreational)
- Family communication patterns
- Family decision-making
- Marital conflict
- Marital happiness/satisfaction
- Parent-child conflict
- History of marital separations
- History of family violence
- History of marital counselling

CHARACTERISTICS OF ADULT FAMILY MEMBERS

Adult Respondent or Reference Person	Current Spouse in HH	Current or Former Spouse Not in HH	
●	○	○	Age
●	○	○	Gender
●	○	○	Race
●	○	○	Hispanic origin
○	○	○	Other origin/ethnicity
○	○	○	Religious affiliation
○	○	○	Religious participation
○	○	○	Country of birth
○	○	○	Immigrant status
○	○	○	English fluency
●	○	○	Current marital status
●	○	○	Marital history
○	○	○	Cohabitation status
○	○	○	Cohabitation history
○	○	○	Parental status
○	○	○	Number children ever born/sired
○	○	○	Age at first birth
○	○	○	Age of youngest child
○	○	○	Children living elsewhere
●	○	○	Duration at current address
●	○	○	Residential mobility
●	○	○	Educational attainment
○	○	○	Degrees attained
○	○	○	GED or regular HS diploma
○	○	○	Current enrollment
○	○	○	Current employment status
○	○	○	Hours usually worked (ft/pt)
○	○	○	Weeks worked
●	○	○	Annual employment pattern
●	○	○	Main occupation
○	○	○	Earnings
○	○	○	Wage rate
○	○	○	Payment of child support
○	○	○	Aptitude or achievement score
○	○	○	Health/disability status
●	○	○	Self-esteem
●	○	○	Locus of control or efficacy
●	○	○	Depression or subjective well-being
●	○	○	Work-related attitudes

CHARACTERISTICS OF CHILD FAMILY MEMBERS

Reference Child or Youth Respondent	Other Children (in HH)	
O	O	Age
O	O	Month and year of birth
O	O	Gender
O	O	Race
O	O	Hispanic origin
O	O	Other origin/ethnicity
O	O	Religious affiliation
O	O	Religious participation
O	O	Country of birth
O	O	Immigrant status
O	O	English fluency
O	O	Exact relationship to adult family members
O	O	Exact relationship to other children in HH
O	O	Marital status/history
O	O	Parental status/history
O	O	Current enrollment in regular school
O	O	Current enrollment in preschool/daycare
O	O	Highest grade completed
O	O	Grade now enrolled
O	O	Employment status/history
O	O	Health status
O	O	Handicapping conditions
O	O	Grade repetition
O	O	Aptitude or achievement score
O	O	Pregnancy/birth history
O	O	Psychological well-being
O	O	Delinquency

Stanford Child Custody Study and Stanford Adolescent Custody Study

PURPOSE In the early 80's, many states revised their divorce statutes, eliminating any maternal preference in child custody decisions, and diminishing the role of the courts in decision-making, requiring instead that the parental couple should make their own custody decisions whenever possible. In addition, in California and certain other states, a preference for joint custody was embodied in the new divorce law. The Stanford Child Custody Study was undertaken to examine how custody decisions were being made in this new legal context: i.e., by what means divorcing parents were able to arrive at their custody decisions; the role of attorneys, mediators, and courts; the stability of arrangements once arrived at; the amount of legal conflict; and the nature of the co-parenting processes that come into being over time in each of the different custodial arrangements. The first study examines how custodial arrangements are established and how they work out over time. The second study, the Stanford Adolescent Custody Study, examines the adjustment of youth 4½ years after their parents' divorce.

SPONSORSHIP Study 1 was directed by Eleanor E. Maccoby and Robert H. Mnookin and funded by the National Institute of Child Health and Human Development and the Stanford Center for the Study of Families, Children & Youth. Study 2 was directed by Christy M. Buchanan, Eleanor E. Maccoby, and Sanford M. Dornbusch and received funding from the Grant Foundation and the Stanford Center.

DESIGN The initial study is a cohort design focusing on 1,124 California families who filed for divorce in either San Mateo or Santa Clara counties in California between September 1984 and April 1985, and who had at least one child under age 16. To trace the process of divorce, three separate telephone interviews were conducted with parents over a three-year time span. In addition, court records were examined to determine the sequence of legal events and their relationship to the day-to-day lives of families. Efforts were made to locate and recruit both parents for the study; however, dual participation was not a prerequisite for inclusion in the sample. At the initial interview, 44% of the families had both parents participating, 39% had the mother only, and 17% involved the father only. Information is collected about all children born into the reference marriage. The sample is diverse in terms of family characteristics, including the age, number, and sex of children and the socioeconomic status of the parents.

The adolescent study was designed to explore the post-divorce functioning of youth whose parents participated in the original child custody study. The decision to focus on adolescents who were under 19 was motivated by an interest in obtaining recent information about their experiences living with one or both parents. Most youth older than 18 would no longer be residing with their parents.

PERIODICITY The design of the child custody study was short-term longitudinal. The first parent interview was conducted shortly after the petition for divorce was filed. The second interview took place one year after the first (about one and a half years after separation) when many of the divorces had been completed. Of the 1,079 families that remained eligible (e.g., had not reconciled), 978 were re-interviewed. The third interview occurred after two more years had passed—three and a half years after separation. A total of 917 families, of the estimated 1,002 families from the first wave who were still eligible, participated in the third wave. A followup study consisting of telephone interviews with 522 children aged 10½ to 18 was also conducted between November 1988 and June 1989—four and one half years after their parents separated. This adolescent custody study represents 81% of the 647 age-eligible respondents.

CONTENT Information was collected regarding family background; number, age, and sex of children; financial resources; and education, occupation, and work schedule of the two parents. The interviews in the child custody study were designed to address four major themes:

340

1) the division of parental responsibilities after divorce, the factors affecting decisions about the amount of time children are to spend with each parent, and the extent of similarity between mothers and fathers in their post-separation roles;

2) the extent of legal conflict surrounding custody, visitation, and financial support and the negotiation and dispute-resolution process, and the involvement of attorneys, mediators and other professionals;

3) the viability of different arrangements for custody and visitation over time, the nature and extent of changes in children's residence and factors producing change, and the extent of flexibility families have in adapting arrangements to changing situations; and

4) cooperation of divorced parents in the day-to-day lives of their children, including logistical problems, the extent of coordination in childrearing efforts, sources of conflict, and communication patterns.

The data are structured such that both parents were interviewed whenever possible with each answering some questions about each child individually. Therefore, variables can be constructed at the child level, at the parent level, or at the family level.

The adolescent interview collected information about parents' current or new partners, including the length of time they had been living in the same house; stability of residential arrangements over time; their experience of specific life stressors in the past 12 months, their impressions of the interparental relationship, parent-child closeness, and identification with parents; joint activities pursued with parents, extent of disengagement from the residential home; parental control and management; household organization and routines; and the adolescent's characteristics and psychological adjustments.

LIMITATIONS The study is an excellent source of information about the pragmatic aspects of child custody arrangements following marital disruption. Unlike most studies of divorcing families, father-custody and joint-custody arrangements are represented in addition to the more frequent mother-custody arrangement. The longitudinal design of the studies allows the investigators to view marital dissolution as a dynamic process that transpires through a series of stages. A further advantage of the study is that it collects information from multiple family members. Moreover, because the study employs a cohort design it allows one to observe the status of families across a comparable set of marker points.

Despite its considerable strengths, the design poses certain limitations as well. Because the sample is a cohort created by the onset of divorce the design did not permit collection of information about the children and families prior to the divorce. The absence of antecedent measures limits possibilities for examining the impact of pre-existing characteristics of families or their situations, although some retrospective information is available. Further, while followup interviews gather important information about the relationship between new spouses or partners and children from the reference marriage, the sociodemographic data collected about these new spouses or partners is limited.

Finally, like other samples of its kind drawn from court records, the investigators faced the usual challenges associated with locating the eligible families. They were successful in locating one parent in 61% of the eligible families — a rate that compares favorably with location rates disclosed by other researchers.

AVAILABILITY
Data files and documentation have been archived by:

> Sociometrics Corporation
> 170 State Street, Suite 260
> Los Altos, CA 94022-2812
> 800/846-3475

Substantive questions regarding the Child Custody Study should be directed to:

> Dr. Eleanor E. Maccoby
> Professor of Psychology (Em.)
> Department of Psychology
> Stanford University
> Stanford, California 94305-2130
> 415/725-2421

For questions related to California law and legal conflict issues, contact:

> Dr. Robert H. Mnookin
> Stanford Law School
> Stanford University
> Stanford, CA 94305-8610
> 415/723-1931

The primary reference person for the Adolescent Custody Study is:

> Dr. Christy M. Buchanan
> Department of Psychology
> Winston Hall, Rm. 244
> Wake Forest University
> Winston-Salem, NC 27109
> 919/759-5424

PUBLICATIONS

Albiston, C.R., Maccoby, E.E., & Mnookin, R.H. (1990). Does joint legal custody matter? *Stanford Law and Policy Review* (Spring).

Buchanan, C.M., Maccoby, E.E., & Dornbusch, S.M. (1991). Caught between parents: Adolescents' experience in divorced homes. *Child Development, 62,* 1008-1029.

Buchanan, C.M., Maccoby, E.E., & Dornbusch, S.M. (1992). Adolescents and their families after divorce: Three residential arrangements compared. *Journal of Research on Adolescence* 2(3), 261-291.

Maccoby, E.E., Depner, C.E., & Mnookin, R.H. (1988). Custody of children following divorce. In E.M. Hetherington & J.D. Arasteh (Eds.), *Impact of divorce, single parenting, and stepparenting on children*. Hillsdale, NJ: Lawrence Erlbaum Associates.

Maccoby, E.E., Depner, C.E., & Mnookin, R.H. (1990). Coparenting in the second year after divorce. *Journal of Marriage and the Family, 52,* 141-155.

Maccoby, E.E., & Mnookin, R.H. (1992). *Dividing the child: Social and legal dilemmas of custody*. Cambridge, MA: Harvard University Press.

Monahan, S.C., Buchanan, C.M., Maccoby, E.E., & Dornbusch, S.M. (1993). Sibling differences in divorced families. *Child Development* 64(1), 152-168.

Mnookin, R.H., Maccoby, E.E., Albiston, C.R., & Depner, C.E. (1990). Private ordering revisited: What custodial arrangements are parents negotiating? In S.D. Sugarman & H.H Kay (Eds.), *Divorce reform at the crossroads*. New Haven, CT: Yale University Press.

Stanford Child Custody Study and Stanford Adolescent Custody Study

Years of Questionnaire: Child Study in 1985, followups in 1986-88; Adolescent Study in 1988-89
Sample size: 800 families in Child Study/522 youths in Adolescent Study

FAMILY LEVEL CHARACTERISTICS

Family Composition

- ○ Full roster of household members (first name, age, sex, and relationship to reference person of each member)
- ● Partial roster of household members
- ● Number of adults in household
- ● Number of children in household
- ● Approximate relationship of family members to householder, child, or one another
- ● Exact relationship of family members to householder, child, or one another
- ● Information about part-time household member
- ● Information about family members no longer living in household[1]
- ○ Information about relatives who live nearby but not in household

Socioeconomic

- ○ Total family income
- ○ Number of persons who depend on family income
- ● Sources of income
- ○ Income amounts identified separately by source
- ○ Poverty status
- ● Welfare status
- ● Food Stamps receipt
- ● Child support receipt
- ○ Medicaid coverage
- ● Private health insurance
- ○ Home ownership/renters
- ○ Assets (other than home ownership)
- ○ Public housing status
- ○ Telephone in household
- ○ Language other than English spoken in home

Geographic/Community Variables

- ● Region of country
- ● State of residence
- ● County/city/MSA of residence
- ○ Size/type of community
- ○ Zip code
- ○ Telephone area code
- ○ Metropolitan residence
- ○ Neighborhood quality
- ○ Local labor market

Stage in Family Life Cycle

- ● Age of adult respondent or spouse/partner
- ● Marital status of adult respondent or spouse/partner
- ● Employment status of adult respondent or spouse/partner
- ● Presence of own children in household
- ● Age of youngest own child in household
- ● Age of oldest own child in household
- ● Existence of own children who have left home
- ○ Intention to have (more) children in future

345

Family Functioning

- Family activities or time use
- ○ Community involvement (civic, religious, recreational)
- Family communication patterns
- Family decision-making
- Marital conflict
- ○ Marital happiness/satisfaction
- Parent-child conflict
- ○ History of marital separations
- ○ History of family violence
- History of marital counselling

CHARACTERISTICS OF ADULT FAMILY MEMBERS

Adult Respondent or Reference Person	Current Spouse in HH[2]	Current or Former Spouse Not in HH[3]	
●	○	●	Age
●	○	●	Gender
●	○	●	Race
●	○	●	Hispanic origin
○	○	○	Other origin/ethnicity
●	○	●	Religious affiliation
○	○	○	Religious participation
○	○	○	Country of birth
○	○	○	Immigrant status
●	○	○	English fluency
●	○	●	Current marital status
●	○	○	Marital history
●	●	●	Cohabitation status
○	○	○	Cohabitation history
●	●	○	Parental status
○	●	○	Number children ever born/sired
○	○	○	Age at first birth
●	○	○	Age of youngest child
●	○	○	Children living elsewhere
●	○	○	Duration at current address
○	○	○	Residential mobility
●	○	●	Educational attainment
○	○	○	Degrees attained
○	○	○	GED or regular HS diploma
●	○	○	Current enrollment
●	○	●	Current employment status
●	○	○	Hours usually worked (ft/pt)
○	○	○	Weeks worked
○	○	○	Annual employment pattern
●	○	●	Main occupation
●	●	●	Earnings
○	○	○	Wage rate
●	○	●	Payment of child support
○	○	○	Aptitude or achievement score
○	○	○	Health/disability status
○	○	○	Self-esteem
○	○	○	Locus of control or efficacy
●	○	○	Depression or subjective well-being
○	○	○	Work-related attitudes

CHARACTERISTICS OF CHILD FAMILY MEMBERS

Reference Child or Youth Respondent[4]	Other Children (in HH)[5]	
●	●	Age
●	●	Month and year of birth
●	●	Gender
○	○	Race
○	○	Hispanic origin
○	○	Other origin/ethnicity
○	○	Religious affiliation
○	○	Religious participation
○	○	Country of birth
○	○	Immigrant status
○	○	English fluency
●	●	Exact relationship to adult family members
○	○	Exact relationship to other children in HH
○	○	Marital status/history
○	○	Parental status/history
○	○	Current enrollment in regular school
●	○	Current enrollment in preschool/daycare
○	○	Highest grade completed
●	○	Grade now enrolled
○	○	Employment status/history
○	○	Health status
●	○	Handicapping conditions
○	○	Grade repetition
○	○	Aptitude or achievement score
○	○	Pregnancy/birth history
●	○	Psychological well-being
○	○	Delinquency

NOTES

Item availability varies by survey year.

1. Ascertained about children from reference marriage who live elsewhere.
2. New spouse if remarried, or new live-in partner.
3. Former spouse from reference marriage.
4. Children from reference marriage (i.e., filed for divorce between September 1984 and March 1985).
5. Children belonging to respondent or spouse from another marriage.

347

Study of American Families

PURPOSE This is a longitudinal panel study of mothers and children. A probability sample was drawn from the July 1961 birth records of white first, second, and fourth-born children (in approximately equal numbers) in Wayne, Oakland and MaComb counties (the Detroit metropolitan area). It was originally known as the Family Growth in Detroit Study and was sometimes called the Detroit Area Study, but it was renamed in 1980 to reflect the scattering of participating families throughout the U.S. Documentation of changes in the attitudes and behavior of mothers and children over time as well as intergenerational differences are possible with these data.

SPONSORSHIP The Survey Research Center of the Institute for Social Research and the Population Studies Center at the University of Michigan conducted the study. The fifth wave of interviews was funded by the National Institute of Child Health and Human Development.

DESIGN Mothers were interviewed in person in 1962 from 92% of the sampled families in an eighty-minute interview covering a wide range of information. Subsequent telephone interviews were conducted in the fall of 1962, and again in 1963, 1966, 1977, 1980, and 1985 (seven waves in all). There were therefore seven interviews covering childbearing, marital, educational, economic, labor force, religious, and attitudinal topics with the mothers over an 18-year period. Mothers were to be interviewed about their children's "nest-leaving" and the resulting changes in parental lifestyles. Mothers whose marriages had dissolved were not interviewed in the fall 1962, 1963, and 1966 waves. However, their history and experiences were updated subsequent to their earlier exclusion.

Children born in 1961 were interviewed in 1980 and 1985 when they were 18 and 23 years of age. Most children were interviewed in person; some were interviewed by telephone or by mail. These questions were to include their life experiences between 1980 and 1985, their educational, occupational, and social activities, together with attitudes regarding family formation and personal development.

In 1980 there were full interviews with the mother and her 18-year-old child for 916 families, or 85% of the families interviewed in 1962. In 1985, 932 children responded (85% of children whose mothers were interviewed in 1962).

PERIODICITY Following the initial 1962 survey, there have been 6 subsequent telephone interviews in the fall of 1962, and again in 1963, 1966, 1977, 1980, and 1985. A 1993 reinterview wave is currently planned.

CONTENT While the investigators originally designed the study to gather information on the childbearing behavior of the mothers, the focus widened over the years to include the young persons across a wide variety of academic, work, sexual, political, social, and attitudinal areas. Marriage, living arrangements, childbearing, schooling, and employment and military experience histories, especially as related to each other, are primary orientations of the data set.

There is considerable data on the mother's marriage experience, the mother's contact with and financial assistance from her parents, financial and other assistance given to the child respondent and other adult children, and the child's relationships with parents, religiosity, childbearing behavior, sexuality, cohabitation, marriage, employment, and attitudes on these general areas of life. For example, questions asked of both mothers and children in 1980 include, "It's better for a person to get married than to go through life being single," and "All in all, there are more advantages to being single than to being married."

LIMITATIONS The original survey was limited to white couples who were living in the Detroit metropolitan area in 1962. There is some material missing for families who separated prior to the 1962, 1963, and 1966 waves. However, their files have been updated with considerable success subsequent to this period.

AVAILABILITY Data will be made available through:

Sociometrics Corporation
170 State Street, Suite 260
Los Altos, CA 94022-2812
800/846-3475

For substantive questions, contact:

Linda Young-DeMarco
Institutes for Social Research
University of Michigan
Ann Arbor, MI 48106
313/763-1500

PUBLICATIONS

Freedman, R., Freedman, D.S., & Thornton, A.D. (1980). Changes in fertility expectations and preferences between 1962 and 1977: their relation to final parity. *Demography, 17*(4), 365-378.

Freedman, D.S. & Thornton, A. (1982). Income and fertility: the elusive relationship. *Demography, 19*(1), 65-78.

Freedman, D., Thornton, A., Camburn, D. Alwin, D. & Young-De-Marco, L. (1988). The life history calendar: A technique for collecting retrospective data. *Sociological Methodology, 18*, 37-68.

Thornton, A. (1988). Cohabitation and marriage in the 1980s. *Demography, 25*(4), 497-508.

Thornton, A. & Camburn, D. (1987). The influence of the family on premarital sexual attitudes and behavior. *Demography, 24*(3), 323-40.

Thornton, A. Freedman, R. & Freedman, D. (1984). Further reflections on changes in fertility expectations and preferences. *Demography, 21*(3), 423-29.

Study of American Families
Year of Questionnaire: 1985
FAMILY LEVEL CHARACTERISTICS
Sample size: 929

Family Composition
O Full roster of household members (first name, age, sex, and relationship to reference person of each member)
O Partial roster of household members
● Number of adults in household
● Number of children in household
O Approximate relationship of family members to householder, child, or one another
● Exact relationship of family members to householder, child, or one another
O Information about part-time household member
● Information about family members no longer living in household[1]
● Information about relatives who live nearby but not in household

Socioeconomic
● Total family income
● Number of persons who depend on family income
O Sources of income
O Income amounts identified separately by source
● Poverty status
O Welfare status
O Food Stamps receipt
O Child support receipt
O Medicaid coverage
O Private health insurance
● Home ownership/renters
● Assets (other than home ownership)
O Public housing status
O Telephone in household
O Language other than English spoken in home

Geographic/Community Variables
O Region of country
O State of residence
O County/city/MSA of residence
O Size/type of community
O Zip code
O Telephone area code
O Metropolitan residence
O Neighborhood quality
O Local labor market

Stage in Family Life Cycle
O Age of adult respondent or spouse/partner
● Marital status of adult respondent or spouse/partner
● Employment status of adult respondent or spouse/partner
O Presence of own children in household
O Age of youngest own child in household
O Age of oldest own child in household
● Existence of own children who have left home
O Intention to have (more) children in future

Family Functioning

- ○ Family activities or time use
- ○ Community involvement (civic, religious, recreational)
- ● Family communication patterns
- ● Family decision-making
- ● Marital conflict
- ● Marital happiness/satisfaction
- ● Parent-child conflict
- ○ History of marital separations
- ○ History of family violence
- ○ History of marital counselling

CHARACTERISTICS OF ADULT FAMILY MEMBERS
Sample size: 929

Adult Respondent or Reference Person	Current Spouse in HH	Current or Former Spouse Not in HH	
●	●	○	Age
●	○	○	Gender
●	○	○	Race²
○	○	○	Hispanic origin
○	○	○	Other origin/ethnicity
●	○	○	Religious affiliation
●	○	○	Religious participation
○	○	○	Country of birth
●	○	○	Immigrant status
○	○	○	English fluency
●	○	○	Current marital status
●	○	○	Marital history
●	○	○	Cohabitation status
●	○	○	Cohabitation history³
●	○	○	Parental status
●	○	○	Number children ever born/sired
○	○	○	Age at first birth
○	○	○	Age of youngest child
●	○	○	Children living elsewhere
○	○	○	Duration at current address
○	○	○	Residential mobility
○	●	○	Educational attainment
○	●	○	Degrees attained
○	○	○	GED or regular HS diploma
○	○	○	Current enrollment
●	●	○	Current employment status
●	○	○	Hours usually worked (ft/pt)
○	○	○	Weeks worked
○	○	○	Annual employment pattern
●	●	○	Main occupation
○	○	○	Earnings
○	○	○	Wage rate
○	○	○	Payment of child support
○	○	○	Aptitude or achievement score
○	○	○	Health/disability status
●	○	○	Self-esteem³
○	○	○	Locus of control or efficacy
○	○	○	Depression or subjective well-being
○	○	○	Work-related attitudes

CHARACTERISTICS OF CHILD FAMILY MEMBERS
Sample size: 923

Reference Child or Youth Respondent	Other Children (in HH)	
●	○	Age
●	○	Month and year of birth
●	○	Gender
●	○	Race[2]
○	○	Hispanic origin
○	○	Other origin/ethnicity
●	○	Religious affiliation
●	○	Religious participation
●	○	Country of birth
●	○	Immigrant status
○	○	English fluency
●	○	Exact relationship to adult family members
○	○	Exact relationship to other children in HH
●	○	Marital status/history
●	○	Parental status/history
○	○	Current enrollment in regular school
○	○	Current enrollment in preschool/daycare
●	○	Highest grade completed
●	○	Grade now enrolled
●	○	Employment status/history
○	○	Health status
○	○	Handicapping conditions
○	○	Grade repetition
●	○	Aptitude or achievement score
●	○	Pregnancy/birth history
●	○	Psychological well-being
○	○	Delinquency

NOTES

1. Information is available for children of mother-respondent who are over 18 years of age in 1985.

2. All mother respondents are white.

3. Self-esteem and cohabitation questions are available for 23-year-old "child" respondents.

Study of the National Incidence and Prevalence of Child Abuse and Neglect

PURPOSE The main purpose of the National Incidence Study is to obtain a clear picture of the incidence, severity, and demographic/geographic distribution of recognized child abuse and neglect in the United States. In addition, it examines how well the official reporting system is working. The second wave of the study also enables researchers to investigate how the severity, frequency and character of child maltreatment have changed since the time of the first study.

SPONSORSHIP The study is sponsored by The National Center on Child Abuse and Neglect, located within the Department of Health and Human Services.

DESIGN The first study (NIS-1), conducted in 1979-1980, used a national probability sample of 26 counties clustered within 10 states. The sample was stratified by urban, suburban, and rural areas. In each county, data were collected from the Child Protective Services (CPS) agency, the primary agency legally responsible for investigating reports of suspected child abuse and neglect; and from non-CPS agencies. Non-CPS agencies were grouped into two categories: (1) investigatory agencies—juvenile probation department or equivalent, local police/sheriff's departments, office of the county coroner/medical examiner, and county public health departments; and (2) other study agencies—short-stay general hospitals, public schools, mental health agencies, and other social service agencies. Information was collected from 26 CPS agencies and 528 non-CPS agencies.

The second study (NIS-2), conducted in 1986, sampled a total of 29 counties (in 28 PSUs) representing different regions of the country and varying levels of county urbanization. Overall, 29 CPS agencies and 706 non-CPS agencies participated in the study.

PERIODICITY The National Study of the Incidence and Severity of Child Abuse and Neglect (NIS-1) was conducted in 1979-1980.

354

The Study of the National Incidence and Prevalence of Child Abuse and Neglect (NIS-2) was conducted in 1986. NIS-3 has been initiated as well.

CONTENT In NIS-1, the study design for CPS data collection called for completion of a "family-level" data form for each report of suspected child abuse or child neglect received by the county CPS agency between May 1, 1979 and April 30, 1980, excluding reports immediately referred to other agencies or otherwise screened out with no attempt at investigations. Two CPS data forms were used, a long form containing all information needed for statistical analysis and a short form containing only enough information to permit identification of duplicates. Non-CPS agencies were given concrete guidelines describing the kinds of child maltreatment situations which were of interest to the study and were asked to provide certain narrative and demographic information about any children they suspected to have experienced one or more of these situations during a specified four month period.

In NIS-2, the study period began September 7, 1986, for all agencies other than schools and day care centers, where it began September 28. The period continued through December 6, 1986 for all agencies. Like NIS-1, CPS data forms were family-level forms, which documented allegations concerning all children in a report on a given household or family, and the non-CPS data form was a child-level form which recorded suspected maltreatment of an individual child.

LIMITATIONS One minor limitation of this study is that there were some slight differences between the CPS forms and the non-CPS forms which result in some incongruities for data analysis. For example, on the non-CPS forms we know the relationship between the mother/mother figure in the home and the child. However, on the CPS forms, we only know that there is a mother or a mother figure in the home; we do not know if she is a natural or a step-mother.

In addition, for researchers wanting to do family-level analyses, the information from the CPS agencies will be quite valuable, but the data from the non-CPS agencies are measured with respect to the individual, not the family.

AVAILABILITY The data set is available through the Clearinghouse on Child Abuse and Neglect. They suggest that researchers using the data set request the following publications: A User's Guide for the Second National Incidence Study, Study Findings, Report on Data Collection, and Report on Data Processing and Analysis. All questions and requests for publications on the study should be done through the Clearinghouse at the following number:

Clearinghouse on Child Abuse and Neglect
P.O. Box 1182
Washington, DC 20013
703/385-7565 or
800/FYI-3366

PUBLICATIONS

Ards, S. & Harrell, A. (1991). *Reporting of child maltreatment: A secondary analysis of the National Survey of Child Abuse and Neglect*. Washington, DC: Urban Institute.

Besharov, D. (1990). Improved research on child abuse and neglect through better definitions. In D. Besharov (Ed.), *Family violence: Research and public policy issues*. Washington, DC: American Enterprise Institute.

Hampton, R.L. (1987). Violence against black children: Current knowledge and future research needs. In R.L. Hampton (Ed.), *Violence in the black family: Correlates and consequences*. Lexington, MA: Lexington Press.

Hampton, R.L. & Newberger, E.H. (1988). Child abuse incidence and reporting by hospitals: Significance of severity, class, and race. In G.T. Hotaling, D. Finkelhor, J.T. Kirkpatrick, & M. Straus (Eds.), *Coping with family violence: Research and policy perspectives*. Newbury Park, CA: Sage.

Miller, C.A., Fine, A., & Adams-Taylor, S. (1989). *Monitoring children's health: Key indicators*. Washington, DC: American Public Health Association.

National Incidence and Prevalence of Child Abuse and Neglect

Years of Questionnaire: 1986-87   Sample size: 5,317

FAMILY-LEVEL CHARACTERISTICS

Family Composition

- ○ Full roster of household members (first name, age, sex, and relationship to reference person of each member)
- ○ Partial roster of household members
- ○ Number of adults in household
- ● Number of children in household
- ○ Approximate relationship of family members to householder, child, or one another
- ○ Exact relationship of family members to householder, child, or one another
- ○ Information about part-time household member
- ○ Information about family members no longer living in household
- ○ Information about relatives who live nearby but not in household

Socioeconomic

- ● Total family income
- ○ Number of persons who depend on family income
- ○ Sources of income
- ○ Income amounts identified separately by source
- ○ Poverty status
- ● Welfare status
- ○ Food Stamps receipt
- ● Child support receipt[1]
- ○ Medicaid coverage
- ○ Private health insurance
- ○ Home ownership/renters
- ○ Assets (other than home ownership)
- ○ Public housing status
- ○ Telephone in household
- ○ Language other than English spoken in home

Geographic/Community Variables

- ○ Region of country
- ○ State of residence
- ○ County/city/MSA of residence
- ○ Size/type of community
- ○ Zip code
- ○ Telephone area code
- ○ Metropolitan residence
- ○ Neighborhood quality
- ○ Local labor market

Stage in Family Life Cycle

- ○ Age of adult respondent or spouse/partner
- ○ Marital status of adult respondent or spouse/partner
- ○ Employment status of adult respondent or spouse/partner
- ○ Presence of own children in household
- ○ Age of youngest own child in household
- ○ Age of oldest own child in household
- ○ Existence of own children who have left home
- ○ Intention to have (more) children in future

357

Family Functioning
O Family activities or time use
O Community involvement (civic, religious, recreational)
O Family communication patterns
O Family decision-making
O Marital conflict
O Marital happiness/satisfaction
● Parent-child conflict
O History of marital separations
● History of family violence
O History of marital counselling

CHARACTERISTICS OF ADULT FAMILY MEMBERS

Adult Respondent or Reference Person	Current Spouse in HH	Current or Former Spouse Not in HH	
●	●	O	Age
●	●	O	Gender
●	●	O	Race[2]
●	●	O	Hispanic origin[2]
O	O	O	Other origin/ethnicity
O	O	O	Religious affiliation
O	O	O	Religious participation
O	O	O	Country of birth
O	O	O	Immigrant status
O	O	O	English fluency
O	O	O	Current marital status
O	O	O	Marital history
O	O	O	Cohabitation status
O	O	O	Cohabitation history
O	O	O	Parental status
O	O	O	Number children ever born/sired
O	O	O	Age at first birth
O	O	O	Age of youngest child
O	O	O	Children living elsewhere
O	O	O	Duration at current address
O	O	O	Residential mobility
O	O	O	Educational attainment
O	O	O	Degrees attained
O	O	O	GED or regular HS diploma
O	O	O	Current enrollment
●	●	O	Current employment status
O	O	O	Hours usually worked (ft/pt)
O	O	O	Weeks worked
O	O	O	Annual employment pattern
O	O	O	Main occupation
O	O	O	Earnings
O	O	O	Wage rate
O	O	O	Payment of child support
O	O	O	Aptitude or achievement score
O	O	O	Health/disability status
O	O	O	Self-esteem
O	O	O	Locus of control or efficacy
O	O	O	Depression or subjective well-being
O	O	O	Work-related attitudes

358

CHARACTERISTICS OF CHILD FAMILY MEMBERS
Sample size: 5,317

Reference Child or Youth Respondent	Other Children (in HH)	
●	O	Age
●	O	Month and year of birth
●	O	Gender
●	O	Race[3]
●	O	Hispanic origin[3]
O	O	Other origin/ethnicity
O	O	Religious affiliation
O	O	Religious participation
O	O	Country of birth
O	O	Immigrant status
O	O	English fluency
●	O	Exact relationship to adult family members[2]
O	O	Exact relationship to other children in HH
O	O	Marital status/history
O	O	Parental status/history
O	O	Current enrollment in regular school
O	O	Current enrollment in preschool/daycare
O	O	Highest grade completed
O	O	Grade now enrolled
O	O	Employment status/history
O	O	Health status
O	O	Handicapping conditions
O	O	Grade repetition
O	O	Aptitude or achievement score
O	O	Pregnancy/birth history
O	O	Psychological well-being
O	O	Delinquency

NOTES
1. Only court-ordered child support; only on the CPS form.
2. Only on the CPS form.
3. On non-CPS form only; the CPS form uses the race of the parent to infer the race of the child.

Survey of Children and Parents

PURPOSE The Congress and the President created the National Commission on Children in late 1987 to assess the status of children and families in the United States and to propose policy and program changes and initiatives. This survey is a part of that assessment.

SPONSORSHIP The National Commission on Children sponsored this 1990 survey with partial support from the Foundation for Child Development.

DESIGN Princeton Survey Research Associates supervised the design of the questionnaire. Members of the Commission, together with the Commission staff and Child Trends, Inc., assisted in developing the content. Interviewers from DataStat, Inc., conducted telephone interviews between September and November 1990 using a national sample of 1,738 parents in the continental United States who live with their children. Also interviewed were 929 of the children aged 10 to 17 living in the households of these parents. The parent sample included 709 parents of non-black, non-Hispanic children, 483 parents of black, non-Hispanic children, and 546 parents of Hispanic children. African American and Hispanic children, as well as all children in the age group 10 to 17, were oversampled. The distribution of interviews with children aged 10 to 17 consists of 387 non-black, non-Hispanic children, 259 black, non-Hispanic children, and 283 Hispanic children.

Three sampling parts were used to yield a representative sample of the general population, a representative sample of the Hispanic surname population, and a representative sample of the black population living in areas with significant black population. The first used a random digit sample of telephone numbers, with exchanges selected with probabilities proportional to their size. Census tracts that were at least 30% black were used to obtain randomly listed telephone numbers, "1" was added, and persons were screened to confirm their race.

Hispanic surnames also were selected at random from listed telephone numbers of households where the telephone subscriber had one of 11,000 Hispanic surnames, "1" was added, and then persons were screened to confirm their ethnic background.

Up to 15 telephone calls were made in order to complete screening, parent, and child interviews. An initial refusal was re-contacted at least once in an effort to persuade nonrespondents to participate.

About 82% of eligible children of respondent parents were also respondents; respondent parents cooperated about 85-88% of the time once they were contacted, with a completion rate of about 90% of the respondents.

Weights were developed deriving from a special analysis of the March 1989 Current Population Survey (known as the Annual Demographic File). Results based on the total sample of children have a +/- 3% accuracy at the 95% confidence level.

PERIODICITY There are no current plans to resurvey.

CONTENT The survey covers a wide variety of questions, with many asked of both parent and child. Questions are included which cover parental and child worries about physical safety, harm, pregnancy, AIDS, alcohol, drug use, drunk drivers, and meeting family expenses. There are questions about the neighborhood, parental involvement with children's activities, parent-child relationships, and discipline. The child's contact and relationship with nonresidential parents, the availability of non-school activities, their friends' delinquent activities, and their admired figures are also included. There are numerous school-related questions, such as the type of school attended, reasons for changing to a different school, the child's feelings about school, and specific topics studied. Child's and parent's aspirations for further schooling are also included. A number of questions address the types of child care used and the amount of self care, together with the feelings of both parent and child on the adequacy of time spent together.

LIMITATIONS Children under age ten are not surveyed, although their parents are. African Americans who do not live in predominantly black neighborhoods are underrepresented as are Hispanics without Hispanic surnames. Response rates were about 70%, slightly higher for the oversampled groups. Parents with children aged 10 to 17 are overrepresented.

AVAILABILITY Data may be obtained from any of the following data archives:

Inter-University Consortium for
 Political and Social Research
P.O. Box 1248
Ann Arbor, MI 48106-1248
313/763-5010

Roper Center for Public Opinion Research
P.O. Box 440
Storrs, CT 06268
203/486-4440

Sociometrics Corporation
170 State Street, Suite 260
Los Altos, CA 94022-2812
800/846-3475

For questions about the survey, contact:

Carol Emig
National Commission on Children
1111 Eighteenth Street NW, Suite 810
Washington, DC 20036
202/254-3800

Questions about survey construction may also be answered by:

Kristin A. Moore
Child Trends, Inc.
2100 M Street NW, Suite 610
Washington DC 20037
202/223-6288

PUBLICATIONS

National Commission on Children. (1991). *Speaking of kids: A National Survey of Children and Parents.* Washington, DC: NCC.

Survey of Children and Parents
Year of Questionnaire: 1990
FAMILY LEVEL CHARACTERISTICS
Sample size: 1,738

Family Composition
- Full roster of household members (first name, age, sex, and relationship to reference person of each member)
- ○ Partial roster of household members
- Number of adults in household
- Number of children in household
- ○ Approximate relationship of family members to householder, child, or one another
- Exact relationship of family members to householder, child, or one another
- ○ Information about part-time household member
- Information about family members no longer living in household[1]
- ○ Information about relatives who live nearby but not in household

Socioeconomic
- Total family income[2]
- ○ Number of persons who depend on family income
- ○ Sources of income
- ○ Income amounts identified separately by source
- ○ Poverty status
- Welfare status
- Food Stamps receipt
- Child support receipt
- Medicaid coverage
- Private health insurance
- Home ownership/renters
- ○ Assets (other than home ownership)
- ○ Public housing status
- Telephone in household
- Language other than English spoken in home

Geographic/Community Variables
- Region of country
- ○ State of residence
- ○ County/city/MSA of residence
- Size/type of community
- ○ Zip code
- Telephone area code
- Metropolitan residence
- Neighborhood quality
- ○ Local labor market

Stage in Family Life Cycle
- Age of adult respondent or spouse/partner
- Marital status of adult respondent or spouse/partner
- Employment status of adult respondent or spouse/partner
- Presence of own children in household
- Age of youngest own child in household
- Age of oldest own child in household
- Existence of own children who have left home
- ○ Intention to have (more) children in future

364

Family Functioning
- ● Family activities or time use
- ● Community involvement (civic, religious, recreational)
- ● Family communication patterns
- ● Family decision-making
- ○ Marital conflict
- ● Marital happiness/satisfaction
- ○ Parent-child conflict
- ○ History of marital separations
- ○ History of family violence
- ○ History of marital counselling

CHARACTERISTICS OF ADULT FAMILY MEMBERS
Sample size: 1,738

Adult Respondent or Reference Person	Current Spouse in HH	Current or Former Spouse Not in HH	
●	○	○	Age
●	●	○	Gender
●	○	○	Race
●	○	○	Hispanic origin
○	○	○	Other origin/ethnicity
●	○	○	Religious affiliation
●	○	○	Religious participation
○	○	○	Country of birth
●	○	○	Immigrant status
●	○	○	English fluency
●	○	○	Current marital status
●	○	○	Marital history
○	○	○	Cohabitation status
○	○	○	Cohabitation history
●	●	○	Parental status
○	○	○	Number children ever born/sired
○	○	○	Age at first birth
○	○	○	Age of youngest child
●	●	○	Children living elsewhere
●	○	○	Duration at current address
○	○	○	Residential mobility
●	●	○	Educational attainment
○	○	○	Degrees attained
○	○	○	GED or regular HS diploma
○	○	○	Current enrollment
●	●	○	Current employment status
●	●	○	Hours usually worked (ft/pt)
○	○	○	Weeks worked
●	●	○	Annual employment pattern
○	○	○	Main occupation
○	○	○	Earnings
○	○	○	Wage rate
●	●	○	Payment of child support
○	○	○	Aptitude or achievement score
○	○	○	Health/disability status
○	○	○	Self-esteem
○	○	○	Locus of control or efficacy
●	○	○	Depression or subjective well-being
○	○	○	Work-related attitudes

CHARACTERISTICS OF CHILD FAMILY MEMBERS
Sample size: 929

Reference Child or Youth Respondent	Other Children (in HH)	
●	●	Age[3]
●	○	Month and year of birth
●	○	Gender
●	○	Race
●	○	Hispanic origin
○	○	Other origin/ethnicity
○	○	Religious affiliation
○	○	Religious participation
○	○	Country of birth
○	○	Immigrant status
○	○	English fluency
●	○	Exact relationship to adult family members
○	○	Exact relationship to other children in HH
○	○	Marital status/history
○	○	Parental status/history
●	○	Current enrollment in regular school
○	○	Current enrollment in preschool/daycare
●	○	Highest grade completed
●	○	Grade now enrolled
●	○	Employment status/history
●	○	Health status
●	○	Handicapping conditions
○	○	Grade repetition
○	○	Aptitude or achievement score
○	○	Pregnancy/birth history
●	○	Psychological well-being
●	○	Delinquency[4]

NOTES

1. Aged 17 or younger.
2. In $10,000 increments to $60,000+.
3. Ages of other children in household are given in ranges of 9 and under, 10-13, and 14-17.
4. Friends who are delinquent and pressures to be delinquent are included.

Survey of Income and Program Participation— Core Survey

PURPOSE The Survey of Income and Program Participation (SIPP) is a major source of information on the demographic and economic situation of persons and families in the United States. Analysis of the data provides a better understanding of the distribution of income, wealth, and poverty in the society, and of the effects of federal and state programs on the well-being of families and individuals. It also serves as a tool for managing and evaluating government transfer and service programs. The gathering of more detailed information on earned, unearned, and asset income sources, coupled with the measurement of monthly variations in such contributing factors as household structure, the determinants of program eligibility, and actual participation, assists researchers and policymakers as they grapple with ways to reform welfare, improve entitlement programs, and otherwise monitor and influence the policies and programs designed to help the needy of this country.

SPONSORSHIP The survey is funded and conducted by the U.S. Bureau of the Census.

DESIGN The survey uses a multi-stage stratified sample of the U.S. civilian, non-institutionalized population. The first panel of SIPP (the 1984 panel) was initiated in October 1983. Original plans called for a sample size of approximately 20,000 households per panel. Budgetary constraints, however, forced panels after 1984 to be reduced to approximately 13,000 households per panel. Although the 1990 panel was increased to approximately 21,500 households, the 1991 panel was again reduced in size to approximately 14,000 households.

In general, each assigned household is interviewed once every four months for a period of two and a half years, resulting in eight interviews per household. To simplify interviewing and data processing, each panel of households is divided into four smaller groups of approximately equal size called rotation groups. These groups are interviewed during four consecutive months. The four-month period of interviewing that it takes to give the entire panel the same interview schedule is called a wave. The reference period for a particular rotation group is the preceding four months. Thus the four rotation groups each have a different reference period for each interviewing wave.

The primary focus of SIPP is adults, defined as persons 15 years of age or older in the initial sample household. Individuals are followed even if they change addresses or move out of the sample household. However, there is differential attrition among persons who have households. Departing fathers, for example, are more likely to be lost to followup than adult children forming their own families. Individuals who move into a sample household are included in the survey only as long as they reside with panel members. Prior to 1992, interviews were generally conducted in person by personnel from the 12 permanent regional offices of the Census Bureau. Beginning in February 1992, waves 1, 2, and 6 are personal interviews, but waves 3, 4, 5, 7, and 8 are conducted by telephone. Proxy respondents are used for individuals who are not present at the time of the interview. The panel nature of SIPP allows year-to-year change estimates to be made using the same individuals. In addition, the overlapping nature of the sample design allows for cross-sectional estimates to be produced on combined panels, thereby substantially increasing sample sizes and the reliability of the estimates produced.

The Census Bureau is redesigning SIPP. The proposed new design calls for panels of approximately 50,000 households. Each panel will be followed for 52 months. The new design is scheduled to be implemented in 1996.

PERIODICITY This is a continuous survey in which overlapping panels are added and existing panels are rotated out after completing their period of approximately two and a half years in the sample. The proposed new design calls for a single panel to be in the field at a time, with each panel followed for 52 months.

CONTENT The survey consists of four major questionnaire components: the control card, the core set of questions repeated ducted one or two times during a panel, and variable topical modules to be added from time to time. In addition, the content of the survey questionnaire may be supplemented by administrative record data.

The control card is used to obtain and maintain information on the basic characteristics associated with households and persons, such as age, race, ethnic origin, sex, marital status, and educational level of each adult member of the household, as well as information on the housing unit and the relationship of the householder to other members. The core portion of the questionnaire includes four major sections: (1) labor force and recipiency, (2) earnings and employment, (3) amounts of income received, and (4) a short set of program questions. Section one obtains general information about labor force activity and recipiency, while sections two and three gather more detailed information about type of employment, earnings, and income. Section four is only asked of the reference person at each address. Among the items included in this section are whether any children aged 5 to 18 in the household participate in subsidized school lunch or breakfast programs.

Among the fixed topical modules are a personal history module and a school enrollment and financing module (see their descriptions in this volume for more detailed information on their purpose and content).

Variable topical modules comprise the final component of the questionnaire. These modules include supplemental questions designed by or for other federal agencies and are added to one or more waves of interviewing. Variable topical modules include: child care arrangements, child support agreements, functional limitations and disability, utilization of health care services, support for nonhousehold members, work-related expenses, job offers, long-term care, shelter costs/energy usage, work schedule, home health care, and spells outside the workforce.

SIPP offers the opportunity to examine short-term economic consequences of divorce, the addition of a baby, or other changes in family configuration. Moreover, by combining information from the core with the extensive information collected in the various topical modules, detailed profiles of families in a variety of circumstances can be made.

LIMITATIONS The sample size is relatively small (compared to the Current Population Survey, for example), leading to relatively large standard errors. The complexity of the survey, an advantage from the viewpoint of providing detailed and accurate information, may impair user access to microdata tapes which may be complicated and expensive to process. For example, the use of more than one file and the merging of data will be needed if a user wishes to combine in one analysis information from topical modules collected in different waves. Even when using only one file, certain types of analyses may require appending information from one person's record onto another person's record. For example, to create a child file containing pertinent parental information, it will be necessary to append appropriate variables from the parents' records onto each child's record. Similarly, to create a family file containing pertinent information on all family members, it will be necessary to identify the parents, children, and any other family members and append appropriate variables from each person's record onto a new family record. In 1990 the unit of observation changed from one record for each person to one record for each person for each month. It remains to be seen whether this new format is preferred by users. Another limitation is that SIPP does not oversample groups of special interest, such as African Americans, Hispanics, or low-income households. Thus, sample sizes for these groups can be small for some types of analyses.

AVAILABILITY Questions about publications, data products, and their availability should be directed to:

> Customer Services Branch
> Data User Services Division
> U.S. Bureau of the Census
> Washington, DC 20233
> 301/763-4100

Access to SIPP public use files is also available through the Inter-University Consortium for Political and Social Research (ICPSR) at the University of Michigan (313/763-5010) and through SIPP ON-CALL at the Census Bureau. SIPP ON-CALL is an electronic data extraction system that provides users with remote access to SIPP data. As of April 1992, only the core data for 1990 are available through this system. Topical modules and future panels of SIPP will be added to the system.

For more information about SIPP ON-CALL, contact:

> Edward Bean, SIPP ON-CALL Staff
> U.S. Bureau of the Census
> 301/763-8389 or 8378

For substantive questions about SIPP, contact:

> Enrique Lamas
> Special Assistant to SIPP
> HHES Division, I-MAIL 307-1
> U.S. Bureau of the Census
> Washington, DC 20233
> 301/763-8018

PUBLICATIONS

Bianchi, S., & McArthur, E. (1991). Family disruption and economic hardship: The short-run picture for children. *Current Population Reports* (Series P-70, No.23). Washington, DC: U.S. Bureau of the Census, GPO.

Jabine, T.B. (1990). Survey of Income and Program Participation: Quality profile. Washington, DC: U.S. Bureau of the Census, GPO.

Jennings, J.T., & Bennefield, R.L. (1992). Who's helping out? Support networks among American families: 1988. *Current Population Reports* (Series P-70, No. 28). Washington, DC: U.S. Bureau of the Census, GPO.

U.S. Bureau of the Census. (1989). Characteristics of persons receiving benefits from major assistance programs. *Current Population Reports* (Series 70, No. 14). Washington, DC: GPO.

U.S. Bureau of the Census. (1990). Work and family patterns of American women. *Current Population Reports* (Series P-23, No. 165). Washington, DC: GPO.

U.S. Bureau of the Census. (1991). What's available from the Survey of Income and Program Participation. Washington, DC: GPO.

Recent SIPP Working Papers include the following:

Long, S.K. (1990). Welfare participation and welfare recidivism: The role of family events. SIPP Working Paper #9018.

Speare, A., Avery, R., & Goldscheider, F. (1990). An analysis of leaving home using data from the 1984 Panel of the SIPP. SIPP Working Paper #9002.

Survey of Income and Program Participation—Core Survey (1990)
Sample size: 21,500 households
FAMILY LEVEL CHARACTERISTICS
Sample size: 55,000 persons

Family Composition
- Full roster of household members (first name, age, sex, and relationship to reference person of each member)
○ Partial roster of household members
- Number of adults in household
- Number of children in household
○ Approximate relationship of family members to householder, child, or one another
○ Exact relationship of family members to householder, child, or one another
○ Information about part-time household member
○ Information about family members no longer living in household
○ Information about relatives who live nearby but not in household

Socioeconomic
- Total family income
○ Number of persons who depend on family income
- Sources of income
- Income amounts identified separately by source
- Poverty status
- Welfare status
- Food Stamps receipt
- Child support receipt
- Medicaid coverage
- Private health insurance
- Home ownership/renters
- Assets (other than home ownership)
- Public housing status
○ Telephone in household
○ Language other than English spoken in home

Geographic/Community Variables
- Region of country[1]
- State of residence
- County/city/MSA of residence
○ Size/type of community
○ Zip code
○ Telephone area code
- Metropolitan residence
○ Neighborhood quality
○ Local labor market

Stage in Family Life Cycle
- Age of adult respondent or spouse/partner
- Marital status of adult respondent or spouse/partner
- Employment status of adult respondent or spouse/partner
- Presence of own children in household
- Age of youngest own child in household
- Age of oldest own child in household
○ Existence of own children who have left home
○ Intention to have (more) children in future

373

Family Functioning

○ Family activities or time use
○ Community involvement (civic, religious, recreational)
○ Family communication patterns
○ Family decision-making
○ Marital conflict
○ Marital happiness/satisfaction
○ Parent-child conflict
○ History of marital separations
○ History of family violence
○ History of marital counselling

CHARACTERISTICS OF ADULT FAMILY MEMBERS
Sample size: 40,000 persons 18 and older

Adult Respondent or Reference Person	Current Spouse in HH	Current or Former Spouse Not in HH	
●	●	○	Age
●	●	○	Gender
●	●	○	Race
●	●	○	Hispanic origin
●	●	○	Other origin/ethnicity
○	○	○	Religious affiliation
○	○	○	Religious participation
○	○	○	Country of birth
○	○	○	Immigrant status
○	○	○	English fluency
●	●	○	Current marital status
○	○	○	Marital history
○	○	○	Cohabitation status
○	○	○	Cohabitation history
○	○	○	Parental status
○	○	○	Number children ever born/sired
○	○	○	Age at first birth
○	○	○	Age of youngest child
○	○	○	Children living elsewhere
○	○	○	Duration at current address
○	○	○	Residential mobility
●	●	○	Educational attainment
○	○	○	Degrees attained
○	○	○	GED or regular HS diploma
●	●	○	Current enrollment
●	●	○	Current employment status
●	●	○	Hours usually worked (ft/pt)
●	●	○	Weeks worked
●	●	○	Annual employment pattern[2]
●	●	○	Main occupation
●	●	○	Earnings
●	●	○	Wage rate
○	○	○	Payment of child support
○	○	○	Aptitude or achievement score
○	○	○	Health/disability status
○	○	○	Self-esteem
○	○	○	Locus of control or efficacy
○	○	○	Depression or subjective well-being
○	○	○	Work-related attitudes

CHARACTERISTICS OF CHILD FAMILY MEMBERS
Sample size: 15,000 children under 18

Reference Child or Youth Respondent	Children (in HH)	
O	●	Age
O	●	Month and year of birth
O	●	Gender
O	●	Race
O	●	Hispanic origin
O	●	Other origin/ethnicity
O	O	Religious affiliation
O	O	Religious participation
O	O	Country of birth
O	O	Immigrant status
O	O	English fluency
O	O	Exact relationship to adult family members
O	O	Exact relationship to other children in HH
O	●	Marital status/history[3]
O	O	Parental status/history
O	O	Current enrollment in regular school
O	O	Current enrollment in preschool/daycare
O	●	Highest grade completed[3]
O	O	Grade now enrolled
O	●	Employment status/history[3]
O	O	Health status
O	O	Handicapping conditions
O	O	Grade repetition
O	O	Aptitude or achievement score
O	O	Pregnancy/birth history
O	O	Psychological well-being
O	O	Delinquency

NOTES
Due to the design of SIPP, the time frame refers to the four months prior to a particular survey wave. Annual information can be obtained by combining information across appropriate waves and rotation groups.

1. Region of country can be created from state codes. However, some states are collapsed because of small population size.

2. Need to combine information across waves.

3. Available for persons 15 and older.

SIPP—Child Care Topical Module

PURPOSE The child care topical module to SIPP is designed to establish an ongoing data base of child care statistics that has heretofore been lacking at the national level.

SPONSORSHIP The topical module is funded and conducted by the U.S. Bureau of the Census. An advisory panel with representatives from selected federal agencies oversees the questionnaire design and frequency of interviewing.

DESIGN The description of the main SIPP survey provides an overview of the basic design. The topical module on child care is asked of respondents who are the designated parents or guardians of children under 15 who are living in the household. The respondents must also either be working or enrolled in school (this criterion did not apply the first time the module was asked in the fifth wave of the 1984 panel) to be eligible for the module. The survey was expanded in the 1988 panel to include persons looking for a job. The questions pertain to the three youngest children under 15 years of age.

PERIODICITY The child care module is asked of every panel. The 1986 through 1989 Panels received the module twice — in the third and sixth waves. By asking the module twice, the Census was able to obtain data from overlapping panels and thereby double the sample size and increase the reliability of the estimates obtained. Beginning in 1990, however, child care items are only asked once each panel in the third wave.

CONTENT The child care module obtains basic information on child care arrangements for the three youngest children of eligible respondents while the respondents are working or are in school. The reference period is the month prior to the interview. For each of the three youngest children, the respondent is asked about the main type of arrangement used (that is, the one where the child was cared for during most of the hours that the respondent worked or was in class), where the child was usually cared for under the arrangement, and the number of hours per week the child usually spent in the arrangement. Information about the type and location of the second major type of arrangement is also gathered. Respondents are also asked about the total cost of child care arrangements in a typical week. They are also asked if either they or their spouse have lost time from work because the person responsible for taking care of their child or children was not available.

In addition to the typical child care arrangements used in the last month, respondents are asked if they have made any changes in child care arrangements during the last year and all the reasons that they had for making any changes, such as reliability of care provider, availability of hours of care provider, and cost.

Also asked in the third wave of the 1990 panel is a topical module on work schedules. Because the topical modules in a particular wave are released together, information gathered in the work schedule module is available for analysis with the child care data. The work schedule module gathers information on hours worked including the time that respondents usually began and ended work and the days of the week that the respondents usually worked. Respondents are asked to characterize their schedules as regular daytime, regular evening shifts, irregular schedules, or some other schedule. With these data it is possible to examine how parents' work schedules are related to their child care needs and the extent to which parents arrange their schedules so that one parent can take care of the children while the other is working.

In addition to the Child Care and Work Schedule Topical Modules, the third wave of the 1990 panel contains the following topical modules: Child Support, Support for Nonhousehold Members, Functional Limitations and Disability, and Utilization of Health Care Services.

LIMITATIONS Even when the overlapping panels are analyzed together, the sample size is still relatively small compared, for example, to the Current Population Survey. Thus estimates may have large standard errors. Moreover, SIPP does not oversample African Americans or Hispanics, so sample sizes for these groups can also be small for some purposes. The complexity of the survey, an advantage from the viewpoint of providing detailed and accurate information, may impair user access to microdata tapes which may be complicated and expensive to process. For some analyses, the use of more than one file and the merging of data may be necessary. See the SIPP "Core" description for more details.

AVAILABILITY As of December 1992, the child care modules available are from the fifth wave of the 1984 panel through the third wave of the 1990 panel. The child care module from the 1991 panel is due to be released early in 1993.

Questions about data products and their availability should be directed to:

> Customer Services Branch
> Data User Services Division
> U.S. Bureau of the Census
> Washington, DC 20233
> 301/763-4100

For substantive question on the child care topical module, contact:

> Martin O'Connell
> Fertility Statistics Branch
> Population Division
> U.S. Bureau of the Census
> Washington, DC 20233
> 301/763-5303

For substantive questions about other aspects of SIPP contact:

> Enrique Lamas
> Special Assistant to SIPP
> HHES Division, I-MALL 307-1
> U.S. Bureau of the Census
> Washington, DC 20233
> 301/763-8018

PUBLICATIONS

U.S. Bureau of the Census. (1987). Who's minding the kids? Child care arrangements: Winter 1984-1985. *Current Population Reports* (Series P-70, No.9). Washington, DC: GPO.

O'Connell, M., & Bachi, A. (1990). Who's minding the kids? Child care arrangements: 1986-87. *Current Population Reports* (Series P-70, No. 20). Washington, DC: U.S. Bureau of the Census, GPO.

SIPP—Child Care

Year of Questionnaire: 1990 Panel
Sample size: 21,500 households

FAMILY LEVEL CHARACTERISTICS

Sample size: 55,000 persons

Family Composition

O Full roster of household members (first name, age, sex, and relationship to reference person of each member)
O Partial roster of household members
O Number of adults in household
O Number of children in household
O Approximate relationship of family members to householder, child, or one another
O Exact relationship of family members to householder, child, or one another
O Information about part-time household member
O Information about family members no longer living in household
O Information about relatives who live nearby but not in household

Socioeconomic

O Total family income
O Number of persons who depend on family income
O Sources of income
O Income amounts identified separately by source
O Poverty status
O Welfare status
O Food Stamps receipt
● Child support receipt
O Medicaid coverage
O Private health insurance
O Home ownership/renters
O Assets (other than home ownership)
O Public housing status
O Telephone in household
O Language other than English spoken in home

Geographic/Community Variables

O Region of country
O State of residence
O County/city/MSA of residence
O Size/type of community
O Zip code
O Telephone area code
O Metropolitan residence
O Neighborhood quality
O Local labor market

Stage in Family Life Cycle

● Age of adult respondent or spouse/partner
● Marital status of adult respondent or spouse/partner
● Employment status of adult respondent or spouse/partner
● Presence of own children in household
O Age of youngest own child in household
O Age of oldest own child in household
O Existence of own children who have left home
O Intention to have (more) children in future

Family Functioning
○ Family activities or time use
○ Community involvement (civic, religious, recreational)
○ Family communication patterns
○ Family decision-making
○ Marital conflict
○ Marital happiness/satisfaction
○ Parent-child conflict
○ History of marital separations
○ History of family violence
○ History of marital counselling

CHARACTERISTICS OF ADULT FAMILY MEMBERS
Sample size: 40,000 persons 18 and older

Adult Respondent or Reference Person	Current Spouse in HH	Current or Former Spouse Not in HH	
●	●	○	Age
●	●	○	Gender
●	●	○	Race
●	●	○	Hispanic origin
●	●	○	Other origin/ethnicity
○	○	○	Religious affiliation
○	○	○	Religious participation
○	○	○	Country of birth
○	○	○	Immigrant status
○	○	○	English fluency
●	●	○	Current marital status
○	○	○	Marital history
○	○	○	Cohabitation status
○	○	○	Cohabitation history
○	○	○	Parental status
○	○	○	Number children ever born/sired
○	○	○	Age at first birth
○	○	○	Age of youngest child
○	○	○	Children living elsewhere
○	○	○	Duration at current address
○	○	○	Residential mobility
●	●	○	Educational attainment
○	○	○	Degrees attained
○	○	○	GED or regular HS diploma
○	○	○	Current enrollment
○	○	○	Current employment status
●	●	○	Hours usually worked (ft/pt)
○	○	○	Weeks worked
○	○	○	Annual employment pattern
○	○	○	Main occupation
○	○	○	Earnings
○	○	○	Wage rate
●	●	○	Payment of child support
○	○	○	Aptitude or achievement score
●	●	○	Health/disability status
○	○	○	Self-esteem
○	○	○	Locus of control or efficacy
○	○	○	Depression or subjective well-being
○	○	○	Work-related attitudes

CHARACTERISTICS OF CHILD FAMILY MEMBERS

Sample size: 15,000 children under 18

Reference Child or Youth Respondent	Children (in HH)	
O	●	Age
O	O	Month and year of birth
O	●	Gender
O	●	Race
O	●	Hispanic origin
O	●	Other origin/ethnicity
O	O	Religious affiliation
O	O	Religious participation
O	O	Country of birth
O	O	Immigrant status
O	O	English fluency
O	O	Exact relationship to adult family members
O	O	Exact relationship to other children in HH
O	●	Marital status/history[1]
O	O	Parental status/history
O	O	Current enrollment in regular school
O	O	Current enrollment in preschool/daycare
O	●	Highest grade completed[1]
O	O	Grade now enrolled
O	O	Employment status/history
O	O	Health status
O	O	Handicapping conditions
O	O	Grade repetition
O	O	Aptitude or achievement score
O	O	Pregnancy/birth history
O	O	Psychological well-being
O	O	Delinquency

NOTES

Topical module data are released separately from the core. Variables needed for matching core data with topical module data are contained on both files. See the core description for a listing of types of variables that are available in the core.

1. Asked of persons 15 and older.

SIPP—Child Support Topical Module

PURPOSE The Child Support Topical Module is designed to supplement and round out similar data collected by the Current Population Survey (CPS). Because SIPP collects detailed information on related topics such as assets, child care, and support for non-household members, SIPP data provide a richer context for viewing the receipt of child support.

Furthermore, in the core part of the SIPP, for each of the four months preceding the interview, respondents are asked if they received any income from child support, and, if so, how much income they received. Whereas the CPS only collects annual amounts of child support received, in theory the SIPP data provide the opportunity to examine patterns of monthly payments using data collected in the core part of the survey, as well as data contained in the module. Hence, insights into the consequences of, for example, regular versus irregular receipt of child support could be gained.

SPONSORSHIP The topical module is funded and conducted by the U.S. Bureau of the Census. An advisory panel with representatives from selected federal agencies oversees the questionnaire design and frequency of interviewing.

DESIGN The description of the SIPP Core Survey provides an overview of the basic design. The topical module on child support is asked of parents with children under 21 years of age who live in their household and whose second parent lives elsewhere.

PERIODICITY The topical module on child support is asked of every panel. Beginning with the 1986 panel, the module is asked twice — in the third and sixth waves. By asking the module twice, the Census Bureau is able to obtain data from overlapping panels and thereby increase the sample size and the reliability of the estimates produced. At present, there are no plans to continue the child support module beyond the 1990 panel.

CONTENT The module was substantially revised and expanded with the 1990 panel. Whereas formerly the questions were asked only of eligible women, beginning in the 1987 panel the questions are now asked of custodial parents regardless of their gender. Thus, this module can be used to examine child support received by both men and women who have custody.

Respondents who have ever had a child support agreement are asked a series of questions about their most recent agreement and any modifications that might have been made to that agreement. They are asked how many children are covered by the agreement, the type of agreement it is (e.g., voluntary written agreement ratified by the court, a court ordered agreement, some other type of written agreement, or a non-written agreement), the year in which the agreement was first reached, the dollar amount of the agreement, whether the dollar amount of the agreement has ever changed, what year the amount was last changed, and what the dollar amount was after the last change.

Respondents are then asked if any payments were due in the last 12 months. If no payments were due, they are asked why not. They are also asked what kinds of provisions for health care costs were included in their child support agreement, the type of child custody arrangements specified by their most recent agreement, whether the agreement specified visitation arrangements between the child or children covered and the other parent, the amount of time spent by all the children (if they all spent the same amount of time) or by the oldest child (if the time differs) visiting the other parent in the last 12 months, where that other parent lives (e.g., same county/city, same state, different state, other), and how the respondent contacts the other parent if they need to (e.g., directly, through a friend, through a relative, by some other means).

If payments were due in the last 12 months, respondents are asked what the total amount was that they were supposed to receive, what amount they actually received, how their payments were received (e.g., directly from the other parent, through a court, through the welfare or child support agency, or by some other method), how regularly their child support payments were received, and how many child support payments were paid within 30 days of when they were due (all, most, some, or none). They are then asked the same series of questions described above about what kinds of provisions for health care costs are included in their child support agreement, the type of child custody arrangements that they have, whether visitation arrangements were specified, the amount of time spent by their children visiting the other parent in the last 12 months, where the other parent lives, and how the respondent contacts the other parent.

In addition to these questions, respondents are asked about other child support agreements that pertain to children in the household not covered by the agreement already described, the children covered by this separate agreement, the dollar amount that was supposed to be received in the last 12 months, the dollar amount actually received, and where the other parent for this agreement now lives.

Respondents are also asked whether they have ever asked a public agency (such as the child support enforcement office or welfare agency) for help in obtaining child support for any of their children. If yes, they are asked in what year they last asked for help, the type of help they asked for (e.g., locate the other parent, establish paternity/maternity, establish support obligation, establish medical support, enforce support, modify an order), whether they received help from the agency, and the type of help that they received.

Respondents are also asked how many children in their household do not have a child support award from an absent parent, whether these children have the same absent parent (if there are different parents, the respondents are asked about their oldest and youngest children not covered by an award in the remaining questions), why child support payments were not agreed to, where the other parent for these children now live, and how they would contact the other parent.

The module concludes by asking about any child support payments that were received in the last 12 months without a written child support agreement, the total amount of such payments received in the last 12 months, and whether any non-cash items or services for child support were received for any of the respondent's children.

Topical modules asked in the same wave are released together. In addition to the child support topical modules, the third wave of the 1990 panel contains topical modules on support for nonhousehold members, functional limitations and disability, utilization of health care services, work schedules, and child care. The sixth wave of the 1990 panel contains the child support topical module as well as modules on support for non-household members, utilization of health care services, functional limitations and disability, and time spent outside the work force.

LIMITATIONS Even when the overlapping panels are analyzed together, the sample size is still relatively small compared, for example, to the Current Population Survey. Thus, estimates may have large standard errors. Moreover, SIPP does not oversample African Americans or Hispanics, so sample sizes for these groups may be small for some analyses. The complexity of the survey, an advantage from the viewpoint of providing detailed and accurate information, may impair user access to microdata tapes which may be complicated and expensive to process. For some analyses, using more than one file and merging data may be necessary. See the SIPP Core Survey description for more details.

For some items there may be high allocation rates, but, overall, the quality of the module appears good.

Persons 15 and older who are interviewed in the first wave are followed if they leave the original household. Thus, it is theoretically possible to track couples who disrupt during the course of the survey and match responses on support paid by absent parents with support received by custodial parents. Such couples, however, will represent only a small fraction of SIPP households. Moreover, because the divorce process takes time, a formal support agreement may not be in place by the end of the panel.

AVAILABILITY Questions about publications, data products, and their availability should be directed to:

Customer Services Branch
Data User Services Division
U.S. Bureau of the Census
Washington, DC 20233
301/763-4100

For substantive questions about the Child Support Topical Module, contact:

> Gordon Lester
> Housing and Household
> Economic Statistics Division
> U.S. Bureau of the Census
> Washington, DC 20233
> 301/763-8576

For substantive questions about other aspects of SIPP contact:

> Enrique Lamas
> Special Assistant to SIPP
> HHES Division, I-MALL 307-1
> U.S. Bureau of the Census
> Washington, DC 20233
> 301/763-8018

PUBLICATIONS

Bianchi, S., & McArthur, E. (1991). Family disruption and economic hardship: The short-run picture for children. *Current Population Reports* (Series P-70, No. 23). Washington, DC: U.S. Bureau of the Census, GPO.

Jennings, J.T., & Bennefield, R.L. (1992). Who's helping out? Support networks among American families: 1988. *Current Population Reports* (Series P-70, No. 28). Washington, DC: U.S. Bureau of the Census, GPO.

Peterson, J.L., & Nord, C. Winquist. (1990). The regular receipt of child support: A multistep process. *Journal of Marriage and the Family, 52*(2), 539-551.

SIPP—Child Support
Year of Questionnaire: 1990 Panel
Sample size: 21,500 households
FAMILY LEVEL CHARACTERISTICS
Sample size: 55,000 persons

Family Composition
O Full roster of household members (first name, age, sex, and relationship to reference person of each member)
O Partial roster of household members
O Number of adults in household
O Number of children in household
O Approximate relationship of family members to householder, child, or one another
O Exact relationship of family members to householder, child, or one another
O Information about part-time household member
O Information about family members no longer living in household
O Information about relatives who live nearby but not in household

Socioeconomic
O Total family income
O Number of persons who depend on family income
O Sources of income
O Income amounts identified separately by source
O Poverty status
O Welfare status
O Food Stamps receipt
● Child support receipt
O Medicaid coverage
O Private health insurance
O Home ownership/renters
O Assets (other than home ownership)
O Public housing status
O Telephone in household
O Language other than English spoken in home

Geographic/Community Variables
O Region of country
O State of residence
O County/city/MSA of residence
O Size/type of community
O Zip code
O Telephone area code
O Metropolitan residence
O Neighborhood quality
O Local labor market

Stage in Family Life Cycle
● Age of adult respondent or spouse/partner
● Marital status of adult respondent or spouse/partner
O Employment status of adult respondent or spouse/partner
● Presence of own children in household
O Age of youngest own child in household
O Age of oldest own child in household
O Existence of own children who have left home
O Intention to have (more) children in future

Family Functioning
O Family activities or time use
O Community involvement (civic, religious, recreational)
O Family communication patterns
O Family decision-making
O Marital conflict
O Marital happiness/satisfaction
O Parent-child conflict
O History of marital separations
O History of family violence
O History of marital counselling

CHARACTERISTICS OF ADULT FAMILY MEMBERS
Sample size: 40,000 persons 18 and older

Adult Respondent or Reference Spouse	Current Spouse in HH	Current or Former Spouse Not in HH	
●	●	O	Age
●	●	O	Gender
●	●	O	Race
●	●	O	Hispanic origin
●	●	O	Other origin/ethnicity
O	O	O	Religious affiliation
O	O	O	Religious participation
O	O	O	Country of birth
O	O	O	Immigrant status
O	O	O	English fluency
●	●	O	Current marital status
O	O	O	Marital history
O	O	O	Cohabitation status
O	O	O	Cohabitation history
O	O	O	Parental status
O	O	O	Number children ever born/sired
O	O	O	Age at first birth
O	O	O	Age of youngest child
O	O	O	Children living elsewhere
O	O	O	Duration at current address
O	O	O	Residential mobility
●	●	O	Educational attainment
O	O	O	Degrees attained
O	O	O	GED or regular HS diploma
O	O	O	Current enrollment
O	O	O	Current employment status
O	O	O	Hours usually worked (ft/pt)
O	O	O	Weeks worked
O	O	O	Annual employment pattern
O	O	O	Main occupation
O	O	O	Earnings
O	O	O	Wage rate
●	●	O	Payment of child support
O	O	O	Aptitude or achievement score
●	●	O	Health/disability status
O	O	O	Self-esteem
O	O	O	Locus of control or efficacy
O	O	O	Depression or subjective well-being
O	O	O	Work-related attitudes

CHARACTERISTICS OF CHILD FAMILY MEMBERS
Sample size: 15,000 children under 18

Reference Child or Youth Respondent	Children (in HH)	
O	●	Age
O	O	Month and year of birth
O	●	Gender
O	●	Race
O	●	Hispanic origin
O	●	Other origin/ethnicity
O	O	Religious affiliation
O	O	Religious participation
O	O	Country of birth
O	O	Immigrant status
O	O	English fluency
O	O	Exact relationship to adult family members
O	O	Exact relationship to other children in HH
O	●	Marital status/history[1]
O	O	Parental status/history
O	O	Current enrollment in regular school
O	O	Current enrollment in preschool/daycare
O	●	Highest grade completed[1]
O	O	Grade now enrolled
O	O	Employment status/history
O	●	Health status
O	●	Handicapping conditions
O	O	Grade repetition
O	O	Aptitude or achievement score
O	O	Pregnancy/birth history
O	O	Psychological well-being
O	O	Delinquency

NOTES
Topical module data are released separately from the core. Variables needed for matching core data with topical module data are contained on both files. See the core description for a listing of types of variables that are available in the core.

1. Asked of persons 15 and older.

SIPP—Functional Limitations and Disability Topical Module

PURPOSE The Functional Limitations and Disability Topical Module to SIPP is intended to provide estimates of the number and characteristics of persons in the United States who are physically or mentally limited in some capacity.

SPONSORSHIP The topical module is funded and conducted by the U.S. Bureau of the Census. An advisory panel with representatives from selected federal agencies oversees the questionnaire design and frequency of interviewing.

DESIGN The description of the SIPP Core survey provides an overview of the basic design. The functional limitations and disability topical module is asked of all persons 15 years of age and older in the household. In addition, questions on the disability status of children under 21 are asked of the designated parent or guardian of such children who live in the household.

PERIODICITY The functional limitations and disability topical module, as of 1990, is asked twice in every panel — in the third and sixth waves. The interview schedule of the SIPP panels allows for several panels to be interviewed during the same time period. For questions that are asked in appropriate waves of overlapping panels, it is possible to combine information from adjacent panels and thereby increase the sample size and reliability of the resulting estimates. It is possible to take advantage of this feature with the functional limitations and disability topical module by combining the sixth wave data with the third wave data of the subsequent panel. When the 1990 and 1991 panels are combined, the sample size increases to approximately 40,000 households.

CONTENT The questions geared towards persons 15 and older ask about a person's overall health, their use of aids such as canes, crutches, walkers, or a wheelchair, and the length of time they have needed an aid. Eligible persons are also asked whether they have difficulty seeing words in a newspaper, hearing normal conversations, or if they have trouble making their speech understood because of a health condition or problem. In addition to these questions, they are asked about difficulty in carrying out normal everyday activities such as lifting or carrying something as heavy as ten pounds, climbing a flight of stairs, walking a quarter of a mile, or using the telephone. Persons 15 and older are also asked if a physical or mental health condition hinders their ability to take care of themselves, including performing such activities as bathing, dressing, eating, preparing meals, or keeping track of money.

Parents or guardians of children under 21 in the household are asked a series of questions that are dependent upon the ages of their children. Parents or guardians of children under 6 are asked whether any of their children have a physical, learning, or mental condition that limits their children in the usual kind of activities done by most children their age, and whether any of their young children have received therapy or diagnostic services to meet their developmental needs. Parents of children between the ages of 6 and 21 are asked about whether their children have a physical, learning, or mental health condition that limits their children in their ability to do regular school work. They are also asked whether any of their children between the ages of 6 and 21 have ever received special education services. Parents of children between the ages of 3 and 14 are asked whether any of their children have a long-standing condition that limits their children's ability to walk, run, or use stairs.

The third and sixth waves of the 1990 panel also contain a topical module on utilization of health care services. Because topical modules asked in the same wave are released together, it is possible to analyze the data from the two modules jointly. In addition to the functional limitations and disability module, the third wave of the 1990 panel contains topical modules on the utilization of health care services, work schedules, child care, child support agreements, and support for nonhousehold members. The sixth wave of the 1990 panel contains the functional limitations and disability module as well as modules on utilization of health care services, time spent outside the work force, child support agreements, and support for nonhousehold members.

LIMITATIONS Even when the overlapping panels are analyzed together, the sample size is still relatively small compared, for example, to the Current Population Survey. Thus, estimates may have large standard errors. Moreover, SIPP does not oversample African Americans or Hispanics, so sample sizes for these groups can also be small for some purposes. The complexity of the survey, an advantage from the viewpoint of providing detailed and accurate information, may impair user access to microdata tapes which may be complicated and expensive to process. For example, to estimate the number of persons living in a family in which at least one member is functionally limited, it would be necessary to identify all family members, scan their records to determine whether they were functionally limited, and create a variable that indicates whether anyone in the family is limited. This variable could then be appended to each family member's record. Unless an analyst has access to a computer package that can retain information from previous cases, such a procedure would involve the creation of a family level file containing pertinent information from each person and then appending family level variables back onto the original person records of family members.

Another limitation, although one common to all surveys asking these types of questions, is that there is substantial inconsistency of reporting when household members are asked to describe disability status.

AVAILABILITY Questions about publications, data products, and their availability should be directed to:

> Customer Services Branch
> Data User Services Division
> U.S. Bureau of the Census
> Washington, DC 20233
> 301/763-4100

For substantive questions on the functional limitations and disability module, contact:

> Jack McNeil
> Population Division
> U.S. Bureau of the Census
> Washington, DC 20233
> 301/763-8300

For substantive questions about other aspects of SIPP contact:

> Enrique Lamas
> Special Assistant to SIPP
> HHES Division, I-MAIL 307-1
> U.S. Bureau of the Census
> Washington, DC 20233
> 301/763-8018

PUBLICATIONS

McNeil, J.M., Lamas, E.J., & Harpine, C.J. (1986). Disability, functional limitations, and health insurance coverage: 1984-85. *Current Population Reports* (Series P-70, No. 8). Washington, DC: U.S. Bureau of the Census, GPO.

Harpine, C.J., McNeil, J.M., & Lamas, E.J. (1990). The need for personal assistance with everyday activities: Recipients and caregivers. *Current Population Reports* (Series P-70, No. 19). Washington, DC: U.S. Bureau of the Census, GPO.

Data from the 1990 third wave module will appear in a forthcoming Census Bureau "Statistical Brief", and data from the 1990 sixth wave/1991 third wave modules will appear in a forthcoming P-70 report.

SIPP—Functional Limitations and Disability
Year of Questionnaire: 1990 Panel
Sample size: 21,500 households
FAMILY LEVEL CHARACTERISTICS
Sample size: 55,000 persons

Family Composition
○ Full roster of household members (first name, age, sex, and relationship to reference person of each member)
○ Partial roster of household members
○ Number of adults in household
○ Number of children in household
○ Approximate relationship of family members to householder, child, or one another
○ Exact relationship of family members to householder, child, or one another
○ Information about part-time household member
○ Information about family members no longer living in household
○ Information about relatives who live nearby but not in household

Socioeconomic
○ Total family income
○ Number of persons who depend on family income
○ Sources of income
○ Income amounts identified separately by source
○ Poverty status
○ Welfare status
○ Food Stamps receipt
● Child support receipt
○ Medicaid coverage
○ Private health insurance
○ Home ownership/renters
○ Assets (other than home ownership)
○ Public housing status
○ Telephone in household
○ Language other than English spoken in home

Geographic/Community Variables
○ Region of country
○ State of residence
○ County/city/MSA of residence
○ Size/type of community
○ Zip code
○ Telephone area code
○ Metropolitan residence
○ Neighborhood quality
○ Local labor market

Stage in Family Life Cycle
● Age of adult respondent or spouse/partner
● Marital status of adult respondent or spouse/partner
○ Employment status of adult respondent or spouse/partner
● Presence of own children in household
○ Age of youngest own child in household
○ Age of oldest own child in household
○ Existence of own children who have left home
○ Intention to have (more) children in future

Family Functioning
- Family activities or time use
- Community involvement (civic, religious, recreational)
- Family communication patterns
- Family decision-making
- Marital conflict
- Marital happiness / satisfaction
- Parent-child conflict
- History of marital separations
- History of family violence
- History of marital counselling

CHARACTERISTICS OF ADULT FAMILY MEMBERS
Sample size: 40,000 persons 18 and older

Adult Respondent or Reference Person	Current Spouse in HH	Current or Former Spouse Not in HH	
●	●	○	Age
●	●	○	Gender
●	●	○	Race
●	●	○	Hispanic origin
●	●	○	Other origin/ethnicity
○	○	○	Religious affiliation
○	○	○	Religious participation
○	○	○	Country of birth
○	○	○	Immigrant status
○	○	○	English fluency
●	●	○	Current marital status
○	○	○	Marital history
○	○	○	Cohabitation status
○	○	○	Cohabitation history
○	○	○	Parental status
○	○	○	Number children ever born/sired
○	○	○	Age at first birth
○	○	○	Age of youngest child
○	○	○	Children living elsewhere
○	○	○	Duration at current address
○	○	○	Residential mobility
●	●	○	Educational attainment
○	○	○	Degrees attained
○	○	○	GED or regular HS diploma
○	○	○	Current enrollment
○	○	○	Current employment status
○	○	○	Hours usually worked (ft/pt)
○	○	○	Weeks worked
○	○	○	Annual employment pattern
○	○	○	Main occupation
○	○	○	Earnings
○	○	○	Wage rate
●	●	○	Payment of child support
○	○	○	Aptitude or achievement score
●	●	○	Health/disability status
○	○	○	Self-esteem
○	○	○	Locus of control or efficacy
○	○	○	Depression or subjective well-being
○	○	○	Work-related attitudes

CHARACTERISTICS OF CHILD FAMILY MEMBERS
Sample size: 15,000 children under 18

Reference Child or Youth Respondent	Children (in HH)	
O	●	Age
O	O	Month and year of birth
O	●	Gender
O	●	Race
O	●	Hispanic origin
O	●	Other origin/ethnicity
O	O	Religious affiliation
O	O	Religious participation
O	O	Country of birth
O	O	Immigrant status
O	O	English fluency
O	O	Exact relationship to adult family members
O	O	Exact relationship to other children in HH
O	●	Marital status/history[1]
O	O	Parental status/history
O	O	Current enrollment in regular school
O	O	Current enrollment in preschool/daycare
O	●	Highest grade completed[1]
O	O	Grade now enrolled
O	O	Employment status/history
O	●	Health status
O	●	Handicapping conditions
O	O	Grade repetition
O	O	Aptitude or achievement score
O	O	Pregnancy/birth history
O	O	Psychological well-being
O	O	Delinquency

NOTES

Topical module data are released separately from core. Variables needed for matching core data with topical module data are contained in both files. See the core description for a listing of types of variables that are available in the core.

1. Asked of persons 15 and older.

397

SIPP—Personal History Topical Module

PURPOSE The Personal History Topical Module to SIPP, as of the second wave of the 1990 panel, consists of eight submodules. The topics are (1) welfare recipiency history and insurance coverage, (2) employment history, (3) work disability history, (4) education and training history, (5) marital history, (6) migration history, (7) fertility history, and (8) household relationships. These submodules are described in detail in the "Content" section below. In previous panels, the content of the submodules has varied.

The goal of this topical module is to gather a broad range of information on individuals that will help in understanding the dynamics of social change and the effectiveness of public programs.

SPONSORSHIP The topical module is funded and conducted by the U.S. Bureau of the Census. An advisory panel with representatives from selected federal agencies oversees the questionnaire design and frequency of interviewing.

DESIGN The description of the SIPP Core Survey provides an overview of the basic design. The Personal History Topical Module is asked of all persons 15 years of age and older in the household.

PERIODICITY The Personal History Topical Module is asked once in every panel. Because it is always asked in the second wave (since the 1986 panel), there is no possibility of combining panels to obtain a larger sample size. However, for the same reason, problems with sample attrition have been minimized compared to the 1984 and 1985 SIPP panels, where such questions were asked in later modules.

CONTENT *Welfare Recipiency Submodule*: The Welfare Recipiency submodule obtains information on the receipt of food stamps, Aid to Families with Dependent Children (AFDC), Supplemental Security Income (SSI) benefits, and Medicaid among persons 18 years and older in the household. It also obtains information about health insurance coverage for everyone living in the household, and about subsidized housing.

Employment History Submodule: The Employment History submodule obtains information on the work history of household members 18 to 64 years old. Information is also collected about spells of not working among individuals who are currently working or who have ever worked six months or longer. The module has been expanded since it became part of the Personal History module in the second wave of the 1986 panel.

Individuals 18 to 64 years old who were employed at least part of the time during the four months prior to the first or second wave are asked the name of their main employer and when they began to work for their main employer. In the 1990 panel, individuals who have a main employer are also asked about characteristics of their employer, such as how many persons are employed by that employer, if the employer operates in more than one location, and the number of persons that are employed at all the locations. Individuals are also asked if they were a member of a labor union, if they were covered by a union contract at their job, and for how many years they have done the kind of work that they do on their job. Persons 18 to 64 who have ever worked two consecutive weeks or longer are asked several questions about their most recent job or business other than their current one, including the name of the employer or business, the type of company, business or industry it was (e.g., manufacturing, wholesale, trade, retail trade, or some other kind of business), the type of work the individual did on the job, and what their main activities or duties were. They are also asked the main reason why they stopped working in that job or business.

Work Disability History Submodule: The Work Disability History submodule gathers information about any health or physical conditions that may affect an individual's ability to work. It is asked of individuals 16 to 67 years old. Individuals are asked if they have a physical, mental, or other health condition which limits the kind or amount of work they can do. If they respond yes, they are asked a series of questions, including when they first became limited in the kind or amount of work they could do, if they were employed at the time their limitation began, and when they last worked before their limiting condition began. To learn more about the types of conditions that interfere with work, individuals with limiting conditions are also asked what health condition is the main reason for their inability to work and if this condition was caused by an accident or injury. If their condition was caused by an accident or injury, they are asked where it took place — on their job, during service in the Armed Forces, in their home, or somewhere else.

Education and Training History Submodule: This submodule gathers basic information on the educational background and work training received by persons 15 years of age and older in the household. The education questions in the submodule are asked of everyone in the household 15 years of age and older. The training questions are only asked of individuals 15 to 64 years of age. Individuals who have ever received training designed to help them find a job, improve their job skills, or learn a new job are asked whether their training was sponsored by such programs as the Job Training Partnership Act (JTPA) or the Comprehensive Employment Training Act (CETA), and the type of training program they attended (e.g., classroom training - job skills; classroom training - basic education; on the job training; job search assistance; work experience; or other training program).

Marital History Submodule: The Marital History submodule is asked of all ever-married persons 15 years old and older. Such persons are asked how many times they have been married. They are then asked when their first, second, and most recent marriages began and ended (if applicable) and how they ended (widowhood or divorce). Individuals whose marriages ended in divorce are also asked when they actually stopped living with their spouses from these marriages.

Migration History Submodule: The Migration History submodule that appeared in the eighth wave of the 1984 panel and the fourth wave of the 1985 panel is substantially different from the submodule that appears in subsequent panels after the second wave. The description of the contents of this submodule applies to its form in the panels since 1985. All individuals 15 and older in a household are asked when they first moved into their current residence. If they have not always lived in their current residence, they are asked where they lived before and for what period of time they lived there. They are also asked if they have ever lived in another state or in a foreign country. If they have, they are asked which one (the most recent one if they have lived in more than one) and for what period of time they lived there. Finally, they are asked where they were born. If they were born in a foreign country, they are asked if they are a naturalized citizen of the United States and when they came to the United States to stay.

Fertility History Submodule: Beginning in the second wave of the 1986 panel, this submodule has been modified. The description of its content is based on its form in the second wave of the panels after 1985.

The submodule is primarily designed to gather information on children of women 15 to 64 years of age. However, women 65 and older are asked how many children they have ever had, and men 18 years of age and older are asked how many children, if any, they have fathered.

Women 15 to 64 years of age are not only asked how many children they have ever had (not counting stillbirths, adopted, foster, or stepchildren), but they are also asked whether all their children are currently living in their household. If some of their children live elsewhere, the women are asked the birth dates of their first and last child and with whom these particular children are now living.

Household Relationships Submodule: This submodule is actually a large matrix. It is only filled out on the reference person's questionnaire, however. It establishes the exact relationship of each person in the household to every other person living in the household. Thus, a variety of complex living arrangements can be identified with the aid of this submodule.

LIMITATIONS SIPP has a relatively small sample size compared, for example, to the Current Population Survey. Furthermore, because the Personal History module is only asked in one wave of each panel, there is no possibility of combining panels to increase sample size. However, the wealth of information that is gathered offsets this limitation to a large extent. Another limitation is that SIPP does not oversample African Americans, Hispanics, or low-income persons. Thus, sample sizes for these groups may be small for some analyses. Finally, the complexity of the survey, an advantage from the viewpoint of providing detailed and accurate information, may impair user access to micro data tapes which may be complicated and expensive to process. For some analyses, using more than one file and merging data may be necessary. The SIPP Core description has more details.

AVAILABILITY Questions about SIPP reports and data products and their availability should be directed to:

>Customer Services Branch
>Data User Services Division
>U.S. Bureau of the Census
>Washington, DC   20233
>301/763-4100

For substantive questions on the Personal History Module contact:

>Martin O'Connell
>Fertility Statistics Branch
>Population Division
>U.S. Bureau of the Census
>Washington, DC   20233
>301/763-5303

For substantive questions about other aspects of SIPP contact:

>Enrique Lamas
>Special Assistant to SIPP
>HHES Division, I-MALL 307-1
>U.S. Bureau of the Census
>Washington, DC   20233
>301/763-8018

PUBLICATIONS

O'Connell, M. (1990). Maternity leave arrangements: 1965-1985. *Current Population Reports* (Series P-23 No. 165). Washington, DC: U.S. Bureau of the Census, GPO.

SIPP—Personal History
Years of Questionnaire: Asked since inception of SIPP in 1984
Sample size: 21,500 households
FAMILY LEVEL CHARACTERISTICS
Sample size: 55,000 persons

Family Composition
- ○ Full roster of household members (first name, age, sex, and relationship to reference person of each member)
- ○ Partial roster of household members
- ○ Number of adults in household
- ○ Number of children in household
- ○ Approximate relationship of family members to householder, child, or one another
- ● Exact relationship of family members to householder, child, or one another
- ○ Information about part-time household member
- ○ Information about family members no longer living in household
- ○ Information about relatives who live nearby but not in household

Socioeconomic
- ○ Total family income
- ○ Number of persons who depend on family income
- ○ Sources of income
- ○ Income amounts identified separately by source
- ○ Poverty status
- ● Welfare status
- ● Food Stamps receipt
- ○ Child support receipt
- ● Medicaid coverage
- ● Private health insurance
- ○ Home ownership/renters
- ○ Assets (other than home ownership)
- ● Public housing status
- ○ Telephone in household
- ○ Language other than English spoken in home

Geographic/Community Variables
- ○ Region of country
- ○ State of residence
- ○ County/city/MSA of residence
- ○ Size/type of community
- ○ Zip code
- ○ Telephone area code
- ○ Metropolitan residence
- ○ Neighborhood quality
- ○ Local labor market

Stage in Family Life Cycle
- ● Age of adult respondent or spouse/partner
- ● Marital status of adult respondent or spouse/partner
- ○ Employment status of adult respondent or spouse/partner
- ○ Presence of own children in household
- ● Age of youngest own child in household[1]
- ● Age of oldest own child in household[1]
- ● Existence of own children who have left home[2]
- ○ Intention to have (more) children in future

403

Family Functioning
○ Family activities or time use
○ Community involvement (civic, religious, recreational)
○ Family communication patterns
○ Family decision-making
○ Marital conflict
○ Marital happiness/satisfaction
○ Parent-child conflict
○ History of marital separations
○ History of family violence
○ History of marital counselling

CHARACTERISTICS OF ADULT FAMILY MEMBERS
Sample size: 40,000 persons 18 and older

Adult Respondent or Reference Person	Current Spouse in HH	Current or Former Spouse Not in HH	
●	●	○	Age
●	●	○	Gender
●	●	○	Race
●	●	○	Hispanic origin
●	●	○	Other origin/ethnicity
○	○	○	Religious affiliation
○	○	○	Religious participation
○	○	○	Country of birth
○	○	○	Immigrant status
○	○	○	English fluency
●	●	○	Current marital status
●	●	○	Marital history
○	○	○	Cohabitation status
○	○	○	Cohabitation history
●	●	○	Parental status
●	●	○	Number children ever born/sired[1]
●	●	○	Age at first birth[2]
●	●	○	Age of youngest child[2]
●	●	○	Children living elsewhere[3]
○	○	○	Duration at current address
○	○	○	Residential mobility
●	●	○	Educational attainment
●	●	○	Degrees attained
○	○	○	GED or regular HS diploma
○	○	○	Current enrollment
○	○	○	Current employment status
○	○	○	Hours usually worked (ft/pt)
○	○	○	Weeks worked
○	○	○	Annual employment pattern
○	○	○	Main occupation
○	○	○	Earnings
○	○	○	Wage rate
○	○	○	Payment of child support
○	○	○	Aptitude or achievement score
○	○	○	Health/disability status
○	○	○	Self-esteem
○	○	○	Locus of control or efficacy
○	○	○	Depression or subjective well-being
○	○	○	Work-related attitudes

CHARACTERISTICS OF CHILD FAMILY MEMBERS
Sample size: 15,000 children under 18

Reference Child or Youth Respondent	Children (in HH)	
O	●	Age
O	O	Month and year of birth
O	●	Gender
O	●	Race
O	●	Hispanic origin
O	●	Other origin/ethnicity
O	O	Religious affiliation
O	O	Religious participation
O	O	Country of birth
O	O	Immigrant status
O	O	English fluency
O	O	Exact relationship to adult family members
O	O	Exact relationship to other children in HH
O	●	Marital status/history[4]
O	●	Parental status/history[1]
O	O	Current enrollment in regular school
O	O	Current enrollment in preschool/daycare
O	●	Highest grade completed[4]
O	O	Grade now enrolled
O	O	Employment status/history
O	O	Health status
O	O	Handicapping conditions
O	O	Grade repetition
O	O	Aptitude or achievement score
O	O	Pregnancy/birth history
O	O	Psychological well-being
O	O	Delinquency

NOTES
Topical module data are released separately from the core. Variable needed for matching core data with topical module data are contained on both files. See the core description for a listing of the types of variables that are available in the core.
1. Fertility questions asked of females 15 and older and of males 18 and older.
2. Asked of females 15 and older.
3. If the first or last born children of females 15 and older are not living in the households, the women are asked where those children now live.
4. Asked of persons 15 and older.

SIPP—School Enrollment and Financing Topical Module

PURPOSE The purpose of the School Enrollment and Financing Topical Module is to gather detailed information on the way individuals finance their education. This information is gathered not only for financing attendance at regular schools such as high school or college, but also for financing attendance at vocational, technical, and business schools.

SPONSORSHIP The topical module is funded and conducted by the U.S. Bureau of the Census. An advisory panel with representatives from selected federal agencies oversees the questionnaire design and frequency of interviewing.

DESIGN The description of the main SIPP survey gives an overview of the basic design. The topical module on school enrollment and financing is asked of all individuals 15 years of age and older who were enrolled in school anytime during the 12 months prior to the survey. As noted above, the definition of school in the topical module includes regular schools such as elementary, high school, or college as well as vocational, technical, or business schools.

PERIODICITY The school enrollment and financing topical module was first asked in the ninth wave of the 1984 panel. Beginning in the 1985 panel, the module was scheduled to be asked twice in each panel—in the fifth and eighth waves. This design would allow two panels to overlap, thereby nearly doubling the sample size and increasing the reliability of the estimates produced. However, budgetary constraints forced the eighth wave to be dropped entirely from the 1986 and 1987 panels. The module was only administered once in the fifth wave of the 1988 panel and was not asked at all in the 1989 panel. The module was administered twice - in the fifth and eighth waves — in the 1990 and the 1991 panels.

CONTENT Individuals 15 years of age and older who were enrolled in school at any time in the 12 months prior to the survey are asked at what level or grade they were enrolled. If they were enrolled in elementary or high school, they are asked if the school they attended was a public school. Except for individuals who attended a public elementary or high school, all other eligible respondents are asked what the total cost of tuition and fees for their school was during the past 12 months and also what the total cost of books and supplies was during the same time period. They are also asked if they lived away from home while attending school and, if so, what the total cost for room and board was while they were at school. Finally they are asked if they received financial assistance from the GI Bill, some other veteran's educational assistance program, a college work-study program, a Pell Grant, a Supplemental Educational Opportunity Grant (SEOG), a National Direct Student Loan (NDSL), a guaranteed student loan (or Stafford Loan), a JTPA Training Program, their employer, a fellowship or scholarship, a tuition reduction, or anything else such as assistance from relatives or friends. If they did receive assistance from any of these sources or from any other source, they are asked how much they received.

Topical modules asked in the same wave are released together. In addition to the School Enrollment and Financing Topical Modules, the fifth and eighth waves of the 1990 panel contain topical modules on annual income and retirement accounts and taxes.

LIMITATIONS The sample size is relatively small compared, for example, to the Current Population Survey. Thus even when two panels can be combined, estimates may have large standard errors. Moreover, SIPP does not oversample African Americans, Hispanics, or low-income populations, so sample sizes for these groups may be small for some analyses. The complexity of the survey, an advantage from the viewpoint of providing detailed and accurate information, may impair user access to microdata tapes which may be complicated and expensive to process. For some analyses, using more than one file and merging data may be necessary. The SIPP Core description has more details.

In addition, the quality of the estimates obtained from the 1984 panel were poor. An edit procedure for the financing data was introduced with the 1985 panel. This edit has substantially improved the quality of the data.

From the perspective of studying the family, it is not possible to determine how families allocate their resources among their children's education because data on children under 15 are not collected.

AVAILABILITY Questions about publications, data products, and their availability should be directed to:

> Customer Services Branch
> Data User Services Division
> U.S. Bureau of the Census
> Washington, DC 20233
> 301/763-4100

For substantive questions on the school enrollment and financing topical module, contact:

> Robert Kominski
> Education and Social Stratification Branch
> U.S. Bureau of the Census
> Washington, DC 20233
> 301/763-1154

For substantive questions about other aspects of SIPP contact:

> Enrique Lamas
> Special Assistant to SIPP
> HHES Division, I-MALL 307-1
> U.S. Bureau of the Census
> Washington, DC 20233
> 301/763-8018

PUBLICATIONS No official Census publications have been produced with these data.

SIPP-School Enrollment and Financing
Year of Questionnaire: 1990   Sample size: 21,500 households
FAMILY LEVEL CHARACTERISTICS
Sample size: 55,000 persons

Family Composition
○ Full roster of household members (first name, age, sex, and relationship to reference person of each member)
○ Partial roster of household members
○ Number of adults in household
○ Number of children in household
○ Approximate relationship of family members to householder, child, or one another
○ Exact relationship of family members to householder, child, or one another
○ Information about part-time household member
○ Information about family members no longer living in household
○ Information about relatives who live nearby but not in household

Socioeconomic
○ Total family income
○ Number of persons who depend on family income
○ Sources of income
○ Income amounts identified separately by source
○ Poverty status
○ Welfare status
○ Food Stamps receipt
○ Child support receipt
○ Medicaid coverage
○ Private health insurance
○ Home ownership/renters
○ Assets (other than home ownership)
○ Public housing status
○ Telephone in household
○ Language other than English spoken in home

Geographic/Community Variables
○ Region of country
○ State of residence
○ County/city/MSA of residence
○ Size/type of community
○ Zip code
○ Telephone area code
○ Metropolitan residence
○ Neighborhood quality
○ Local labor market

Stage in Family Life Cycle
● Age of adult respondent or spouse/partner
● Marital status of adult respondent or spouse/partner
○ Employment status of adult respondent or spouse/partner
○ Presence of own children in household
○ Age of youngest own child in household
○ Age of oldest own child in household
○ Existence of own children who have left home
○ Intention to have (more) children in future

Family Functioning

○ Family activities or time use
○ Community involvement (civic, religious, recreational)
○ Family communication patterns
○ Family decision-making
○ Marital conflict
○ Marital happiness/satisfaction
○ Parent-child conflict
○ History of marital separations
○ History of family violence
○ History of marital counselling

CHARACTERISTICS OF ADULT FAMILY MEMBERS
Sample size: 40,000 persons 18 and older

Adult Respondent or Reference Person	Current Spouse in HH	Current or Former Spouse Not in HH	
●	●	○	Age
●	●	○	Gender
●	●	○	Race
●	●	○	Hispanic origin
●	●	○	Other origin/ethnicity
○	○	○	Religious affiliation
○	○	○	Religious participation
○	○	○	Country of birth
○	○	○	Immigrant status
○	○	○	English fluency
●	●	○	Current marital status
○	○	○	Marital history
○	○	○	Cohabitation status
○	○	○	Cohabitation history
○	○	○	Parental status
○	○	○	Number children ever born/sired
○	○	○	Age at first birth
○	○	○	Age of youngest child
○	○	○	Children living elsewhere
○	○	○	Duration at current address
○	○	○	Residential mobility
●	●	○	Educational attainment
○	○	○	Degrees attained
○	○	○	GED or regular HS diploma
○	○	○	Current enrollment
○	○	○	Current employment status
○	○	○	Hours usually worked (ft/pt)
○	○	○	Weeks worked
○	○	○	Annual employment pattern
○	○	○	Main occupation
○	○	○	Earnings
○	○	○	Wage rate
○	○	○	Payment of child support
○	○	○	Aptitude or achievement score
○	○	○	Health/disability status
○	○	○	Self-esteem
○	○	○	Locus of control or efficacy
○	○	○	Depression or subjective well-being
○	○	○	Work-related attitudes

CHARACTERISTICS OF CHILD FAMILY MEMBERS
Sample size: 15,000 children under 18

Reference Child or Youth Respondent	Children (in HH)	
O	●	Age
O	O	Month and year of birth
O	●	Gender
O	●	Race
O	●	Hispanic origin
O	●	Other origin/ethnicity
O	O	Religious affiliation
O	O	Religious participation
O	O	Country of birth
O	O	Immigrant status
O	O	English fluency
O	O	Exact relationship to adult family members
O	O	Exact relationship to other children in HH
O	●	Marital status/history[1]
O	O	Parental status/history
O	O	Current enrollment in regular school
O	O	Current enrollment in preschool/daycare
O	●	Highest grade completed[1]
O	O	Grade now enrolled
O	O	Employment status/history
O	O	Health status
O	O	Handicapping conditions
O	O	Grade repetition
O	O	Aptitude or achievement score
O	O	Pregnancy/birth history
O	O	Psychological well-being
O	O	Delinquency

NOTES
Topical module data are released separately from the core. Variables needed for matching core data with topical module data are contained on both files. See core description for a listing of types of variables that are available in the core.
1. Asked of persons 15 and older.

411

SIPP—Support for Nonhousehold Members Topical Module

PURPOSE The support for Nonhousehold Members Topical Module is designed to provide information about cash assistance by adult household members to persons residing elsewhere. Much of the information gathered has not previously been available. Furthermore, because respondents are asked about payments they make to support children living elsewhere, it is possible for the first time to obtain detailed characteristics about persons who pay child support.

SPONSORSHIP The topical module is funded and conducted by the U.S. Bureau of the Census. An advisory panel with representatives from selected federal agencies oversees the questionnaire design and frequency of interviewing.

DESIGN The description of the SIPP Core Survey gives an overview of the basic design. The topical module on support for nonhousehold members is asked of all persons 15 years of age and older in the household.

PERIODICITY The support for nonhousehold members topical module is asked twice in every panel. With the exception of the first time the module was asked (1984 panel, fifth wave), the pattern of the interview schedule means that two panels will always overlap, thereby nearly doubling the sample size and increasing the reliability of the estimates produced. The modules have been asked twice since the 1986 panel.

CONTENT The module has undergone several modifications since its inception. Common to all of the modules to date have been two basic sets of questions — one regarding the support of children, the other regarding the support of other persons not residing in the household. Except for the eighth wave of the 1984 panel and the fourth wave of the 1985 panel, children are persons

412

under 21 years of age. In those two panels, the question is only asked of support for children under 18.

The set of questions on child support asks not only how much child support was paid during the past 12 months, but also the number of children being supported. Also asked are conditions of payment (e.g., court-ordered payments, health care provisions, and method of payment).

The set of questions about payments to other persons asks for the number of such persons, their relationship to the respondent, where they live (private home or apartment, nursing home, someplace else), and the amount paid to them during the past 12 months for the first two persons mentioned. If more than two people are mentioned, a question is asked about how much total support is paid for the other persons not already mentioned.

Beginning in the sixth wave of the 1986 panel and for all subsequent panels, the respondents are asked if they make regular payments, lump-sum payments, or both. Also, if the respondent has a family plan health insurance policy, they are asked if it covers anyone not living in the household. If so, they are asked how many nonhousehold members the plan covers and their relationship to the respondent (child, spouse, other).

Topical modules asked in the same wave are released together. In addition to the Support for Nonhousehold Members topical module, the third wave of the 1990 panel contains topical modules on child support, functional limitations and disability utilization of health care services, work schedules, and child care. The sixth wave of the 1990 panel contains the support for nonhousehold members topical module as well as modules on utilization of health care services, time spent outside the workforce, child support agreements, and functional limitations and disability.

LIMITATIONS Even when the overlapping panels are analyzed together, the sample size is still relatively small compared, for example, to the Current Population Survey. Thus, estimates may have large standard errors. Moreover, SIPP does not oversample African Americans, Hispanics, or low-income populations. Thus, sample sizes for these groups may be small for some analyses. The complexity of the survey, an advantage from the viewpoint of providing detailed and accurate information, may impair user access to microdata tapes which may be complicated and expensive to process. For some analyses, using more than one file and merging data may be necessary. See the SIPP Core Survey description for more details.

AVAILABILITY Public use files are available for the modules that appeared in the fifth and eighth waves of the 1984 panel and for all modules from the third wave of the 1986 panel through the third wave of the 1988 panel.

Questions about publications, data products, and their availability should be directed to:

> Customer Services Branch
> Data User Services Division
> U.S. Bureau of the Census
> Washington, DC 20233
> 301/763-4100

For substantive questions on the Support for Nonhousehold Members topical module contact:

> Martin O'Connell
> Fertility Statistics Branch
> Population Division 301/763-5303 or

> Jack McNeil
> Population Division
> U.S. Bureau of the Census
> Washington, DC 20233
> 301/763-8300

For substantive questions about other aspects of SIPP, contact:

> Enrique Lamas
> Special Assistant to SIPP
> HHES Division, I-MAIL 307-1
> U.S. Bureau of the Census
> Washington, DC 20233
> 301/763-8018

PUBLICATIONS

Jennings, J.T., & Bennefield, R.L. (1992). Who's helping out? Support networks among American families: 1988. *Current Population Reports* (Series P-70, No. 28). Washington, DC: U.S. Bureau of the Census, GPO.

O'Connell, M.O., Jennings, J.T., Lamas, E.J., & McNeil, J.M. (1988). Who's helping out? Support networks among American families? *Current Population Reports* (Series P-70, No. 13). Washington, DC: U.S. Bureau of the Census, GPO.

SIPP: Support for Nonhousehold Members
Year of Questionnaire: 1990 Panel   Sample size: 21,500 households
FAMILY LEVEL CHARACTERISTICS
Sample size: 55,000 persons

Family Composition
O Full roster of household members (first name, age, sex, and relationship to reference person of each member)
O Partial roster of household members
O Number of adults in household
O Number of children in household
O Approximate relationship of family members to householder, child, or one another
O Exact relationship of family members to householder, child, or one another
O Information about part-time household member
O Information about family members no longer living in household
O Information about relatives who live nearby but not in household

Socioeconomic
O Total family income
O Number of persons who depend on family income
O Sources of income
O Income amounts identified separately by source
O Poverty status
O Welfare status
O Food Stamps receipt
● Child support receipt
O Medicaid coverage
O Private health insurance
O Home ownership/renters
O Assets (other than home ownership)
O Public housing status
O Telephone in household
O Language other than English spoken in home

Geographic/Community Variables
O Region of country
O State of residence
O County/city/MSA of residence
O Size/type of community
O Zip code
O Telephone area code
O Metropolitan residence
O Neighborhood quality
O Local labor market

Stage in Family Life Cycle
● Age of adult respondent or spouse/partner
● Marital status of adult respondent or spouse/partner
O Employment status of adult respondent or spouse/partner
● Presence of own children in household
O Age of youngest own child in household
O Age of oldest own child in household
O Existence of own children who have left home
O Intention to have (more) children in future

Family Functioning
○ Family activities or time use
○ Community involvement (civic, religious, recreational)
○ Family communication patterns
○ Family decision-making
○ Marital conflict
○ Marital happiness/satisfaction
○ Parent-child conflict
○ History of marital separations
○ History of family violence
○ History of marital counselling

CHARACTERISTICS OF ADULT FAMILY MEMBERS
Sample size: 40,000 persons 18 and older

Adult Respondent or Reference Person	Current Spouse in HH	Current or Former Spouse Not in HH	
●	●	○	Age
●	●	○	Gender
●	●	○	Race
●	●	○	Hispanic origin
●	●	○	Other origin/ethnicity
○	○	○	Religious affiliation
○	○	○	Religious participation
○	○	○	Country of birth
○	○	○	Immigrant status
○	○	○	English fluency
●	●	○	Current marital status
○	○	○	Marital history
○	○	○	Cohabitation status
○	○	○	Cohabitation history
○	○	○	Parental status
○	○	○	Number children ever born/sired
○	○	○	Age at first birth
○	○	○	Age of youngest child
○	○	○	Children living elsewhere
○	○	○	Duration at current address
○	○	○	Residential mobility
●	●	○	Educational attainment
○	○	○	Degrees attained
○	○	○	GED or regular HS diploma
○	○	○	Current enrollment
○	○	○	Current employment status
○	○	○	Hours usually worked (ft/pt)
○	○	○	Weeks worked
○	○	○	Annual employment pattern
○	○	○	Main occupation
○	○	○	Earnings
○	○	○	Wage rate
●	●	○	Payment of child support
○	○	○	Aptitude or achievement score
●	●	○	Health/disability status
○	○	○	Self-esteem
○	○	○	Locus of control or efficacy
○	○	○	Depression or subjective well-being
○	○	○	Work-related attitudes

CHARACTERISTICS OF CHILD FAMILY MEMBERS
Sample size: 15,000 children under 18

Reference Child or Youth Respondent	Children (in HH)	
O	●	Age
O	O	Month and year of birth
O	●	Gender
O	●	Race
O	●	Hispanic origin
O	●	Other origin/ethnicity
O	O	Religious affiliation
O	O	Religious participation
O	O	Country of birth
O	O	Immigrant status
O	O	English fluency
O	O	Exact relationship to adult family members
O	O	Exact relationship to other children in HH
O	●	Marital status/history[1]
O	O	Parental status/history
O	O	Current enrollment in regular school
O	O	Current enrollment in preschool/daycare
O	●	Highest grade completed[1]
O	O	Grade now enrolled
O	O	Employment status/history
O	●	Health status
O	●	Handicapping conditions
O	O	Grade repetition
O	O	Aptitude or achievement score
O	O	Pregnancy/birth history
O	O	Psychological well-being
O	O	Delinquency

NOTES

Topical module data are released separately from the core. Variables needed for matching core data with topical module date are contained on both files. See the core description for a listing of types of variables that are available in the core.
1. Asked of persons 15 and older.

Survey of Inmates
of Local Jails

PURPOSE Two percent of the U.S. adult population is under correctional supervision (jail, probation, prison, or parole). Jails are locally administered confinement facilities which incarcerate a wide variety of sentenced and unsentenced persons. They temporarily detain juveniles pending transfer to juvenile authorities and hold inmates awaiting transfer to other jurisdictions or authorities.

SPONSORSHIP The 1989 Survey of Inmates of Local Jails was conducted for the U.S. Dept. of Justice, Bureau of Justice Statistics by the Field Division of the U.S. Bureau of the Census.

DESIGN The sample is drawn from 424 local jails selected from a universe of 3,312 jails that were enumerated in the 1988 National Jail Census. Facilities were selected via a two stage design, stratified according to populations of male and female inmates. About 1 in 70 of males in each were selected, and either that proportion or about 1 in 15 of the women were chosen, with 5,675 interviews overall, or a 92.3 percent response rate. Weights were developed. Only national level estimates may be derived from this survey.

PERIODICITY Similar surveys were conducted in 1972, 1978, and 1983.

CONTENT Personal interviews during July, August, and September of 1989 yielded data on age, sex, marital status, race and Hispanic origin, education, military service, pre-arrest income, offenses, sentences, criminal histories, probation and employment status at arrest, jail activities, and prior drug and alcohol use and treatment. Family structure is known, such as whether the inmate grew up in a household without either parent (10.5%), in a single-parent household (39.1%), the number of siblings, their mother's age at her first birth, and the presence of a stepparent. Respondents were surveyed on whether they had ever been physically or sexually abused, whether they had ever taken medication for an emotional or mental problem or received court-ordered mental treatment. They were asked whether another family member had served time in jail or prison, and whether a parent or guardian had abused alcohol or drugs.

LIMITATIONS It is not known to what extent the interviewers from the Bureau of the Census were able to gain the trust of the respondents. Criminal history data were provided the interviewer from file data; however, other questions, including drug use and treatment history, were based on self reports. Unconvicted inmates awaiting trial were not asked about drug use during the month prior to incarcerated periods.

Family data are very limited. Number of siblings are included, but not by sex or by exact relationship. While the respondent is asked whether physical of sexual abuse occurred before age 18, the abuser is not identified.

AVAILABILITY The data (the Survey of Inmates in Local Jails, 1989, ICPSR 9419) are available from:

> National Archives of Criminal Justice Data
> University of Michigan
> P.O. Box 1248
> Ann Arbor, MI 48106-1248
> 800/999-0960

For substantive questions, contact:

> Tracy Snell
> Bureau of Justice Statistics
> 633 Indiana Ave., NW
> Room 1007
> Washington, DC 20531
> 202/616-3288

PUBLICATIONS

Information is available from the Bureau of Justice Statistics, including the following Special Reports:

Beck, A.J. (1991). *Profile of jail inmates, 1989* (Report No. NCJ-129097). Washington, DC: U. S. Department of Justice.

Harlow, C.W. (1991). *Drugs and jail inmates, 1989* (Report No. NCJ-130836).

Snell, T.L. (1992). *Women in jail, 1989* (Report No. NCJ-134732)

Publications may be ordered through:

> Justice Statistics Clearinghouse
> National Criminal Justice Reference Service
> Box 6000
> Rockville, MD 20850
> 800/732-3277
> 301/251-5500 in the Washington, DC area

Survey of Inmates of Local Jails
Year of Questionnaire: 1989
Sample size: 5,675 inmates[1]

FAMILY LEVEL CHARACTERISTICS

Family Composition
○ Full roster of household members (first name, age, sex, and relationship to reference person of each member)
○ Partial roster of household members
○ Number of adults in household
○ Number of children in household
● Approximate relationship of family members to householder, child, or one another
○ Exact relationship of family members to householder, child, or one another
○ Information about part-time household member
○ Information about family members no longer living in household
○ Information about relatives who live nearby but not in household

Socioeconomic
○ Total family income
● Number of persons who depend on family income[2]
● Sources of income
○ Income amounts identified separately by source
○ Poverty status
● Welfare status
○ Food Stamps receipt
○ Child support receipt
○ Medicaid coverage
○ Private health insurance
○ Home ownership/renters
○ Assets (other than home ownership)
○ Public housing status
○ Telephone in household
○ Language other than English spoken in home

Geographic/Community Variables
○ Region of country
○ State of residence
○ County/city/MSA of residence
○ Size/type of community
○ Zip code
○ Telephone area code
○ Metropolitan residence
○ Neighborhood quality
○ Local labor market

Stage in Family Life Cycle
● Age of adult respondent or spouse/partner
● Marital status of adult respondent or spouse/partner
● Employment status of adult respondent or spouse/partner[3]
● Presence of own children in household[4]
○ Age of youngest own child in household
○ Age of oldest own child in household
● Existence of own children who have left home
○ Intention to have (more) children in future

422

Family Functioning

- Family activities or time use
- Community involvement (civic, religious, recreational)
- Family communication patterns
- Family decision-making
- Marital conflict
- Marital happiness/satisfaction
- Parent-child conflict
- History of marital separations
- History of family violence
- History of marital counselling

CHARACTERISTICS OF ADULT FAMILY MEMBERS

Adult Respondent or Reference Person	Current Spouse in HH	Current or Former Spouse Not in HH	
●	○	○	Age
●	○	○	Gender
●	○	○	Race
●	○	○	Hispanic origin
○	○	○	Other origin/ethnicity
○	○	○	Religious affiliation
○	○	○	Religious participation
●	○	○	Country of birth
●	○	○	Immigrant status
○	○	○	English fluency
●	○	○	Current marital status
○	○	○	Marital history
○	○	○	Cohabitation status
○	○	○	Cohabitation history
●	○	○	Parental status[4]
●	○	○	Number children ever born/sired[4]
○	○	○	Age at first birth
○	○	○	Age of youngest child[4]
●	○	○	Children living elsewhere[4]
●	○	○	Duration at current address
○	○	○	Residential mobility
●	○	○	Educational attainment
○	○	○	Degrees attained
●	○	○	GED or regular HS diploma
○	○	○	Current enrollment
●	○	○	Current employment status[2]
●	○	○	Hours usually worked (ft/pt)[2]
○	○	○	Weeks worked
○	○	○	Annual employment pattern
●	○	○	Main occupation
●	○	○	Earnings[3]
○	○	○	Wage rate
○	○	○	Payment of child support
○	○	○	Aptitude or achievement score
●	○	○	Health/disability status
○	○	○	Self-esteem
○	○	○	Locus of control or efficacy
○	○	○	Depression or subjective well-being
○	○	○	Work-related attitudes

CHARACTERISTICS OF CHILD FAMILY MEMBERS

Reference Child or Youth Respondent	Other Children (in HH)	
O	O	Age
O	O	Month and year of birth
O	O	Gender
O	O	Race
O	O	Hispanic origin
O	O	Other origin/ethnicity
O	O	Religious affiliation
O	O	Religious participation
O	O	Country of birth
O	O	Immigrant status
O	O	English fluency
O	O	Exact relationship to adult family members
O	O	Exact relationship to other children in HH
O	O	Marital status/history
O	O	Parental status/history
O	O	Current enrollment in regular school
O	O	Current enrollment in preschool/daycare
O	O	Highest grade completed
O	O	Grade now enrolled
O	O	Employment status/history
O	O	Health status
O	O	Handicapping conditions
O	O	Grade repetition
O	O	Aptitude or achievement score
O	O	Pregnancy/birth history
O	O	Psychological well-being
O	O	Delinquency

NOTES
1. 1.5% of inmates were 17 or younger.
2. Some respondents may have interpreted "your total income" to mean family income.
3. Before arrest.
4. Exact relationship to respondent of children cannot be determined. Question asks whether respondent has children but does not prompt respondent to included step- or adopted children.

Survey of Inmates of State Correctional Facilities

PURPOSE This survey is one of a series of data gathering efforts undertaken during the 1970s to help policy makers assess and overcome deficiencies in the nation's correctional institutions. Currently there is an emphasis on understanding the background characteristics of the offenders and associated situational factors which may be associated with their criminal activities and apprehension. There are related surveys of inmates of local jails, inmates of federal prisons (forthcoming with sample size of about 8,500), and a survey of those in juvenile correctional facilities.

SPONSORSHIP The 1991 Survey of Inmates of State Correctional Facilities was conducted for the U.S. Dept. of Justice, Bureau of Justice Statistics by the Field Division of the U.S. Bureau of the Census.

DESIGN The data were collected in August 1991 through about 15,000 personal interviews with a probability sample of inmates. Facilities are selected in the first stage; inmates are selected from rosters of sampled facilities in the second stage. The sample design allowed for separate sampling frames for males and an oversampling of females. The Census of State Adult Correctional Facilities makes the sampling design for the survey of inmates possible.

PERIODICITY Similar surveys were conducted in 1974, 1979, and 1986, when 275 facilities were selected and 13,711 inmates were successfully interviewed.

CONTENT Personal interviews yielded data on personal characteristics, number of siblings (including half and step), current offenses, pretrial release, trial, current sentence, victims, criminal history, gun acquisition and use, prison infractions and work assignments, socieconomic characteristics, frequency of calls, visits and mail from children while in prison, drug use and treatment, peer activities, sexual and physical abuse history, and prison treatment programs and testing.

LIMITATIONS It cannot be determined whether siblings or children of the respondent are biologically related to the respondent, nor can it be determined whether any children are now living with stepparents or biological parents, or some combination. There is no information on community or family functioning.

It is not known to what extent the interviewers from the Bureau of the Census were able to gain the trust of the respondents. Criminal history and incarceration data are taken from files and used during the course of the interview, so are not subject to bias introduced by self reports. However, considerable activity that is self reported is illegal.

AVAILABILITY The data will be available from:

> National Archives of Criminal Justice Data
> University of Michigan
> P.O. Box 1248
> Ann Arbor, MI 48106-1248
> 800/999-0960

For substantive questions, contact:

> Tracy Snell
> Bureau of Justice Statistics
> 633 Indiana Ave, NW
> Room 1007
> Washington, DC 20531
> 202/616-3288

PUBLICATIONS Publications based on the previous (1986) survey include several Bureau of Justice Statistics Special Reports:

Greenfeld, L.A., & Minor-Harper, S. (1991). *Women in prison* (Report No. NCJ-127991).

Innes, C.A., & Greenfeld, L.A. (1991). *Violent state prisoners and their victims* (Report No. NCJ-124133). Washington, DC: U.S. Dept. of Justice.

These and forthcoming publications using the 1991 data may be ordered from:

> Justice Statistics Clearinghouse
> National Criminal Justice Reference Service
> Box 6000
> Rockville, MD 20850
> 800/732-3277
> 301/251-5500 in the Washington, DC area

Survey of Inmates
of State Correctional Facilities
Year of Questionnaire: 1991   Sample size: 13,990 inmates
FAMILY LEVEL CHARACTERISTICS

Family Composition
O Full roster of household members (first name, age, sex, and relationship to reference person of each member)
O Partial roster of household members
O Number of adults in household
O Number of children in household
● Approximate relationship of family members to householder, child, or one another
O Exact relationship of family members to householder, child, or one another
O Information about part-time household member
O Information about family members no longer living in household
O Information about relatives who live nearby but not in household

Socioeconomic[1]
O Total family income
● Number of persons who depend on family income[2]
● Sources of income
O Income amounts identified separately by source
O Poverty status
● Welfare status[3]
O Food Stamps receipt
O Child support receipt
O Medicaid coverage
O Private health insurance
O Home ownership/renters
O Assets (other than home ownership)
O Public housing status
O Telephone in household
O Language other than English spoken in home

Geographic/Community Variables
O Region of country
O State of residence
O County/city/MSA of residence
O Size/type of community
O Zip code
O Telephone area code
O Metropolitan residence
O Neighborhood quality
O Local labor market

Stage in Family Life Cycle
● Age of adult respondent or spouse/partner
● Marital status of adult respondent or spouse/partner
● Employment status of adult respondent or spouse/partner[3]
● Presence of own children in household[4]
O Age of youngest own child in household
O Age of oldest own child in household
O Existence of own children who have left home
O Intention to have (more) children in future

Family Functioning

- O Family activities or time use
- O Community involvement (civic, religious, recreational)
- O Family communication patterns
- O Family decision-making
- O Marital conflict
- O Marital happiness/satisfaction
- ● Parent-child conflict
- O History of marital separations
- ● History of family violence
- O History of marital counselling

CHARACTERISTICS OF ADULT FAMILY MEMBERS

Adult Respondent or Reference Person	Current Spouse in HH	Current or Former Spouse Not in HH	
●	O	O	Age
●	O	O	Gender
●	O	O	Race
●	O	O	Hispanic origin
O	O	O	Other origin/ethnicity
O	O	O	Religious affiliation
O	O	O	Religious participation
O	O	O	Country of birth
●	O	O	Immigrant status[6]
O	O	O	English fluency
●	O	O	Current marital status
O	O	O	Marital history
O	O	O	Cohabitation status
O	O	O	Cohabitation history
●	O	O	Parental status[4]
O	O	O	Number children ever born/sired
O	O	O	Age at first birth
●	O	O	Age of youngest child[4,5]
●	O	O	Children living elsewhere
●	O	O	Duration at current address
●	O	O	Residential mobility
●	O	O	Educational attainment
O	O	O	Degrees attained
●	O	O	GED or regular HS diploma
O	O	O	Current enrollment
●	O	O	Current employment status[1]
●	O	O	Hours usually worked (ft/pt)[1]
O	O	O	Weeks worked
O	O	O	Annual employment pattern
●	O	O	Main occupation[1]
●	O	O	Earnings[1]
O	O	O	Wage rate
O	O	O	Payment of child support
O	O	O	Aptitude or achievement score
●	O	O	Health/disability status
O	O	O	Self-esteem
O	O	O	Locus of control or efficacy
O	O	O	Depression or subjective well-being
O	O	O	Work-related attitudes

CHARACTERISTICS OF CHILD FAMILY MEMBERS

Reference Child or Youth Respondent	Other Children (in HH)	
O	O	Age
O	O	Month and year of birth
O	O	Gender
O	O	Race
O	O	Hispanic origin
O	O	Other origin/ethnicity
O	O	Religious affiliation
O	O	Religious participation
O	O	Country of birth
O	O	Immigrant status
O	O	English fluency
O	O	Exact relationship to adult family members
O	O	Exact relationship to other children in HH
O	O	Marital status/history
O	O	Parental status/history
O	O	Current enrollment in regular school
O	O	Current enrollment in preschool/daycare
O	O	Highest grade completed
O	O	Grade now enrolled
O	O	Employment status/history
O	O	Health status
O	O	Handicapping conditions
O	O	Grade repetition
O	O	Aptitude or achievement score
O	O	Pregnancy/birth history
O	O	Psychological well-being
O	O	Delinquency

NOTES

1. During the period before incarceration.
2. Persons supported by the respondent before incarceration.
3. Welfare status refers to persons depending upon respondent's income, before and after arrest. Their approximate relationship to respondent is provided.
4. Exact relationship to respondent of children cannot be determined. Respondent is asked to include step- or adopted children.
5. Respondent is asked for information only about the six youngest children.
6. U.S. Citizenship is available, not immigration.

Survey of Juveniles in Custody

PURPOSE This study interviewed juveniles and young adults in custody, with the Children in Custody census providing the universe for this study of youth in long-term, state-operated juvenile facilities.

SPONSORSHIP The Survey of Juveniles in Custody was conducted by the Bureau of the Census for the Bureau of Justice Statistics of the U.S. Department of Justice.

DESIGN This pilot survey was based on personal interviews with a nationally representative sample of 2,621 residents from among the more than 25,000 individuals confined in long-term, state-operated juvenile institutions. Interviews were carried out in 50 institutions in 26 states. More than a quarter of the sample was young adults aged 18 or older (primarily as a result of the inclusion of California's Youth Authority facilities). The sample design was a stratified sample based on the size of the correctional facility. Long-term and state-operated facilities with institutional environments were included in the sampling frame. The majority of these institutions described themselves as training schools. The survey excluded institutions that were locally operated state facilities not designed for secure custody, all short-term facilities, and all those being privately operated. Although participation was voluntary, the response rate was 89 percent.

PERIODICITY This youth based survey has only been conducted in 1987. The Children in Custody census of facilities, which obtains aggregate level descriptive information, is conducted every two years.

CONTENT Personal interviews yielded data on how the young person became a facility resident, personal characteristics, the current offense, victim information and acquaintance with or relationship to the offender, criminal history, drug and alcohol

431

use, peer group and gang involvement, family structure, family's criminal involvement, and victimization status.

LIMITATIONS Self reports of criminal activities are subject to underreporting and also to overreporting. Difficulties connected with accurate recall of events in the past are also a problem for most survey data. Family information is very limited. Whether the parent or foster parent sent the respondent to the facility is known, as is whether the most recent offense occurred at home, and whether the victim(s) were family members. Victimization by family members, the type of family structure, and incarceration of family members is known. Otherwise, there is no information available on any socioeconomic indicators, on geographic variables, or even on the presence of siblings, unless they were victims of current offense(s) or had served time in jail.

AVAILABILITY Public use tapes of BJS data sets are available from:

> National Archives of Criminal Justice Data
> University of Michigan
> P.O. Box 1248
> Ann Arbor, MI 48106-1248
> 800/999-0960

For substantive questions, contact:

> Tracy Snell
> Bureau of Justice Statistics
> 202/616-3288

PUBLICATIONS Thirty-two descriptive tables and a copy of the questionnaire are included in the publication:

Bureau of Justice Statistics. (1989). *Correctional Populations in the United States, 1987* (Report No. NCJ-118762).

It may be obtained by calling 800/732-3277 (301/251-5500 in the Washington area).

Survey of Juveniles in Custody
Year of Questionnaire: 1987
Sample size: 2,621 juveniles[1]
FAMILY LEVEL CHARACTERISTICS

Family Composition
- O Full roster of household members (first name, age, sex, and relationship to reference person of each member)
- O Partial roster of household members
- O Number of adults in household
- O Number of children in household
- O Approximate relationship of family members to householder, child, or one another
- O Exact relationship of family members to householder, child, or one another
- O Information about part-time household member
- O Information about family members no longer living in household
- O Information about relatives who live nearby but not in household

Socioeconomic
- O Total family income
- O Number of persons who depend on family income
- O Sources of income
- O Income amounts identified separately by source
- O Poverty status
- O Welfare status
- O Food Stamps receipt
- O Child support receipt
- O Medicaid coverage
- O Private health insurance
- O Home ownership/renters
- O Assets (other than home ownership)
- O Public housing status
- O Telephone in household
- O Language other than English spoken in home

Geographic/Community Variables
- O Region of country
- O State of residence
- O County/city/MSA of residence
- O Size/type of community
- O Zip code
- O Telephone area code
- O Metropolitan residence
- O Neighborhood quality
- O Local labor market

Stage in Family Life Cycle
- O Age of adult respondent or spouse/partner
- O Marital status of adult respondent or spouse/partner
- O Employment status of adult respondent or spouse/partner
- O Presence of own children in household
- O Age of youngest own child in household
- O Age of oldest own child in household
- O Existence of own children who have left home
- O Intention to have (more) children in future

433

Family Functioning
○ Family activities or time use
○ Community involvement (civic, religious, recreational)
○ Family communication patterns
○ Family decision-making
○ Marital conflict
○ Marital happiness/satisfaction
● Parent-child conflict
○ History of marital separations
● History of family violence
○ History of marital counselling

CHARACTERISTICS OF ADULT FAMILY MEMBERS

Adult Respondent or Reference Person	Current Spouse in HH	Current or Former Spouse Not in HH	
○	○	○	Age
○	○	○	Gender
○	○	○	Race
○	○	○	Hispanic origin
○	○	○	Other origin/ethnicity
○	○	○	Religious affiliation
○	○	○	Religious participation
○	○	○	Country of birth
○	○	○	Immigrant status
○	○	○	English fluency
○	○	○	Current marital status
○	○	○	Marital history
○	○	○	Cohabitation status
○	○	○	Cohabitation history
○	○	○	Parental status
○	○	○	Number children ever born/sired
○	○	○	Age at first birth
○	○	○	Age of youngest child
○	○	○	Children living elsewhere
○	○	○	Duration at current address
○	○	○	Residential mobility
○	○	○	Educational attainment
○	○	○	Degrees attained
○	○	○	GED or regular HS diploma
○	○	○	Current enrollment
○	○	○	Current employment status
○	○	○	Hours usually worked (ft/pt)
○	○	○	Weeks worked
○	○	○	Annual employment pattern
○	○	○	Main occupation
○	○	○	Earnings
○	○	○	Wage rate
○	○	○	Payment of child support
○	○	○	Aptitude or achievement score
○	○	○	Health/disability status
○	○	○	Self-esteem
○	○	○	Locus of control or efficacy
○	○	○	Depression or subjective well-being
○	○	○	Work-related attitudes

CHARACTERISTICS OF CHILD FAMILY MEMBERS

Reference Child or Youth Respondent	Other Children (in HH)	
●	○	Age
●	○	Month and year of birth
●	○	Gender
●	○	Race
●	○	Hispanic origin
○	○	Other origin/ethnicity
○	○	Religious affiliation
○	○	Religious participation
○	○	Country of birth
○	○	Immigrant status
○	○	English fluency
○	○	Exact relationship to adult family members
○	○	Exact relationship to other children in HH
○	○	Marital status/history
○	○	Parental status/history
○	○	Current enrollment in regular school
○	○	Current enrollment in preschool/daycare
●	○	Highest grade completed
○	○	Grade now enrolled
○	○	Employment status/history
○	○	Health status
○	○	Handicapping conditions
○	○	Grade repetition
○	○	Aptitude or achievement score
○	○	Pregnancy/birth history
○	○	Psychological well-being
●	●	Delinquency

NOTES

1. About one-fourth of respondents were over the age of 18.

Urban Poverty and Family Life Survey of Chicago

PURPOSE The Urban Poverty and Family Life Study was designed to describe and understand the lives of African American, Mexican, Puerto Rican, and white families living in impoverished Chicago neighborhoods.

SPONSORSHIP The survey was designed by a team of researchers from the University of Chicago, headed by William Julius Wilson. Field work was carried out by the National Opinion Research Center (NORC). Sponsors were: the Carnegie Corporation of New York, the Chicago Community Trust, the Ford Foundation, the Joyce Foundation, the Lloyd A. Fry Foundation, the MacArthur Foundation, the Rockefeller Foundation, the Spencer Foundation, the U.S. Department of Health and Human Services, the William T. Grant Foundation, and the Woods Charitable Trust.

DESIGN The sample was a multi-stage, stratified probability sample of 2,490 adult parents, aged 18 - 44, who were living in high-poverty census tracts in the city of Chicago in 1986. A small sample of black non-parents was also interviewed. A high-poverty census tract was defined as a tract in which at least 20% of the 1980 population had family incomes below the federal poverty line. The final parent sample contained 1,183 black, 489 Mexican, 454 Puerto Rican, and 364 white respondents. One quarter of the interviews were conducted in Spanish. The overall completion rate was 79%.

PERIODICITY This was a one time survey, fielded in 1987.

CONTENT Information was collected on: marriage and childbearing, work experience and welfare use, household composition and social networks, and attitudes and values. Particularly rich data were gathered on friends, kin, social networks, and characteristics of the local community. Information on participation in the "underground" economy was also gathered. The survey was designed specifically to address issues related to family life in poor neighborhoods, to allow for the exploration of various theories of poverty, and to allow for racial and ethnic comparisons.

LIMITATIONS Generalizability of research findings may be limited by the fact that the survey was conducted in only one city, Chicago. In addition, there are few measures of family functioning.

AVAILABILITY For copies of the data and documentation:

> Inter-University Consortium for Political
> and Social Research
> Institute for Social Research
> P.O. Box 1248
> Ann Arbor, Michigan 48106-1248
> 313/763-5010

For technical questions about the survey, contact:

> Joleen Kirschenman
> Irving B. Harris Graduate School
> of Public Policy Studies
> University of Chicago
> 1313 East 60th St., Rm. 145
> Chicago, IL 60637
> 312/702-0894

PUBLICATIONS

Testa, M., & M. Krogh. (1990). *Nonmarital parenthood, male joblessness and AFDC participation in inner-city Chicago.* Final report prepared for the Assistant Secretary of Planning and Evaluation, DHHS, under Grant No. 88ASPE204A.

Testa, M., Astone N., Krogh, M., & Neckerman, K. (1989). Employment and marriage among inner-city fathers. *The Annals of the American Academy of Political and Social Science*, 79-91.

There is a working paper series associated with this data set. To receive a current list of available papers which use this data, contact:

> Center for the Study of Urban Inequality
> Irving B. Harris Graduate School
> of Public Policy Studies
> University of Chicago
> 1313 East 60th St., Rm. 145
> Chicago, IL 60637
> 312/702-0894

The Urban Family Life Survey
Year of Questionnaire: 1987
Sample size: 2,490 respondents
FAMILY LEVEL CHARACTERISTICS

Family Composition
- Full roster of household members (first name, age, sex, and relationship to reference person of each member)
○ Partial roster of household members
- Number of adults in household
- Number of children in household
○ Approximate relationship of family members to householder, child, or one another
- Exact relationship of family members to householder, child, or one another
- Information about part-time household member
- Information about family members no longer living in household
○ Information about relatives who live nearby but not in household

Socioeconomic
- Total family income
○ Number of persons who depend on family income
- Sources of income[1]
- Income amounts identified separately by source[1]
○ Poverty status
- Welfare status
- Food Stamps receipt[1]
- Child support receipt
- Medicaid coverage
- Private health insurance
- Home ownership/renters
- Assets (other than home ownership)
- Public housing status
○ Telephone in household
- Language other than English spoken in home

Geographic/Community Variables
○ Region of country
○ State of residence
○ County/city/MSA of residence
- Size/type of community
- Zip code
○ Telephone area code
○ Metropolitan residence
- Neighborhood quality
○ Local labor market

Stage in Family Life Cycle
- Age of adult respondent or spouse/partner
- Marital status of adult respondent or spouse/partner
- Employment status of adult respondent or spouse/partner
- Presence of own children in household
- Age of youngest own child in household
- Age of oldest own child in household
- Existence of own children who have left home
- Intention to have (more) children in future

439

Family Functioning

○ Family activities or time use
● Community involvement (civic, religious, recreational)
○ Family communication patterns
○ Family decision-making
○ Marital conflict
○ Marital happiness/satisfaction
○ Parent-child conflict
○ History of marital separations
○ History of family violence
○ History of marital counselling

CHARACTERISTICS OF ADULT FAMILY MEMBERS

Adult Respondent or Reference Person	Current Spouse in HH	Current or Former Spouse Not in HH	
●	●	●	Age
●	●	●	Gender
●	●	○	Race
●	○	○	Hispanic origin
○	○	○	Other origin/ethnicity
●	○	○	Religious affiliation
●	○	○	Religious participation
●	○	○	Country of birth
●	○	○	Immigrant status
●	○	○	English fluency
●	●	○	Current marital status
●	○	○	Marital history
●	○	○	Cohabitation status
●	○	○	Cohabitation history
●	○	○	Parental status
●	○	○	Number children ever born/sired
●	○	○	Age at first birth
●	○	○	Age of youngest child
●	○	○	Children living elsewhere
●	○	○	Duration at current address
●	○	○	Residential mobility
●	●	●	Educational attainment
●	○	○	Degrees attained
●	○	○	GED or regular HS diploma
●	○	○	Current enrollment
●	●	○	Current employment status
●	○	○	Hours usually worked (ft/pt)
○	○	○	Weeks worked
○	○	○	Annual employment pattern
●	●	●	Main occupation
●	●	○	Earnings[1]
○	○	○	Wage rate
●	○	●	Payment of child support
○	○	○	Aptitude or achievement score
●	○	○	Health/disability status
○	○	○	Self-esteem
○	○	○	Locus of control or efficacy
○	○	○	Depression or subjective well-being
●	○	○	Work-related attitudes

CHARACTERISTICS OF CHILD FAMILY MEMBERS

Reference Child or Youth Respondent	Children (in HH)	
O	●	Age
O	●	Month and year of birth
O	●	Gender
O	O	Race
O	O	Hispanic origin
O	O	Other origin/ethnicity
O	O	Religious affiliation
O	O	Religious participation
O	O	Country of birth
O	O	Immigrant status
O	O	English fluency
O	●	Exact relationship to adult family members
O	O	Exact relationship to other children in HH
O	O	Marital status/history
O	O	Parental status/history
O	O	Current enrollment in regular school
O	O	Current enrollment in preschool/daycare
O	●	Highest grade completed[2]
O	●	Grade now enrolled[2]
O	●	Employment status/history[2]
O	O	Health status
O	O	Handicapping conditions
O	O	Grade repetition
O	O	Aptitude or achievement score
O	O	Pregnancy/birth history
O	O	Psychological well-being
O	O	Delinquency

NOTES
1. Available only for the month preceeding the interview.
2. Information given for all living children over the age of 12, both in and out of household.

Vital Statistics—Natality

PURPOSE The purpose of the natality reporting system is to collect and tabulate at the federal, state, and sub-state levels data on births from the 50 states and the District of Columbia. Demographic and health information from birth certificates can be analyzed by researchers and policymakers interested in assessing the health of infants and pinpointing health problems, making population projections and estimates, following trends in non-marital and teenage childbearing, and measuring progress made by national health programs. In addition, the birth certificate provides legal proof of the birth.

SPONSORSHIP The National Center for Health Statistics, Division of Vital Statistics, collects and publishes natality data.

DESIGN A certificate of live birth is completed by the attending physician or other health personnel for each birth. Birth certificates are sent by local registrars to the state registrar. States report the data to the Division of Vital Statistics on state coded data tapes. In 1989, one hundred percent of the births were reported to NCHS in the form of state coded data tapes for all states and the District of Columbia.

PERIODICITY Data collection is continuous. Monthly and annual reports of provisional data and annual and special subject reports based on final data are issued. All states have been included in the birth registration area since 1933.

CONTENT The certificate of live birth, which is the source of vital registration data, has been revised effective with the 1989 data and includes more information. A significant change is that birth data for 1989 were tabulated primarily by race of mother, a departure from previous tabulations by race of child (which had assigned the child to the race of the non-white parent, if any; to the race of the father, if both were non-white; or to Hawaiian, if either parent were Hawaiian). In addition to race, Hispanic origin (Hispanics may be of any race) was identified for both parents in

47 states and D.C. In 1989, parent education was reported for 48 states and D.C. (not for Washington or New York states), again including this information from California and Texas. In 1989, the mother's marital status was reported for 44 states and D.C.; it was inferred for 6 states (California, Connecticut, Michigan, Nevada, New York, and Texas) by comparing parent and child surnames. Also included in 1989 was information on congenital defects, health risks of mother, and obstetric procedures and method of delivery.

LIMITATIONS Not all states obtain all information and the range of data is limited (see above). Trend data by race will be reported by both new and previous classifications for 1989 and 1990.

AVAILABILITY Data tapes may be purchased from:

> National Technical Information Service
> 5285 Port Royal Road
> Springfield, VA 22161
> 703/487-4650

For substantive questions, contact:

> Stephanie Ventura, Selma Taffel, or Bob Heuser
> Natality Branch/Division of Vital Statistics
> National Center for Health Statistics
> 6525 Belcrest Road, Room 840
> Hyattsville, MD 20782
> 301/436-8954

PUBLICATIONS

National Center for Health Statistics. (1992). Advance report of new data from the 1989 birth certificate. *Monthly Vital Statistics Report, 40*(12, suppl.). Public Health Service, Washington, DC.

National Center for Health Statistics. (1990). *Vital statistics of the United States, 1988, Vol. 1, Natality.* (DHHS Publication No. (PHS) 90-1100). Public Health Service, Washington, DC: GPO.

Moore, K.A. (1992). *Facts at a glance*. (Annual fact sheet on teenage childbearing). Washington, DC: Child Trends.

Moore, K.A., Snyder, N.O., & Daly, M. (1991). *A state-by-state look at teenage childbearing in the United States*. Flint, MI: Charles Stewart Mott Foundation.

Vital Statistics—Natality
Year of Questionnaire: 1989 Birth Certificates
Sample size: Total U.S. Births (4,040,958 in 1989)

FAMILY LEVEL CHARACTERISTICS

Family Composition

○ Full roster of household members (first name, age, sex, and relationship to reference person of each member)
○ Partial roster of household members
○ Number of adults in household
○ Number of children in household
○ Approximate relationship of family members to householder, child, or one another
○ Exact relationship of family members to householder, child, or one another
○ Information about part-time household member
○ Information about family members no longer living in household
○ Information about relatives who live nearby but not in household

Socioeconomic

○ Total family income
○ Number of persons who depend on family income
○ Sources of income
○ Income amounts identified separately by source
○ Poverty status
○ Welfare status
○ Food Stamps receipt
○ Child support receipt
○ Medicaid coverage
○ Private health insurance
○ Home ownership/renters
○ Assets (other than home ownership)
○ Public housing status
○ Telephone in household
○ Language other than English spoken in home

Geographic/Community Variables

● Region of country
● State of residence
● County/city/MSA of residence
○ Size/type of community
● Zip code
○ Telephone area code
● Metropolitan residence
○ Neighborhood quality
○ Local labor market

Stage in Family Life Cycle

● Age of adult respondent or spouse/partner
● Marital status of adult respondent or spouse/partner[1]
○ Employment status of adult respondent or spouse/partner
○ Presence of own children in household
○ Age of youngest own child in household
○ Age of oldest own child in household
○ Existence of own children who have left home
○ Intention to have (more) children in future

445

Family Functioning
- Family activities or time use
- Community involvement (civic, religious, recreational)
- Family communication patterns
- Family decision-making
- Marital conflict
- Marital happiness/satisfaction
- Parent-child conflict
- History of marital separations
- History of family violence
- History of marital counselling

CHARACTERISTICS OF ADULT FAMILY MEMBERS

Child's Mother	Child's Father	Current or Former Spouse Not in HH	
●	●	○	Age
●	●	○	Gender
●	●	○	Race
●	●	○	Hispanic origin[2]
○	○	○	Other origin/ethnicity
○	○	○	Religious affiliation
○	○	○	Religious participation
●	●	○	Country of birth
○	○	○	Immigrant status
○	○	○	English fluency
●	○	○	Current marital status[3]
○	○	○	Marital history
○	○	○	Cohabitation status
○	○	○	Cohabitation history
○	○	○	Parental status
●	○	○	Number children ever born/sired[3]
○	○	○	Age at first birth
●	○	○	Age of youngest child[4]
○	○	○	Children living elsewhere
○	○	○	Duration at current address
○	○	○	Residential mobility
●	●	○	Educational attainment[5]
○	○	○	Degrees attained
○	○	○	GED or regular HS diploma
○	○	○	Current enrollment
○	○	○	Current employment status
○	○	○	Hours usually worked (ft/pt)
○	○	○	Weeks worked
○	○	○	Annual employment pattern
○	○	○	Main occupation
○	○	○	Earnings
○	○	○	Wage rate
○	○	○	Payment of child support
○	○	○	Aptitude or achievement score
○	○	○	Health/Disability status
○	○	○	Self-esteem
○	○	○	Locus of control or efficacy
○	○	○	Depression or subjective well-being
○	○	○	Work-related attitudes

CHARACTERISTICS OF CHILD FAMILY MEMBERS

Reference Child or Youth Respondent	Other Children (in HH)	
●	○	Age
●	○	Month and year of birth
●	○	Gender
●	○	Race[6]
●	○	Hispanic origin[2]
○	○	Other origin/ethnicity
○	○	Religious affiliation
○	○	Religious participation
●	○	Country of birth
○	○	Immigrant status
○	○	English fluency
○	○	Exact relationship to adult family members
○	○	Exact relationship to other children in HH
○	○	Marital status/history
○	○	Parental status/history
○	○	Current enrollment in regular school
○	○	Current enrollment in preschool/daycare
○	○	Highest grade completed
○	○	Grade now enrolled
○	○	Employment status/history
●	○	Health status
●	○	Handicapping conditions[7]
○	○	Grade repetition
○	○	Aptitude or achievement score
○	○	Pregnancy/birth history
○	○	Psychological well-being
○	○	Delinquency

NOTES
1. Marital status is reported for 44 states and D.C., and inferred for the remaining six states by comparing parent and child surnames.
2. Data for Hispanic origin are for 47 states and D.C.
3. For 44 states and D.C.
4. Date of previous live birth.
5. For 48 states and D.C.
6. As of 1989, race of child is calculated by race of mother.
7. Some conditions, such as Down's Syndrom, are believed to be underreported.

447

Vital Statistics—Marriage and Divorce

PURPOSE These statistics are designed to provide information on marriages and divorces and on the people involved in marriages and divorces (including children involved in divorce) for the largest possible number of states.

SPONSORSHIP The National Center for Health Statistics (NCHS) obtains from state and local officials complete counts of marriages and divorces by county of occurrence and marriages by month of occurrence. NCHS also obtains sample records from microfilm copies of the original certificates received from the registration offices of states and areas comprising the marriage registration area (MRA) and the divorce registration area (DRA).

DESIGN Marriage and divorce statistics for the United States, for the registration areas, and for individual states are limited to events occurring during the year and registered within the specified area. All tabulations are by place of occurrence and include events occurring to nonresidents. Marriages and divorces of members of the Armed Forces or other U.S. nationals that occur outside the United States are excluded.

Registration areas for the collection of marriage and divorce statistics were established in 1957 and 1958, respectively. These areas include states with adequate programs for collecting marriage and divorce statistics. Criteria for participation in the registration areas are:
- A central file of marriage or divorce records;
- A statistical report form conforming closely in content to the Standard License and Certificate of Marriage or Standard Certificate of Divorce, Dissolution of Marriage or Annulment;
- Regular reporting to the state office by all local areas in which marriages or divorces are recorded; and
- Test for completeness and accuracy of marriage or divorce registration carried out in cooperation with NCHS.

448

In 1988 the MRA comprised 42 states, New York City, the District of Columbia, Puerto Rico, and the Virgin Islands. The DRA included 31 states, the District of Columbia, and the Virgin Islands. Marriages in the MRA accounted for 80 percent of all marriages in the United States in 1988, and divorces in the DRA accounted for 49 percent of all divorces.

The marriage sample was designed to yield estimates of state totals as well as frequency distributions by characteristics of the bride and groom. These estimates were made for the total MRA and each state in the MRA. A sampling rate was designated for each of the MRA states so that the selected sample for it would consist of at least 2,500 records. Five different sampling rates were used: All records, 1/2, 1/5, 1/10, and 1/20. Sampling procedures for the divorce sample parallel those for the marriage sample. Overall, in 1988 about 41 percent of all marriages in the MRA were included in the sample, and about 49 percent of all divorces in the DRA were included.

Samples of marriages for 47 states are available for the census years of 1970 and 1980.

PERIODICITY Annual data from the MRA have been compiled since 1957. Annual data from the DRA have been compiled since 1958. Complete counts of events or estimates for the entire United States have been compiled since 1920.

CONTENT The Marriage Data Tape is a microdata computer file consisting of records that include data on the bride and groom, including age or date of birth, race, education, previous marital status, number of this marriage, date last marriage ended, state (or foreign country) of birth, state of marriage, state of residence, type of ceremony, and related characteristics. The Divorce Data Tape is a microdata computer file consisting of records that include data for date of marriage, date of separation, plaintiff, state of marriage, state of divorce, total number of living children, and for each husband and wife: age at decree, age at separation, date of birth, state (or country) of birth, education, race, number of this marriage, and related items.

Data are classified by various demographic characteristics. *Vital Statistics of the United States* contains a section on marriages, divorces and annulments, marriages and divorces in Puerto Rico and the Virgin Islands, and the Technical Appendix.

LIMITATIONS Many states are not included in the MRA and the DRA.

AVAILABILITY Provisional data on marriages and divorces are published in the NCHS *Monthly Vital Statistics Report*. Final data are published in *Vital Statistics of the United States, Volume III: Marriage and Divorce*, and are available in Federal Depository Libraries. The National Center for Health Statistics will respond to requests for unpublished data whenever possible. Requests should be sent to the Scientific and Technical Information Branch at the address below.

Data tapes may be purchased from:

> National Technical Information Service
> Springfield, VA 22161
> 703/487-4780

For information on tape specifications, price, and stock numbers, contact:

> Scientific and Technical Information Branch
> National Center for Health Statistics
> 6525 Belcrest Road, Rm. 1067
> Hyattsville, MD 20782
> 301/436-8500

For substantive questions concerning marriage or divorce registration and analysis, contact:

> Barbara Foley Wilson
> 301/436-8954

PUBLICATIONS

National Center for Health Statistics. (1991). Advance report of final marriage statistics, 1988. *Monthly Vital Statistics Report*, *40*(4, suppl.). Hyattsville, MD: Public Health Service.

National Center for Health Statistics. (1992). Births, marriages, divorces, and deaths for 1991. *Monthly Vital Statistics Report*, *40*(12). Hyattsville, MD: Public Health Service.

Vital Statistics on Marriage and Divorce
Years of Questionnaire: 1968-1988
Sample size: 200,000 to 800,000 marriages and divorces
FAMILY LEVEL CHARACTERISTICS
Family Composition
○ Full roster of household members (first name, age, sex, and relationship to reference person of each member)
○ Partial roster of household members
○ Number of adults in household
○ Number of children in household
○ Approximate relationship of family members to householder, child, or one another
○ Exact relationship of family members to householder, child, or one another
○ Information about part-time household member
○ Information about family members no longer living in household
○ Information about relatives who live nearby but not in household

Socioeconomic
○ Total family income
○ Number of persons who depend on family income
○ Sources of income
○ Income amounts identified separately by source
○ Poverty status
○ Welfare status
○ Food Stamps receipt
○ Child support receipt
○ Medicaid coverage
○ Private health insurance
○ Home ownership/renters
○ Assets (other than home ownership)
○ Public housing status
○ Telephone in household
○ Language other than English spoken in home

Geographic/Community Variables
● Region of country
● State of residence
○ County/city/MSA of residence
○ Size/type of community
○ Zip code
○ Telephone area code
○ Metropolitan residence
○ Neighborhood quality
○ Local labor market

Stage in Family Life Cycle
● Age of adult respondent or spouse/partner
● Marital status of adult respondent or spouse/partner
○ Employment status of adult respondent or spouse/partner
○ Presence of own children in household
○ Age of youngest own child in household
○ Age of oldest own child in household
○ Existence of own children who have left home
○ Intention to have (more) children in future

Family Functioning

- Family activities or time use
- Community involvement (civic, religious, recreational)
- Family communication patterns
- Family decision-making
- Marital conflict
- Marital happiness/satisfaction
- Parent-child conflict
- History of marital separations
- History of family violence
- History of marital counselling

CHARACTERISTICS OF ADULT FAMILY MEMBERS

Adult Respondent or Reference Person	Current Spouse in HH	Current or Former Spouse Not in HH	
●	●	○	Age
●	●	○	Gender
●	●	○	Race
○	○	○	Hispanic origin
○	○	○	Other origin/ethnicity
○	○	○	Religious affiliation
○	○	○	Religious participation
●	●	○	Country of birth
○	○	○	Immigrant status
○	○	○	English fluency
●	●	○	Current marital status
●	●	○	Marital history
○	○	○	Cohabitation status
○	○	○	Cohabitation history
○	○	○	Parental status
●	●	○	Number children ever born/sired[1]
○	○	○	Age at first birth
○	○	○	Age of youngest child
○	○	○	Children living elsewhere
○	○	○	Duration at current address
○	○	○	Residential mobility
●	●	○	Educational attainment
○	○	○	Degrees attained
○	○	○	GED or regular HS diploma
○	○	○	Current enrollment
○	○	○	Current employment status
○	○	○	Hours usually worked (ft/pt)
○	○	○	Weeks worked
○	○	○	Annual employment pattern
○	○	○	Main occupation
○	○	○	Earnings
○	○	○	Wage rate
○	○	○	Payment of child support
○	○	○	Aptitude or achievement score
○	○	○	Health/disability status
○	○	○	Self-esteem
○	○	○	Locus of control or efficacy
○	○	○	Depression or subjective well-being
○	○	○	Work-related attitudes

CHARACTERISTICS OF CHILD FAMILY MEMBERS

Reference Child or Youth Respondent	Other Children (in HH)	
O	O	Age
O	O	Month and year of birth
O	O	Gender
●	●	Race[2]
O	O	Hispanic origin
O	O	Other origin/ethnicity
O	O	Religious affiliation
O	O	Religious participation
O	O	Country of birth
O	O	Immigrant status
O	O	English fluency
O	O	Exact relationship to adult family members
O	O	Exact relationship to other children in HH
O	O	Marital status/history
O	O	Parental status/history
O	O	Current enrollment in regular school
O	O	Current enrollment in preschool/daycare
O	O	Highest grade completed
O	O	Grade now enrolled
O	O	Employment status/history
O	O	Health status
O	O	Handicapping conditions
O	O	Grade repetition
O	O	Aptitude or achievement score
O	O	Pregnancy/birth history
O	O	Psychological well-being
O	O	Delinquency

NOTES

1. Can only determine children ever born to relevant marriage; for divorce statistics only.
2. Race of children inferred from race of parents; for divorce statistics only.

454

Vital Statistics—Mortality

PURPOSE The primary goal of the vital registry system within the United States is to provide legal documentation of vital events such as birth and mortality. Statistical information is then provided to federal, state, and local authorities to aid in planning and evaluating programs and social services, assessing rates of population growth, and measuring changes in population composition.

SPONSORSHIP The Public Health Service provides recommended standards for collecting death certificates and recording information. Most, if not all, recommended data are collected by states on their own certificate forms. The National Center for Health Statistics (NCHS) compiles, analyzes, and publishes mortality data from all 50 states, including the District of Columbia, Puerto Rico, Guam, and the Virgin Islands.

SAMPLING DESIGN Mortality data are taken directly from death certificates sent to NCHS from each state and territory. Health officials are required to report all deaths and fetal deaths (deaths at 20 weeks or more gestation). While accurate assessments of the completeness of the vital registry system are available, it is believed that death registration in the United States is nearly 99% complete. Underreporting of fetal deaths is greater than for non-fetal deaths.

PERIODICITY Mortality statistics were first published by the federal government in 1850 based on data taken from the Census. Mortality estimates were first collected in 1880 for two states and several cities. Mortality registration expanded steadily to include all 50 states, the District of Columbia, and territories. Data are collected continually, with monthly and annual summaries. Monthly summaries are based on provisional data which includes non-residents. Summaries are estimated from the Current Mortality Sample, a 10% sample of certificates received each month by NCHS. All certificates received during that month, regardless of the date of death, are sampled.

CONTENT Basic demographic characteristics of the deceased such as age at death, date of birth, race, gender, and occupation are collected. All tables are broken down by ten-year age groups, with sex, race, and age in specific proportions and rates. Also included is the cause of death and cause-specific death rates. Each death is attributed to one primary cause or underlying condition and reported as such on the death certificate. The scheme for classifying underlying cause of death is the International Classification of Diseases (ICD). Since 1979, reported conditions have been classified using the Ninth Revision of the ICD, or ICD-9. The annual report, *Vital Statistics of the United States, Mortality*, contains nine sections: general mortality, infant mortality, fetal mortality, perinatal deaths, accidents, life tables, death by geographic region, deaths in Puerto Rico, Guam and the Virgin Islands, and a technical appendix.

LIMITATIONS In general, the family related data collected for death certificates, such as marital status, is inapplicable to children. The parents' names of deceased children, however, are usually available. The death registration systems can vary from state to state in terms of the consistency, completeness, and accuracy of recorded information, particularly with respect to cause of death. In addition, changes in the classification of diseases may limit the comparability of cause-specific death rates over time. Accidental deaths later determined to be homicide or suicide are not typically reclassified. The ICD-9 includes categories for deaths due to poisoning or drug or alcohol abuse, although the actual number of deaths due to such causes is probably underreported. Deaths to U.S. residents that occur outside the United States are excluded.

AVAILABILITY Provisional mortality estimates are published in the *Monthly Vital Statistics Report*.

Provisional death rates by cause of death, age, race, sex, age by sex, age by race, age by sex by race, and age by leading causes, are provided in the Current Mortality Sample (see description above). Final data are published in *Vital Statistics of the United States, Volume II: Mortality*.

Public use data tapes are available for purchase through the

National Technical Information Service
5285 Port Royal Road
Springfield, VA 22161
703/487-4780

For information on tape specifications, price, and stock numbers, contact:

Scientific and Technical Information Branch
National Center for Health Statistics
6525 Belcrest Road, Rm. 1067
Hyattsville, MD 20782
301/436-8500

For specific mortality data, contact:

Statistical Resources Branch (address as above)
301/436-8980

For information about mortality registration system, contact:
Mortality Statistics Branch (address as above)
301/436-8884

PUBLICATIONS

National Center for Health Statistics. (1993). Advance report of final mortality statistics, 1990. *Monthly Vital Statistics Report, 41*(7, suppl.). Hyattsville, MD: Public Health Service.

National Center for Health Statistics. (1992). *Vital statistics of the United States 1989, Vol. II, Mortality.* Washington, DC: Public Health Service.

Vital Statistics — Mortality
Year of Questionnaire: 1989
Sample size: 2,150,466 reported deaths
FAMILY LEVEL CHARACTERISTICS

Family Composition
O Full roster of household members (first name, age, sex, and relationship to reference person of each member)
O Partial roster of household members
O Number of adults in household
O Number of children in household
O Approximate relationship of family members to householder, child, or one another
O Exact relationship of family members to householder, child, or one another
O Information about part-time household member
O Information about family members no longer living in household
O Information about relatives who live nearby but not in household

Socioeconomic
O Total family income
O Number of persons who depend on family income
O Sources of income
O Income amounts identified separately by source
O Poverty status
O Welfare status
O Food Stamps receipt
O Child support receipt
O Medicaid coverage
O Private health insurance
O Home ownership/renters
O Assets (other than home ownership)
O Public housing status
O Telephone in household
O Language other than English spoken in home

Geographic/Community Variables
● Region of country
● State of residence
● County/city/MSA of residence
O Size/type of community
● Zip code
O Telephone area code
O Metropolitan residence
O Neighborhood quality
O Local labor market

Stage in Family Life Cycle
● Age of adult respondent or spouse/partner
● Marital status of adult respondent or spouse/partner
O Employment status of adult respondent or spouse/partner
O Presence of own children in household
O Age of youngest own child in household
O Age of oldest own child in household
O Existence of own children who have left home
O Intention to have (more) children in future

458

Family Functioning

- Family activities or time use
- Community involvement (civic, religious, recreational)
- Family communication patterns
- Family decision-making
- Marital conflict
- Marital happiness/satisfaction
- Parent-child conflict
- History of marital separations
- History of family violence
- History of marital counselling

CHARACTERISTICS OF ADULT FAMILY MEMBERS
Sample size: 2,078,473 deaths to persons 20 and older

Adult Respondent or Reference Person	Current Spouse in HH	Current or Former Spouse Not in HH	
●	○	○	Age
●	○	○	Gender
●	○	○	Race
●	○	○	Hispanic origin
●	○	○	Other origin/ethnicity
○	○	○	Religious affiliation
○	○	○	Religious participation
●	○	○	Country of birth
○	○	○	Immigrant status
○	○	○	English fluency
●	○	○	Current marital status
○	○	○	Marital history
○	○	○	Cohabitation status
○	○	○	Cohabitation history
○	○	○	Parental status
○	○	○	Number children ever born/sired
○	○	○	Age at first birth
○	○	○	Age of youngest child
○	○	○	Children living elsewhere
○	○	○	Duration at current address
○	○	○	Residential mobility
●	○	○	Educational attainment
○	○	○	Degrees attained
○	○	○	GED or regular HS diploma
○	○	○	Current enrollment
○	○	○	Current employment status
○	○	○	Hours usually worked (ft/pt)
○	○	○	Weeks worked
○	○	○	Annual employment pattern
●	○	○	Main occupation
○	○	○	Earnings
○	○	○	Wage rate
○	○	○	Payment of child support
○	○	○	Aptitude or achievement score
●	○	○	Health/disability status[1]
○	○	○	Self-esteem
○	○	○	Locus of control or efficacy
○	○	○	Depression or subjective well-being
○	○	○	Work-related attitudes

CHARACTERISTICS OF CHILD FAMILY MEMBERS
Sample size: 71,431 deaths to persons under 20

Reference Child or Youth Respondent	Other Children (in HH)	
●	○	Age
●	○	Month and year of birth
●	○	Gender
●	○	Race
●	○	Hispanic origin
●	○	Other origin/ethnicity
○	○	Religious affiliation
○	○	Religious participation
●	○	Country of birth
○,	○	Immigrant status
○	○	English fluency
○	○	Exact relationship to adult family members
○	○	Exact relationship to other children in HH
●	○	Marital status/history
○	○	Parental status/history
○	○	Current enrollment in regular school
○	○	Current enrollment in preschool/daycare
●	○	Highest grade completed
○	○	Grade now enrolled
○	○	Employment status/history
●	○	Health status[1]
○	○	Handicapping conditions
○	○	Grade repetition
○	○	Aptitude or achievement score
○	○	Pregnancy/birth history
○	○	Psychological well-being
○	○	Delinquency

NOTES
1. Limiting conditions.

NOTES

NOTES